THE AMERICAN NEGRO
HIS HISTORY AND LITERATURE

MINUTES

OF THE

PROCEEDINGS

OF THE

NATIONAL
NEGRO CONVENTIONS

1830-1864

Edited by Howard Holman Bell

ARNO PRESS and THE NEW YORK TIMES

NEW YORK 1969

General Editor
WILLIAM LOREN KATZ

THE PROCEEDINGS

1830—Philadelphia
Constitution of the American Society of
Free Persons of Colour
and
The Proceedings of the Convention

1831—Philadelphia
Minutes and Proceedings of the
First Annual Convention

1832—Philadelphia
Minutes and Proceedings of the
Second Annual Convention

1833—Philadelphia
Minutes and Proceedings of the
Third Annual Convention

1834—New York
Minutes of the Fourth Annual Convention

1835—Philadelphia
Minutes of the Fifth Annual Convention

1843—Buffalo
Minutes of the National Convention of
Colored Citizens

1847—Troy
Proceedings of the National Convention of
Colored People and Their Friends

1848—Cleveland
Report of the Proceedings of the
Colored National Convention

1853—Rochester
Proceedings of the
Colored National Convention

1855—Philadelphia
Proceedings of the
Colored National Convention

1864—Syracuse
Proceedings of the National Convention of
Colored Men

THIRTY YEARS BEFORE THE CIVIL WAR A SMALL GROUP OF FREE Negroes, old and young, met at Philadelphia to consider the problem of possible expatriation of blacks from Cincinnati where friction had developed over job competition. Present were Hezekiah Grice, young Baltimore activist; Richard Allen, venerable revolutionary against segregated worship; James W. C. Pennington, escaped slave and minister of the gospel. These and others who might be mentioned at this first national convention were successful not only in taking action on the subject at hand, but also in establishing the precedent of national assemblies that were to be called, sometimes annually, sometimes at irregular intervals during the three and one-half decades before the end of the Civil War. Meeting annually during the next five years, the National Negro Convention performed acceptably in so many areas that it could well be said to be the first "national association for the advancement of colored people."

The National Convention met twelve times before the end of the Civil War, but never after 1830 with so limited an agenda. While favorable to most of the reforms that a reform oriented America cherished, the free Negro felt that there were certain things which were more specifically applicable to him than to other Americans; he chose naturally to pay particular attention to those needs.

Emanating from these national conventions was the repeated reminder that slavery still sullied the image of a Christian democratic nation; that those blacks who were free were in all too many cases only nominally free; that the nation judged a man not by his capabilities but prejudged him by the color of his skin. During the

i

entire era there was seldom a national conclave that did not preach the value of temperance, morality, education, economy and self help. They asked not for special considerations but for equality of opportunity. They wanted an education that would fit them for competition in the contemporary world, and they demanded the opportunity to practice the skills acquired through that education or training. They wanted the right to bear witness in court and they wanted access to the jury box. They insisted that freedom of the body without full and unrestricted suffrage would leave the black man half slave and only half free.

Although the national conventions of the 1830's were sometimes almost overrun by whites pleading a particular cause or offering gratitous advice on a multiplicity of subjects, those of the 1840's were more independent of white influence and more militant in their approach to problems. There was less talk of moral reform and more of using the ballot to accomplish desired ends. There was growing tolerance of, even respect for, violence in freeing those in bondage. By the 1850's a significant minority of blacks were disenchanted enough with the land of their birth to resort to seeking ways to bypass the usual government controls through organization of some form of a state-within-a-state, or, more militantly, to seeking ways to establish or support a Negro nation beyond the borders of the United States. In fact, interest in emigration was undergoing one of its several peaks of the decade when the opening of hostilities concentrated the attention of all upon the fate of the nation and thus caused all factions to reevaluate their respective positions.

The last of the national conventions to meet before the end of the Civil War was at Syracuse on the eve of the presidential election of 1864. That meeting left no doubt of a united black front with a determination to see that they would no longer be excluded from the advantages of liberty and democracy. By that time full citizenship, including suffrage, had become the dominant issue, for without suffrage there was no assurance of redress of grievances.

Although some few men remained active throughout the thirty-five years covered in the accompanying documents, most of those in leadership positions in the 1830's dropped out during the following decades as younger and more militant men moved into positions of authority. Death took the usual toll with the Reverend Richard Allen leading the way. Emigration, though not making heavy inroads into national convention leadership, did claim one of the founders, Hezekiah Grice, who spent a quarter of a century in Haiti, where he was at one time high in government. Alexander Crummell spent a similar number of years as an emigrant in Africa, but perhaps the most celebrated of the early emigrants was John Russwurm, whose editorship of *Freedom's Journal* from 1827 to 1829 had allowed him to examine all sides of the plight of the American whose skin happened to be black. Before he departed for Africa he had also printed the early suggestions of cooperative action that had been developed into the national conventions beginning in 1830.

As the problems of the 1850's made the Negro American even more uncertain of the future, it was emigration that came to hold a very substantial influence on the minds of many strong convention men. It attracted the attention of Henry Highland Garnet, Martin R. Delany, William Howard Day, James Theodore Holly, and many others in greater or lesser degree as the dark days of the Kansas Nebraska Act, the Dred Scott decision, and the uncertain stance of the Republican party on slavery foretold troublous times ahead. Whether they chose to remain in America, as most blacks did, or whether they chose to cast their lot beyond the borders, as a very vocal minority wished, it was obvious to most in the late 1850's that the land of promise was still far in the distance.

Some men of talent and leadership ability were able to ride with the changing tide of reform. William Whipper of Pennsylvania was active in the conventions of the early 1830's as the group wrestled with the problems of education and possible expatriation to Canada; he became one of the leading exponents of the more theoretical moral reform ideas of the latter part of the decade; veered gradually to a position recognizing emigration as a legitimate avenue of progress in the 1850's; and was active in the national conventions of that decade when the pro- and anti-slave interpretation of the constitution was a matter of debate. Other long-term participants included James W. C. Pennington and Amos G. Beman. Both were ministers, as were many of the others who made the national conventions work, for the Negro minister, perhaps more than his white counterpart, was often the man who could travel more readily than his flock; he was usually better educated; he was more accustomed to dealing with public matters.

Generally speaking, it was the generation that took control in the 1840's that was to contine in command until the close of the Civil War. It was this decade that ushered in such names as Henry Highland Garnet, Martin R. Delany, James McCune Smith, and the great Frederick Douglass. Although working with the still younger and equally well-educated men of the West like the Langstons and William H. Day, they dominated the conventions to the end of the era, and thus left their stamp on the fate of the Negro and the fate of the nation in 1865. More mature in the 1850's, even statesmanlike in 1864, the men who stood responsible for the voice of the black man in America could rest content that they had given much to the cause of freedom and justice.

Perhaps freedom and justice should be delimited by indicating that it pertained chiefly to the male. The national conventions had not dealt more gently with women's rights than had most other reform organizations of the era. It is true that women had addressed some conventions, but so had men who were considered to be almost enemies. At the Cleveland National Convention in 1848 women had managed, through the intercession of Martin R. Delany, to get some points across. But if women had been deprived of a voice throughout most of the era, the convention of 1864 made some amends by inviting both Edmonia Highgate and Frances E. W. Harper to speak.

Whether it was in the conventions of the 1830's or in that of 1864, there was a compelling similarity in motivation and an equally compelling similarity in outcome. The desire to lift the entire black population—slave and nominally free—to a position of equality under constitutional government was motivation enough. But beyond this the men of the convention movement were idealists, and they sought constantly to make the black man, as well as the white, more worthy of the blessings of liberty and equality in a land in which they deemed mankind to be so capable of being elevated to a position akin almost to that of the gods.

If somewhat long on idealism, the conventions had always to settle for something less than success if one is to judge from immediate and demonstrable improvements growing out of convention demands. But who can say what produces what effect in a fluid situation? Was the convention movement responsible for the end of slavery? It had its influence. Did it bring about citizenship and suffrage for the Negro? It helped. Did it create a better educational climate for white and black alike? It would be hard to prove that it did not.

During these years the national convention met an average of once in three years. Meanwhile there were numerous regional state and local conventions advocating generally the same things publicized in the national meetings. All were publicized to the extent that the press would cooperate, and in many cases the convention itself assumed responsibility for publishing the record of the meeting. Three and one-half decades of continuous education through any means available, especially when the people and the causes were both somewhat controversial in the public eye, must have had its impact. The wit, the oratory, the philosophical argumentation, the plans for self betterment reached a substantial audience because whites and blacks alike listened avidly to the public speeches which were usually presented at the evening sessions, and were often taken up and copied from paper to paper. The Negro in convention shared with the Negro on the battlefield of the Civil War and with all Americans, black and white, the victory over slavery and disunion. The fact that that victory was turned into the hell of post reconstruction need not dim the brilliance of the moment when slavery ended and all Americans looked forward to a better life.

The work of this first "national association for the advancement of colored people" was well done. The official documents, sometimes too restricted as official documents often are, lie before you in the following pages. A careful perusal reveals the genuine effort of the men who sacrificed their time, their money, and their talents to building a better life. And when you turn to the messages to the Negro Americans or to all Americans you will seldom find a page which does not show the intense feeling, the patience, the pathos, the utter rightness of the black man's position as he appeals to his own people to live justly, serve God, create a better community for himself; and to the broader American audience to be fair enough to give the downtrodden a chance to prove themselves in the land where liberty and equality are the watchwords. Over and over the Negro American pointed out to all who had eyes to see that the enslavement of one was the enslavement of all—that the debasement of the black American was the debasement of all Americans.

There are few American pioneers who have given more than

these men gave. They lived in the era sometimes labeled as the age of the Common Man, but the Common Man had not yet learned enough democracy to accept their contributions to the welfare of the nation. America learned that lesson in the deaths of over 600,000 men on the field of battle. And if today we wonder why progress has not been more rapid, we can perhaps find the answer in that we do not always live at the pace that these men did as they, along with other Americans, battled for the cause of righteousness. One thing is obvious. They did not reach their great goal by the same route. Each man marched to the sound of his own drum, but the overall goal was never forgotten—all Americans must be free and equal. Reformers today may find that they have something in common with a William Whipper, who could follow the winds of reform wherever they might lead; with a Frederick Douglass or George T. Downing, who seldom allowed their gaze to pass beyond the American horizon, but who demanded complete acceptance and complete equality in the land of their birth; or a Henry Highland Garnet or Martin R. Delany, who dreamed of a great nation for black people somewhere beyond the borders of the United States. The record, except for the emigration interest that seldom appeared in the minutes of the national conventions, is here for those who will read.

Howard H. Bell
PROFESSOR OF HISTORY
MORGAN STATE COLLEGE

The following article appeared in the October 1859 issue of *The Anglo-African Magazine* and is reprinted here because of the light it throws on the genesis of the Negro convention movement.

THE

Anglo-African Magazine.

| VOL. I. | OCTOBER, 1859. | NO. 10. |

The First Colored Convention.

On the fifteenth day of September, 1830, there was held at Bethel Church, in the city of Philadelphia, the first Convention of the colored people of these United States. It was an event of historical importance; and, whether we regard the times or the men of whom this assemblage was composed, we find matter for interesting and profitable consideration.

Emancipation had just taken place in New York, and had just been arrested in Virginia by the Nat Turner rebellion and Walker's pamphlet. Secret sessions of the legislatures of the several Southern States had been held to deliberate upon the production of a colored man who had coolly recommended to his fellow blacks the only solution to the slave question, which, after twenty-five years of arduous labor of the most hopeful and noble-hearted of the abolitionists,* seems the forlorn hope of freedom to-day—insurrection and bloodshed. Great Britain was in the midst of that bloodless revolution which, two years afterwards, culminated in the passage of the Reform Bill, and thus prepared the joyous and generous state of the British

heart which dictated the West India Emancipation Act. France was rejoicing in the not bloodless *trois jours de Juliet*. Indeed, the whole world seemed stirred up with a universal excitement, which, when contrasted with the universal panics of 1837 and 1857, leads one to regard as more than a philosophical speculation the doctrine of those who hold the life of mankind from the creation as but one life, beating with one heart, animated with one soul, tending to one destiny, although made up of millions upon millions of molecular lives, gifted with their infinite variety of attractions and repulsions, which regulate, or crystallize them into evanescent substructures or organizations, which we call nationalities and empires and peoples and tribes, whose minute actions and reactions on each other are the histories which absorb our attention, whilst the grand universal life moves on beyond our ken, or only guessed at, as the astronomers shadow out movements of our solar system around or towards some distant unknown centre of attraction.

If the times of 1830 were eventful, there were among our people, as well as among other peoples, men equal to the occasion. We had giants in those days! There were Bishop Allen, the founder of the great

* See letter of Hon. Gerrit Smith to Convention of Jerry Rescuers, dated Sept. 3, 1859.

Bethel connection of Methodists, combining in his person the fiery zeal of St. Francis Xavier with the skill and power of organizing of a Richelieu; the meek but equally efficient Rush (who yet remains with us in fulfilment of the scripture), the father of the Zion Methodists; Paul, whose splendid presence and stately eloquence in the pulpit, and whose grand baptisms in the waters of Boston Harbor, are a living tradition in all New England; the saintly and sainted Peter Williams, whose views of the best means of our elevation are in triumphant activity to-day; William Hamilton, the thinker and actor, whose sparse specimens of eloquence we will one day place in gilded frames as rare and beautiful specimens of Etruscan art—William Hamilton, who, four years afterwards, during the New York riots, when met in the street, loaded down with iron missiles, and asked where he was going, replied, "to die on my threshold!" Watkins, of Baltimore, Frederick Hinton, with his polished eloquence, James Forten, the merchant prince, * William Whipper, just essaying his youthful powers, Lewis Woodson and John Peck, of Pittsburgh, Austin Steward, then of Rochester, Samuel E. Cornish, who had the distinguished honor of reasoning Gerrit Smith out of colonizationism, and of telling Henry Clay that he would never be president of anything higher than the American Colonization Society, Philip A. Bell, the born *sabreur*, who never feared the face of clay, and a hundred others, were the worthily leading spirits among the colored people.

And yet the idea of the first colored Convention did not originate with any of these distinguished men: it came from a young man of Baltimore, then, and still, unknown to fame. Born in that city in 1801, he was in 1817 apprenticed to a man some two hundred miles off in the Southeast. Arriving at his field of labor, he worked hard nearly a week and received poor fare in return. One day while at work near the house, the mistress came out and gave him a furious scolding, so furious, indeed, that her husband mildly interfered; she drove the latter away, and threatened to take the Baltimore out of the lad with cow-hide, &c., &c.; at this moment, to use his own expression, the lad became *converted*, that is, he determined to be his own master as long as he lived. Early nightfall found him on his way to Baltimore, which he reached after a severe journey which tested his energy and ingenuity to the utmost. At the age of twenty-three he was engaged in the summer time in supplying Baltimore with ice from his cart, and in winter in cutting up pork for Ellicots' etablishment. He must have been strong and swift with knife and cleaver, for in one day he cut up and dressed some four hundred and fifteen porkers.*

In 1824, our young friend fell in with Benjamin Lundy,† and in 1828–9, with

---

* It is a profitable comparison of 1830 with 1859 to remember that up to 1834–5, Mr. James Forten, of Philadelphia, was held up as an extraordinary instance of a colored man's ability, and because he had amassed $20,000 at his business.

* In the year of grace 1855, professional duties threw the writer of this into an acquaintance with Rutherford, a lineal descendant of *the* Rutherford of the Scotch Reformation : he was engaged at a thousand dollars a year in "cutting up" for a pork establishment in New York city ; he was a splendid fellow (physically) of five-and-twenty, and a magnificent Greek scholar ; it was a strange enchantment, to sit in the airy loft over-looking the Hudson, and hear him, cleaver in hand, recite and criticize the glowing lines of Homer Pindar and Anacreon !

† Mr. Goodell, in his "Slavery and Anti-Slavery in the United States," page 385, states that Benjamin Lundy started his first anti-slavery paper in Baltimore. This is not correct. Shortly after the discussion on the Missouri Compromise, a Mr. Lambert, residing in Tenneseee, published the "EMANCIPATOR," in that State, a thorough-going anti-slavery journal, which gave the best account extant of the insurrection in Charleston in 1822.

Wm. Lloyd Garrison, editors and publishers of the "Genius of Universal Emancipation;" a radical anti-slavery paper—whose boldness would put the "National Era" to shame—printed and published in the slave State of Maryland. In 1829–30, the colored people of the free States were much excited on the subject of emigration: there had been an emigration to Hayti, and also to Canada, and some had been driven to Liberia by the severe laws and brutal conduct of the fermenters of colonization in Virginia and Maryland. In some districts of these States, the disguised whites would enter the houses of free colored men at night, and take them out and give them from thirty to fifty lashes, to get them to consent to go to Liberia.

It was in the spring of 1830, that the young man we have sketched, HEZEKIAH GRICE, conceived the plan of calling together a meeting or convention of colored men, in some place north of the Potomac, for the purpose of comparing views and of adopting a harmonious movement either of emigration, or of determination to remain in the United States; convinced of the hopelessness of contending against the oppressions in the United States, living in the very depth of that oppression and wrong, his own views looked to Canada; but he held them subject to the decision of the majority of the convention which might assemble.

On the 2nd of April, 1830, he addressed a written circular to prominent colored men in the free States, requesting their opinions on the necessity and propriety of holding such convention, and stated that if the opinions of a sufficient number warranted it, he would give notice of the time and place at which duly elected delegates might assemble. Four months passed away, and his spirit almost died within him, for he had received not a line from any one in reply. When he visited Mr. Garrison in his office, and stated his project, Mr. Garrison took up a copy of Walker's Appeal, and said, although it might be right, yet it was too early to have published such a book.

On he 11th of August, however, he received a sudden and peremptory order from Bishop Allen, to come instantly to Philadelphia, about the emigration matter. He went, and found a meeting assembled to consider the conflicting reports on Canada of Messrs. Lewis and Dutton; at a subsequent meeting held the next night, and near the adjournment, the Bishop called Mr. Grice aside, and gave him to read a printed circular, issued from New York city, strongly approving of Mr. Grice's plan of a convention, and signed by Peter Williams, Peter Vogelsang and Thomas L. Jinnings. The Bishop added, "my dear child, we must take some action immediately, *or else these New Yorkers will get ahead of us.*" The Bishop left the meeting to attend a lecture on chemistry by Dr. Wells,[*] of Baltimore. Mr. Grice introduced the subject of the convention; and a committee consisting of Bishop Allen, Benjamin Pascal, Cyrus Black, James Cornish, and Junius C. Morel, were appointed to lay the matter before the colored people of Philadelphia. This committee, led, doubtless, by Bishop Allen, at once issued a call for a convention of the colored men of the United States, to be held in the city of Philadelphia on the 15th September, 1830.

Mr. Lundy was, at that time, a saddler, working at his bench, in the same place where this paper was published; he became deeply interested in the cause and soon associated himself with with Mr. Lambert. The latter died before his journal had completed its first year, and his mantle fell upon the shoulders of Benjamin Lundy, and there "found nothing less pure, less noble, or less energetic than itself."

---

[*] A black man of talent, who was instructed in medicine at a medical college in Baltimore, on condition that he would go to Africa.

At that time, in the prime of his young manhood, he must have presented the front of one equal to any fortune, able to achieve any undertaking. Standing six feet high, well-proportioned, of a dark bronze complexion, broad brow, and that stamp of features out of which the Greek sculptor would have delighted to mould the face of Vulcan—he was, to the fullest extent, a working man of such sort and magnetism as would lead his fellows where he listed.

In looking to the important results that grew out of this Convention, the independence of thought and self-assertion of the black man are the most remarkable. Then the union of purpose and union of strength which grew out of the acquaintanceship and mutual pledges of colored men from the different States. Then the subsequent conventions, where the great men we have already named, and others, appeared and took part in the discussions with manifestations of zeal, talent and ability, which attracted Garrison, the Tappans, Jocelyn, and others of that noble host, who, drawing no small portion of their inspiration from their black brethren in bonds, did manfully fight in the days of anti-slavery which tried men's souls, and when, to be an abolitionist, was, to a large extent, to be a martyr.

We cannot help adding the thought, that had these conventions of the colored people of the United States continued their annual sittings from 1830 until the present time, the result would doubtless have been greater general progress among our people themselves, a more united front to meet past and coming exigencies, and a profounder hold upon the public attention, and a deeper respect on the part of our enemies than we now can boast of. Looking at public opinion as it is, the living law of the land, and yet a malleable, ductile entity, which can be moulded, or, at least, affected, by the thoughts of any masses vigorously expressed, we should have become

a power on earth, of greater strength and influence than in our present scattered and dwindled state we dare even dream of. The very announcement' "Thirtieth Annual Convention of the Colored People of the United States," would bear a majestic front. Our great gathering at Rochester in 1853, commanded not only public attention but respect and admiration. Should we have such a gathering even now, once a year, not encumbered with elaborate plans of action, with too many wheels within wheels, we can yet regain much of the ground lost. The partial gathering at Boston, the other day, has already assumed its place in the public mind, and won its way into the calculations of the politicians.

Our readers will doubtless be glad to learn the subsequent history of Mr. Grice He did not attend the second Convention, but, in the interval between the second and third, he formed, in the city of Baltimore, a " LEGAL RIGHTS ASSOCIATION," for the purpose of ascertaining the legal status of the colored man in the United States, It was entirely composed of colored men, among whom were Mr. Watkins (the colored Baltimorean), Mr. Deaver, and others. Mr. Grice called on William Wirt, and asked him " what he charged for his opinion on a given subject?" " Fifty dollars." " Then, sir, I will give you fifty dollars if you will give me your opinion on the legal condition of a free colored man in these United States."

Mr. Wirt required the questions to be written out in proper form before he could answer them. Mr. Grice employed Tyson, who drew up a series of questions based upon the Constitution of the United States, and relating to the rights and citizenship of the free black. He carried the questions to Mr. Wirt, who, glancing over them, said, "really, sir, my position as an officer under the government renders it a delicate matter for me to answer these questions as they should be answered, but I'll tell you

Mr. Grice returned to Baltimore rejoicing at the success of his project; but, in the same boat which bore him down the Chesapeake, he was accosted by Mr. Zollickoffer, a member of the Society of Friends, a Philadelphian, and a warm and tried friend of the blacks. Mr. Zollickoffer used arguments and even entreaties, to dissuade Mr. Grice from holding the Convention, pointing out the dangers and difficulties of the same should it succeed, and the deep injury it would do the cause in case of failure. Of course it was reason and entreaty thrown away.

On the fifteenth of September, Mr. Grice again landed in Philadelphia, and in the fulness of his expectation asked every colored man he met about the Convention; no one knew anything about it; the first man did not know the meaning of the word, and another man said, "who ever heard of colored people holding a convention—convention, indeed!" Finally, reaching the place of meeting, he found, in solemn conclave, the five gentlemen who had called the Convention, and who had constituted themselves delegates: with a warm welcome from Bishop Allen, Mr. Grice, who came with credentials from the people of Baltimore, was admitted as delegate. A little while after, Dr. Burton, of Philadelphia, dropped in, and demanded by what right the six gentlemen held their seats as members of the Convention. On a hint from Bishop Allen, Mr. Pascal moved that Dr. Burton be elected an honorary member of the Convention, which softened the Doctor. In half an hour, five or six tall, grave, stern-looking men, members of the Zion Methodist body in Philadelphia, entered, and demanded by what right the members present held their seats and undertook to represent the colored people. Another hint from the Bishop and it was moved that these gentlemen be elected honorary members. But the gentlemen would submit to no such thing, and would accept nothing short of full membership, which was granted them.

Among the delegates were Abraham Shadd, of Delaware, J. W. C. Pennington, of Brooklyn, Austin Steward, of Rochester, Horace Easton, of Boston, and — Adams, of Utica.

The main subject of discussion was emigration to Canada; Junius C. Morel, Chairman of a committee on that subject, presented a report, on which there was a two days' discussion; the point discussed was, that the report stated that "the lands in Canada were *synonymous* with those of the Northern States." The word *synonymous* was objected to, and the word similar proposed in its stead. Mr. Morel, with great vigor and ingenuity, defended the report, but was finally voted down, and the word *similar* adopted. The Convention recommended emigration to Canada, passed strong resolutions against the American Colonization Society, and at its adjournment appointed the next annual Convention of the people of color to be held in Philadelphia, on the first Monday in June, 1831.

At the present day, when colored conventions are almost as frequent as church-meetings, it is difficult to estimate the bold and daring spirit which inaugurated the Colored Convention of 1830. It was the right move, originating in the right quarter and at the right time. Glorious old Maryland, or, as one speaking in the view that climate grows the men, would say, Maryland—Virginia region, which has produced Benjamin Banneker, Nat. Turner, Frederick Douglass, the parents of Ira Aldrige, Henry Highland Garnett, and Sam. Ringold Ward,[*] also produced the founder of colored conventions, Hezekiah Grice!

_____

[*] All the black men yet mentioned in Appleton's new Encyclopedia—Aldridge, Banneker and Frederick Douglass—were either natives or immediate descendants of this *regio in terris.*

what to do: they should be answered, and by the best legal talent of the land; do you go to Philadelphia, and present my name to Horace Binney, and he will give you an answer satisfactory to you, and which will command the greatest respect throughout the land." Mr. Grice went to Philadelphia, and presented the questions and request to Horace Binney. This gentleman pleaded age and poor eye-sight, but told Mr. Grice that if he would call on John Sargent, he would get answers of requisite character and weight. He called on John Sargent, who promptly agreed to answer the questions if Mr. Binney would allow his name to be associated as an authority in the replies. Mr. Binney again declined, and so the matter fell through. This is what Mr. Grice terms his "*Dred Scott case*"—and so it was.

He attended the Convention of 1832, but by some informality, or a want of credentials, was not permitted to sit as a full member!—Saul ejected from among the prophets!—Yet he was heard on the subject of rights, and the doctrine of "our rights," as well as the first colored convention, are due to the same man.

In 1832, chagrined at the colored people of the United States, he migrated to Hayti, where, until 1843, he pursued the business of carver and gilder. In the latter year he was appointed Director of Public Works in Port-au-Prince, which office he held until two years ago. He is also engaged in, and has wide knowledge of, machinery and engineering. Every two or three years he visits New York, and is welcomed to the arcana of such men as James J. Mapes, the Bensons, Dunhams, and at the various works, where steam and iron obey human ingenuity in our city. He is at present in this city, lodg-

ing at the house of the widow of his old friend and coadjuter Thomas L. Jinnings, 133 Reade street. We have availed ourselves of his presence among us to glean from him the statements which we have imperfectly put together in this article.

We cannot dismiss this subject without the remark, of peculiar pertinence at this moment, that it would have been better for our people had Mr. Grice never left these United States. The twenty-seven years he has passed in Hayti, although not without their mark on the fortunes of that island, are yet without such mark as he would have made in the land and upon the institutions among which he was born. So early as his thirty-second year, before he had reached his intellectual prime, he had inaugurated two of the leading ideas on which our people have since acted, conventions to consider and alleviate their grievances, and the struggle for legal rights. If he did such things in early youth, what might he not have done with the full force and bent of his matured intellect? And where, in the wide world, in what region, or under what sun, could he so effectually have labored to elevate the black man, as on this soil and under American institutions?

So profoundly are we opposed to the favorite doctrine of the Puritans and their co-workers, the colonizationists— *Ubi Libertas, ibi Patria*—that we could almost beseech Divine Providence to reverse some past events, and to fling back into the heart of Virginia and Maryland their Sam. Wards, Highland Garnets, J. W. Penningtons, Frederick Douglasses, and the twenty thousand who now shout hosannas in Canada—and we would soon see some stirring in the direction of *Ubi Patria, ibi Libertas!*

The Conventions
of the 1830's

IN 1830 THE BLACK AMERICAN HAD NO PRECEDENT TO FOLLOW IN organizing a national assembly to discuss topics of concern to all, but the time was ripe for such a meeting. Between 1827 and 1829, *Freedom's Journal,* the first Negro newspaper, had acted as the medium through which Negro Americans communicated. There they reported local assemblies, discussed problems, and even made some suggestions for a national assembly. This new-found outlet died when its editor, John Russwurm (reputedly the first Negro graduate from an American college [Bowdoin]), decided to cast his lot with the colonizationalists, but the latent idea of a national assembly seemed the natural answer to an emergency that threatened expatriation of free Negroes from Cincinnati.

The question of what could be done to aid those forced to seek a home elsewhere carried over into succeeding conventions, and was eventually settled by general acceptance of the idea that if expatriation must take place, then it should be to Canada but that emigration should not be encouraged. Thereafter, not only during the 1830's but throughout the entire era to the close of the Civil War, the national conventions tended to shy away from the subject of emigration or to reiterate the stand taken earlier. However, the rising militancy of the Negro in the 1850's, coupled with the Negro Nationalism of the era, tended to keep the issue of emigration active in black America in the decade before the Civil War.

During the 1830's, the very natural desire for an institution of higher education open to Negroes, or more specifically, a Negro school, had moved into a position of prominence in the discussions at the annual conventions, where it motivated efforts of Negroes and their white friends to provide such a school. That effort ended in failure, and so did early efforts at integrated schools, even in areas later to be the hallowed ground of abolitionism.

A third area of interest, which would extend on through the decade and to a lesser extent throughout the entire era, was that of moral reform. Always aware of the plight of the average Negro, free or slave, and always aware of the finger of the white community that pointed in scorn at the exterior trappings of poverty but seldom in love and understanding at the efforts of the black folk to rise in spite of their poverty, the national conventions placed tremendous emphasis on morality and correct living. It is in these passages that one can find some of the most beautiful prose of the entire era, as men schooled in adversity poured out their yearnings for a better life, a better America, and a better world.

CONSTITUTION

OF THE

AMERICAN SOCIETY

OF

FREE PERSONS OF COLOUR,

FOR IMPROVING THEIR CONDITION IN THE UNITED STATES;
FOR PURCHASING LANDS; AND FOR THE ESTABLISH-
MENT OF A SETTLEMENT IN UPPER CANADA.

ALSO

THE PROCEEDINGS OF THE CONVENTION,

WITH THEIR

ADDRESS

TO

THE FREE PERSONS OF COLOUR

IN THE

UNITED STATES.

PHILADELPHIA:
PRINTED BY J. W. ALLEN, NO 26, STRAWBERRY-ST.
1831.

MINUTES OF THE CONVENTION.

AT a Convention held by adjournments from the 20th day of September, to the 24th of the same inclusive, 1830, in accordance with a public notice issued on behalf of the Coloured Citizens of Philadelphia, and addressed to their brethren throughout the U. States, inviting them to assemble by delegation, in Convention, to be held in the city of Philadelphia, on the 20th day of September, 1830, and signed, on behalf, by the Rev. Bishop *Allen, Cyrus Black, Junius C. Morel, Benjamin Paschall*, jr. and *James Cornish*—

The delegation accordingly met in Bethel church, on the 20th September, at 10 o'clock, A. M. and after a chaste and appropriate prayer by the venerable Bishop *Allen*, the Convention was organized by electing

Rt. Rev. RICHARD ALLEN, President.
Dr. BELFAST BURTON, of Philadelphia, ⎱ Vice Presidents.
AUSTIN STEWARD, of Rochester, N. Y. ⎰
JUNIUS C. MOREL, of Philadelphia, Secretary, and
ROBERT COWLEY, of Maryland, Assistant Secretary.

On motion it was

Resolved, That this Convention do recommend the formation of a Parent Society; and that immediately after its organization, to appoint a general corresponding Agent, to reside at or near the intended purchase in Upper Canada.

On motion it was

Resolved, That this Convention enjoins and requires of each of its members to use their utmost influence in the formation of of societies, *auxiliary* to the Parent Society about being established in the city of Philadelphia; and also to instruct the auxiliary societies when formed, to send delegates to the next General Convention.

On motion it was

Resolved, That the next General Convention shall be composed of delegates appointed by the Parent Society and its auxiliaries: provided always, that the number of delegates from each society, shall not exceed *five*, and all other places, where there are no auxiliaries, are hereby invited to send one delegate.

On motion it was

Resolved, That this Convention address the Free People of Colour throughout the United States, and publish in one of the daily papers of this city.

On motion it was

Resolved, That the Convention do adjourn at the invitation of one of the managers of the Lombard-street Free School for coloured children. The Convention were highly gratified at the order, regularity and improvement discoverable in the various departments, among a collection of children, male and female, rising four hundred. Their specimens in writing, needlework, &c. &c. made a deep impression on the Convention, with a desire that the People of Colour may availingly appreciate every extended opportunity for their improvement in the various situations where they may reside.

On motion, the House adjourned *sine die*.

Rt. Rev. RICHARD ALLEN, President.
JUNIUS C. MOREL, Secretary.

-◄◉►-

The following Delegates composed the Convention, viz.

Pennsylvania—Rev. Richard Allen, Dr. Belfast Burton, Cyrus Black, Junius C. Morel, Benjamin Paschall, jr. James Cornish, Wm. S. Whipper, Peter Gardiner, John Allen, James Newman, Charles H. Leveck, Frederick A. Hinton.

New-York—Austin Steward, Jos. Adams, George L. Brown.

Connecticut—Scipio C. Augustus.

Rhode-Island—George C. Willis, Alfred Niger.

Maryland—James Deavour, Hezekiah Grice, Aaron Willoon, Robert Cowley.

Delaware—Abraham D. Shad.

Virginia—Arthur M. Waring, Wm. Duncan, James West, jr.

HONORARY MEMBERS.

Robert Brown, William Rogers, John Bowers, Richard Howell, Daniel Peterson, Charles Shorts, of Pennsylvania; Leven Williams, of New-York; James P. Walker, of Maryland; John Robinson, of Ohio; Rev. Samuel Todd, of Maryland; John Arnold, of New-Jersey; Sampson Peters, of New-Jersey; Rev. Anthony Campbell, of Delaware; Don Carolos Hall, of Delaware.

CONSTITUTION.

PREAMBLE.

In conformity to a resolution of the Delegates of Free Persons of Colour, in General Convention assembled, in the City of Philadelphia, September 20th, 1830, recommending the formation and establishment of a Parent Society in the City of Philadelphia, for the purpose of purchasing land, and locating a settlement in the Province of Upper Canada; and to which all other Societies formed for that purpose, may become auxiliary—We therefore have adopted the following Constitution.

ARTICLE I.

This Society shall be called "The American Society of Free Persons of Colour, for improving their condition in the United States; for purchasing lands; and for the establishment of a settlement in the Province of Upper Canada:" and shall consist of such Persons of Colour as shall pay not less than *twenty five cents* on entering, and thereafter quarterly, *eighteen and three quarter cents.*

ARTICLE II.

The Officers of the Society shall be, a President, and Vice Presidents, four of whom to be chosen out of the city and county of Philadelphia ; a Corresponding, Recording, and two Assistant Secretaries, and a Treasurer: a Board of Managers of fifteen members, a Corresponding Committee of five, a Financial Committee of three, a Soliciting Committee of thirteen, and a Publishing Committee of three; all of whom shall be elected by Ballot, at the annual meeting in October.

The Society shall meet quarterly in the city of Philadelphia. on the first Monday in October, January, April, and July.

The Board of Managers shall meet to transact business on the last Monday of every month; they shall have power to fill all vacancies occurring during the year, in their body, or any of the committees Nine of their number shall constitute a quorum.

ARTICLE III.

The President shall preside at all meetings of the Society, and sign all orders on the Treasurer.

The Vice Presidents shall preside at all meetings of the Society, in the absence of the President.

The President, Vice Presidents, Secretaries, and Treasurer, shall be *ex officio* members of the Board of Managers.

ARTICLE IV.

The duty of the Coresponding Secretary shall be to attend the meetings of the Corresponding Committee, keep the minutes of their proceedings; he shall be subject to their order, and shall report and present all letters or communications directed to him, to the chairman of the committee, that they may be convened together. He shall also keep a true copy of all his letters or communications.

The Committee of Correspondence shall open an exchange of views with the different Auxiliary Societies that may be formed ; receive intelligence concerning the operations of the different societies throughout the United States, and from other persons aiming to improve the situation and condition of the people of colour ; and also receive all essays on the subject, with such other information as may conduce to the accomplishment of the great object of the Society.

All communications shall be directed to the Corresponding Secretary.

ARTICLE V.

The Recording Secretary shall attend the meetings of the Society and keep their minutes.

He shall be provided with a book. wherein shall be recorded the proceedings of the Society, of the Board of Managers, and of the Committees, or any persons entrusted with the care or concerns of the Society.

Therefore it shall be the duty of the chairmen of the several committees to aid the Recording Secretary in the discharge of his official duty.

The Assistant Secretaries shall attend the meetings and keep the minutes of the Board of Managers, and assist the Recording Secretary when required.

ARTICLE VI.

The Treasurer on entering upon the duties of his office, shall give such security for the faithful performance of his trust as the Board of Managers shall require.

The Treasurer shall not retain in his possession more than $100. All monies above that sum shall be deposited in the United States Bank, that all persons interested in the prosperity of the Institution, may be satisfied as to the safety of their funds; and no sum so deposited shall be withdrawn without an order signed by the President, Vice President, and Secretary of the Parent Society, and four of the Board of Managers thereof.

He shall keep fair accounts of his transactions, hold all papers belonging to the Society, and pay, (if in funds,) all such orders drawn by the Board of Managers, signed by the President, and attested by the Recording Secretary.

He shall annually report to the Board of Managers the state of the treasury, or as often as they may direct; and at the expiration of his term, if not re-elected, shall hand over all the books, papers and funds of the Society to his successor, within thirty days.

ARTICLE VII.

The Financial Committee shall have under their care the pecuniary concerns of the Society, and every thing in relation thereto: they shall also audit the accounts of the Treasurer.

They shall report to the Board of Managers, from time to time, bills or provisions for the increase of the funds, or appropriations of the same, as they may deem in their judgment expedient, that the same may be considered or approved.

ARTICLE VIII.

The Soliciting Committee shall be provided with books for the purpose of receiving subscriptions or donations, wherein shall be registered the names, and amount so received.

ARTICLE IX.

The several Committees shall record, for the future use of the Society, all important observations that may relate to the subject of their charge.

The Board of Managers shall report to the Society quarterly; and at the annual meeting, their report shall be printed in pamphlet form.

ARTICLE X.

All Societies, auxiliary to this, shall, when formed, duly notify the Board of Managers of the Parent Society, through its Corresponding Secretary, taking care to forward a copy of their organization and proceedings, to be entered upon the records of the Society.

And with the view of more effectually strengthening a general union among the Free People of Colour, it shall be the duty of each auxiliary Society respectively, to elect from among their own members, one individual as Vice President of the Parent Society.

—◄●►—

At a meeting of the Parent Society, held on Monday the 30th of November, 1830, the following persons were elected Officers for the ensuing year, viz.

President—Rev. Richard Allen.

Vice Presidents—Messrs. John Bowers, Rob't Brown, Daniel D. Brownhill, Peter Gardiner.

Corresponding Secretary—William Whipper.

Recording Secretary—Charles H. Leveck.

Assistant Secretaries—John P. Thompson, Samuel D. Potts.

Treasurer—James Johnson.

Board of Managers—Dr. Belfast Burton, Messrs. John P. Burr, Scipio Sewell, John Allen, (Porter,) Richard Howell, Joseph Cassey, Shedrich Basset, James Gibson, Jeremiah Bowser, Richard B. Johnson, James Newman, Henry Beckett, Peter Mc Neal, James Bird, Abraham Williams.

Corresponding Committee—Dr. Belfast Burton, Messrs. Daniel B. Brownhill, John B. Sammons, Frederick A. Hinton, Rev. Richard Allen.

Financial Committee—Messrs. Charles W. Gardner, John B. Sammons, Thomas Butler.

Soliciting Committee—Rev. Richard Allen, Messrs. Samuel Nickels, William James, Joseph Cassey, Thomas Channock, Thomas Butler, William C. West, Robert Johnson, Joshua Brown, Edward Johnson, Jeremiah Bowser, Prince G. Laws, Samuel Combegy.

Publishing Committee—Dr. Belfast Burton, Messrs. William Whipper, John Dutton.

CONVENTION OF PEOPLE OF COLOUR.

AS much anxiety has prevailed on account of the enactment of laws in several States of the Union, especially that of Ohio, abridging the liberties and privileges of the Free People of Colour, and subjecting them to a series of privations and sufferings, by denying them a right of residence, unless they comply with certain requisitions not exacted of the Whites, a course altogether incompatible with the principles of civil and religious liberty.

In consideration of which, a delegation* was appointed from the states of Connecticut, New York, Pennsylvania, Delaware, and Maryland, to meet in Convention in Philadelphia, to consider the propriety of forming a settlement in the province of Upper Canada, in order to afford a place of refuge to those who may be obliged to leave their homes, as well as to others inclined to emigrate with the view of improving their condition.

The said Convention accordingly met in Bethel Church, city of Philadelphia, on the 20th of September, 1830; and having fully considered the peculiar situation of many of their brethren, and the advantages to be derived from the proposed settlement, adopted the following

ADDRESS

To the Free People of Colour of these United States.

Brethren,

Impressed with a firm and settled conviction, and more especially being taught by that inestimable and invaluable instrument, namely, the Declaration of Independence, that all men are born free and equal, and consequently are endowed with unalienable rights, among which are the enjoyments of life, liberty, and the pursuits of happiness.

Viewing these as incontrovertable facts, we have been led to the following conclusions; that our forlorn and deplorable situation earnestly and loudly demand of us to devise and pursue all legal means for the speedy elevation of ourselves and brethren to the scale and standing of men.

* In consequence of not having had timely notice, delegates from other sections of the country did not attend; though it is hoped that at the Convention on the first Monday in June next, there will be a more general representation.

And in pursuit of this great object, various ways and means have been resorted to; among others, the African Colonization Society is the most prominent. Not doubting the sincerity of many friends who are engaged in that cause ; yet we beg leave to say, that it does not meet with our approbation. However great the debt which these United States may owe to injured Africa, and however unjustly her sons have been made to bleed, and her daughters to drink of the cup of affliction, still we who have been born and nurtured on this soil, we, whose habits, manners, and customs are the same in common with other Americans, can never consent to take our lives in our hands, and be the bearers of the redress offered by that Society to that much afflicted country.

Tell it not to barbarians, lest they refuse to be civilised, and eject our christian missionaries from among them, that in the nineteenth century of the christian era, laws have been enacted in some of the states of this great republic, to compel an unprotected and harmless portion of our brethren, to leave their homes and seek an asylum in foreign climes : and in taking a view of the unhappy situation of many of these, whom the oppressive laws alluded to, continually crowd into the Atlantic cities, dependent for their support upon their daily labour, and who often suffer for want of employment, we have had to lament that no means have yet been devised for their relief.

These considerations have led us to the conclusion, that the formation of a settlement in the British province of Upper Canada, would be a great advantage to the people of colour. In accordance with these views, we pledge ourselves to aid each other by all honourable means, to plant and support one in that country, and therefore we earnestly and most feelingly appeal to our coloured brethren, and to all philanthropists here and elsewhere, to assist in this benevolent and important work.

To encourage our brethren earnestly to co-operate with us, we offer the following, viz. 1st. Under that government no invidious distinction of colour is recognised, but there we shall be entitled to all the rights, privileges, and immunities of other citizens. 2d. That the language, climate, soil, and productions are similar to those in this country, 3d. That land of the best quality can be purchased at the moderate price of one dollar and fifty cents per acre, by the one hundred acres. 4th. The market for different kinds of produce raised in that colony, is such as to render a suitable reward to the industrious farmer, equal in our opinion to that of the United States. And lastly, as the erection of buildings must necessarily claim the attention of the emigrants, we would invite the mechanics from our large cities to embark in the enterprise ; the advancement of architecture depending much on their exertions, as they must consequently take with them the arts and improvements of our well regulated communities.

It will be much to the advantage of those who have large families, and desire to see them happy and respected, to locate themselves in a land where the laws and prejudices of society will have no effect in retarding their advancement to the summit of civil and religious improvement. There the diligent student will have ample opportunity to reap the reward due to industry and perseverence ; whilst those of moderate attainments, if properly nurtured, may be enabled to take their stand as men in the several offices and situations necessary to promote union, peace, order and tranquility. It is to these we must look for the strength and spirit of our future prosperity.

Before we close, we would just remark, that it has been a subject of deep regret to this convention, that we as a people, have not availingly appreciated every opportunity placed within our power by the benevolent efforts of the friends of humanity, in elevating our condition to the rank of freemen. That our mental and physical qualities have not been more actively engaged in pursuits more lasting, is attributable in a great measure to a want of unity among ourselves; whilst our only stimulus to action has been to become domestics, which at best is but a precarious and degraded situation.

It is to obviate these evils, that we have recommended our views to our fellow-citizens in the foregoing instrument, with a desire of raising the moral and political standing of ourselves; and we cannot devise any plan more likely to accomplish this end, than by encouraging agriculture and mechanical arts : for by the first, we shall be enabled to act with a degree of independence, which as yet has fallen to the lot of but few among us ; and the faithful pursuit of the latter, in connection with the sciences, which expand and ennoble the mind, will eventually give us the standing and condition we desire.

To effect these great objects, we would earnestly request our brethren throughout the United States, to co-operate with us, by forming societies *auxiliary* to the Parent Institution, about being established in the city of Philadelphia, under the patronage of the GENERAL CONVENTION. And we further recommend to our friends and brethren, who reside in places where, *at present*, this may be impracticable, so far to aid us, by contributing to the funds of the Parent Institution ; and, if disposed, to appoint one delegate to represent them in the next Convention, to be held in Philadelphia the first Monday in June next, it being fully understood, that organized societies be at liberty to send any number of delegates not exceeding *five*.

Signed by order of the Convention,

Rev. RICHARD ALLEN, *President,*
Senior Bishop of the African Methodist Episcopal Churches.

JUNIUS C. MOREL, *Secretary.*

MINUTES

AND

PROCEEDINGS

OF THE

FIRST ANNUAL CONVENTION

OF THE

PEOPLE OF COLOUR,

HELD BY ADJOURNMENTS

IN THE CITY OF PHILADELPHIA,

FROM THE SIXTH TO THE ELEVENTH OF JUNE, INCLUSIVE, 1831.

Philadelphia:

PUBLISHED BY ORDER OF THE COMMITTEE

OF ARRANGEMENTS.

. . . .

1831.

MINUTES AND PROCEEDINGS

OF THE

FIRST ANNUAL CONVENTION

OF THE

PEOPLE OF COLOUR.

———————

The Delegates met on Monday, the 6th of June, in the brick Wes
leyan Church, Lombard Street, pursuant to public notice, signed, on
behalf of the Parent Society, at Philadelphia, by Dr. Belfast Burton
and William Whipper.

Present, the following gentlemen, viz :—

John Bowers,
Dr. Belfast Burton,
James Cornish, 〉Philadelphia.
Junius C. Morel,
Wm. Whipper,

Rev. Wm. Miller,
Henry Sipkins,
Thos. L. Jennings, 〉New-York.
Wm. Hamilton,
James Pennington,

Rev. Abner Coker, 〉 Maryland.
Robert Cowley,

Abraham D. Shad, 〉 Delaware.
Rev. Peter Gardiner,

Wm. Duncan, Virginia.

Who presented their credentials, and took their seats accordingly.

After an appropriate prayer by the Rev. W. Miller, on motion, the
Convention proceeded to business, by electing

JOHN BOWERS, *President.*

ABRAHAM D. SHAD, 〉 *Vice-Presidents.*
WILLIAM DUNCAN,

WILLLIAM WHIPPER, *Secretary.*

THOS. L. JENNINGS, *Assistant Secretary.*

When the house was declared organized, on motion, the Rev. Charles W. Gardiner, and the Rev. Samuel Todd, were appointed Chaplains for this Convention, they not being of the delegation.

On motion, Resolved, That a Committee be appointed to institute an inquiry into the condition of the free people of colour throughout the United States, and report their views upon the subject at a subsequent meeting.

On motion, Resolved, That Messrs. Morel, Shad, Duncan, Cowley, Sipkins, and Jennings, compose that Committee.

The Committee on the Condition of the Free People of Colour of the United States, reported as follows:—

Brethren and Fellow-Citizens:—

We, the Committee of Inquiry, would suggest to the Convention the propriety of adopting the following resolutions, viz:—Resolved,

That, in the opinion of this Convention, it is highly necessary that the different Societies engaged in the *Canadian Settlement,* be earnestly requested to persevere in their praiseworthy and philanthropic undertaking; firmly believing, that, at a future period, their labours will be crowned with success.

The Committee would also recommend this Convention to call on the free people of colour, to assemble *annually* by delegation, at such place as may be designated as suitable.

They would also respectfully submit to your wisdom, the necessity of your deliberate reflection on the dissolute, intemperate, and ignorant condition of a large portion of the coloured population of the United States. They would not, however, refer to their unfortunate circumstances to add degradation to objects already degraded and miserable; nor, with some others, improperly class the virtuous of our colour with the abandoned, but with the most sympathizing and heartfelt commiseration, show our sense of obligation as the true guardians of our interests, by giving wholesome advice and good counsel.

The Committee consider it as highly important, that the Convention recommend the necessity of creating a general fund, to be denominated the CONVENTIONAL FUND, for the purpose of advancing the objects of this and future conventions, as the public good may require.

They would further recommend, that the Declaration of Independence and Constitution of the United States, be read in our Conventions; believing, that the truths contained in the former are incontrovertible, and that the latter guarantees in letter and spirit to every freeman born in this country, all the rights and immunities of citizenship.

Your Committee with regret have witnessed the many oppressive, unjust and unconstitutional laws, which have been enacted in different parts of the Union, against the free people of colour, and they would call upon this convention as possessing the rights of freemen, to recommend to the people through their delegation, the propriety of memorializing the proper authorities, whenever they may feel themselves aggrieved, or their rights invaded, by any cruel or oppressive laws.

And your Committee would further report, that, in their opinion, *Education*, *Temperance* and *Economy*, are best calculated to promote the elevation of mankind to a proper rank and standing among men, as they enable him to discharge all those duties enjoined on him by his Creator. We would therefore respectfully request an early attention to those virtues among our brethren, who have a desire to be useful.

And lastly, your Committee view with unfeigned regret, and respectfully submit to the wisdom of this Convention, the operations and misrepresentations of the American Colonization Society, in these United States.

We feel sorrowful to see such an immense and wanton waste of lives and property, not doubting the benevolent feelings of some individuals engaged in that cause.—But we cannot for a moment doubt, but that the cause of many of our unconstitutional, unchristian, and unheard of sufferings, emanate from that unhallowed source ; and we would call on Christians of every denomination firmly to resist it.— When, on motion, the report of the committee was unanimously accepted and adopted.

The convention was favoured with a visit from the Rev. S. S. Jocelyn of New-Haven, (Conn.,) Messrs. Arthur Tappan, of New-York, Benjamin Lundy, of Washington, (D. C.,) William L. Garrison, of Boston, (Mass.,) Thomas Shipley and Charles Pierce, of Philadelphia. When, on motion, it was unanimously resolved, that the afore-mentioned gentlemen have permission to make any inquiries or communications, which they might deem proper.

In pursuance of this privilege, Messrs. Jocelyn, Tappan and Garrison, severally addressed the Convention on the subject of Education, and informed the Convention that their chief business with them was to submit to their body a plan for establishing a College, for the education of Young Men of Colour, on such basis, as cannot but elevate the general character of the coloured population—

They, therefore, solicited the favour of the Convention to appoint a committee to confer with them on the subject.

The Convention, feeling the importance of the communication, appointed a committee to consult with the above gentlemen.

The Committee, to whom was submitted the duty of conferring with Messrs. Tappan, Jocelyn and Garrison, reported as follows :—

That a plan had been submitted to them by the above-named gentlemen, for the liberal education of Young Men of Colour, on the Manual Labour System, all of which they respectfully submit to the consideration of the Convention, and are as follow :

The plan proposed is, that a College be established at New-Haven, Conn., as soon as $20,000 are obtained, and to be on the Manual Labour System, by which, in connexion with a scientific education, they may also obtain a useful Mechanical or Agricultural profession, and, (they farther report, having received information,) that a benevolent individual has offered to subscribe one thousand dollars towards this object, provided, that a farther sum of nineteen thousand dollars can be obtained in one year.

After an interesting discussion, the above report was unanimously adopted; one of the inquiries by the Convention was, in regard to the place of location. On interrogating the gentlemen why New-Haven should be the place of location, they gave the following as their reasons :—

1st. The site is healthy and beautiful.

2d. Its inhabitants are friendly, pious, generous, and humane.

3d. Its laws are salutary and protecting to all, without regard to complexion.

4th. Boarding is cheap and provisions are good.

5th. The situation is as central as any other that can be obtained with the same advantages.

6th. The town of New-Haven carries on an extensive West India trade, and many of the wealthy coloured residents in the Islands, would, no doubt, send their sons there to be educated, and thus a fresh tie of friendship would be formed, which might be productive of much real good in the end.

And last, though not the least, the literary and scientific character of New-Haven, renders it a very deisrable place for the location of the College.

The Convention, having received the report of the committee, and being deeply impressed with the importance of such an institution, do hereby resolve, that it is highly expedient to make an effort to carry the same into effect, under due regulations. Therefore, resolved, that this Convention earnestly recommend to our Brethren, to contribute as God has given them the ability, to aid in carrying into operation the proposed institution; and the Convention would wish it to be distinctly understood, that the Trustees of the contemplated Institution, shall a majority of them be coloured persons; the number proposed is seven, three white, and four coloured; who shall be elected by the subscribers, contributors, or their representatives: the elections to be held in the city of New-York, unless ordered otherwise by the Convention.

The Trustees shall annually report the state and condition, with all other necessary information relating to the Institution, to the Annual Convention.

On motion, the Rev. Samuel E. Cornish, was unanimously elected General Agent, to collect funds, in aid of the contemplated Institution, (his necessary compensation being gurranteed by the liberality of the benevolent individual before alluded to) with power to appoint sub-agents, at such places where the Convention may have made no appointments.

On motion, Resolved, That Arthur Tappan, Esq., at New-York, be appointed to receive as Treasurer, all moneys that may be collected for the purpose of establishing the proposed Institution at New-Haven, he satisfying the Executive Committee at New-York.

And on motion, it was Resolved, That there be Provisional Committees appointed, whose duty it shall be to aid and assist the Agent or Agents that may be appointed in the discharge of their duties.

And that the Provisional Committee at New-York shall be the Executive Committee until the Trustees are appointed.

Here follow the several Provisional Committees: viz.

Boston.—Rev: Hosea Reiston, Robert Roberts, James G. Barbadoes, and Rev. Samuel Snowden.

New-York.—Rev. Peter Williams, Boston Cromwell, Philip Bell, Thomas Downing, Peter Voglesang.

Philadelphia.—Joseph Cassey, Robert Douglass, Senr., James Forten, Richard Howell, Robert Purvis.

Baltimore.—Thomas Green, James P. Walker, Samuel G. Mathews, Isaac Whipper, Samuel Hiner.

New Haven.—Biars Stanley, John Creed, Alexander C. Luca.

Brooklyn, L. I.—Jacob Deyes, Henry Thomson, Willis Jones.

Wilmington, Del.—Rev. Peter Spencer, Jacob Morgan, William S. Thomas.

Albany.—Benjamin Latimore, Captain Schuyler, Captain Francis March.

Washington, D. C.—William Jackson, Arthur Waring, Isaac Carey.

Lancaster, Pa.—Charles Butler and Jared Grey.

Carlisle, Pa.—John Peck, and Rowland G. Roberts.

Chambersburg, Pa.—Dennis Berry.

Pittsburg.—John B. Vashon, Lewis Gardiner, Abraham Lewis.

Newark, N. J.—Peter Petitt, Charles Anderson, Adam Ray.

Trenton.—Sampson Peters, Leonard Scott.

On motion, it was Resolved, That the convention appoint a President, Vice-President, Treasurer, Corresponding Secretary, and Recording Secretary, to hold their office for one year or until the next Convention, all of whom shall reside in the city or county of Philadelphia, and be styled the Conventional Board, who shall act as the representatives of the Convention during its recess.

Whereupon the following persons were duly elected.

John Bowers, President.

Frederick A. Hinton, Vice-President, Joseph Casey, Treasurer, Junius C. Morel, Corresponding Secretary, Charles H. Leveck, Recording Secretary.

On motion, Resolved, That there be a Vice-President and Corresponding Secretary in each state, to hold their offices for the term of one year, or until others are appointed, whose duties it shall be to use every exertion to obtain moneys and remit the same to the Treasurer of the Conventional Fund at Philadelphia, and that the officers have power to fill any vacancies that may occur in their body by resignation or otherwise.

Whereupon the Convention appointed the following officers—

New-York.—Thomas L. Jennings, Vice-President ; Peter Voglesang, Corresponding Secretary.

Massachusetts.—James G. Barbadoes, Vice-President; Henry H. Mondy, Corresponding Secretary.

Maryland.—Rev. Abner Cocker, Vice-President; Robert Cowley, Corresponding Secretary.

Rhode Island.—George C. Willis, Vice-President; Alfred Niger, Corresponding Secretary.

District of Columbia.—William Wormley, Vice-President; John W. Prout, Corresponding Secretary.

Delaware.—Rev. Peter Spencer, Vice-President; Abraham D. Shad, Corresponding Secretary.

Virginia.—James Wilkins, Vice-President; William Duncan, Corresponding Secretary.

New Jersey.—Leonard Scott, Vice-President; with permission to appoint his Secretary.

Connecticut.—Scipio C. Augustus.

Ohio.—Charles Hatfield, Vice-President; John Liverpool, Corresponding Secretary.

On motion of Mr. Jennings, it was Resolved, That the Vice-Presidents and Secretaries of each state are hereby requested to use every exertion in recommending the formation of Associations for the purpose of raising funds for the great object in view, and that each Society appoint its own Treasurer, who shall pay over all moneys so collected to the Treasurer of the General Fund at Philadelphia.

RULES AND REGULATIONS

TO BE OBSERVED BY

THE CONVENTIONAL BOARD OF OFFICERS.

1st. The funds shall be under the immediate control of the Officers of the Convention during their continuance in office, subject to the following restrictions, viz:—

They shall pay all moneys appropriated by the Convention, and for that purpose they are hereby invested with authority to draw on the Treasurer for the same.

They shall pay all the ordinary expenses of the Convention that may be necessary and proper, and shall with proper vouchers account to the Annual Convention for the same at each session.

The President shall preside at each meeting of the Board of Officers which shall form a Council for the transaction of the business of the Convention during its recess.

During the absence or inability of the President to preside, the Vice-President shall be competent to discharge all of his duty in the Council.

The Recording Secretary shall keep accurate minutes of the meetings of the officers at any time or times, which minutes, with all other useful matter that may come under his observation, shall be laid before the Annual Conventions from time to time.

The Treasurer shall receive all moneys that may be collected by all the different societies, (which now are or hereafter may be subject to the order of the Convention,) for which the president shall take his receipt. He shall pay all moneys as the Council may draw on him for the order, being signed by each of the Council.

The Corresponding Secretary shall notify the Vice-Presidents and Secretaries of their appointments, together with the general views of the Convention in relation to the Canadian settlement.

He shall, also, hold the most extensive and faithful correspondence with the Committees and Agents appointed to advance the interests of the proposed College, holding his correspondence subject to the inspection of the President and Vice-Presidents only.

No moneys shall be drawn from the funds, but by consent of a majority of the Council.

The Convention recommends the Parent Society at Philadelphia, and all others engaged in the Canadian purchase, to alter their Constitutions and by-laws, so as to become auxiliary to the Convention, to the Treasurer of which they shall remit their funds at stated times.

On motion of Mr. Jennings, Resolved, That this Convention highly approve of the exertions of the Parent Society and its Auxiliaries, (recommended by the last Convention,) for the able and zealous manner in which they have discharged their duties, far exceeding the most sanguine expectations of its friends.

Resolved, That this Convention approves and highly appreciates the laudable intention of (Junius C. Morel and John P. Thompson,) to establish a weekly Journal in the city of Philadelphia, in aid of the cause of our oppressed brethren, and pledge ourselves to use our influence in promoting it to public patronage.

Resolved, That the thanks of this Convention be given to Messrs. Shipley, Lundy, Tappan, Garrison, Jocelyn and Peirce, for the friendship evinced by them towards this Convention, and its constituents.

On motion, Resolved, That the Convention recommend to the People of Colour *throughout the United States*, to set apart the fourth day of July, as a day of humiliation, fasting and prayer—and to beseech Almighty God to interpose on our behalf, that the shackles of slavery may be broken, and our sacred rights obtained, and that there be appropriate addresses delivered on that day, and collections taken and forwarded to the Treasurer at Philadelphia, for the general purposes of the Convention.

It was further Resolved, That the editors of the "Genius of Universal Emancipation," "The Liberator," and "African Sentinel," are our tried friends, and fearless advocates of our rights and promoters of our best interests, are entitled to a prominent place in our affections.

That the principles emanating from said presses, ought to be proclaimed throughout the world, and read by every friend of the rights of man—and that we pledge ourselves to use all our influence in promoting the support and circulation of such vehicles.

On motion, it was Resolved, That the next Annual Convention be held in the city of Philadelphia, on the first Monday in June, 1832.

On motion, it was Resolved, that each Society in the United States, (organized by the recommendation of this Convention) be authorized to send delegates, not exceeding *five* in number, to represent them in the General Convention to be held aforesaid ; and that in places where it is not practicable at present to form Societies, the people shall have the same privilege, *provided* they contribute to the furtherance of the objects of the Convention.

On motion, the Convention recommends to the People of Colour throughout the United States, the discontinuance of public processions on *any* day, considering it as highly injurious to our interests as a people.

On motion, it was unanimously Resolved, That this Convention feels grateful for the kind services rendered by the American Society for the Abolition of Slavery, in the United States—also, to the Anti-Slavery Society in Great Britain, and to the friends of the rights of man wherever dispersed.   Adjourned, sine die.

JOHN BOWERS, *President.*

WILLIAM WHIPPER,
THOMAS L. JENNINGS,   } *Secretaries.*

Philadelphia, June 11th, 1831.

CONVENTIONAL ADDRESS.

Respected Brethren and Fellow Citizens—

In accordance with a resolution of the last Convention, we have again been assembled, in order to discharge those duties which have devolved upon us by your unanimous voices.

Our attention has been called to investigate the political standing of our brethren wherever dispersed, but more particularly the situation of those in this great Republic.

Abroad, we have been cheered with pleasant views of humanity, and the steady, firm, and uncompromising march of equal liberty to the human family. Despotism, tyranny, and injustice have had to retreat, in order to make way for the unalienable rights of man. Truth has conquered prejudice, and mankind are about to rise in the majesty and splendour of their native dignity.

The cause of general emancipation is gaining powerful and able friends abroad. Britain and Denmark have performed such deeds as will immortalize them for their humanity, in the breasts of the philanthropists of the present day; whilst, as a just tribute to their virtues, after ages will yet erect unperishable monuments to their memory. (Would to God we could say thus of our own native soil!)

And it is only when we look to our own native land, to the birthplace of our *fathers*, to the land for whose prosperity their blood and our sweat have been shed and cruelly extorted, that the Convention has had cause to hang its head and blush. Laws, as cruel in themselves as they were unconstitutional and unjust, have in many places been enacted against our poor unfriended and unoffending brethren; laws, (without a shadow of provocation on our part,) at whose bare recital the very savage draws him up for fear of the contagion—looks noble, and prides himself because he bears not the name of a Christian.

But the Convention would not wish to dwell long on this subject, as it is one that is too sensibly felt to need description.

We would wish to turn you from this scene with an eye of pity, and a breast glowing with mercy, praying that the recording angel may drop a tear, which shall obliterate for ever the remembrance of so foul a stain upon the national escutcheon of this great Republic.

This spirit of persecution was the cause of our Convention. It was that first induced us to seek an asylum in the Canadas; and the Convention feel happy to report to their brethren, that our efforts to establish a settlement in that province have not been made in vain. Our prospects are cheering; our friends and funds are daily increasing; wonders have been performed far exceeding our most sanguine expectations: already have our brethren purchased eight hundred acres of land—and two thousand of them have left the soil of their birth, crossed the lines, and laid the foundation for a structure which promises to prove an asylum for the coloured population of these United States. They have erected two hundred log houses, and have five hundred acres under cultivation.

And now it is to your fostering care the Convention appeal, and we appeal to you as to men and brethren, yet to enlarge their borders.

We therefore ask of you, brethren—we ask of you, philanthropists, of every colour, and of every kindred, to assist us in this undertaking. We look to a kind Providence, and to you, to say whether our desires shall be realized, and our labours crowned with success.

The Convention has done its duty, and it now remains for you, brethren, to do yours. Various obstacles have been thrown in our way by those opposed to the elevation of the human species; but, thanks to an all-wise Providence, his goodness has as yet cleared the way, and our advance has been slow but steady. The only thing now wanted, is an accumulation of funds, in order to enable us to make a purchase agreeable to the direction of the first Convention; and, to effect that purpose, the Convention has recommended, to the different Societies engaged in that cause, to persevere and prosecute their designs with doubled energy; and we would earnestly recommend to every coloured man, (who feels the weight of his degradation,) to consider himself in duty bound to contribute his mite towards this great object. We would say to all, that the prosperity of the rising generation mainly depends upon our active exertions.

Yes, it is with us to say whether they shall assume a rank and standing among the nations of the earth, as men and freemen, or whether they shall still be prized and held at market price. Oh, then, by a brother's love, and by all that makes man dear to man—awake in time! Be wise! Be free! Endeavour to walk with circumspection: be obedient to the laws of our common country; honour and respect its lawmakers and lawgivers: and, through all, let us not forget to respect ourselves.

During the deliberations of this Convention, we had the favour of advising and consulting with some of our most eminent and tried philanthropists—men of unblemished character and of acknowledged rank and standing. Our sufferings have excited their sympathy; our ignorance appealed to their humanity; and, brethren, we feel that gratitude is due to a kind and benevolent Creator, that our excitement and appeal have neither been in vain. A plan has been proposed to the Convention for the erection of a College for the instruction of young men of colour, on the manual labour system, by which the children of the poor may receive a regular classical education, as well as those of their more opulent brethren, and the charge will be so regulated as to put it within the reach of all. In support of this plan, a benevolent individual has offered the sum of one thousand dollars, provided that we can obtain subscriptions to the amount of nineteen thousand dollars in one year.

The Convention has viewed the plan with considerable interest, and after mature deliberation, on a candid investigation, feel strictly justified in recommending the same to the liberal patronage of our brethren, and respectfully solicit the aid of those philanthropists who feel an interest in sending light, knowledge, and truth, to all of the human species.

To the friends of general education, we do believe that our appeal will not be in vain. For, the present ignorant and degraded condition of many of our brethren in these United States (which has been a subject of much concern to the Convention,) can excite no astonishment, (although used by our enemies to show our inferiority in the scale of human beings;) for, what opportunities have they possessed for mental cultivation or improvement? Mere ignorance, however, in a people divested of the means of acquiring information by books, or an extensive connexion with the world, is no just criterion of their intellectual incapacity; and it has been actually seen, in various remarkable instances, that the degradation of the mind and character, which has been too hastily imputed to a people kept, as we are, at a distance from those sources of knowledge which abound in civilized and enlightened communities, has resulted from no other causes than our unhappy situation and circumstances.

True philanthrophy disdains to adopt those prejudices against any people which have no better foundation than accidental diversities of colour, and refuses to determine without substantial evidence and incontestible fact as the basis of her judgment. And it is in order to remove these prejudices, which are the actual causes of our ignorance, that we have appealed to our friends in support of the contemplated Institution.

The Convention has not been unmindful of the operations of the American Colonization Society, and it would respectfully suggest to that august body of learning, talent, and worth, that, in our humble opinion, strengthened, too, by the opinions of eminent men in this country, as well as in Europe, that they are pursuing the direct road to perpetuate slavery, with all its unchristianlike concomitants, in this boasted land of freedom; and, as citizens and men whose best blood is sapped to gain popularity for that Institution, we would, in the most feeling manner, beg of them to desist : or, if we must be sacrificed to their philanthrophy, we would rather die at home. Many of our fathers, and some of us, have fought and bled for the liberty, independence, and peace which you now enjoy ; and, surely, it would be ungenerous and unfeeling in you to deny us an humble and quiet grave in that country which gave us birth !

In conclusion, the Convention would remind our brethren that knowledge is power, and to that end, we call on you to sustain and support, by all honourable, energetic, and necessary means, those presses which are devoted to our instruction and elevation, to foster and encourage the mechanical arts and sciences among our brethren, to encourage simplicity, neatness, temperance, and economy in our habits, taking due care always to give the preference to the production of freemen wherever it can be had. Of the utility of a General Fund, the Convention believes there can exist but one sentiment, and that is for a speedy establishment of the same. Finally, we trust our brethren will pay due care to take such measures as will ensure a general and equal representation in the next Convention.

Signed—

> Belfast Burton,
> Junius C. Morel,   } *Publishing Committee.*
> William Whipper,

DELEGATES' NAMES.

> John Bowers,
> Dr. Belfast Burton,
> James Cornish,   } Philadelphia.
> Junius C. Morel,
> Wm. Whipper,
> John Peck,   Carlisle, Pa.

Rev. Abner Coker, Robert Cowley,	} Maryland.
Rev. Wm. Miller, Henry Sipkins, Thos. L. Jennings, Wm. Hamilton,	} New-York.
James Pennington,	Long-Island.
Abraham D. Shad, Rev. Peter Gardiner,	} Delaware.
William Duncan,	Virginia.

The Conventional Board of Officers beg leave to give their unfeigned thanks to their friend and brother, the Rev. Lewis G. Wells, of Baltimore, for his liberality in appropriating the gross proceeds of one night's lecturing on Phrenology to the benefit of the Fund.

JOHN BOWERS, *President.*

CHARLES H. LEVECK, *Secretary.*

MINUTES

AND

PROCEEDINGS

OF THE

SECOND ANNUAL CONVENTION,

FOR THE IMPROVEMENT

OF THE FREE PEOPLE OF COLOR

In these United States,

HELD BY ADJOURNMENTS

IN THE CITY OF PHILADELPHIA,

From the 4th to the 13th of June inclusive, 1832.

☙☙☙☙☙☙☙

PHILADELPHIA:
PUBLISHED BY ORDER OF THE CONVENTION.
Benj. Paschal, Thos. Butler, and Jas. C. Matthews, Publishing Com.
Martin & Boden, Printers.

1832.

MINUTES.

AGREEABLY to public notice, the Delegates to the Second Annual General Convention, for the improvement of the condition of the free people of color in these United States, met at the Benezett Hall, in Seventh Street, and commenced business at 9 o'clock A. M.—Mr. John Bowers, President of the Conventional Board appointed at the last meeting of the Convention to transact its business during its recess, took the Chair, and Junius C. Morel, acted as Secretary. After a most eloquent and appropriate prayer by the Rev. Charles W. Gardner, the following Delegates presented their credentials, which were read and approved, and they admitted to seats in the Convention, viz:—

PENNSYLVANIA.

Pittsburg.—John B. Vashon.

Philadelphia.

John Bowers,	Benjamin Paschal,
William Whipper,	F. A. Hinton.
J. C. Morel,	

Carlisle.—John Peck.

Lewistown, Mifflin county.—Samuel Johnson.

NEW YORK.

New York City.

William Hamilton,	Henry Sipkins,
Thomas L. Jennings,	Philip A. Bell.

Brooklyn.—James Pennington.

DELAWARE.

Wilmington.

Joseph Burton,	William Johnson,
Jacob Morgan,	Peter Gardiner.
Abm. D. Shad,	

MARYLAND.
Baltimore.

Samuel Elliott,   Robert Cowley,   Samuel Hiner.

NEW JERSEY.
Gloucester.

Thomas D. Coxsin,   Thomas Banks,
Trenton.—Aaron Roberts.

MASSACHUSETTS.
Boston.—Hosea Easton.
New Bedford.—Nathan Johnson.

CONNECTICUT.
Hartford.—Paul Drayton.
New Haven.—Scipio C. Augustus.

RHODE ISLAND.
Providence.—Ichabod Northrop.

On motion, the Convention proceeded to the election of officers for its present sessions, when the following persons were duly elected:

HENRY SIPKINS, President.
JOHN B. VASHON, 1st Vice President.
FREDERICK A. HINTON, 2d Vice President.
PHILIP A. BELL, Secretary,
JUNIUS C. MOREL, Assistant Secretary.
CHARLES H. LEVECK, Clerk.

After the election of the President and 1st Vice President, Mr. Frederick A. Hinton, Vice President of the Conventional Board, announced to the house the election of Mr. Henry Sipkins of New York, President of the Convention, and Mr. John B. Vashon of Pittsburg, first Vice President. On the election of the second Vice President, Mr. John Bowers announced to the house the election of Mr. F. A. Hinton of Philadelphia, second Vice President. The election of the Secretaries and Chaplain were announced by the President of the Convention.

On motion, resolved that the list of names of the Delegates be read. It was accordingly read, and each member answered to his name. Moved and seconded that we adjourn to meet in this Hall at half past three o'clock this afternoon. Agreed.

Afternoon Session.

. The Convention met agreeably to adjournment, Mr. Sipkins in the Chair, Philip A. Bell, Secretary. After prayer by the Rev. C. W. Gardner, it was, on motion, agreed that the Secretary proceed to call the roll, and read the minutes of the forenoon session; which being done, it was moved and seconded that the name of the mover and seconder of each motion shall be attached to the same. Agreed.

On motion of William Hamilton, seconded by John Bowers, the following persons were appointed a Committee to draft rules to govern this Convention, viz:— Benjamin Paschal, John Peck, James Pennington, Thos. L. Jennings, and Thomas D. Coxsin, and to report the same as soon as possible.

The second Vice President announced and introduced to the Convention the Rev. R. R. Gurley of Washington City, and Mr. Brackenridge of Kentucky, and several other distinguished gentlemen.

The President of the Conventional Board appointed at the last meeting of the Convention, presented a report of the proceedings of the Board during its recess.

Moved by William Whipper, seconded by Benjamin Paschal, that the report of the President of the Conventional Board be referred to a Committee of three persons, with full power to enquire for all documents concerning the same, or connected with the business thereof, and report the same to-morrow morning. Agreed.

William Whipper, Benjamin Paschal, and William Hamilton were appointed.

On motion of John Peck, seconded by Benjamin Paschal, agreed that the Rev. Charles W. Gardner be requested to officiate as Chaplain to this Convention.

On motion of John Bowers, seconded by John Peck, that the Rev. Hosea Easton be assistant Chaplain. Agreed.

Moved by William Hamilton, seconded by John Peck, that a committee of three persons be appointed to write an Address to the free people of color in these United States, expressive of the views of this Convention; that they shall be nominated by the President and appointed by the Convention; and that they shall present the same for approval on Friday morning next. Messrs. Abraham

1*

D. Shad, William Hamilton, and William Whipper were appointed.

Moved by Thomas L. Jennings, and seconded by Jas. Pennington, that a committee of five be appointed who shall report to this Convention such subjects as they may deem essntial for it to act upon. The following persons were appointed—Thomas L. Jennings, James Pennington, Junius C. Morel, Thomas D. Coxsin, and John B. Vashon.

Moved by John Bowers, seconded by John Peck, that all monies paid to this Convention shall be received by Frederick A. Hinton, until a treasurer be appointed. Agreed.

On motion, adjourned to 9 o'clock, Tuesday morning.

Tuesday, June 5th.—Morning Session.

Agreeably to adjournment, the Convention met in the Benezett Hall. The President took his seat, and the house was opened with prayer by the Rev. Charles W. Gardner.

Mr. John Bowers informed the Convention that the Trustees of the First African Presbyterian Church, in Seventh street, had consented to let us have the same for one dollar and fifty cents per day.

On motion the terms were agreed to.

The Rev. C. W. Gardner informed the Convention that the Rev. Mr. Gurley, of Washington City, Secretary and General agent of the Colonization Society, desired permission to address the meeting in the afternoon.

On motion of Mr. Hamilton, seconded by Mr. Bell, the request of Mr. Gurley was granted.

Benjamin Paschâl offered an amendment, seconded by William Whipper—Resolved that the Rev. R. R. Gurley deliver his sentiments in writing to this Convention, and that we answer him in the same. The President decided the same as not an amendment.

On motion, resolved that the committee appointed to draft rules for the government of this Convention, report. The same was presented, read and adopted. The report and rules were as follows:—

We, your committee, appointed to draft rules and regulations for the government of this Convention, beg leave to report—

1. The President shall take the chair at the time to which the House may be adjourned, and upon the appearance of a quorum shall direct the roll to be called and the previous minutes read.

2. The President shall have full power to keep order and decorum; shall decide questions of order, subject to an appeal to the Convention, and appoint or nominate committees when ordered by the Convention.

3. In case of the absence of the President, the first Vice President shall perform his duty, and in his absence it shall devolve upon the second Vice President.

4. If two or more members rise to speak at one time, the President shall decide who shall be entitled to the floor.

5. Every member who shall be in the House at the time the question is put, shall give his vote, unless the House, for special reasons, shall excuse him.

6. No member shall be permitted to leave the House without the permission of the President.

7. No member shall be interrupted while speaking, except by a call to order by the President; when such member may appeal to the House.

8. When a motion is stated by the President, it shall be deemed to be in possession of the House, but may be withdrawn at any time before a decision.

9. While the President is stating any question, or addressing the House, no member shall walk out, or cross the floor, nor when any member is speaking entertain private discourse.

10. No member shall speak more than twice on the same subject without leave of the house.

11. No motion or proposition on a subject different from that under consideration shall be admitted under color of amendment.

12. No motion for reconsideration shall be in order unless made by a member who voted in the majority.

13. A motion for adjournment shall always be in order after 1 o'clock, P. M. or 6 o'clock. P. M. All of which your committee respectfully submit.

THOMAS L. JENNINGS,
JAMES PENNINGTON,
JOHN PECK,
THOMAS D. COXSIN,
BENJAMIN PASCHAL.

Adopted, June 5th, 1832.

The committee appointed to report such business as might be essential to be acted upon by the Convention, signified their readiness to submit the same, which was read.

On motion of Mr. Paschal, seconded by Mr. Hamilton, the report was returned to the committee for reconsideration.

It was, on motion, agreed that the committee be enlarged to seven persons. Robert Cowley and Benjamin Paschal were appointed.

Report of the Committee.

Resolved—That in the opinion of this committee, the plan suggested by the first General Convention, of purchasing land or lands in Upper Canada, for the avowed object of forming a settlement in that province, for such colored persons as may choose to emigrate there, still merits and deserves our united support and exertions, and further, that the appearances of the times, in this our native land, demands an immediate action on that subject. Adopted.

Resolved—That in the opinion of this committee, we still solemnly and sincerely protest against any interference, on the part of the American Colonization Society, with the free colored population in these United States, so long as they shall countenance or endeavor to use coercive measures, (either directly or indirectly,) to colonize us in any place which is not the object of our choice. And we ask of them respectfully, as men and as Christians, to cease their unhallowed persecutions of a people already sufficiently oppressed, or if, as they profess to have our welfare and prosperity at heart, to assist us in the object of our choice,—Resolved, that this committee would recommend to the members of this Convention, to discountenance, by all just means in their power, any emigration to Liberia or Hayti, believing them only calculated to distract and divide the whole colored family.

Moved by Wm. Hamilton, seconded by Thomas D. Coxsin, that the following motion of Mr. T. D. Coxsin, seconded by Robert Cowley, viz:—

Resolved, That the members of this Convention take into consideration the propriety of affecting the purch se of Lands in the Province of Upper Canada, as a permanent home for the people of color, when they may be compelled to remove from these United States, be laid on the table, to be taken up on Wednesday morning.—Agreed.

Moved by Wm. Whipper, seconded by Abraham D. Shad, that a committee of three be appointed to invite such of our white brethren in the city of Philadelphia as may feel disposed to attend our deliberations, and that they be at liberty to make such communications, as in their opinion, will advance the objects of the Convention. Agreed. The following persons constitute that committee—John Bowers, Wm. Whipper and Peter Gardiner.

On motion, adjourned to meet in the First African Presbyterian Church in Seventh Street.

Afternoon Session.

Met agreeably to adjournment in the First African Presbyterian Church. The President took the chair. The house was opened with prayer by the Rev. Hosea Easton. The roll being called and the minutes read, the committee to whom was returned the report of such business as might be essential to be acted on by this Convention, for reconsideration, asked of the house a longer time, which was granted.

Moved by William Hamilton, seconded by Thomas L. Jennings, that the President appoint a committee of three to examine and correct the minutes after each adjournment.—Agreed. The following persons were appointed. —Wm. Hamilton, Frederick A. Hinton and Abraham D. Shad.

The Rev. Mr. Gurley, Secretary of the American Colonization Society appeared, and by permission of the President, conformably to a resolution of the Convention, addressed the meeting at considerable length, in his usual tone of eloquence, with a view, as he said, of removing some erroneous impressions in the minds of the people of color, in relation to the Colonization Society. He was followed by Mr. Wm. Lloyd Garrison in reply, who in a most eloquent and convincing speech, proved that the operations of that Society militate against the interest of the people of color in these United States.

Mr. Vashon, a delegate from Pittsburg, in a speech of considerable length, represented the views and feelings of the people generally, in relation to that Society.

Mr. Thomas Shipley, who is a strenuous friend to the

abolition of Slavery, then addressed the Convention in an excellent speech.

The hour of adjournment having arrived, at half past six, adjourned to meet next morning at nine o'clock. Prayer by the Rev. Charles W. Gardner.

Wednesday Morning, 6th June.

Met agreeably to adjournment. The President took his chair. Prayer by the Rev. Hosea Easton.

The Secretary having called the roll and read the minutes of the previous Session, it was moved by Junius C. Morel, seconded by Thos. L. Jennings, that any member making a motion, shall, at the request of the President or any member, commit the same to writing.—Agreed.

On motion, the resolution of Mr. Coxsin, respecting the purchase of lands in the province of Upper Canada, as a permanent home for those of our brethren who may be compelled to leave these United States, was called up for consideration, when a most animated discussion took place, and brought into requisition the almost entire talent of the Convention; the greater part insisting that any recommendation of the Convention to emigrate from the United States, was calculated to impress the public mind, that we relinquished our claim to this being the land of our nativity. The principal speakers on that side of the motion, were Messrs. Hamilton, Shad, Jennings, Bell, Vashon, Johnson, of Lewistown, Pennington, and Peck. The supporters of the motion, were Messrs. Cowley, Morel, Paschal, Coxsin, Elliot, Roberts, Banks, and Hiner. When Mr. A. D. Shad, seconded by Mr. Bell, offered, as an amendment, the following resolution, viz:—

That the members of the Convention take into consideration the propriety of affecting the purchase of lands in Upper Canada, as an Assylum for those of our brethren who may be compelled to remove from these United States.

Moved by Benjamin Paschal, and seconded by Thomas D. Coxsin, that a committee of five be appointed to consider the amendment offered by Mr. A. D. Shad, and that they report to morrow morning. Messrs. Robert Cowley, Wm. Hamilton, Junius C. Morel, John Peck and Wm. Whipper, were appointed.

On motion, adjourned to 3 o'clock, P. M.

Wednesday, Afternoon Session.

The President took the chair at three o'clock. Prayer by the Rev. William Johnson.

The roll having been called, and the minutes of the morning session read, the Committee appointed to report to the Convention such business as might be essential to be acted upon, and to whom was returned the report for reconsideration, signified that they were ready to submit the same.

Moved by Mr. Easton, seconded by Mr. Paschal, that the report be read.—Agreed.

On motion, it was agreed that the same be taken up by sections and considered for adoption; but the same was postponed to give the Rev. Mr. Patterson, an advocate of the Colonization Society, an opportunity of expressing his sentiments before the Convention. The Reverend gentleman evinced a liberality of feeling toward those who differ with him as to the most efficient means of improving the condition of the people of color, and declared his readiness to assist in any plan that promised their elevation. Mr. Patterson was followed by Mr. Garrison who exhibited, by a large number of facts, taken from the proceedings of the Colonization Society, that the sentiments cherished by it in relation to us, as citizens of the United States, are hostile to our interests. Mr. Junius C. Morel followed on the same side, in a very eloquent speech. Mr. Evan Lewis, of the city of Philadelphia, a strenuous advocate of the general emancipation of the people of color, addressed the meeting in a most excellent discourse. Some remarks were also made by Captain ———, of a vessel that took out emigrants to Liberia.

Adjourned at 7 o'clock. Prayer by the Rev. C. W. Gardner.

Thursday Morning, 7th June.

Convened according to adjournment. The President took his seat. Prayer by the Rev. Samuel Elliott.

The Secretary called the roll, and read the minutes of the previous session ; when a lady most friendly to the attainment of the rights of the people of color, delivered a most feeling address on the miseries attendant on our present situation ; when it was agreed that a vote of thanks be tendered the lady, for her friendly expression of feelings toward us. The President in the name of the Convention, presented the same.

On motion, Resolved, that any communications to the Convention, from places represented shall be presented by a delegate from that place.

Moved by Thos. L. Jennings, seconded by John Peck, that the Vice Presidents and Committees, appointed by the last Convention, report their proceedings during the year, in the order of their appointment, and present the same as soon as convenient.—Agreed.

On motion, adjourned to meet at 3 o'clock.

Thursday June 7th, Afternoon Session.

The President took his seat at the time appointed. Prayer by the Rev. C. W. Gardner. The roll was called, and the minutes of the Convention of the forenoon session read.

Mr. John B. Vashon presented a letter containing a proclamation of Major General Andrew Jackson, to the free colored inhabitants of Louisiana, in the year 1814, and also one by his order, by his Aid-de-Camp, Thos. Butler.

After reading the same, Mr. Vashon moved, and was seconded by T. D. Coxsin, that 3000 copies be printed for gratuitous distribution.

After a very protracted discussion on the propriety of entering the proclamation upon the minutes, a suspension of a vote on it was granted with a view to enable some of the members who were absent on committee business, to give their votes. The members having returned, Mr. Peck moved, and was seconded by Thomas L. Jennings, that the sentiments contained in the proclamation of Gen. Jackson, are in accordance with those of every philanthropist in these United States, and are entitled to a prominent place in the minutes of the Convention. This motion provoked considerable debate and was eventually negatived.

Mr. Vashon's motion for printing 3000 copies, was again called up, and the letter again read; the debate was renewed as to the propriety of printing. The hour of adjournment having arrived, the motion was withdrawn.

On motion, adjourned to meet in this place to-morrow morning at nine o'clock. Prayer by the Rev. Charles W. Gardner.

Friday Morning, June 8th, 1832.

The Convention met agreeably to adjournment. The President took his seat and called the house to order. Prayer by the Rev. Samuel Johnson.

Mr. James Pennington presented a list of resolutions for the consideration of the Convention, which produced very tedious debates, and it was finally deemed inexpedient that the same should, at present, engage the deliberation of this meeting.

The committee on the subject of the Canada purchase, was called on for its report on the same, which was submitted and read.

The report was signed by William Whipper, William Hamilton and John Peck. A counter report was presented by a minority of the committee, signed Robert Cowley and Junius C. Morel. The reports produced a very long discussion. Adjourned to meet at three o'clock.

June 8th, Afternoon Session.

Met as by adjournment; the house being called to order, was opened with prayer by the Rev. Samuel Johnson.

On motion of Benjamin Paschal, seconded by Thomas D. Coxsin—Resolved that the rule of adjournment be postponed for one hour this evening.

On motion of Thomas D. Coxsin, seconded by Benjamin Paschal, the report of the minority of the committee, was called for a second reading, which being done, a motion that the same be adopted, produced a long debate and was finally negatived.

Mr. John B. Vashon, having had the proclamation of Gen. Jackson and his Aid-de-Camp, printed, presented the Convention with two hundred copies, for which he received its thanks.

Adjourned at 6 o'clock, to meet at 9 to-morrow morning. Prayer by the Rev. C. W. Gardner.

Saturday Morning, June 9th, 1832.

Met in the First African Presbyterian Church in 7th street; the house being called to order, prayer by the Rev. C. W Gardner.

2

14

Moved by Thomas L. Jennings, and seconded by Benjamin Paschal, that two persons be added to the committee on the Canada question, and that the reports of the majority and minority be referred to the same, and that they report with all convenient despatch.—Agreed. T. Coxsin and Benj. Paschal were added to the committee.

Moved by John Peck, and seconded by J. C. Morel, that the report of Thomas L. Jennings, Vice President of the Convention for the State of New York be read.—Agreed.

The report set forth that a Society, auxiliary to the Convention, had been established in the city of New York on the 13th day of July last, and at the present time, contains between one hundred and twenty and thirty members; that in Brooklyn, Long Island, a Society for the same purpose, had been formed, consisting of from sixty to seventy members; that in Catskill, a Society was formed; in Albany preparations were making to form a like Society; and that although the Corresponding Secretary, had written to the colored inhabitants of Newburg and Hudson, no answer had been received from the two latter places.

The Secretary had taken an early opportunity, after the adjournment of the previous Convention, to open a correspondence with the colored inhabitants of New York and New Jersey, but that no written communication from that place had transpired.

Mr. John Bowers apprised the meeting, that in consequence of the Trustees wishing to have the Church cleaned for the service on the Sabbath, that the Convention would not be able to meet in that house in the afternoon; whereupon he moved, and was seconded by Mr. Peck, that this session continue one hour beyond the ordinary time of adjournment, which was agreed to unanimously.

Moved by Thos. L. Jennings, and seconded by James Pennington, that we proceed to the appointment of a Vice President and a Corresponding Secretary in each of the States, where the same may be safely done, to hold their offices for one year or until others are appointed. They shall have power to fill any vacancy that may happen, and make such appointments in the different parts of the state, as they may deem conducive to our interests. The following were appointed.

New York—Thomas L. Jennings, V. P.—Henry Sipkins, Cor. Sec.
Massachusetts—Jas. G. Barbadoes, V. P.—H. H. Manday, Cor. Sec.
Rhode Island—Geo. C. Willis, V. P.—Alfred Niger, Cor. Sec.
Connecticut—Scipio C. Augustus, V. P.—Peter Osborn, Cor. Sec.
Ohio—John Liverpool, Cor. Sec.
New Jersey—Aaron Roberts, V. P.
Maryland—Rev. Abner Crocker, V. P.—Robert Cowley, Cor. Sec.
Delaware—Rev. Peter Spencer, V. P.—A. D. Shad, Cor. Sec.

Moved and seconded, that the Vice Presidents and Secretaries be requested to employ their best endeavors in recommending the formation of associations to aid the objects of the Convention, and, at stated periods, transmit to the Treasurer of the general fund, such sums as circumstances may admit.

The committee on the joint reports, returned and presented the same, which was read, and the same was unanimously adopted, as follows:—

CANADIAN REPORT.

The Committee, to whom was submitted the following resolution for their consideration—viz:—

Resolved—That the members of this Convention take into consideration the propriety of effecting the purchase of Lands in the province of Upper Canada as an Asylum for those of our brethren who may be compelled to remove from these United States, beg leave, most respectfully to report—

That, after due consideration, they believe the resolution embraces three distinct enquiries for the consideration of this Convention, which should be duly weighed before they can adopt the sentiments contained in the above named resolution—Therefore your Committee conceive the resolution premature, and now proceed to state the enquiries separately—

First—Is it proper for the Free People of Color in this Country, under existing circumstances, to remove to any distant territory beyond these United States?

Secondly—Does Upper Canada possess superior advantages and conveniences to those held out in these United States or elsewhere?

Thirdly—Is there any certainty that the people of color will be compelled by oppressive legislative enactments to abandon the land of their birth for a home in a distant region?

Your committee before examining those inquiries, would most respectfully take a retrospective view of the object for which the Convention was first associated, and the causes which have actuated their deliberations.

The expulsory laws of Ohio, in 1829, which drove our people to seek a new home in Upper Canada, and their impoverished situation afterwards, excited a general burst of sympathy for their situation, by the wise and good, over the whole country. This awakened public feeling on their behalf, and numerous meetings were called to raise funds to alleviate their present miseries. The bright prospects that then appeared to dawn on the new settlement, awakened our people to the precariousness of their situations, and, in order more fully to be prepared for future exigencies, and to extend the system of benevolence still further to those who should remove to Upper Canada, a Circular was issued by five individuals, viz:—the Rev. Richard Allen, Cyrus Black, Junius C. Morel, Benjamin Pascal, and James E. Cornish, in behalf of the citizens of Philadelphia, calling a Convention of the colored delegates from the several States, to meet on the 20th day of September, 1830, to devise plans and means for the establishment of a colony in Upper Canada, under the patronage of the general Convention, then called.

That Convention met, pursuant to public notice, and recommended the formation of a parent Society, to be established, with auxiliaries, in the different towns where they had been represented in *general* Convention, for the purpose of raising monies to defray the object of purchasing a Colony in the province of Upper Canada, for those who should hereafter wish to emigrate thither, and that immediately after its organization, a Corresponding Agent should be appointed to reside at or near the intended purchase.

Our then limited knowledge of the manners, customs, and privileges, and rights of aliens in Upper Canada, together with the climate, soil and productions thereof, rendered it necessary to send out Agents to examine the same, who returned with a favorable report, except that citizens of these United States could not purchase lands in Upper Canada, and legally transfer the same to other individuals.

The Convention resolved to reassemble on the first Monday in June, 1831, during which time the order of the Convention had been carried into operation, relative to establishing Societies for the promotion of said object; and the sum and total of their proceedings were, that the Convention recommended to the colored people generally, when persecuted as were our brethren in Ohio, to seek an Asylum in Upper Canada. During which time, information having been received that a part of the white inhabitants of said province had, through prejudice and the fear of being overburthened with an ejected population, petitioned the provincial parliament to prohibit the general influx of colored population from entering their limits, which threw some consternation on the prospect. The Convention did not wholly abandon the subject, but turned its attention more to the elevation of our people in this, our native home.

The recent occurrences at the South, have swelled the tide of prejudice until it has almost revolutionized public sentiment, which has given birth to severe legislative enactments in some of the States, and almost ruined our interests and prospects in others, in which, in the opinion of your Committee, our situation is more precarious than it has been at any other period since the Declaration of Independance.

The events of the past year have been more fruitful in persecution, and have presented more inducements than at any other period of the history of our country, for the men of color to fly from the graves of their fathers, and seek new homes, in a land where the roaring billows of prejudice are less injurious to their rights and privileges.

Your Committee would now approach the present Convention and examine the resolution under consideration, beginning with the first interrogatory, viz: Is it proper for the Free people of color, in this country, under existing circumstances, to remove to any distant territory beyond the United States?

If we admit the first interrogatory to be true, as it is the exact spirit of the margin of this resolution, now under consideration, it is altogether unnecessary for us to make further preparation for either our moral, intellectual or political advancement in this our own, our native land.

Your committee also believe that if this Convention shall adopt a resolution that will, as soon as means can be obtained, remove our colored population to the province of Upper Canada, the best and brightest prospect of the philanthropists who are laboring for our elevation in this country will be thwarted, and that they will be brought to the conclusion that the great object which actuated their labors would now be removed, and that they might now rest from their labors, and have the painful feeling of transmitting to future generations, that an oppressed people, in the land of their birth, supported by the genuine philanthropists of the age, amidst friends, companions, and their natural attachments, a genial clime, a fruitful soil—amidst the rays of as proud institutions as ever graced the most favored spot that has ever received the glorious rays of a meridian sun—have abandoned their homes on account of their persecutions, for a home almost similarly precarious, for an abiding place among strangers!

Your committee further believe that any express plan to colonize our people beyond the limits of these United States, tends to weaken the situation of those who are left behind, without any peculiar advantage to those who emigrate. But it must be admitted, that the rigid oppression abroad in the land is such, that a *part* of our suffering brethren cannot live under it, and that the compulsory laws and the inducements held out by the American Colonization Society are such as will cause them to alienate all their natural attachments to their homes, and accept of the only mode left open, which is to remove to a distant country to receive those rights and privileges of which they have been deprived. And as this Convention is associated for the purpose of recommending to our people the best mode of alleviating their present miseries,

Therefore, your committee would, most respectfully, recommend to the general Convention, now assembled, to exercise the most vigorous means to collect monies through their auxiliaries, or otherwise, to be applied in such manner, as will advance the interests, and contribute to the wants of the free colored population of this country generally.

Your committee would now most respectfully approach

the *second inquiry,* viz:—Does Upper Canada possess superior advantages and conveniences to those held out in the United States or elsewhere?

Your committee, without summing up the advantages and disadvantages of other situations, would, most respectfully answer in the affirmative. At least they are willing to assert that the advantage is much in favor of those who are obliged to leave their present homes. For your more particular information on that subject we would, most respectfully, refer you to the interesting account given by our real and indefatigable friend, Benjamin Lundy, in a late number of the " Genius of Universal Emancipation." Vide Genius of Universal Emancipation, No. 10, Vol. 12.

From the history there laid down, your committee would, most respectfully, request the Convention to aid, so far as in their power lies, those who are obliged to seek an asylum in the province of Upper Canada; and, in order that they may more effectually carry their views into operation, they would respectfully request them to appoint an Agent in Upper Canada, to receive such funds as may be there transmitted for their use.

Your committee have now arrived at the *third* and last inquiry, viz:—Is there any certainty that we, as a people, will be compelled to leave this our native land, for a home in a distant region? To this inquiry your committee are unable to answer; it belongs to the fruitful events of time to determine. The mistaken policy of some of the friends of our improvement, that the same could be effected on the shore of Africa, has raised the tide of our calamity until it has overflowed the vallies of peace and tranquillity—the dark clouds of prejudice have rained persecution—the oppressor and the oppressed have suffered together—and we have yet been protected by that Almighty arm, who holds in his hands the destinies of nations, and whose presence is a royal safeguard, should we place the utmost reliance on his wisdom and power.

Your committee, while they rejoice at the noble object for which the Convention was first associated, have been unable to come to any conclusive evidence that lands can be purchased by this Convention and legall transferred to individuals, residents of said colony, so long as the present laws exist. But, while they deem it inexpedient for the Convention to purchase lands in Upper Canada for the purpose of erecting a colony thereon, do again, most respectfully, hope that they will exercise the same laudable exertions to collect funds for the comfort and happiness of our people there situated, and those who may hereafter emigrate, and pursue the same judicious measures in the appropriation of said funds, as they would in procuring a tract of land, as expressed by the resolution.

Your committee, after examining the various circumstances connected with our situation as a people, have come, unanimously, to the conclusion to recommend to this Convention to adopt the following resolution, as the best mode of alleviating the miseries of our oppressed brethren.

Resolved—That this Convention recommend the establishment of a Society, or Agent, in Upper Canada, for the purpose of purchasing lands and contributing to the wants of our people generally, who may be, by oppressive legislative enactments, obliged to flee from these United States and take up residence within her borders. And that this Convention will employ its Auxiliary Societies, and such other means as may lie in its power, for the purpose of raising monies, and remit the same for the purpose of aiding the proposed object.

Signed—

ROBERT COWLEY,
JOHN PECK,
WM. HAMILTON,
WM. WHIPPER, } COMMITTEE.
BENJ. PASCHAL,
THOS. D. COXSIN,
J. C. MOREL,

Moved by William Hamilton, seconded by Robt. Cowley, that William Whipper, and Thomas L. Jennings, be appointed to transcribe the report, and hand the same to the Clerk, to be entered on the minutes.

At half past two o'clock, Mr. P. A. Bell moved, and was seconded by Mr. Peck, that we adjourn to meet in the same place on Monday morning at 9 o'clock; the same prevailed.

Monday Morning, June 11th 1832.

The Convention, as per adjournment, met at 9 o'clock in the First Presbyterian Church. The house was called to order by the President, and prayer performed by the Rev. C. W. Gardner.

Moved and seconded that the committee appointed to revise the minutes, proceed immediately to the fulfilment of their appointment, and report the same as soon as possible.—Carried.

On motion, Resolved, that a committee of three be appointed for attending to the publication of the minutes of this Convention, as soon as they are returned by the correcting committee. Messrs. J. B. Vashon, Benj. Paschal and John Peck, were appointed.

Moved by Wm. Hamilton, and seconded by Thomas L. Jennings, that the next annual Convention of the free people of color, be held in the city of New York. The same after some debate was lost. When, on motion of Mr. Morel, seconded by Mr. Cowley, it was agreed that the same should be held in the city of Philadelphia, on the first Monday in June next.

Moved by J. C. Morel, seconded by B. Paschal, that a committee of conference, consisting of seven, be added to the conventional board, to assist in the transaction of its business during the year.

The following persons were appointed a committee to nominate suitable candidates for the offices, viz :—John Bowers, Frederick A. Hinton, Benjamin Paschal, J. C. Morel and Robert Cowley, who returned the under written persons, who were duly elected.

Robert Brown, President.
Benjamin Paschal, Vice President.
Charles H. Leveck, Recording Secretary.
J. C. Morel, Corresponding Secretary.
Frederick A. Hinton, Treasurer.

Committee.—Thomas Butler, J. C. Mathews, John Bowers, Jr. George Johnson, James Bird, Wm. C. West, Stephen H. Gloucester.

Mr. Pennington presented a summary of resolutions for the consideration of the Convention, which the advanced stage of its session prevented its acting upon, but which was thought a proper subject for the ensuing Convention. Adjourned to meet at three o'clock.

Monday Afternoon, June 11th, 1832.

According to adjournment met. By request of the President, the Rev. Simeon S. Jocelyn, of New Haven, delivered a very impressive prayer. Mr. T. L. Jennings, by desire, called the roll and read the minutes of the morning session.

The Rev. Mr. Harrison, of the Island of Antigua, was at his desire, permitted to address the Convention. His discourse was an elegant description of the great improvement in the religious, literary and civil condition of the people of color in several of the West India Islands, within a few years, and of the prospects of their general extension and increase.

Moved by Wm. Whipper, seconded by F. A. Hinton, that the sincere thanks of this Convention be returned to the Rev. Mr. Harrison, for his amiable and eloquent address, disclosing the situation of our colored brethren in the West Indies; and that we, the representatives of the free colored people of this country, do, in their behalf, request him to bear unto them our sympathy and prayers for their success, assuring them that we, as children of the same persecuted family, do possess those kindred feelings which should vibrate in the heart of the christian and philanthropist, and that we cheerfully rejoice at their prosperity, and mourn over their adversities.

The Rev. S. S. Jocelyn, of New Haven, then gave an elaborate history of the number of colored schools, the number of scholars, and a general description of the state of improvement among them. He read compositions of two young men in New York, remarkable for their chasteness of conception and expression. He spoke fervently and affectionately on the advantages to be derived by us, from learning, temperance, industry and frugality, and seriously admonished us, to recommend to our brethren, by precept and example, to the extent in our power, their advancement in the above virtues, and to particularly inculcate the early education of our children. He also adverted to the various proceedings in relation to the contemplated college, but recommended perseverance:

Mr. Jocelyn received the thanks of the house, on motion of Mr. Coxsin, seconded by Mr. Paschal, for his praiseworthy and unremitted exertions to promote the character of the colored people.

The committee appointed to examine whether any, or what alterations are, or may be necessary, in the arrangements of the last year, for the erection of a college, made the following statement.

We, the committee, to whom was referred so much of the tenth section of the report of the Convention of last year, as relates to the establishment of a college, most respectfully report—That we have duly reflected on the importance of establishing such an institution for the education of colored youth, and on the necessity of persevering in our endeavors to effect its erection, and do recommend the plan, prescribed by the Convention of last year, to continue the Rev. Samuel E. Cornish, general agent to solicit subscriptions, as the most efficient means of producing the object desired. It is further suggested, that in the event of his refusing to serve, or a vacancy happening, power shall be vested in the executive committee at New York, by and with advice and consent of the conventional board; but that all advice or instructions to the Agent, shall emanate from the committee, whose duty it shall be to provide for the payment of the Agent.

Your committee would also inform the Convention, that in consequence of some hostility manifested by some of the inhabitants of New Haven, against the location of the establishment in that place, it became prudent to alter the address, so as to read "New Haven or elsewhere." We would present to this Convention, the propriety of investing the executive committee with power to appoint additional committees when they judge them useful. Your committee in conclusion, would state that no report having been received from the General Agent by the executive committee, nor by the conventional board, it is not in their power to enter into further detail.

Signed, JOHN PECK,
PAUL DRAYTON,
WM. HAMILTON, } Committee.
PHILIP A. BELL,
FRED'K. A. HINTON,

Mr. Philip A. Bell, a member of the executive committee at New York, presented the following, viz:

The committee appointed at the last meeting of the Convention, to attend to the raising of funds for the establishment of a Manual Labor College for the instruction of coloured youth, beg leave to report,—That soon after their appointment, they met, and instructed the Rev. Samuel E. Cornish, the agent appointed by the Convention, to proceed to the soliciting of subscriptions, to commence with the city and vicinity of Philadelphia.

That at his setting out, Mr. Cornish met with great encouragement from the liberal subscriptions of those on whom he called, but that speedily such an opposition was raised by the white citizens of New Haven, the place contemplated by the Convention to *locate the College, that they were convinced that it would be more suitable to suspend the operations of the Agent, until a pamphlet, written on the subject, by the Rev. S. S. Jocelyn should be extensively circulated; after which a renewed attempt was made to obtain subscriptions, but with so little success that they determined not to prosecute the work any further until the present meeting of the Convention.

They now submit the subject to your consideration, believing it to be of too great importanse to be abandoned without further efforts being made to effect it, and such an Agent or Agents as are not only well qualified for the soliciting of subscriptions, but as would devote their whole attention to it during the ensuing year. We strongly entertain the opinion that the plan may be accomplished. All of which is respectfully submitted.

Signed, PETER WILLIAMS,
THOMAS DOWNING,
PETER VOGLESANG,
BOSTON CRUMMEL, and
PHILIP A. BELL.

New York, June 1st, 1832.

On motion, Resolved, That Arthur Tappan, Esq. at New York, be appointed to receive, as Treasurer, all monies that may be collected for the purpose of establishing the proposed institution at New Haven or elsewhere, he satisfying the Executive Committee at New York.

On motion of Wm. Whipper, and seconded by T. I. Jennings,—Resolved, That the contemplated College, proposed by the last Convention to be established at New Haven, be established elsewhere; and that the rules and regulations then adopted, is hereby ackı wledged and confirmed by this Convention.

And on motion, it was resolved, That there be provisional committees appointed, whose duty it shall be to aid and assist the Agent or Agents, that may be appointed in the discharge of their duties. And that the provisional committee at New York shall be the executive committee vntil the Trustees are appointed.

Here follow the several provisional committees, viz:

STATE OF NEW YORK.—*New York*—Rev. Peter Williams, Boston Crommel, Philip A. Bell, Thomas Downing, Peter Voglesang. *Albany*—Benjamin Latimore, Charles Morton, Captain Francis March. *Brooklyn*—Jacob Deyes, Henry Thompson, Willis Jones. *Newtown*—Thomas Johnson, John Potter.

PENNSYLVANIA.—*Philadelphia*—Joseph Cassey, Robert Douglass, sen. James Forten, Frederick A. Hinton, Robert Purvis. *Pittsburg*—John B. Vashon, Geo. Gardiner, Abraham Lewis, Lewis Woodson. *Lancaster*—Charles Butler, Benj. Simmons. *Carlisle*—John Peck, Roland G. Robinson. *Chambersburg*—Dennis Berry.

MASSACHUSETTS—*Boston*—Rev. Hosea Easton, Robert Roberts, James G. Barbadoes, Rev. Samuel Snowden. *New Bedford*—Charles K. Kook, Morris Anderson, Richard C. Johnson.

CONNECTICUT.—*Hartford*—H. Foster, Mason Freeman, Wm. C. Munroe. *New Haven*—Biars Stanley, John Creed, Alexander C. Lucas. *Middletown*—J. C. Bemen, Geo. Penny, Joseph Gilbert,

NEW JERSEY—*Trenton*—Aaron Roberts, Robert Henson. *New Brunswick*—James C. Cowes, ——— Reesner, John Barclay. *Newark*—Peter Petit, Charles Anderson, Adam Ray. *Gloucester co.*—Thomas Banks, Thomas D. Coxsin, John Kelly.

MARYLAND.—*Baltimore*—Thomas Green, James P. Walker, Samuel G. Mathews, Isaac Whipper, Samuel Hiner.

DELAWARE.—*Wilmington*—Rev. Peter Spencer, Jacob Morgan, Wm. S. Thomas.

DISTRICT OF COLUMBIA,—*Washington City.*—Wm. Jackson, Arthur Waring, Isaac Garey.

3

Agreeably to previous notice a collection was taken up for defraying the expenses of the Convention, which from its long continuance were considerable. An invitation was received from Mr. Kennedy, Principal of the Adelphia School, to attend an exhibition of his pupils to-morrow morning at 8 o'clock, which was accepted, and resulted in extreme gratification to those who visited it.

Adjourned to meet at 9 o'clock to-morrow.

Tuesday morning, June 12th, 9 o'clock.

Met in the first African Presbyterian Church. The house was called to order and prayer performed by the Rev. Samuel Johnson.

On motion of Mr. Hinton, Resolved—That a committee of three be appointed by the President, to wait on the Rev. Samuel E. Cornish, and request him to furnish the Convention with such information, in regard to the progress of the business of the College, as he may possess. Messrs. Samuel Johnson, P. Drayton, and T. D. Coxsin were appointed. Mr. Wm. Lloyd Garrison having, on Tuesday last, presented a congratulatory letter to the Convention, from the New England Anti-Slavery Society, on the probability, from present prospects, of our condition being improved by the joint efforts of our friends and ourselves; and recommending our continued exertions to improve our children at the tenderest age in habits of morality and industry,

On motion, Resolved—That this Convention highly appreciate the sentiments and measures of the Society, and that we request Mr. William L. Garrison to tender to the members thereof, assurances of our distinguished regard.

Moved and seconded that the following persons, viz: Henry Sipkins, James Pennington, and F. A Hinton, constitute a committee to draw up an Address to the citizens of the United States, exhibiting the oppressed condition of the colored people, and requesting their propitiousness towards us, and the same to be published in the most extensively circulated daily papers. Agreed.

Resolved—That Mr. Austin Stewart, of Wilberforce Settlement, Upper Canada, be requested to act as Corresponding Agent for the different Societies that now are, or may be established, for the assistance of those emigrating to that place, and to furnish the Conventional Board, through their Corresponding Secretary, such information as may be deemed necessary.

Moved by Mr. Pennington, seconded by Mr. Easton, that this Convention recommend to the Auxiliary Societies to obtain all the information possible, relative to the state and number of schools in their respective sections; the branches of education taught in each, with the number of scholars, and make returns of the same through their delegates, to the next Convention.

Adjourned to meet at 3 o'clock.

Afternoon Session.

The Convention, pursuant to adjournment, met.— Prayer by the Rev. Hosea Easton. The report of the persons who were to call on the General Agent was asked for, when the following was presented.

The committee appointed to call on the Rev. Samuel E. Cornish, most respectfully report, that they have, in conformity to their instruction, made known to him the desire of the Convention, and that he will be in attendance this afternoon.

Moved by William Whipper, seconded by Mr. Pennington, that the following resolution on the minutes of the last Convention be adopted by this, viz:—

That the Convention recommend to the people of color throughout the United States, the discontinuance of public processions on any day. We considering them as highly prejudicial to our interests as a people. Agreed.

It was moved that the documents or interrogatories of Mr. Grice, a representative of the Legal Right Society of Baltimore be reconsidered. After considerable debate on the subject, it was resolved that we tender to Mr. Hezekiah Grice, our sincere thanks for the valuable information contained therein, but that we respectfully decline any interference, as a body; but we sincerely hope that the Society will persevere in its laudable undertaking, and that as individuals we will give it our best support.

On motion, Resolved—That the consideration of the Bill for the establishment of a High School on the Munual Labor System, to be located in the State of Pennsylvania, be referred to the Provisional Committee at Philadelphia, and that they are hereby requested to collect all necessary information relative thereto and report the same to the next annual Convention.

The Convention and auditors were feelingly impressed by a farewell address delivered by their indefatigable friend William Lloyd Garrison, of which a copy was requested for publication.

The Rev. Samuel E. Cornish, General Agent for obtaining subscriptions for the contemplated College at New Haven, appeared, and stated that through unavoidable causes, he was not prepared to produce a written report. He therefore made a verbal statement of the affairs connected with his agency, and presented his subscription book, which upon examination was found to contain subscriptions to the amount of between two and three thousand dollars. The book was returned.

Moved and Seconded, that the conventional board be required to submit an Annual Message or Report containing an account of their proceedings, the information received from the different parts of the States in regard to the movements of the Colonization Society, the increase of Anti-Slavery Societies, and such general intelligence as may be thought serviceable, at the opening of each succeeeding Convention. Agreed. Prayer by the Rev. Chs. W. Gardner.

Adjourned to meet at 9 o'clock to morrow morning.

Wednesday Morning, June 13th 1832.

Met according to adjournment, Mr. Vashon (V. P.) in the chair. The meeting being called to order, the Rev. Samuel Johnson performed prayer. The President informed the house that business might proceed; whereupon Mr. Jennings moved, and was seconded by Mr. Whipper, that we recommend, as far as practicable, the use of free productions in preference to other productions. Agreed.

Moved by Wm. Whipper, seconded by Thomas L. Jennings, that this Convention recommend to our people generally, the formation of Societies for the promotion of Temperance, on the plan of total abstinence from the use of ardent spirits. Agreed.

On motion of John Peck, seconded by Benjamin Paschal, Resolved that this Convention highly recommend to the free people of color of these United States, where it may be practicable, to call meetings and have appropriate discourses delivered on the Sabbath most convenient, near the Fourth of July, and take up collections to assist the objects contemplated by this Convention. Prayer by the Rev. Charles W. Gardner.

Adjourned to meet at 3 o'clock.

Wednesday Afternoon Session.

Met conformably to adjournment in the First African Presbyterian Church in Seventh street. The President called the house to order. Prayer by the Rev. Hosea Easton.

On motion, the committee appointed to draw up a Conventional address to the free people of color, presented the same, which was read and adopted. (The same will appear at the end of these minutes.)

A communication in behalf of the free people of color of Lewistown, Mifflin county, Pa. signed Thomas Williams, and J. G. Smith, was read and referred to the Conventional Board.

Moved by Thomas D. Coxsin, seconded by Paul Drayton, that this Convention take into consideration the propriety of adopting such measures as in their opinion may be most expedient for bettering the condition of mechanics of color, by our general encouragement to them. Referred.

Moved by Thomas L. Jennings, seconded by Paul Drayton, that the Corresponding Secretary of the Conventional Board, as soon as possible, shall give notice to all the absent officers and committees in the different States, of their respective appointments, in a printed circular, to be provided by the Board for that purpose.— Agreed.

Several other motions were made and debated, and finally laid over until the next Convention.

At 7 o'clock moved and seconded that this Convention rise, and that the next Annual Convention meet in the City of Philadelphia, on the first Monday in June, 1833.

Mr. John Bowers having been appointed to receive and retain some of the monies belonging to the Convention, on motion the President drew a draft on him to pay over to the treasurer, all monies in his hands, over and above the expenses at present due by the Convention, which expenses he was authorized to pay.

3*

Mr. J. C. Morel introduced Major Barbour of Liberia. to the Convention.

Mr. Dennison, an advocate of the rights of the people of color, came in the moment after the adjournment, and was very attentively listened to by a considerable number who had remained, in some most excellent remarks.

————◉◐————

RULES AND REGULATIONS

TO BE OBSEERVED BY

The Conventional Board of Officers.

1. The funds shall be under the immediate control of the officers of the Convention during their contiuuance in office, subject to the following restrictions, viz:—

2 They shall pay all monies appropriated by the Convention, and for that purpose they are hereby invested with authority to draw on the Treasurer for the same.

3. They shall pay all the ordinary expenses of the Convention that may be necessary and proper, and shall with proper vouchers account to the Annual Convention for the same at each session.

4. The President shall preside at each meeting of the board of officers which shall form a council for the transaction of the business of the Convention during its recess.

5. During the absence or inability of the President to preside, the Vice President shall be competent to discharge all of his duty in the Council.

6. The Recording Secretary shall keep accurate minutes of the meetings of the officers at any time or times, which minutes, with all other useful matter that shall come under his observation, shall be laid before the Annual Conventions from time to time.

7. The Treasurer shall receive all monies that may be sent by the different Societies, (which now are or hereafter may be subject to the order of the Convention,) for which the President shall take his receipt. He shall pay all monies as the Council may draw on him for the order, being signed by the President and Sectreary.

8. The Corresponding Secretary shall notify the Vice Presidents and Secretaries of their appointments, together with the general views of the Convention in relation to the Canadian Settlement.

9. He shall, also, hold the most extensive and faithful correspondence with the Committees and Agents appointed to advance the interests of the proposed College, holding his correspondence subject to the inspection of the President and Vice President only.

10. No monies shall be drawn from the funds but by consent of a majority of the Council.

11. The Convention recommends the Parent Society at Philadelphia, and all others engaged in the Canadian Purchase, to alter their Constitutions and by-laws, so as to become auxiliary to the Convention, to the Treasurer of which they shall remit their funds at stated times.

12. It was resolved, That the Editors of the "Liberator," and "Genius of Universal Emancipation," are our tried friends, and fearless advocates of our rights and promoters of our best interests, and are entitled to a prominent place in our affections.

13. That the principles emanating from said presses, ought to be proclaimed throughout the world, and read by every friend of the rights of man—and that we pledge ourselves to use all our influence in promoting the support and circulation of such periodicals.

On motion of Wm. Whipper, seconded by F. A. Hinton, Resolved—That this Convention recognize in the representative of the Anti-Slavery Society, Wm. Lloyd Garrison, the bold and uncompromising advocate of the rights of man, as an editor and advocate of the free colored population, an able and fearless declaimer against oppression, as a man, a true and faithful friend, possessing honesty, virtue, and piety. For his exertions rendered to us as a people—therefore we do *ourselves*, and in behalf of *those* we represent; present him our sincere thanks, wishing that success and prosperity may attend him through life.

14. On motion, it was Resolved, that each Society in the Unied States, (organized by the recommendation of this Convention) be authorized to send delegates, not exceeding *five* in number, to represent them in the General Convention to be held as aforesaid; and that in places where it is not practicable at present to form Societies, the people shall have the same privilege, *provided* they contribute to the furtherance of the objcets of the Convention.

On motion, it was unanimously resolved, That this Convention feels grateful for the kind services rendered by the American Soctety for the Abolition of Slavery in the United States; also to the New England Anti-Slavery Society, to the Anti-Slavery Societies of Great Britain, and to the friends of the Rights of Man wherever dispersed. Adjourned, *sine die.*

HENRY SIPKINS, President.

Philip A. Bell,
Junius C. Morel, } Secretaries.

Philadelphia, June 13th 1832.

CONVENTIONAL ADDRESS

To the Free Colored inhabitants of these United States.

FELLOW CITIZENS:—

We have again been permitted to associate in our representative character, from the different sections of this Union, to pour into one common stream, the afflictions, the prayers, and sympathies of our oppressed people; the axis of time has brought around this glorious, annual event. And we are again brought to rejoice that the wisdom of Divine Providence has protected us during a year, whose autumnal harvest, has been a reign of terror and persecution, and whose winter has almost frozen the streams of humanity, by its frigid legislation. It is under the influence of times and feelings like these, that we now address you. Of a people situated as we are, little can be said, except that it becomes our duty, strictly to watch those causes that operate against our interests and privileges; and to guard against whatever measures that will either lower us in the scale of being, or perpetuate our degredation in the eyes of the civilized world.

The effects of Slavery on the bond, and Colonization on the free. Of the first we shall say but little, but will here repeat the language of a high minded Virginian in the Legislature of that state, on the recent discussion of the slave question before that honorable body, who declared, that man could not hold property in man and that the master held no right to the slave, either by a law of nature or a patentee from God, but by the will of society; which we declare to be an unjust usurpation of the rights and privileges of men.

But how beautiful must the prospect be to the philanthropist, to view us, the children of persecution, grown to manhood, associating in our delegated character, to devise plans and means for our moral elevation, and attracting the attention of the wise and good, over the whole country, who are anxiously watching our deliberations.

We have here to inform you, that we have patiently listened to the able and eloquent arguments produced by

the Rev. R. R. Gurley, Secretary of the American Colonization Society, in behalf of the doings of said Society,
and Wm. Lloyd Garrison, Esq. in opposition to its action.

A more favorable opportunity to arrive at truth seldom
has been witnessed, but while we admire the distinguished piety and christian feelings, with which he so solemnly
pourtrayed the doctrines of that institution; we do now
assert, that the result of the same, has tended more deeply to rivet our solid conviction, that the doctrines of said
Society, are at enmity with the principles and precepts
of religion, humanity and justice, and should be regarded
by every man of color in these United States, as an evil
for magnitude, unexcelled, and whose doctrines aim at
the entire extinction of the free colored population and the
riviting of Slavery.

We might here repeat our protest against that institution, but it is unnecessary, your views and sentiments
have long since gone to the world, the wings of the wind
have borne your disapprobation to that institution. Time
itself cannot erase it. You have dated your opposition
from its beginning, and your views are strengthened by
time and circumstances, and they hold the uppermost
seat in your affections. We have not been unmindful of the compulsory laws which caused our brethren in
Ohio, to seek new homes in a distant land, there to share
and suffer all the inconveniencies of exiles in an unculti-
vated region, which has led us to admire the benevolent
feelings of a rival government in its liberal protection to
strangers, which has induced us to recommend to you, to
exercise your best endeavors, to collect monies to secure
the purchase of lands in the Canadas, for those who may
by oppressive legislative enactments, be obliged to move
thither.

In contributing to our brethren that aid which will secure them a refuge in a storm, we would not wish to be
understood, as to possessing any inclination to remove,
nor in the least to impoverish that noble sentiment which
we rejoice in exclaiming—

This is *our* own,
Our native land.

All that we have done, humanity dictated it, neither
inclination nor alienated feelings to our country prescrib-

ed it, but that power which is above all other considerations, viz: The law of necessity.

We yet anticipate in the moral strength of this nation, a final redemption from those evils that have been illegitimately entailed on us as a people. We yet expect by due exertions on our part, together with the aid of the benevolent philanthropists of our country, to acquire a moral and intellectual strength, that will unshaft the calumnious darts of our adversaries, and present to the world a general character, that they will feel bound to respect and admire.

It will be seen by a reference to our proceedings, that we have again recommended the further prosecution of the contemplated college, proposed by the last Convention, to be established at New Haven, under the rules and regulations then established. A place for its location will be selected in a climate and neighborhood, where its inhabitants are less prejudiced to our rights and privileges. The proceedings of the citizens of New Haven, with regard to the erection of the college, were a disgrace to themselves, and cast a stigma on the reputed fame of New England and the country. We are unwilling that the character of the whole country shall sink by the proceedings of a few. We are determined to present to another portion of the country not far distant, and at no very remote period, the opportunity of gaining for them the character of a truly philanthropic spirit, and of retrieving the character of the country, by the disreputable proceedings of New Haven. We must have Colleges and high Schools on the Manual Labor system, where our youth may be instructed in all the arts of civilized ife. If we ever expect to see the influence of prejudice decrease, and ourselves respected, it must be by the blessings of an enlightened education. It must be by being in possession of that classical knowledge which promotes genius, and causes man to soar up to those high intellectual enjoyments and acquirements, which places him in a situation, to shed upon a country and a people, that scientific grandeur which is imperishable by time, and drowns in oblivions cup their moral degredation. Those who think that our primary schools are capable of effecting this, are a century behind the age, when to have proved a question in the rule of three, was considered a higher attainment, than solving the most difficult problem in Euclid is now. They might have at that time performed, what some people expect of them now, in the then barren state of science, but they are now no longer capable of reflecting brilliancy on our national character, which will elevate us from our present situation. If we wish to be respected, we must build our moral character, on a base as broad and high as the nation itself—our country and our character require it—we have performed all the duties from the menial to the soldier—our fathers shed their blood in the great struggle for independence. In the late war between Great Britain and the United States, a proclamation was issued to the free colored inhabitants of Louisiana, Sept. 21st, 1814, inviting them to take up arms in defence of their country, by Gen. Andrew Jackson. And in order that you may have an idea of the manner in which they acquitted themselves on that perilous occasion, we will refer you to the proclamation of Thomas Butler, Aid-de-Camp.

You there see that your country expects much from you, and that you have much to call you into action, morally, religiously and scientifically. Prepare yourselves to occupy the several stations to which the wisdom of your country may promote you. We have been told in this Convention, by the Secretary of the American Colonization Society, that there are causes which forbid our advancement in this country, which no humanity, no legislation and no religion can control. Believe it not. Is not humanity susceptible of all the tender feelings of benevolence? Is not legislation supreme—and is not religion virtuous? Our oppressed situation arises from their opposite causes. There is an awakening spirit in our people to promote their elevation, which speaks volumes in their behalf. We anticipated at the close of the last Convention, a larger representation and an increased number of delegates, we were not deceived, the number has been ten fold. And we have a right to expect that future Conventions will be increased by a geometrical ratio, until we shall present a body, not inferior in number to our state legislatures, and the *phenomena* of an *oppressed people*, deprived of the rights of citizenship, in the midst of an enlightened nation, devising plans and measures, for their personal and mental elevation, by *moral suasion alone.*

In recommending you a path to pursue for our present good and future elevation, we have taken into consideration, the circumstances of the free colored population, so far as it was possible to ascertain their views and sentiments, hoping that at a future Convention, you will all come ably represented, and that your wishes and views, may receive that deliberation and attention, for which this body is particularly associated.

Finally.—Before taking our leave, we would admonish you, by all that you hold dear, beware of that bewitching evil, that bane of society, that curse of the world, that fell destroyer of the best prospects, and the last hope of civilized man,—INTEMPERANCE.

Be righteous, be honest, be just, be economical, be prudent, offend not the laws of your country—in a word, live in that purity of life, by both precept and example—live in the constant pursuit of that moral and intellectual strength, which will invigorate your understandings, and render you illustrious in the eyes of civilized nations, when they will assert, that all that illustrious worth, which was once possessed by the Egyptians, and slept for ages, has now arisen in their descendants, the inhabitants of the new world.

MINUTES

AND

PROCEEDINGS

OF THE

THIRD ANNUAL CONVENTION,

FOR THE IMPROVEMENT

OF THE

FREE PEOPLE OF COLOUR

In these United States,

HELD BY ADJOURNMENTS

IN THE CITY OF PHILADELPHIA,

From the 3d to the 13th of June inclusive, 1833.

———

NEW-YORK:
PUBLISHED BY ORDER OF THE CONVENTION.
—
1833.

MINUTES.

THE Delegates to the third Annual General Convention of the Free People of Colour, for their improvement in these United States, met agreeably to public notice in the Benezett Hall, in the City of Philadelphia, on Monday, June 3, 1833.

Mr. Frederick A. Hinton, was appointed Chairman, and Mr. Charles H. Levick Secretary, until the convention be organized. Prayer by the Rev. Noah Cannon.

The following delegates presented their credentials, and were regularly admitted members of the convention.

PENNSYLVANIA.

Philadelphia.
Frederick A. Hinton,
Abraham Williams,
Stephen H. Gloucester,
Robert Purvis,
William Whipper.
Westchester.
Abraham D. Shadd,
William Lewis,
Caleb Cregg,
Vincent Smith,

Rev. Jeremiah Miller.
Carlisle.
John Peck,
Thomas Butler.
Peter Gardiner,
James Bird,
Samuel C. Hutchins.
Harrisburg.
Rev. J. D. Richardson,
George Galbrecht,
William Brewer, *Wilkesbarre.*

MARYLAND.
Baltimore.
Rev. Samuel Elliott,
William D. Jenkins,

Robert Cowley,
Samuel Hiner.

NEW-JERSEY.
Gloucester.
John Kelly,
Thomas Banks,
Henry Frisby,
Benjamin Stokely,
James C. Matthews.
Henry Ogden, *Newark.*

Burlington.
Emanuel W. Congo,
Robert J. Taylor.

Trenton.
Leonard Scott,
Abner H. Francis.

DELAWARE.
Wilmington.
Peter Hubbard,
Jacob Morgan.

Joseph Burton.
Matthew Draper.

Providence, R. I.—George Spywood.

MASSACHUSETTS.

Boston.
James G. Barbadoes,
George W. Thompson,

Hosea Easton.
New Bedford.
Richard Johnson.

CONNECTICUT.

New-Haven.—Luke Lathrop. *Hartford.*—Mason Freeman.

NEW-YORK.

New-York City.
William Hamilton, Sen.
Thomas L. Jinnings,
Ransom F. Wake,
Charles Mortimer,
James Barnett.

Poughkeepsie.
George Richardson,
David Ruggles.

William Brown, } *Brooklyn.*
H. C. Thompson, }
J. W. C. Pennington. *Newtown.*
Charles Smith, } *Newburgh.*
Wm. P. Johnson. }
William Rich, *Troy.*
John G. Stewart, *Albany.*
Catskill & Hudson.
Henry Sipkins.

In the progress of convention, the following gentlemen were admitted honorary members. Rev. Messrs. Watkins and Douglass of Maryland, Mr. Nathan Johnson of New-Bedford, Mass. and Mr. Thomas Van Renselear, of Princeton, N. J.

On motion the following persons were appointed a committee to nominate suitable officers for the convention, viz. Thos. L. Jinnings, Robert Cowley and John Peck.

After various motions and discussions, Adjourned to meet at 3 o'clock.

Afternoon Session.

Met as per adjournment. Mr. Wm. Hamilton was appointed chairman. Prayer by the Rev. Peter Gardiner.

The roll having been called and the minutes of the morning session read, the convention resolved itself into a committee of the whole, to act upon some controverted points of admitting members.

On the various motions offered, very animated discussions were kept up until the hour of adjournment. Adjourned to meet at 9 o'clock to-morrow morning.

Tuesday Morning, June 4.

Met in the Benezett Hall. The chairman took his seat. Prayer by the Rev. Samuel Elliott. The minutes of the previous meeting having been read, it was, on motion, resolved that the convention immediately adjourn to meet in the **First African Presbyterian Church**—to which they immediately repaired and proceeded to business.

The committee appointed to nominate officers for the convention, reported the following:

ABRAHAM D. SHADD, *President.*
RICHARD D. JOHNSON, *1st. Vice do.*
JOHN G. STEWART, *2d do.*
RANSOM F. WAKE, *Secretary.*
HENRY OGDEN, *Assistant Secretary.*
JOHN B. DUPUY, *Clerk.*

On motion, the report was unanimously adopted, and the persons therein named, declared duly elected, the officers being regularly installed proceeded to the duties of their several appointments.

On motion, resolved, that a committee of five persons be appointed to draft Rules and Regulations for the government of the convention, Messrs. Purvis, Jinnings, Sipkins, Butler, and Peck, were appointed.

On motion, resolved that the President appoint a committee of five for the purpose of correcting the minutes and publishing the same.

On motion of Mr. Spywood, seconded by Mr. Barbadoes, resolved that no person shall be acknowledged as delegates to this convention unless they bring proper credentials from their respective societies or meetings held for the purpose of electing them as such. A petition from the People of Colour of Hartford, to this convention, praying it to take into consideration the constitutionality of a Law lately passed in the State of Connecticut, prohibiting the establishing of Literary institutions in said State, for the instruction of persons of Colour of other States, was read and laid over for further consideration.

Mr. Frederick A. Hinton having requested leave to introduce a preamble and resolution on Wednesday afternoon, on motion of P. C. Matthews, seconded by Robt. Purvis, resolved that F. A. Hinton be permitted to offer to this convention a preamble and resolution, approbatory of the mission of Wm. Lloyd Garrison, Esq. to England.

The committee appointed to draft rules and regulations for

the government of this convention, made the following report, which was adopted.

Your committee appointed to adopt rules and regulations for the
government of this Convention, respectfully report—

1. The President shall take the chair at the time to which the
House may be adjourned, and upon the appearance of a quorum
shall direct the roll to be called and the previous minutes read.

2. The President shall have full power to keep order and decorum; shall decide questions of order, subject to an appeal to the
Convention, and appoint or nominate committees when ordered by
the Convention.

3. In case of the absence of the President, the first Vice President shall perform his duty, and in his absence it shall devolve
upon the second Vice-President.

4. If two or more members rise to speak at one time, the President shall decide who shall be entitled to the floor.

5. Every member who shall be in the House at the time the
question is put, shall give his vote, unless the House, for special
reasons, shall excuse him.

6. No member shall be permitted to leave the House without
the permission of the President.

7. No member shall be interrupted while speaking, except by a
call to order by the President; when such member may appeal to
the House.

8. When a motion is stated by the President, it shall be deemed
to be in possession of the House, but may be withdrawn at any
time before a decision.

9. While the President is stating any question, or addressing the
House, no member shall walk out, or cross the floor, nor when any
member is speaking entertain private discourse.

10. No member shall speak more than twice on the same subject, and shall not occupy more than fifteen minutes at each time,
without permission from the House.

11. No motion or proposition on a subject different from that
under consideration shall be admitted under colour of amendment.

12. No motion for reconsideration shall be in order unless made
by a member who voted in the majority, and approved of by the
President.

13. A motion for adjournment shall always be in order after
1 o'clock, P. M. or 6 o'clock, P. M.

14. All documents and papers, presented for the consideration
of this convention, shall be submitted to a committee of five, appointed for that purpose.

15. All motions to be made shall be submitted to writing, if requested.

(*Signed*)　　HENRY SIPKINS,
ROBERT PURVIS,
THOMAS L. JINNINGS,
JOHN PECK,
THOMAS BUTLER.

Adjourned to meet at 3 o'clock.

Afternoon Session.

Held in the First Presbyterian Church in Seventh-street, the President in the chair. The roll having been called and the minutes of the morning session read, on motion, the president appointed James Barnett, William Brown, Leonard Scott, James G. Barbadoes and Joseph Burton, a committee to examine all documents and papers submitted to the Convention, in conformity to the 14th Article of the Rules and Regulations.

The President also appointed Messrs. Henry Sipkins, Frederick A. Hinton, T. L. Jinnings, Robert Cowley and John Peck, a committee for the purpose of revising the minutes of this convention, and superintending the printing of the same.

On motion, resolved that a committee of five be appointed to lay before this convention such business as may be thought proper to be acted upon. The President appointed Wm. Whipper, John Peck, Robert Cowley, Henry Sipkins, and Wm. Lewis, said committee. Adjourned to meet to-morrow morning at 9 o'clock.

Wednesday Morning, June 5.

President in the chair. Prayer by the Rev. Mr. Elliott.

Moved and seconded that the committee appointed to present the order of business make their report, whereon the following was presented.

The committee appointed to lay before this convention a report of such business as they deem proper to engage its attention, respectfully submit the following :

Moved by R. F. Wake, seconded by David Ruggles, that the report be accepted, carried. Resolved that it be taken up by sections for adoption : viz.

1. That it is the duty of this Convention to inquire into the transactions of the Conventional Board appointed by the last Convention.
2. Whether the recommendation of last Convention have gone into operation, and whether they have or have not had any happy effect in producing an improvement in the condition of our people.
3. Whether there is any prospect that a Manual Labour School for the instruction of coloured youth will shortly be established, and if so *where*, and what progress has been made towards its completion.

4. Whether the resolution attached to the report of the committee on the Canadian subject last year, has been put in operation.

5. The committee most respectfully recommend an expression of sentiment in regard to *colonization*.

6. That a committee be appointed to present some more efficient plan of representation, by which each city, town or village, may be represented according to the respective ratio of numbers.

7. That a committee be appointed to draw up an address to the people of colour, on the subject of *Temperance*, depicting its happy influence on the morals of a community, and likewise declaring the traffic and use of ardent spirits destructive to the morals of a community.

8. They also recommend that the President of the Conventional Board, or in case of his decease, or inability to perform the duties, the Vice-President prepare an annual message depicting the situation of our people, and suggesting for the consideration of the Convention, such matter as he shall deem worthy of their consideration, and also that he shall preside at the opening of the Convention, until it is organized by the appointment of its officers.

9. That there be a committee of five, to prepare an address to the free people of colour of the United States. Adopted.

(*Signed*)   WILLIAM WHIPPER,
JOHN PECK,
HENRY SIPKINS,
ROBERT COWLEY,
WILLIAM LEWIS.

Resolved, that a nominating committee, consisting of five persons, be appointed to nominate committees to act on the different subjects embraced in the report of the committee on the order of business, to be acted on during the sitting of this convention. The president appointed Mess. J. G. Stewart, Henry Sipkins, S. H. Gloucester, J. W. C. Pennington and John Peck, that committee.

Moved by R. F. Wake and seconded by Wm. Hamilton, that a committee consisting of one delegate from the different states represented in this convention, be appointed to draft resolutions expressive of the sentiments of the people of Colour by them represented, in regard to the subject of colonization.

Moved by S. H. Gloucester, seconded by Geo. Spywood, that it shall be the order of the day on Friday next, that the chairman, or one that he shall appoint, of each delegation, to give a short report respecting the condition of the people that they represent. Adopted.

Adjourned to meet at 3 o'clock, P. M.

Afternoon Session.

Held pursuant to adjournment in the First African Presbyterian Church. President in the chair. The roll having been called and minutes of the morning session read :—The following preamble and resolution, was submitted by F. A. Hinton, seconded by Robert Purvis.

Whereas, the Board of Managers of the New England Anti-Slavery society, have sent Wm. Lloyd Garrison, Esq. as their agent to England, for the purpose of procuring funds to aid in the establishment of a Manual Labour School, for the education of coloured youth; and of disseminating in that country, the truth in relation to the objects of the American Colonization Society.

And whereas we deem it proper that the sentiments of the Free Coloured Population of this country, should be expressed in relation to the said mission. Therefore be it Resolved, that this Convention do most heartily approve of the appointment of Mr. Garrison for the objects above mentioned, and having the utmost confidence in his worth and integrity, as well as a sincere interest in the purposes of his mission, we do cordially recommend him to the attention and kindness of the philanthropic inhabitants of Great Britain.

The foregoing preamble and resolution was supported by Mess. F. A. Hinton and R. Purvis, in very excellent addresses, and was carried unanimously.

Moved by T. L. Jinnings, and seconded by Wm. Hamilton, that no person shall be eligible to a seat in the Convention as a delegate, under the age of 21 years, and that he shall be an actual resident of the state from which he shall be returned, at least six months previous to the sitting of the Convention.

The committee appointed to nominate committees to act on the different subjects embraced in the report on the order of business to be acted on during the present session, respectfully report the following:

To draft a preamble and resolutions expressive of the views of the Convention in regard to colonization, James G. Barbadoes of *Massachusetts*, William Hamilton of *New-York;* Luke Lathrop, of *Connecticut;* George Spywood, of *Rhode Island;* Thomas Banks, of *New-Jersey;* William

Whipper, of *Pennsylvania;* Samuel Elliott, of *Maryland;* and Joseph Burton of *Delaware.*

To prepare an address to the Free People of Colour, Wm. Whipper, John G. Stewart, Robert Cowley, Henry Sipkins and Richard Johnson.

To prepare an address on Temperance, James W. C. Pennington, Abraham Williams and William Rich.

On the transactions of the Conventional Board : William Brown, James C. Matthews and James Bird.

To inquire whether the recommendation of last convention has been attended to, and what effect it has had among our people, F. A. Hinton, Henry C. Thompson and Peter Gardiner.

To inquire whether there is any prospect that a Manual Labour School for the instruction of coloured youth, will shortly be established or not; Charles Mortimer, Wm. D. Jenkins, Henry Ogden, George W. Thompson, Matthew Draper, Mason Freeman and Abner Frances.

On the regulation of representation, Thomas L. Jinnings, Abraham D. Shadd, Stephen H. Gloucester, David Ruggles and John Peck.

On the duty of the President and Vice President of the Conventional Board, Henry Sipkins, Robert Cowley, George Richardson, William Brown and William Lewis. Which was adopted.

Moved by Wm. Hamilton, and seconded by Frederick A. Hinton, that Wm. Hamilton have leave to bring in a motion relative to the Phœnix Societies, to be the order of the day on Friday next, in the afternoon. Adopted. Adjourned to meet to-morrow morning at 9 o'clock A. M.

Tursday Morning, June 6.

Convention met pursuant to adjournment, in the first African Presbyterian Church. President in the chair. Prayer by the Rev. Mr. Levington of Baltimore, Md.

The roll having been called, and the Minutes of the last session read, the Rev. Mr. Levington having expressed a desire to address the convention, it was moved by T. L. Jinnings, seconded by William Hamilton, that he be permitted. Carried. The Rev. gentleman then addressed the Convention at considerable length, recommending a monthly concert of prayer among our people throughout the U. S.

A motion for reconsideration of the subjects debated on Monday, and on some documents submitted to the committee of examination, engaged the session until the hour of adjournment. Adjourned to meet at 3 o'clock precisely.

Afternoon Session.

President in the chair. The roll was called, and the minutes of the morning session read.

A letter from Mr. John B. Vashon of Pittsburg was read, expressing his approbation of the objects of the Convention, and enclosing the sum of five dollars, for the furtherance of the objects thereof.

On motion of R. F. Wake, seconded by J. G. Stewart, it was resolved, that this Convention accept the donation sent by Mr. Vashon, of Pittsburg, for which, and the expression of sentiment contained in his letter, we return him our thanks.

Mr. Bacon of Boston was introduced, who very feelingly addressed the Convention, expressive of the deep interest that he personally, and the New England Anti-Slavery Society, of which he is an Agent, felt in our behalf.

Moved by F. A. Hinton, and seconded by John Peck, that a special Committee of three be appointed to return our thanks to Mr. Bacon, Agent of the New England Anti-Slavery Society, for the expression of the sentiments of the said Society in regard to this Convention. Carried. William Whipper, R. F. Wake, and J. G. Stewart, were appointed.

The Committee on the duties of President and Vice-President of the Conventional Board, presented their report, together with rules and regulations to be observed by the Conventional Board of Officers, which was accepted.

On motion, resolved that the report be taken up by sections for adoption. When the following rules were adopted—

RULES AND REGULATIONS

THE CONVENTIONAL BOARD OF OFFICERS.

1. The funds shall be under the immediate control of the officers of the Convention during their continuance in office, subject to the following restrictions, viz:—They shall pay all moneys appropriated by the Convention, and for that purpose they are hereby invested with authority to draw on the Treasurer for the same, and to fill any vacancy that may happen in the board by a vote of the majority at any of their meetings.

2. They shall pay all the ordinary expenses of the Convention that may be necessary and proper, and shall with proper vouchers account to the Annual Convention for the same at each session.

3. The President shall preside at each meeting of the board of officers which shall form a council for the transaction of the business of the Convention during its recess.

4. During the absence or inability of the President to preside, the Vice-President shall be competent to the discharge of all the duties of President in the council.

5. The Recording Secretary shall keep accurate minutes of the meetings of the officers at any time or times, which minutes, with all other useful matter that shall come under his observation, shall be laid before the Annual Conventions from time to time.

6. The corresponding Secretary shall notify the Vice-Presidents and Secretaries of their appointments, together with the general views of the Convention in relation to the Canadian Settlement. He shall, also, hold the most extensive and faithful correspondence with the Committees and Agents appointed to advance the interests of our people, holding his correspondence subject to the inspection of the President and Vice-President only.

7. The Treasurer shall receive all moneys that may be sent by the different societies (which now are or hereafter may be subject to the order of the Convention,) for which the President shall take his receipt. He shall pay all moneys that the council may draw on him for, the order being signed by the President and Secretary.

8. No moneys shall be drawn from the funds, but by the consent of a majority of the council.

9. It shall be the duty of the President of the Conventional Board, (or in case of his death, resignation, or inability to act, the Vice-President,) to prepare and send an annual message to the Convention, at the opening of each session, depicting the situation of our people, and suggesting for the consideration of the Convention such matter as he shall deem worthy of their consideration.

10. The President of the Conventional Board shall preside at the opening of each Annual Convention, until the same is organized by the appointment of its own officers, and in his absence the Vice-President shall preside.

(*Signed*)

WILLIAM BREWER,
WILLIAM LEWIS,
HENRY SIPKINS,
ROBERT COWLEY,
GEORGE R. RICHARDSON.

Adjourned.

Friday Morning, June 7.

President in the Chair.

Prayer by Rev. Jeremiah Miller. The roll was called, and the minutes of the preceding session read.

The order of the day was called up, namely, the reports of the foreman of the several delegations, some of which were presented and accepted. Mr. Arnold Buffom, addressed the Convention, in relation to the High School for coloured females, established in Canterbury, Connecticutt, by Miss Prudence Crandall, and read an extract from a letter from Mr. Arthur Tappen of New-York, *containing important facts relative to said School,* and recommending to the people of colour, the encouragement and support of the same.

Moved by S. H. Gloucester, and seconded by R. Cowley, that a Committee of five persons be appointed to inquire into, and report whether any and how far encouragement ought to be given to the settlement in Upper Canada ; carried. The following persons were appointed, Messrs. Cowley, Butler, Banks, Draper, and Stewart.

Moved by Henry Sipkins, seconded by James W. C. Pennington, that William Hamilton, John Peck, and Peter Gardiner, be a Committee, to whom the reports on the state of Society be submitted for condensation. Adjourned.

Friday Afternoon.

President in the Chair. The roll was called, and the minutes of the morning session being read, the Convention proceeded to business.

Moved by Henry Ogden, seconded by William Whipper, that the next Annual Convention of the free people of colour, be held in the City of New-York.

Mr. Wm. Whipper made the following amendment, provided that it sit in New-York and Philadelphia, alternately, after considerable debate, in which a majority of the delegates took part, it was carried in the affirmative. Yeas 32, Nays 12.

Mr. Hinton, introduced Mr. William Wharton, of Philadelphia, a distinguished philanthropist, and friend of the people of colour, who, after some preliminary remarks, read a highly interesting letter from Mr. Charles Marriott, of Hudson, N. Y.

Moved by John G. Stewart, and seconded by Frederick A. Hinton, that the thanks of this Convention be returned to Messrs. Wharton and Marriott, for the expression of good will manifested in the address, and in the communication. Adjourned to meet at 9 o'clock to-morrow morning.

Saturday Morning, June 8.

President in the Chair.

Prayer by the Rev. Mr. Levington, of Maryland. The roll being called, and the minutes of the preceding session read. several reports of the Foreman of the different delegations were read and accepted. The Committee appointed to inquire whether there is any prospect, that a Manual Labour School, for the instruction of coloured youth will shortly be established, presented their report, which was read and accepted.

REPORT.

The Committee on the above subject, respectfully beg leave to report, that from the best information, they have been able to obtain, the following is the present state of progress, viz : The New England Anti Slavery Society, have proposed the establishment of a Manual Labour School, which will be commenced as soon as ten thousand dollars shall have been subscribed, nearly one thousand has been already raised, and there is reason to believe that it will shortly be carried into operation. There are also great efforts making for the establishment of a Manual Labour School in New York, which will be commenced as soon as an adequate amount is subscribed, and your Committee have been informed that the contributions for this purpose have been liberal, and in the State of Pennsylvania, ten thousand dollars has been left for the establishment of a Manual Labour School, near the City of Philadelphia, subject to the control of the Society of Friends.

(*Signed*)   CHARLES MORTIMER,
HENRY OGDEN,
GEORGE W. THOMPSON,
MATTHEW DRAPER,
MASON FREEMAN,
ABNER H. FRANCIS,
WILLIAM D. JENKINS.

Moved by William Hamilton, seconded by Thomas L. Jinnings, that this Convention earnestly recommends the formation of Phœnix Societies in every State, after the form, and on the principles of the Phœnix Societies of the City of New·York, and that the constitution of said Societies be attached to the printed minutes of this Convention. Carried unanimously. The Committee appointed to inquire into,

and report whether any, and how far encouragement ought to
be given to the settlement of coloured people in Upper Canada, presented their report, which was read and accepted,
to which was appended the following resolution—

Resolved, that Mr. Austin Stewart be requested to continue his agency at the Wilberforce Settlement in Upper Canada, to whom funds may be remitted, by societies or individuals, for the relief of such persons as may leave the
United States, and take up their residence within their borders.

On motion of Mr. Whipper, seconded by Mr. Peck, the
Convention resolved itself into a Committee of the whole,
Mr. Richard Johnson in the chair, for the discussion of the
resolution. Very animated debates on the subject, continued
until near the hour of adjournment, when the Committee
rose, reported progress, and asked leave to sit again, which
was granted for Monday afternoon.

Adjourned till Monday morning, at 9 o'clock, A. M.

Morlay Morning, June 10.

The Conventio. met, pursuant to adjournment, in the first
African Presbyterian Church, at 9 o'clock, A. M.

President in the Chair.

Prayer by the Rev. Mr. Eliott. The roll having been
called, and the minutes of the preceding session read, the
report of the Vice-President of the State of New-York, and
several reports of the different delegations were read and
accepted. The committee on Temperance presented their
report, which was accepted and adopted.

REPORT.

The committee on the subject of Temperance, beg leave to report, that in common with the friends of moral reform throughout
our country, we are called upon for devout aspirations of praise to
God, for that success he has granted to the cause of Temperance,
during the past year.

In every section of our country, and among every class of persons, the principles of the American Temperance Society have
progressed at a ratio, wholly beyond all anticipation.

Intemperance, the great evil which a few years since was seated
in the vitals of our nation, threatening a speedy death to every
interest, whether social, civil, or religious, and baffling every effort
made for its removal, now has, as must be acceded by every intelligent observer, an adequate remedy. That remedy is the simple principle of voluntary associations, on the plan of INTIRE AB-

STINENCE, which is evidently the only safety of the temperate, and the only hope of the intemperate.

In connexion with the earnest and faithful arguments drawn from an array of facts, alike incontestable and appalling, exposing the evils of the traffic, and of the use of Distilled Liquors, the means which have urged forward the reformation in opposition to the ignorance, the prejudice, and the cold selfishness of enemies, and the inactivity and timidity of friends; the providence of God has concurred, in a remarkable manner, so as to place the cause of temperance beyond the possibility of failure. Facts in connexion with the Cholera, the awful judgment, which has "hung sackcloth around the globe," and within the past year, converted our land into one vast house of mourning, have forcibly impressed upon this, and upon other nations, the conviction, that Intoxicating Liquors have an injurious tendency upon the human system, at once establishing the opinion, in which men, the most eminent of the medical profession in both Europe and America, harmonize, "that there is an affinity, between human disease and strong drink," "that it is invariably injurious to persons in health, and therefore the use should be discontinued."

The one million, five hundred thousand individuals, in the United States, and the one hundred thousand in England, arrayed under the banners of Temperance, respond the same sentiment. The one thousand five hundred, who have conscientiously discontinued the manufacturing of, and the five thousand who have ceased to sell *the waters of death*, unitedly rejoice in the principle of TOTAL ABSTINENCE.

The six hundred *American Vessels*, now navigating the ocean, without the use of the poison, are proclaiming to the nations in "trumpet tones," that the monster is soon to be driven from the face of the globe.

The committee are happy to state, that the recommendation on this subject, given by the Convention, last year, has exerted a happy influence, in awakening attention to this subject, although owing to the sparceness of the colored population, we have no means of accurate knowledge of the number, who have pledged themselves to this cause, yet as they are more or less under the influence of Temperance Societies, and from facts before us, we are safe in stating that large numbers have signed the pledge, and are members of societies connected with the different Churches and Sabbath Schools, and of other societies in almost every section of the country.

Distinct societies have been organized in most of the cities and large villages in the states represented in the Convention, though it is not in our power to lay before you all, which in this way has been effected, yet we are gratified in stating, that societies have been formed at Washington, D. C., Philadelphia and Carlisle, Penn., New Haven, Hartford and Middletown, Conn., Boston, Mass., Princeton, N. J., and in the State of New-York, at Albany, Schenectady, Utica, Syracuse, Catskill, Poughkeepsie, Newburg, Newtown, Troy, Brooklyn, and in the City of New-York there are five distinct organizations. These societies for the most part are doing well.

While in view of what has been accomplished, we have cause of gratitude, and of encouragement, yet much, very much, remains to be done. The Rum system, like that of *slavery*, is upheld by ignorance, avarice, and incorrect views of duty. Alike they are exerting a withering influence—both, blessed be God, are receding before omnipotent truth; but the triumph is to be achieved over deep rooted prejudices, and long cherished and stubborn habits, but the light of truth, in its energy and majesty, is adequate for its accomplishment.

While upon other portions of the community, a flood of light is pouring forth from the press and from the pulpit, there is among us a criminal remissness in the diffusion of correct principles on this subject—To free our brethren from the chains of American oppression, and to clear away the mists of prejudice, which so unjustly attempts to withhold from us our rights, as American citizens, our hope and confidence is in the diffusion of correct moral principle; this alone, is adequate to induce those whom we represent, to feel the obligation of banishing, at once, and for ever, the use of strong drink, and with it the fruitful source of the evils which retard our best interests.

That the Convention may act with more efficiency, and assume an attitude to guide public opinion, your Committee have deemed it important to make a few suggestions.

They recommend during the present session of the Convention, the formation of a Conventional Temperance Society, to be styled THE COLOURED AMERICAN CONVENTIONAL TEMPERANCE SOCIETY; that the officers and managers of which be appointed from different sections of the country; and that it hold its Annual Meeting during the time and at the place of the Meeting of the Convention.

The utility of such an organization is obvious; the design of which should not be to descend to the drudgery and minute attention to detail the appropriate work of other societies engaged in this good work, but to give an impulse to, and to exercise a supervision over the Temperance effort, throughout our portion of community. Every member will be a pledged and authorised Agent, happily adapted to exert an influence in the formation of Societies, and in securing the co-operation of the friends of *moral reform*, and of the friends of the people of colour.

Such a Society, from its relative position to our population, will form a medium of statistical information, which cannot be as well procured in any other way. It will promote unity of feeling and action, which in this work are of intrinsic importance. Whatever doubt may be entertained of man's capacity single handed, to do much good, it cannot be doubted when he allies himself to others. "*Union is full of strength and encouragement.*"

Your Committee further suggest, the importance of an *endeavour to call up the attention of our population generally to this momentous subject*, more particularly, that of influential individuals; for at every successive step taken in the investigation of this subject, with its bearing upon our political and moral interests, we have been shocked, and humbled, at the criminal apathy which pervades the minds of many of our intelligent and useful men, and many of our *pious men too*, on this obviously important.

subject. We venture to assert, that no portion of our fellow citizens has as deep an interest in the promotion of the cause of Temperance, as that to which we belong, and no body of men either in their individual or collective capacity, are pressed with weightier responsibilities, than that to whom we now address ourselves—what we are to be as a people is peculiarly suspended upon our moral and intellectual qualities.

For in addition to all those weighty considerations tending so remarkably to correct the public opinion of other portions of community, and are working such moral wonders, there are other considerations which ought deeply to interest the "*Free people of Colour of the United States*," and to rivet the conviction upon every mind, that they of all others ought by every possible means to urge forward this glorious reformation; not that intemperance abounds more among us, than among others, for in the face of the declaration to the contrary, made by the disparagers of an injured people, your committee are prepared to prove, that it does not exist among us even to as great an extent as among others; but notwithstanding, it, more than any thing under our control, tends to perpetuate that *relentless prejudice*, which arrays itself against our dearest interests; frowns us away from the avenues of useful knowledge and of wealth; and which with a cruel hand wrenches from us our political rights.

In all our deliberations, we recognize the idea, that intelligence, industry, economy, and moral worth, in connexion with the purifying power of heaven-born truth, are sufficient alone, to prostrate, this *iron hearted monster*.

Now the destroyer, Intemperance, directly counteracts the influence of these redeeming qualities, and what is worse, nurtures in their stead every thing loathsome.

Those children in tatters, who are cruelly permitted to waste those precious hours, which should be employed in the acquisition of knowledge, who are shivering with cold, or crying for a morsel of bread, are the children of *intemperate parents. These impoverished families, these premature graves*, are the production of strong drink.

What is the foundation of those vile and unreasonable slanders, which are trumpeted throughout this land of freemen? "That the situation of the slave at the south, is far preferable to that of the coloured freeman of the north." It is founded in the opinion of the apologer of slavery, formed, when beholding degraded men, clustering around those fatal corners, where "*liquid fire* is dispensed," or while beholding here and there, the staggering steps of miserable men and women, who with fœtid breath, deride the idea of "TOTAL ABSTINENCE." Here too, we have the source of *four fifths* of the pauperism known among us, and that of the most of those *petty crimes* which, contribute much to keep in countenance those weak men who are for ever prating about *extraneous mass, and African inferiority*.

We take the liberty farther to recommend as powerfully tending to advance the Temperance reformation, the formation of Societies, in religious congregations; in each ward of large cities, and in each large village in the UNITED STATES, where circumstances will admit. We also recommend the organization of Female Societies.

Finally we recommend, as worthy of notice, the following resolution passed in the "United States' Temperance Convention," recently held in this City.

Resolved, that Temperance Societies, and the friends of temperance throughout the country, be requested to hold simultaneous Meetings, on the last Tuesday in February, 1834, to review what has been done during the past year, and to consider what remains to be done, and to take such measures as may be suitable, by the universal diffusion of information, and by kind moral influence, to extend and perpetuate the principles and the blessings of our land.

In conclusion, the Committee beg leave to state, that they have given that attention, to the duty assigned them, as time and circumstances would allow, that while they regret that their Report does not present this *all engrossing subject* as fully as they could wish, still they hope it may in a measure answer the desired object.

In dismissing our subject, we would respectfully impress upon each Member of the Convention, that of all the subjects that come within the range of our deliberations, few, if any, are of greater importance than that of Temperance; it has a claim upon our vigorous support, upon our best feelings and efforts—*If this advances, if this triumphs, every interest* we aim to promote, *every blessing* we seek as men, or as citizens of this our beloved republic, *must advance, must triumph.* MORAL WORTH IS POWERFUL, AND WILL PREVAIL. All of which is respectfully submitted.

JAMES W. C. PENNINGTON,
ABRAHAM WILLIAMS,
WILLIAM RICH.

Moved by T. L. Jinnings, seconded by Samuel C. Hutchins, that there be a Committee of three persons to draft a constitution, in order to carry the resolution of forming a Temperance Society into effect. Whereupon, William Whipper, F. A. Hinton, and T. L. Jinnings, were appointed.

Monday Afternoon.

President in the Chair.

The roll having being called, and the minutes of the morning session read, the Convention resolved itself into a Committee of the whole, to take up the order of the day.

Charles Mortimer in the Chair.

After a very interesting discussion on the Canadian Report and Resolution, the Committee arose, the Convention then resumed its session.

President in the Chair.

The Chairman of the Committee reported progress, and asked leave to sit again, whereon it was moved, that the

Committee have leave to sit again on to-morrow, afternoon, at 3 o'clock.   Adjourned.

Tuesday Morning, June 11.

President in the Chair.

Prayer by the Rev. Mr. Levington, of Maryland.   Roll was called, and minutes of the last sitting read.   The Committee on representation presented their report, which was read, taken up by sections, and adopted, viz :—

REPORT.

Resolved, that in each and every county in which a Society is, or may be formed Auxiliary to the Convention, shall be entitled to send delegates, not exceeding five persons, and it is hereby understood, that under no pretence whatever, will any other body or society be admitted to send delegates as members to the Convention from such county, where a society shall or may exist, without the sanction of the senior society, in their participating in selecting or electing the above mentioned delegates.   Carried.

Resolved, that in any county where no society has been formed, the people shall have the privilege of returning two delegates, provided they contribute to the furtherance of the objects of the Convention.   Carried.

Resolved, that as one of the primary objects of the Convention, is to elicit information in regard to the situation of our people, it is expedient therefore, that no person shall be received as a delegate, who shall not be a resident of the State from which he shall be returned, at least six months previous to his election.   Carried.

Resolved, that it is expedient to have a regular return of each delegate signed by the President and Secretary, or Chairman, and Secretary of every Society, or Public Meeting of any county, at least two weeks previous to the sitting of the Convention, forwarded to the President of the Conventional Board, who shall keep a regular record, and present the same at the opening of the Convention.

Moved by David Ruggles, seconded by James G. Barbadoes, that each delegation pay toward the promotion of the objects of the Convention, when they present their credentials, a sum not less than five dollars.   Carried.   Several reports of the different delegations were read, and accepted.

A very interesting and highly important communication was received from the Rev. Simon S. Jocelyn, of New Haven, which was read and approved of, encouraging us to perseverance in our efforts, for the common benefit, and affording us the consolatory information, than to some of the north, west, and eastern Colleges, he is assured, that properly pre-

pared coloured youth can be admitted, and also, that notwithstanding the persecution and opposition to the establishment
of Miss Prudence Crandall's School, (for the instruction of
coloured females, in Canterbury, Connecticut,) it was in a
flourishing condition, and only required the encouragement
and support of those for whom it was opened, to triumph
over the opposition. The grateful thanks of the Convention
were returned, for the very valuable information contained
therein. Adjourned.

Afternoon Session.

The Convention met agreeably to adjournment.

President in the Chair. Roll called and minutes read.

The Convention went into committee of the whole, to take
up the order of the day, on the Canadian question.

Henry Sipkins in the chair. The report and resolution
was read.

On motion of Mr. Cowley, seconded by Mr. Jenkins, that
the Committee of the whole on the above question be dis-
solved, and beg leave to decline any further consideration of
the subject.

The President then resumed the chair, and the chairman
of the committee reported accordingly. The resolution was
then taken up in Convention and debated, when on motion
of John G. Steward, seconded by William D. Jenkins, that
the report and resolution be adopted, was decided in the affirmative. Ayes 32, Nays 14.

Moved by H. Ogden, seconded by T. L. Jinnings, that
the session of this Convention, be protracted from 9 o'clock,
A. M., to 3 o'clock, P. M., on Wednesday. Carried. Adjourned to meet to-morrow morning, at 9 o'clock.

Wednesday, June 12.

President in the Chair.

Prayer by Mr. Charles Mortimer. The roll was called,
and minutes of the preceding meeting read. A reconsideration of the vote on the Canada Report and Resolution being
called for.

On motion of Henry Sipkins, seconded by Henry Ogden,
it was resolved, that the Canadian Report be returned to the
Committee, with whom it originated, together with the Re-

solutions offered yesterday afternoon, as amendments, to make such use of them in connexion with the report, as they may deem proper.

Mr. T. L. Jinnings, presented some resolutions, to be made the order of the day, which was referred to a Committee of three, to report in one hour. The President appointed Mr. H. Sipkins, R. Cowley, and L. Lathrop. The committee to whom the Canadian Report was returned, together with the resolutions offered by F. A. Hinton, seconded by W. Whipper, presented the report with the said resolutions attached as a substitute for the one adopted yesterday.

On motion of R. F. Wake, seconded by D. Ruggles, that the report and resolutions be adopted, they received a unanimous vote. The following is the report and resolutions—

REPORT.

Resolved, that a Committee of five persons be appointed to inquire into, and report thereon, whether any, and how far encouragement ought to be given to the settlement of coloured people in Upper Canada.

The Committee appointed to take into consideration the foregoing resolution, having had the same under mature deliberation, beg leave to submit the following brief report—

It appears to your Committee, that the call for a Convention of free people of colour, was at first made for the purpose of giving aid and encouragement to a settlement of coloured people in the province of Upper Canada, in consequence of the revival of certain oppressive acts of the Legislature of the State of Ohio. It appears to your Committee, that the unjust operation of those laws, induced many persons of colour to leave, their hitherto peaceful and quiet homes, for one of a transitory and doubtful character. In this situation of affairs, the feelings and sympathies of the free people of colour, were aroused in every part of this widely extended republic, meetings held and means collected to assist those who had precipitately fled the land of their nativity, and left all the endearing associations that make life desirable. The philanthropists of our country, with that liberality of feeling, which has ever characterised the good and great of every clime, came forward with distinguished ardour, and liberally contributed means to alleviate the precarious situation of those who had emigrated. Hence arose the present Convention.

The peculiar situation of a large portion of the free people of colour of this country, has not escaped the observation of your Committee, and the most rigid scrutiny has led to the conclusion, that there is not now, and probably never will be actual necessity for a large emigration of the present race of free coloured people, they therefore refrain from recommending any emigration whatever, but would respectfully say to such as may be desirous to go, that the fertile soil of Upper Canada holds out inducements far more advantageous, than the desolate regions of Africa, where the scorching rays of a meridian sun, blasts by its withering influence the enlivening growth of successful vegetation.

Your Committee are not unmindful of the oppressive laws recently enacted in several of the States, which dooms the free people of colour to inconveniences far more grievous than could have been anticipated, by the enlightened and sincere friends to the happiness of mankind; yet such is the uncertainty of all sublunary concerns, that laws, (which should have slept for ever in the silence of night,) have been enacted in this enlightened day, in a country possessing many beautiful Institutions, that would have been a disgrace to the most barbarous nations of antiquity. Hence, the absolute necessity for opening a door for the voluntary emigration of our people, to a region of country possessing all the advantages of a healthy and salubrious climate, fertile soil, and equitable laws. Your Committee therefore, recommend the adoption of the following resolutions—

Resolved, that this Convention most respectfully recommend to their constituents, to devote their thoughts and energies to the improvement of their condition, and to the elevation of their character, in this their native land, rejecting all plans of colonization any where.

Resolved, that should any State by Legislative enactments, drive our brethren from its jurisdiction, we will give them all the aid in our power to enable them to remove and settle in Upper Canada, or elsewhere, that they may not be compelled to sacrifice their lives in the insalubrious climate of Liberia, provided for them by the American Colonization Society.

Resolved, that for the above purpose, the Societies auxiliary to this Convention, are requested to supply our Treasury with funds.

> ROBERT COWLEY,
> THOMAS BUTLER,
> MATTHEW DRAPER,
> THOMAS BANKS,
> JOHN G. STEWART.

The Committee appointed to condense the reports of the several delegations, presented their report, which was read and accepted, as follows—

The Committee appointed to condense the reports of the heads of Delegations, have had under consideration the subject submitted to them, and after a careful examination of twenty-two reports, are gratified in being enabled to state to the Convention, that an improvement in the general character of their constituents, is beginning to appear in a greater or less degree, every where among them. In some places, several Churches are established, with large congregations; several School Houses, well attended by scholars; many Temperance and Benefit Societies, and there is scarcely any places represented, where there is any considerable number of coloured people, notwithstanding the prevalence of colonization principles in some of them, where some portion of the children are not, where they have no school of their own, admitted among the white, or have the benefit of Sabbath School instruction, and your Committee respectfully submit it as a matter of belief, gathered from remarks contained in the reports, that an increasing desire of improvement is extending itself among us.

(*Signed*)   WILLIAM HAMILTON,
JOHN PECK,
PETER GARDINER.

The Committee appointed to take into consideration, the resolutions presented by T. L. Jinnings, presented their report, which was read and accepted.

Resolved, that the report be adopted. Carried, viz :—

Resolved, that the Vice-President and Secretaries, appointed in the different States, be requested to use their exertions to form Phœnix Societies, similar to those in the City of New-York.

Resolved, that the next Convention be held on the second Monday in August, 1834. Reconsidered and lost.

Resolved, that a Committee of five persons be appointed to nominate the officers of the Conventional Board.

Resolved, that a Vice-President and Corresponding Secretary be appointed in the different States.

(*Signed*)   HENRY SIPKINS,
LUKE LATHROP,
ROBERT COWLEY.

The President appointed Messrs. Barnet, Hamilton, Sipkins, Wake, and Jinnings, a Committee to nominate officers for the Conventional Board.

Resolved, that the Convention proceed to the appointment of Vice-Presidents and Corresponding Secretaries in the different States. The following gentlemen were appointed :—

NEW YORK.
Thomas L. Jinnings, Vice-Pres., city—Henry Sipkins, Cor. Sec., city.

MASSACHUSETTS.
Rich. Johnson, Vice-Pres., New Bedford—J G. Barbadoes, Cor. Sec., Boston.

RHODE ISLAND.
George C. Willis, Vice-President—Alfred Niger, Corresponding Secretary.

CONNECTICUT.
J. W. Creed, Vice-President—Luke Lathrop, Corresponding Secretary.

OHIO.
John Liverpool, Vice-President, with permission to appoint his own Secretary.

NEW JERSEY.
Leonard Scott, Vice-Pres., Trenton—Henry Ogden, Cor. Sec., Newark.

MARYLAND.
Rev. Samuel Eliott, Vice-Pres., Baltimore—R. Cowley, Cor. Sec., Baltimore.

DELAWARE.
Israel Jeffries, Vice-Pres., Wilmington—Pet. Hubbard, Cor. Sec., Wilmington.

PENNSYLVANIA.
John P. Burr, Vice-Pres., Philadelphia—Rob. Purvis, Cor. Sec., Philadelphia.

MAINE.

Mr. Manuel, Vice-President, Portland—Rhuben Rhuben, Cor. Sec., Portland.

DISTRICT OF COLUMBIA.

Arthur Waring, Vice-President—John Cook, Corresponding Secretary.

Moved by John Peck, and seconded by Richard Johnson, that the Convention adjourn (*sine die*) to-morrow, Thursday, afternoon. Carried.

Moved by John Peck, and seconded by Charles Mortimer, that the Convention requests our friends and the people of colour in general, to take such means and measures as may in their wisdom seem most expedient to collect money, to be forwarded to the President of the Conventional Board, in order to form a general Conventional fund, to be applied as the Convention shall deem most beneficial. Approved.

On motion of William Hamilton, seconded by Henry Sipkins, it was resolved, that a committee of five be appointed to bring in a report of all unfinished business, and the same to be acted on to-morrow morning. T. L. Jinnings, William Rich, William Hamilton, W. D. Jenkins, and John Rich, were appointed.

Moved by T. L. Jinnings, seconded by James Barnett, that the Convention prescribe the form in which the reports of the different delegations shall be made, respecting the situation of their different sections of country, and that the same be attached to the printed minutes, arranged under the proper heads to be reported on. Carried.

The following form was adopted, agreeably to the request of the Convention of free people of colour of the United States.

We, the delegates of the town of   in the county of   and state of   respectfully report, that there is in the said town, city, or county,

     "   Inhabitants of Colour,
     "   Churches,
     "   Day Schools,
     "   Sabbath Schools,
     "   Scholars,
     "   Temperance Societies,
     "   Benevolent Societies,
     "   Mechanics,
     "   Store Keepers, &c.

The report of the Conventional Board, exhibiting the amount of receipts and expenditures during the year, was read and accepted.

Moved by T. L. Jinnings, seconded by R. F. Wake, that the thanks of the Convention be returned to the Conventional Board, for their services during the past year. Carried.

Adjourned to meet to-morrow morning, at 9 o'clock.

Thursday Morning, June 13.

President in the Chair.

Prayer by Mr. Charles Mortimer. The roll having been called, and the minutes of the preceding session read, the Committee appointed to bring in a report of all unfinished business, presented their report, which was read, and disposed of in the course of the day.

Moved, that each delegation represented in this Convention, be a Committee, to form Temperance Societies in their respective places which they represent. Ordered to lie on the table.

Moved by John Peck, and seconded by Henry Ogden, that it be recommended to our people, to hold a monthly concert of prayer on the last Monday of every month, to supplicate the Supreme Ruler of the universe, for his blessing upon the efforts which are making, or may hereafter be made for the improvement of the condition of the people of colour. Adopted. Yeas 18, Nays 12.

The Committee on Colonization presented their report, which was read and adopted, viz :—

Report on African Colonization.

The committee consisting of one delegate from each State, for the purpose of reporting the views and sentiments of the people of colour in their respective States, relative to the principles and operations of the American Colonization Society, respectfully beg leave to report :—That all the people of the States they represent, feel themselves aggrieved by its very existence, and speak their sentiments of disapprobation in language not to be misunderstood. The only exception to the rule is, those who are receiving an education, or preparing themselves for some profession, at the expense of the society.

Your committee, therefore, respectfully declare, that they have given the subject that serious consideration which its connexion with the interest of our people, and a proper respect for the opinions of a large portion of the people of the United States, imperiously demand.

After having divested ourselves of all unreasonable prejudice, and reviewed the whole ground of our opposition to the American Colonization Society, with all the candour of which we are capable, we still declare to the world, that we are unable to arrive at any other conclusion, than that the life-giving principles of the association are totally repugnant to the spirit of true benevolence; that the doctrines which the society inculcates, are hostile to those of our holy religion; nay, a direct violation of the golden rule of our Lord, "All things whatsoever ye would that men should do unto you, do ye even so to them."—That the inevitable, if not the designed tendency of these doctrines, is to strengthen the cruel prejudices of our opponents, to steel the heart of sympathy to the appeals of suffering humanity, to retard our advancement in morals, literature and science, in short, to extinguish the last glimmer of hope, and throw an impenetrable gloom over our fairest and most reasonable prospects.

These are not the illusions of a distempered imagination, the ebullitions of inflamed prejudice, or the effusions of fanaticism, as some would unjustly insinuate—No: they are deliberate, irresistible conclusions, founded on facts derived from the official documents of the Colonization Society—the approved declarations and acts of the agents of that association, which we need not here recapitulate, as we presume you are perfectly familiar with them.

The recent discussions on that subject have elicited much light, and an awakening influence is arising in favour of the true interests of our people. Many of its ablest advocates have deserted the cause, and are now busily engaged in tearing down the MONUMENT they assisted in erecting.

The investigations that have been made into that society within the past year, justifies us in believing that that great BABEL of oppression and persecution must soon cease to exist. It has been reared so high, that the light of heaven, the benevolence of true philanthropy, and the voice of humanity, forbid its further ascent; and, as in ancient times, the confusion of tongues has already begun, which speedily promises its final consummation—and although it has but recently been classed with the benevolent enterprises of this age, it must shortly be numbered with the ruins of the past.

The recent appeal of the selectmen of Canterbury, (Conn.) to that Society, but too clearly demonstrates to the eyes of an enlightened public, that they have recognized it as an instrument, by which they might more fully carry into operation their horrible design of preventing innocent and unprotected females from receiving the benefits of a liberal education, without which, the best and brightest prospects of any country or people, must be for ever blasted.

Your committee would recommend to this Convention to adopt the following resolution:—

Resolved, That this Convention discourage, by every means in their power, the colonization of our people, anywhere beyond the limits of this CONTINENT; and those who may be obliged to exchange a cultivated region for a howling wilderness, we would recommend, to retire back into the western wilds, and fell the *native forests of America*, where the *plough-share* of prejudice has as yet been unable to penetrate the soil—and where they can dwell in peaceful retirement, under their own vine and under their own fig tree.

(*Signed*)   JAMES G. BARBADOES, *Mass.*
WILLIAM HAMILTON, *N. Y.*
WILLIAM WHIPPER, *Penn.*
SAMUEL ELLIOTT, *Md.*
GEORGE SPYWOOD, *R. Island,*
THOMAS BANKS, *N. J.*
JOSEPH BURTON, *Del.*
LUKE LATHROP, *Conn.*

Moved by John G. Stewart, seconded by James Bird, that three thousand copies of the Conventional Address, and the Report on African Colonization, be printed in handbills for distribution, by the members of the Convention. Carried unanimously.

The committee appointed to nominate officers for the Conventional Board, presented their report, which was read, and on motion of James Bird, seconded by John G. Stewart, adopted, viz :—

WILLIAM HAMILTON, SEN., *President,*
THOMAS DOWNING, *Vice-President,*
JAMES FIELDS, *Recording Secretary,*
HENRY SIPKINS, *Corresponding Secretary,*
JOHN ROBERTSON, *Treasurer.*

COMMITTEE.

JAMES FRAZER,   WILLIAM C. JEFFERS,
BOSTON CRUMMEL,   RANSOM F. WAKE,
JOHN BERRIAN,   PHILIP A. BELL,
JAMES BARNETT.

Mr. Thomas Shipley, of Philadelphia, addressed the Convention on the subject of Temperance, and the general rules of conduct as connected with our improvement, in an eloquent manner, and received the thanks of the Convention.

Adjourned to meet at 3 o'clock, P. M.

Afternoon Session.

The Convention met pursuant to adjournment.

President in the Chair. The roll was called, and minutes of the morning session read.

A communication from our distinguished friend, Benjamin Lundy, being received, on motion, it was resolved, that the same be read, which by request was done by Mr. Lewis.

On motion of William Hamilton, seconded by David Ruggles, resolved that Mr. Evan Lewis be requested to have the communication of Benjamin Lundy to this Convention, printed in the " Genius of Universal Emancipation."

On motion of S. H. Gloucester, seconded by Wm. Hamilton, It was resolved, that the thanks of the Convention be returned to Mr. Evan Lewis, for reading the communication, and for his able address delivered before the Convention.

Moved by R. F. Wake, seconded by James Barnett, that inasmuch as it is in contemplation, as soon as possible to establish Manual Labour Schools, in different sections of the country, viz : in Pennsylvania, New-York, and New England. We, the delegates of the free people of colour, assembled in Convention in the city of Philadelphia, do earnestly recommend them to the notice of the *liberal*, the philanthropic, and all who are friendly to the cause of the general improvement of our hitherto much neglected and oppressed race, to contribute in aid of the object in view, to the general agents that may be employed for that purpose. Carried.

Resolved, that the Convention require of the Conventional Board, that as soon as the Minutes of this Convention shall have been printed, that they shall distribute to each delegation 50 copies gratis, if required, and for all over they shall exact the sum of one dollar and fifty cents per hundred. Carried.

On motion of William Whipper, seconded by Robert Purvis, It was resolved that this Convention recommend to our people generally, to give all the support in their power to such papers as advocate the cause of our people, that are now in general circulation, such as " The Genius of Universal Emancipation,"—" The Liberator,"—" Emancipator," " Genius of Temperance,"—" Abolitionist," &c.

Mr. David Ruggles, according to leave, presented a preamble and resolution, relative to the High School recently established by Miss Prudence Crandall, which was read.

Resolved, that the preamble and resolution be handed to the committee of revision, for their decision. Carried.

The committee are of opinion that the preceding is included in the two communications before mentioned, but think that the utmost in our power should be done to sustain it, and therefore cheerfully recommend to our brethren, who may have girl children whom they wish to be well educated, to send them to her school.

Moved by J. G. Stewart, seconded by William Rich, that the Convention recommend to the free people of colour in the United States, the formation of free labour produce Societies, wherever it may be practicable, and that each delegate use the utmost exertions in his private capacity, in recommending to coloured capitalists, the establishment of stores on the principles above named. Carried.

Moved by Robert Purvis, seconded by John Peck, that this Convention highly approve of the indefatigable labours of Miss Lydia White, in her establishment of a free labour store, and that the patronage of all who feel an interest in promoting the cause of universal freedom, is cheerfully recommended to her store, *No. 42 North Fourth-Street*, in the city of Philadelphia. Carried unanimously.

The committee to prepare an address, presented the same, which was read and adopted. (See next page.)

Moved by W. Whipper, seconded by R. Purvis, that all the unfinished business of this Convention be referred to the Conventional Board, whose duty it shall be to complete the same. Carried.

Moved by F. A. Hinton, seconded by R. F. Wake, whereas the American Colonization Society, have recently elected the venerable general, La Fayette, and several of our distinguished citizens, their Vice-Presidents, for the purpose as appears to us of suppressing public sentiment, in opposition to their motives, by seeming to give the sanction and countenance of great names to their sinister plans and projects, and conceiving that such apparent approbation may not always be intended on the part of the individuals whose names are so used, or if intended, may be the result of imperfect or incorrect information in relation to the subject; Therefore,

Resolved, that our worthy and highly esteemed fellow-citizens, Mr. James Foster, of Philadelphia, and the Rev. Peter Williams, of the city of New-York, be requested to correspond with such of the gentlemen above alluded to, as they may deem proper, for the purpose of explaining to them, the views and wishes of the people of colour, in reference to the important subject of Colonization, and if possible to counteract the mischievous aims of the American Colonization Society, so adverse to the best interests and happiness of the free people of colour in this country.   Carried.

On motion of S. H. Gloucester, seconded by J. G. Steward, It was resolved, that the thanks of this Convention be, and they are hereby given to Mr. Abraham D. Shadd, President of the Convention, for his impartial and dignified deportment in the discharge of his official duties, during the sitting of this Convention, to which the President made an appropriate reply.

On motion of J. C. Mathews, seconded by R. Purvis, It was resolved, that a vote of thanks be tendered to the Vice-Presidents and Secretaries for their services.

Adjourned to meet in the city of New-York, on the 1st Monday in June, 1834, at 10 o'clock, A. M.

ABRAHAM D. SHADD, Pres.

RANSOM F. WAKE, } <i>Secretaries.</i>
HENRY OGDEN,

Philadelphia, Jnne 13, 1833.

CONVENTIONAL ADDRESS,

To the Free Coloured inhabitants of the United States.

Brethren and Fellow Citizens,

It is a matter of high congratulation that, through the providence of Almighty God, we have been enabled to convene, for the fourth time, as the representatives of the free people of colour of eight of the States of the Union, for the purpose of devising plans for our mutual and common improvement, in this, the land of our nativity.

To that important object the entire attention of the Convention has been directed; but to effect it, as might be expected, a very considerable diversity of sentiment as to the best means, existed. Various circumstances growing out of our local situations operate to produce a great difference of feeling, as well as of judgment, in the course best calculated to insure our advancement in prosperity. Our brethren at the south are subject to many very cruel and oppressive laws, to get clear of which they will consent to go into exile, as promising to them enjoyments from which they are cut off in the land of their birth. Gratitude to the bountiful Bestower of all good, compels us to rejoice in the acknowledgment that the lot of many of us has fallen in a happier and fairer portion of the land, to separate ourselves from which, or to promulgate a wish to do so, without better prospects of improvement before us than has yet come to our knowledge, would be suicidal to the vital interests of the coloured people of the free states, and would justly draw upon us the execration of the thinking part in the slave states.

Ours is a defensive warfare ; on our domicil we meet the aggressor, and if we move, or give our consent to move, and bid them to follow before we are driven, forcibly driven, from our lodgements —which, Heaven be praised, is not probable—their denunciations would be just.

The Canadian Reports, as published in the minutes of this Convention, may be regarded as the unequivocally expressed sentiments of the coloured people of the free states, viz.: improvement, but without emigration, except it be voluntary.

By an attentive perusal of the minutes and proceedings of the Convention, it will be apparent how deeply we sympathize in the distresses of our more unfortunate brethren, and the interest we willingly take, to the extent of our power, to mitigate their sufferings. We feel confident that the course pursued, as presented in this address, will receive the approbation of our constituents, and of those of our fellow citizens who are solicitous that our moral, religious, civil, and political condition should be improved in the United States. To promote our welfare, a great and increasing interest is manifesting itself in various parts of the Union ; and we feel assured that we shall receive the hearty concurrence and support of our brethren, in the measures herein recommended for our general benefit. We supplicate the intercession of Jehovah, to extend this interest to the most remote parts of our country. We think that we cannot make a stronger or more effectual appeal to your judgments to secure your active co-operation in the plans suggested, than by exhibiting to you a brief outline of the efforts making by our friends to elevate the character and condition of the man of colour.

With a view that we may the more clearly understand the duties that now devolve upon us, it may be necessary to advert to times gone by, when in a state of slavery, ignorance, and misery, with scarcely sufficient intellect remaining to wish for freedom: such is the deteriorating effect of the slave system, carried to the extent that it has been and now is in America ; there arose a number of philanthropists, who espoused our cause, and by their continued exertions have effected the entire liberation of the slaves in some of the states; and the salutary influence of those principles has been felt, in some degree, in every part of the U. States, and once bid fair to make every citizen of our country proud of the distinguished appellation of an American. But it is lamentable that a deep and solemn gloom has settled on that once bright anticipation, and that monster, *prejudice*, is stalking over the land, spreading in its course its pestilential breath, blighting and withering the fair and natural hopes of our happiness, resulting from the enjoyment of that invaluable behest of God to man—FREEDOM.

It is not to be expected that we would enter into a disquisition, with a view to satisfy the minds of those who fancy they are interested in prolonging the miseries of their fellow men; on that subject, it is presumed the greatest stretch of human reason has been employed to elucidate its repugnance to the precepts of the Gospel; its infringement on the natural rights of man; its injury to the interests of those who cleave to it on the score of supposed interest, and its repugnance to the happiness, as well as to the interests of society in general. From these considerations, the conviction is forced upon us that they willingly and wilfully shut their eyes against the clearest evidences of reason. In that state of helplessness in which we were, schools were erected for our improvement, and from them great benefit has resulted. Schools have been erected by philanthropists, and many of us have been educated without so much as knowing when, or by whom, the edifices had been reared. But the manifest improvement that we have made, loudly demands we should employ the talents we possess in assisting the philanthropists of the present time in their endeavours for our further advancement. A host of benevolent individuals are at present actively engaged in the praiseworthy and noble undertaking of raising us from the degradation we are now in, to the exalted situation of American freemen. Their success eminently depends upon the succour and encouragement they receive from our united efforts to carry into effect those plans recommended for the government of our conduct. With a strong desire for our improvement in morality, religion, and learning, they have advised us strictly to practise the virtues of temperance and economy, and by all means early to instruct our children in the elements of education. The Convention being perfectly convinced of the impossibility of our moral elevation without a strict adherence to these precepts, has conceived it to be its duty earnestly to call upon our brethren to give their aid and influence in promoting an object so desirable. In conformity to the recommendation of the former Convention, we are happy to have it in our power to state, that several temperance societies have been formed in most, if not in all, the states represented. In the course of the proceedings, will be found an elaborate report on the subject of temperance, to the careful perusal of which we invite the especial attention of our brethren. That societies for mental improvement, particularly among the females, have been established in several places, and a manifest improvement has marked their progress. Some diligence has also been employed in extending the benefits of education to a considerable number of children, who had been before neglected, and mental feasts have been held, of mixed companies of males and females, in some of the cities, on the recommendation of our very worthy friend, the Rev. Simeon S. Jocelyn, of New Haven.

From these promising beginnings we eagerly anticipate a speedy and extensive spread of those principles so justly calculated to dignify human nature; and earnestly hope a universal imitation

5

of those salutary examples, without which the best endeavours of our friends must prove abortive.

The resolution passed at the last Convention, that the auxiliary societies obtain all the information possible relative to the number and state of the schools in their respective sections; the branches of education taught in each, with the number of scholars, and make returns of the same through their delegates, to this Convention, has not been fulfilled to the extent desired; but a general report will be found attached to the proceedings.

A circumstance that we would particularly introduce to the serious consideration of our brethren in general, is, the great efforts that are making by our friends, for the establishment of manual labour schools, for the improvement of our youth in the higher branches of education, for the report on which subject we refer the reader to the minutes. It is not, however, thought to be improper here to state, that in the city of New-York efforts are making to establish, in that state, a school of this description. In the state of Pennsylvania, a benevolent (deceased) individual has bequeathed ten thousand dollars for, or towards, the erection of a similar school. And the New England Anti-Slavery Society, (which has laid a broader base for philanthropic exertion in the cause of the man of colour, than any benevolent institution that has preceded it,) has, in addition to its various other methods to raise the character and condition of the free people of colour, promoted addresses and discussions, oral and written, defending us from the unjust aspersions of our enemies; has opened a subscription, with a determination to raise funds sufficient to establish manual labour schools in New England for the instruction of coloured youth. This most meritorious institution, in the vindication of the natural, civil, and political rights of the coloured people, ought, and we trust does, occupy a distinguished place in the feelings and affections of our people. The more perfectly and securely to carry into effect that part of their plan relating to schools, they deemed it necessary to send our very worthy and highly talented advocate and defender, William Lloyd Garrison, to England, to endeavour to raise funds to aid in that enterprise, but not less to unfold the manifold misrepresentations respecting the people of colour, by Mr. Elliot Cresson, an agent of the American Colonization Society, in his addresses to the British people.

On the subject of the American Colonization Society, the expression of public sentiment has been frequently and clearly given, and as an evidence of our unvaried conviction of its hostility to our interests, we refer to the address and report on that subject. We cannot, however, brethren, pass over this important cause of much of our debasement, without informing you that we have arrived at that point in the examining of the duties submitted for our consideration, that we must necessarily leave the confined borders of our own view of natural, civil, and political rights, growing out of immemorial prescriptive usage, that birth constitutes citizenship. Theories, perfectly new and multiform, are offered for adjudication. We shall decline a decision until we have examined their several merits We shall first call your attention to the most important of these theories, that of the American Colonization Society, not only because it pursues, by its dependent agents, the most irrational course to effect the object they profess to have in view, as unfolded by them to the people of the North, but that the supporters of the system at the South are among the most talented and respectable of their citizens; how these men should advocate a cause so incommensurate to produce the avowed desired effects, seems involved in impenetrable mystery. But it is worse than idle, when the address is made to the common sense of common men, to ask whether a child or person born in the United States of America can be considered a native of England. The philanthropists of this association have endeavoured to establish, as a primary belief, that the coloured child, that is, the child not white, no matter how many generations he may be able to trace in a lineal ascent, is an African, and ought to be sent to the land of his forefathers—Africa. When they have worked up the fancy of their hearers to that pitch that they really believe us to be Africans, it becomes an easy matter to excite their sympathy so that they readily loose their purse-strings, and voluntarily contribute to the beneficent scheme of the Society to restore us to the land of our nativity. The show of seeming seriousness in combatting so ludicrous a position, if it was not upheld by a very respectable portion of the intelligence of the country, might create a doubt of the intent.

But this society has most grossly vilified our character as a people; it has taken much pains to make us abhorrent to the public, and then pleads the necessity of sending us into banishment. A greater outrage could not be committed against an unoffending people; and the hypocrisy that has marked its movements, deserves our universal censure. We have been cajoled into measures by the most false representations of the advantages to be derived from our emigration to Africa. The recommendation has been offered as presenting the greatest and best interests to ourselves. No argument has been adduced, other than that based on prejudice, and that prejudice founded on our difference of colour. If shades of difference in complexion is to operate to make men the sport of powerful caprice, who can pretend to determine how long it may be before, on this principle, the colonists may be again compelled to migrate to the land of their fathers in America.

The conduct of this institution is the most unprincipled that has been realized in almost any civilized country. Based and supported as it was, by some men of the greatest wealth and talent that the country boasts, under the sanction of names so respectable, the common sense of the community was led astray, little imagining that any thing more was designed than appeared on the surface, viz. the improvement of the condition of the people of colour, by their removal to Africa, and the evangelizing of that continent. The hidden insidious design in our removal, political expediency, was confined to the few that organized the society; its secret purposes have been kept as close as possible. But Southern inquisitiveness demanded a developement of the secret, with which they were satisfied, and it received their support—while the North, prompted by sentiments of benevolence towards us, entered heartily into the scheme. But the real objects being now manifest many have withdrawn their support from it, from their conviction of its insufficiency to perform what was expected, and the want of good faith on the part of the society, as to its real object in awakening their sympathy. The deception is discovered, and it is hoped that before long, the man of colour will be reinstated in his natural rights.

In the city of New-York, there has been lately formed an institution called the Phœnix Society, consisting of some of the most wealthy and talented men in that city, white and coloured, the object of which is to unite the whole coloured people into a fraternity for our improvement; and it is hoped, that under the guidance of Almighty God, our most sanguine expectations will be realized.

ABRAHAM D. SHADD, President.

Philadelphia, June 13, 1833.

MINUTES

OF THE

FOURTH ANNUAL CONVENTION,

FOR THE IMPROVEMENT

OF

THE FREE PEOPLE OF COLOUR,

In the United States,

HELD BY ADJOURNMENTS

IN THE ASBURY CHURCH, NEW-YORK,

From the 2d to the 12th of June inclusive, 1834.

———

NEW-YORK:

PUBLISHED BY ORDER OF THE CONVENTION.

—

1834.

MINUTES.

———

THE Delegates to the Fourth Annual Convention for the improvement of the Free People of Colour, in the United States, agreeably to public notice, met at Chatham-street Chapel, at half past 10 o'clock, on Monday, June 2, 1834. Mr. William Hamilton, President of the Conventional Board, took his seat as Chairman of the meeting, and Mr. James Fields, assisted by Mr. Theodore C. Breshaw, officiated as Secretary.

Prayer was offered by the Rev. Mr. Raymond, and a discourse delivered by Rev. Mr. Cornish, after which the President of the Conventional Board addressed the delegates.

GENTLEMEN,

It is with the most pleasing sensations, that I, in behalf of my coloured fellow citizens of New-York, tender you of the Delegation to this Convention, a hearty welcome to our city. And in behalf of the Conventional Board, I repeat the welcome. And, gentlemen, with regard to myself, my full heart vibrates the felicitation.

You have convened to take into consideration what may be the best means for the promotion of the best interest of the people of colour of these United States, particularly of the free people thereof. And that such Convention is highly necessary, I think a few considerations will amply show.

First, the present form of society divides the interest of the community into several parts. Of these, there is that of the white man, that of the slave, and that of the free coloured man. How lamentable, how very lamentable, it is that there should be, any where on earth, a community of castes, with separate interests! That society must be the most happy, where the good of one is the common good of the whole. Civilization is not perfect, nor has reason full sway, until the community shall see that a wrong done to one is a wrong done to the whole; that the interest of one is or ought to be the common interest of the whole. Surely that must be a happy state of society where the sympathies of all are to all alike.

How pleasing, what a compliment to the nation, is the expression of Mons. Vallier, a celebrated traveller in Africa, where, speaking of the Hottentots, he says " There none need to offer themselves as objects of compassion, for all are compassionate." Whatever our early-tutored prejudice may say to the contrary, such a people must be happy. Give me a residence in such a society, and I shall fancy myself in a community the most refined.

But alas for the people of colour in this community! their interest is not identified with that of other men. From them, white men stand aloof. For them the eye of pity hath scarcely a tear.

To them the hand of kindness is palsied, to them the dregs of mercy scarcely are given. To them the finger of scorn is pointed ; contumely and reproach is continually theirs. They are a taunt, a hissing, and a by-word. They must cringe, and crouch, and crawl, and succumb to their peers. Long, long, long has the demon of prejudice and persecution beset their path. And must they make no effort to throw off the evils by which they are beset? Ought they not to meet to spread out their wrongs before one another ? Ought they not to meet to consult on the best means of relief? Ought they not to make one weak effort ; nay, one strong, one mighty moral effort, to roll off the burden that crushes them ?

Under present circumstances it is highly necessary the free people of colour should combine, and closely attend to their own particular interest. All kinds of jealousy should be swept away from among them, and their whole eye fixed, intently fixed, on their own peculiar welfare. And can they do better than to meet thus ; to take into consideration what are the best means to promote their elevation, and after having decided, to pursue those means with unabating zeal until their end is obtained ?

Another reason why this Convention is necessary, is, that there is formed a strong combination against the people of colour, by some who are the master spirits of the day, by men whose influence is of the strongest character, to whom this nation bow in humble submission, and submit to their superior judgment, who turn public sentiment whichever way they please.

You cannot but perceive that I allude to the Colonization Society. However pure the motives of some of the members of that society may be, yet the master spirits thereof are evil minded towards us. They have put on the garb of angels of light. Fold back their covering, and you have in full array those of darkness.

I need not spread before you the proofs of their evil purposes. Of that you have had a quantity sufficient; and were there no other good reason for this Convention, the bare circumstance of the existence of such an institution would be a sufficient one. I do hope, confidently hope, that the time will arrive, and is near at hand, when we shall be in full possession of all the rights of men.

But as long at least as the Colonization Society exists, will a Convention of coloured people be highly necessary. This society is the great Dagon of the land, before whom the people bow and cry, Great Jehovah, and to whom they would sacrifice the free people of colour. That society has spread itself over this whole land; it is artful, it suits itself to all places. It is one thing at the south, and another at the north; it blows hot and cold; it sends forth bitter and sweet; it sometimes represents us as the most corrupt, vicious, and abandoned of any class of men in the community. Then again we are kind, meek, and gentle. Here we are ignorant, idle, a nuisance, and a drawback on the resources of the country. But as abandoned as we are, in Africa we shall civilize and christianize all that heathen country. And by thus preaching continually, they have distilled into the minds of the community a desire to see us removed.

They have resorted to every artifice to effect their purposes, by exciting in the minds of the white community, the fears of insurrection and amalgamation ; by petitioning State legislatures to grant us no favours ; by petitioning Congress to aid in sending us away ; by using their influence to prevent the establishment of seminaries for our instruction in the higher branches of education.

And such are the men of that society that the community are blind to their absurdities, contradictions and paradoxes. They are well acquainted with the ground and the wiles by which to beguile the people.

It is therefore highly necessary we should meet, in order that we may confer on the best means to frustrate the purpose of so awful a foe.

I would beg leave to recommend an attentive consideration to this matter. Already you have done much toward the enervation of this giant: he begins to grow feeble ; indeed he seems to be making his last struggle, if we may judge from his recent movements. Hang around him ; assail him quickly. He is vulnerable. Well pointed darts will fetch him down, and soon he breathes no more.

Cheer up my friends ! Already has your protest against the Colonization Society shown to the world that the people of colour are not willing to be expatriated. Cheer up. Already a right feeling begins to prevail. The friends of justice, of humanity, and the rights of man are drawing rapidly together, and are forming a moral phalanx in your defence.

That hitherto strong-footed, but sore-eyed vixen, prejudice, is limping off, seeking the shade. The Anti-Slavery Society and the friends of immediate abolition, are taking a noble, bold and manly stand, in the cause of universal liberty. It is true they are assailed on every quarter, but the more they are assailed the faster they recruit. From present appearances the prospect is cheering, in a high degree. Anti-Slavery Societies are forming in every direction. Next August proclaims the British dominions free from slaves.

These United States are her children, they will soon follow so good an example. Slavery, that Satanic monster, that beast whose mark has been so long stamped on the forehead of the nations, shall be chained and cast down into blackness and darkness for ever.

Soon, my brethren, shall the judgment be set. Then shall rise in glory and triumph, reason, virtue, kindness and liberty, and take a high exalted stand among the sons of men. Then shall tyranny, cruelty, prejudice and slavery be cast down to the lowest depths of oblivion ; yea, be banished from the presence of God, and the glory of his power for ever. Oh blessed consummation, and devoutly to be desired!

It is for you, my brethren, to help on in this work of moral improvement. Man is capable of high advances in his reasoning and moral faculties. Man is in the pursuit of happiness. And reason, or experience, which is the parent of reason, tells us that the highest state of morality is the highest state of happiness. Aside from a future day of judgment and retribution, there is always a day of retribution at hand. That society is most miserable that is most immoral—that most happy that is most virtuous. Let me therefore recommend earnestly that you press upon our people the necessity and advantage of a moral reformation. It may not produce an excess of riches, but it will produce a higher state of happiness, and render our circumstances easier.

You, gentlemen, can begin here. By managing this conference in a spirit of good will and true politeness ; by constantly keeping in view and cultivating a spirit of peace, order and harmony, rather than satire, wit, and eloquence; by putting the best possible construction on each other's language, rather than charging each other with improper motives. These dispositions will bespeak our character more or less virtuous and refined, and render our sitting more or less pleasant. I will only now add, that the report of the Conventional Board will be submitted at your call ; and my earnest hope is that you may have a peaceful, pleasant sitting.

Leave having been granted, Rev. Mr. Dennison offered the following resolution, and addressed the meeting in its support, viz :

Resolved, that the Conventional Board take measures for holding a public meeting in the chapel during the recesses of the Convention, at which meeting addresses shall be delivered and the citizens invited to attend.

On motion of Mr. Berrian, resolved that this meeting adjourn to meet at 3 P. M. at the Asbury Church, Elizabeth-street. The Benediction was then pronounced by Rev. Mr. Rush.

Monday Afternoon, June 2.
The delegates assembled at the hour to which they were

adjourned, in Asbury Church. The President of the Conventional Board called the house to order, and prayer was offered by Rev. Mr. Hogarth.

On motion of Mr. Vogelsang, resolved, that inasmuch as no rule was laid down by the last Convention held in Philadelphia, respecting the obligation of the Secretary of the Board to perform the duties of Secretary of the Convention, that James Fields be appointed Secretary, and Theodore C. Breshaw, Assistant Secretary.

On motion of Mr. Hughes, resolved, that the credentials of Delegates be called up in geographical order, beginning with the most eastern State. The credentials of Delegates present, were accordingly presented and severally accepted as follows, viz.

MASSACHUSETTS.

Charles L. Remond, *Salem.*
James G. Barbadoes, *Boston.*
John C. Scarlett.

New Bedford.
Jacob Perry,
Nathan Johnson.

CONNECTICUT.

New Haven.
Henry M. Merriman,

Alexander C. Luca,
Hoshea Easton, *Hartford.*

RHODE ISLAND.

Providence, George Spywood.

NEW-YORK.

Robert Jackson, *Catskill.*
Poughkeepsie.
Jared Gray,
Nathan Blount.
Albany.
John G. Stewart,
Charles S. Morton.
Brooklyn.
George Hogarth,
Henry C. Thompson,
Henry Brown,

Thomas S. Thompson,
Abraham Brown.
Newtown.
John K. Jackson,
James W. C. Pennington.
City of New-York.
Benjamin F. Hughes,
William Hamilton, Sen.
Henry Sipkins,
Samuel Hardenburg,
Peter Vogelsang.

NEW-JERSEY.

Abner H. Francis, *Trenton.*
Newark.
John D. Closson,

Henry Drayton.
Amos Freeman, *Rahway.*
Henry Ogden, *Orange.*

PENNSYLVANIA.

Carlisle.
John Peck,
Frederick A. Hinton,
Samuel C. Hutchins.

Columbia.
Stephen Smith,
Joshua P. B. Eddy.
William Brewer, *Wilkesbarre.*
West Chester.
Abraham D. Shadd,

Eli Johnson,
Benjamin Wilson,
Joseph Pierce.
Samuel Van Brackle, *Chester.*
Henry C. Sippins, *Easton.*
City of Philadelphia.
William Whipper,
Thomas Butler,
James Bird,
Peter Gardner.

MARYLAND.
Baltimore, Theodore J. B. London.

OHIO.
Cincinnati, Owen T. B. Nicken.

On motion of Mr. Sipkins, *Resolved,* that a committee of seven be appointed by the President to nominate officers of the Convention, whereupon the following persons were appointed that committee, viz: Mr. Smith, of *Pennsylvania;* Mr. Jackson, of *New-York;* Mr. Hogarth, of *New-York;* Mr. Francis, of *Trenton;* Mr. Hughes, of *New-York;* Mr. Van Brackle, of *Pennsylvania;* Mr. Peck, of *Pennyslvania.*

The Convention then adjourned to meet at 9 o'clock on Tuesday A. M.

Tuesday Morning, June 3.

The Convention met as per adjournment. Prayer by the Rev. Mr. Perry. The Secretary pro. tem. being unavoidably absent, Mr. Ogden, of New-Jersey, was requested to fill his place.

The nominating committee being called upon to report, on motion of Mr. Brewer, *Resolved,* that three persons be appointed inspectors of the election. The President accordingly appointed Messrs. Henry C. Thompson, James Cornish and Thomas Butler, inspectors.

The committee of inspection reported the following gentlemen, as being duly elected officers of the convention, viz:

HENRY SIPKINS, *President.*
WILLIAM HAMILTON, SEN. 1st. *Vice do.*
JOHN D. CLOSSON,   2d *do.*
BENJAMIN F. HUGHES, *Secretary.*
ABNER H. FRANCIS, *Assistant do.*

2

The officers were accordingly announced by the Chairman and invited to their seats.

On motion, *Resolved,* that the rules and regulations of the last, be adopted for the government of this Convention.

Resolved, that any member absent at the call of the roll shall report himself to the President, on his afterwards entering the house.

Resolved, that the hour of adjournment be suspended to a quarter before 2 o'clock, for the purpose of hearing Mr. Peck's resolution.

Mr. Peck then presented the following resolution, viz: That a Committee of seven be appointed, in compliance with a desire mutually expressed on the part of the contending delegations from Philadelphia, to investigate and settle the difference between them ; and that each of the parties shall be permitted to choose three of the committee ; and the President shall appoint the seventh, the parties agreeing to be governed by the decision of the committee so appointed. After much discussion the question was put and decided in the affirmative. The parties then announced their selection as follows, viz: On the one part, Abner H. Francis, Samuel C. Hutchins, Robert Jackson ; and on the other part, Peter Vogelsang, Samuel Van Brackle, Joshua P. B. Eddy. Mr. Hamilton was appointed by the President on the part of the Convention.

Adjourned till 3 o'clock, P. M.

Afternoon Session.

Prayer by the Rev. Hoshea Easton.

President in the chair. The roll having been called and the minutes of the morning session read, *Resolved,* that fifteen be a quorum to proceed to business.

Resolved, that the Secretary be paid twelve shillings per day, for his services during the session of this Convention.

On motion of Mr. Barbadoes, *Resolved,* that 2000 copies of Mr. Hamilton's address be printed for gratuitous distribution, and that a committee of three be appointed to prepare Mr. Hamilton's address for publication.

Messrs. Hamilton, Jackson, and Barbadoes, were appointed said committee.

On motion of Mr. Brewer, *Resolved*, that a committee be appointed to inquire into the expediency of establishing a Manual Labour School for the education of Coloured Youth, and for their instruction in the agricultural and mechanic arts, at some central point in the middle States, and that said committee make a report to this Convention. Laid on the table for further consideration.

On motion of Mr. Pennington, *Resolved*, that a committee of five be appointed by the chair, to lay before this Convention such business as may be necessary for them to act upon, and that they report as soon as possible. Messrs. Pennington, Thompson, Van Brackle, Easton and Remond, were appointed said committee.

On motion of Mr. Peck, *Resolved*, that this Convention adjourn on Friday next.

On motion of Mr. Hamilton, *Resolved*, that Mr. Peck's motion be laid on the table until Friday next.

On motion of Mr. Brewer, *Resolved*, that the Conventional Board report to-morrow morning.

Adjourned to meet to-morrow, at 9 o'clock, A. M.

Wednesday Morning, June 4.

The President in the chair. Prayer by Rev. Mr. Drayton.

The roll was called and the minutes of the preceding session were read.

On motion of Mr. Barbadoes, *Resolved*, that a committee be appointed to make the necessary arrangements for publishing the minutes of the Convention, as speedily as possible.

On motion of Mr. Peck, *Resolved*, that the President appoint a committee of three, to be associated with the Secretary as a publishing committee. The following persons were accordingly appointed, viz : Messrs. Hamilton, Barbadoes and Jackson.

On motion of Mr. Hamilton, *Resolved*, that a committee consisting of one Delegate from each State be appointed by the President, to take measures for holding a public meeting on Monday or Tuesday evening, as may be most convenient, for the purpose of hearing statements from the several Delegations, as to the general state of our cause throughout the county. Messrs. Barbadoes, Spywood, Merriman, Jackson, London, Peck and Nickens were appointed.

The committee appointed to lay before this Convention suitable business to be acted upon, report the following :

1. That a committee be appointed to suggest some plan, by which to remove some of the principal effects of that prejudice which prevails against coloured citizens. Such as exclusion from equal church privileges, and the disadvantages to which we are subjected in travelling by steam boats and stages.

2. Whereas strong combinations are formed for the express purpose of perpetually excluding coloured people from acquiring knowledge in the mechanic arts, that a committee be appointed to point out the most efficient means of making general a knowledge of the above named arts.

3. That a committee be appointed to ascertain what access is granted to people of colour in Manual Labour Schools, already established in different parts of the country ; and whether there is any prospect of other Manual Labour Schools being established, to which we may have access.

4. That a committee be appointed to consider the claims to the Liberator, and to point out the best way in which our influence may be directed for the sustenance of that and other papers pledged to our cause.

5. That a committee be appointed to examine the merits and demerits of the Colonization Society, so far as its advocates claim to have missionary objects in view.

6. That a committee be appointed to inquire whether laws have been passed by any of the State legislatures during the present year, bearing on the rights and liberties of coloured citizens ; and in case such laws have been passed, to propose the proper mode of opposing them, and effecting their repeal.

7. That a committee be appointed to draft a constitution for the government of the Convention of free persons of colour.

8. That a committee be appointed to prepare an address to the free people of colour, expressive of the views of this Convention, relative to the policy they should observe in all public relations in which we are liable to be classed as a people distinct from other portions of the community.

The above report was accepted and taken up by sections for adoption. The merits of each section having been discussed and approved, the entire report was adopted; and by order of the house, the President appointed a committee to report upon each section as follows, viz. Messrs. Easton, Johnson and Spywood on the *first;* Messrs. Ogden, Easton and Hogarth on the *second;* Messrs. Barbadoes, Hinton and London on the *third;* Messrs. Eddy, Shadd and Blount on the *fourth;* Messrs. Whipper, Van Brackle, Easton, Johnson and Luca on the *fifth.* Adjourned to 3 o'clock, P. M.

Afternoon Session.

The President in the chair. Prayer by the Rev. Mr. Perry. Messrs. Israel Lewis of Wilberforce, U. C.; Evan Williams of Port au Prince, Hayti; and Richard Voluntine of Cranbury, N. Y. were admitted honorary members of this Convention.

The heads of the several Delegations reported; and on motion of Mr. Robt. Jackson, the following persons, viz. Messrs. Nickens, Eddy and Drayton were appointed a committee to condense the reports.

Elizur Wright, Jun. Esq., was introduced and leave granted him to address the Convention. Arthur Tappan, Esq. was introduced to the Convention.

Mr. Hinton submitted a resolution to suspend the rule relative to the appointment of Delegates, in order to admit the Philadelphia Delegations to seats as members of the Convention. After some discussion on the propriety of the measure, the resolution was withdrawn. Adjourned to meet to-morrow, at 9 o'clock, A. M.

Thursday Morning, June 5.

The President in the chair. Prayer by the Rev. Mr. Eddy. The roll was called and the Minutes of the preceding session were read. A communication from Utica, N. Y. was received, bearing the signature of Messrs. Brown, Wycoff and

Fountain, and referred to the committee for condensing the Minutes.

Mr. Hughes submitted the following preamble and resolution, seconded by Mr. Hinton, viz. Whereas, it is the duty of this Convention, to guard the general interests of the coloured community of this country ; and whereas, it is conceived that all vain expenditures of time and pomp in dress, are deleterious in their effects, inasmuch as they tend to impoverish us, and to increase the prejudice and contempt of the whites. Therefore, *Resolved*, That we *disapprove, will discountenance and suppress,* so far as we have power or influence, the exhibition and procession usually held on the *fifth* day of July annually, in the city of New-York ; and all other processions of coloured people, not necessary for the interment of the dead.

On motion of Mr. Shadd, *Resolved*, That this resolution be made the order of the day for 3 o'clock to-morrow, P. M.

On motion of Mr. Peck, seconded by Mr. Drayton, *Resolved*, That this Convention organize itself into a National Society, for the general improvement of the free people of colour in the United States, and that a committee of seven be appointed to draft a constitution for the government of said society. After some remarks in favour and against the resolution, it was laid on the table for future consideration.

The committee on the first section of report on business proper to be acted on, reported. The report was accepted, and taken up by sections for adoption. Adjourned till 3 o'clock, P. M.

Afternoon Session.

The President in the chair. Prayer by Rev. Mr. Drayton. The roll was called and the Minutes of the morning session were read. The unfinished business of the morning was taken up for consideration, when, on motion, a suspension was ordered, to receive the report on contested Delegations. The committee reported Messrs. Bird, Butler, Gardner, Whipper and Purvis to be the legally appointed Delegates from Philadelphia ; the report was adopted, and such parts of the Delegation as were present, were admitted to their seats.

On motion of Mr. Hinton, seconded by Mr. Hutchins, *Resolved,* That a committee of seven persons be appointed to consider and report upon the whole subject of Abolition, as set forth by our uncompromising friends of the American Anti-Slavery Society.

The report of the committee on the first section of the above named report, was again called up and discussed; when, on motion, it was *Resolved,* That the recommendations therein contained, with the exception of the last clause of the third section as follows, be rejected, viz. To obviate all difficulty in travelling, *Resolved,* that our people be recommended to patronize those conveyances and establishments only, in which are granted us equal privileges for our money. Adjourned till to-morrow 9 o'clock, A. M.

Friday Morning, June 6.

President in the chair. Prayer by Rev. Mr. Nickens. The roll was called, and the Minutes of the preceding session were read. A communication was received from Mr. Vashon of Pittsburg, Penn., read and ordered on file. A communication was also received from Mrs. Fell of Philadelphia. Read and ordered on file.

Resolved, that the first hour of each morning session be devoted to the reading of communications.

Mr. Peck's resolution on forming a National Society, was taken up and discussed. Adopted by a large majority. Adjourned to meet at 3 o'clock, P. M.

Afternoon Session.

President in the chair. Prayer by the Rev. Theo. S. Wright. The roll was called and the Minutes of the morning session were read.

Resolved, that a committee of seven be appointed to draft a constitution for the government of the contemplated National Society ; and that Messrs. Bird, Drayton, Hogarth, Easton, Van Brackle, Vogelsang and Hamilton be that committee.

Mr. Hughes' resolution on processions being the order of the day for this afternoon, was taken up. After a very protracted debate on its merits, the question was called for. Mr. Brown of Brooklyn, N. Y. magnanimously stated that he had hitherto been favourable to processions, and had taken con siderable share in their arrangement ; but that he was now convinced of their injurious tendency to his brethren, and consequently would have nothing more to do with them. The yeas and nays on the question were then demanded by calling the roll, and it was decided in the affirmative by an overwhelming majority, viz. *Yeas*, Remond, Barbadoes, Scarlett, Perry, Johnson, Merriman, Luca, Easton, Jackson, Hogarth, Brown, Thompson, Thompson, Brown, Hughes, Hamilton, Vogelsang, Jackson, Pennington, Gray, Blount, Peck, Depee, Hinton, Hutchins, Smith, Butler, Gardner, Francis, Closson, Drayton, Freeman, Ogden, Nicken, Lewis, Shadd, Johnson, Wilson, Spywood, Stewart, 40 *Nays*, Hardenburg, Brewer, 2.

A communication was received from the New-York Philomathean Society, praying the Convention to recommend the establishment of Literary Societies ; the prayer of the petitioners was granted.

Saturday Morning, June 7.

President in the chair. Prayer by Rev. Hoshea Easton. The roll was called and the Minutes of the last session were read. The committee appointed to consider the merits, &c. of the Colonization Society, made the following report :

The committee appointed to investigate and report upon the merits of the Colonization Society, so far as its advocates claim to have missionary objects in view, beg leave to report that they have duly investigated the subject confided to them ; and can find nothing worthy of commendation in the missionary operations of the society. They therefore recommend to the Convention the adoption of the following resolutions, viz.

First—Resolved, That in our opposition to the Colonization Society, we have not opposed ourselves to the persons, piety, or good intentions of men, nor to the civilization of Africa ; but to the principles which aim at the root of our liberty ; and so long as these odious principles are adhered to by any of our fellow citizens, we shall deem it our duty to feel and act with uncompromising hostility to the same. The character of the founders, of all who advocate, of those who support, and the popularity of the scheme notwithstanding.

Secondly, That we solemnly submit it to the Colonization

Society, whether under any consideration, and especially in view of our institutions, they have a right to continue our adherence to the project of our colonization.

Thirdly, That the free people of colour in all places, where it may be practicable, are advised to prepare memorials, to be signed by every citizen of their respective regions, who entertain sentiments of opposition ; and to be sent to the Colonization Society at their next annual meeting, most respectfully requesting them to erase the words, *free people of colour,* with their consent, from the constitution.

Resolved, that 3000 copies of the Minutes of this Convention be printed, and that each Delegation be furnished with 50 copies thereof.

On motion of Mr. Jackson, seconded by Mr. Ogden *Resolved,* that committees be appointed to correspond with persons residing at Liberia ; to use every means for ascertaining the true situation of our brethren there colonized, how many are desirous to return to this country, but are prevented for want of means ; and that this committee be authorized to publish from time to time the results of their correspondence.

Resolved, that a committee of *Five* be appointed, to appoint committees to carry into effect the above resolution. Messrs. Hamilton, Gardner, Remond, Easton and London were accordingly appointed.

Resolved, that a standing committee of *Five* be appointed for the city of New-York, to conduct the correspondence with Liberia, viz. Messrs. Vogelsang, Cornish, Williams, Hughes and Downing.

Resolved, that the Committees of correspondence are directed to report to the next Annual Convention, the measures proper to be adopted for the relief of the sufferers at Liberia ; and whether supplies of provisions should be furnished them, or whether means should be raised to aid them in returning to their own country.

On motion of Mr. Francis, seconded by Mr. Barbadoes, *Resolved,* that an extract from the Minutes on the subject of processions, be published three times in three of the leading Daily and other papers in the city of New-York ; and that the treasurer of the Conventional Board is hereby instructed to pay the expenses of such publication.

Resolved, that the publishing committee, viz. Messrs. Hamilton, Barbadoes, Jackson and Hughes are instructed to carry the above resolution into full effect.

Mr. Easton proposed the following preamble and resolution, seconded by Mr. Luca, which was unanimously adopted : Whereas, there are certain grievances connected with the elective franchise, as now enjoyed by a portion of *the free people of colour* in our country, which demand prompt and efficient action ; therefore, *Resolved,* that a committee of one Delegate from each State be appointed to consider and report upon the subject to this Convention. Messrs. Butler, Easton, Closson, Pennington, Hutchins, London, Stewart, Barbadoes, and Brewer were appointed that committee.

On motion of Mr. Hinton, seconded by Mr. Hughes, *Resolved,* that this Convention do most cordially approve of the disinterested and truly philanthropic course of Miss Prudence Crandall of Canterbury, Con., in her devotion to the education of female coloured youth ; and we do most cheerfully commend her to the patronage and affection of the people of colour at large.

On motion of Mr. Luca, seconded by Mr. Easton, *Resolved,* that this Convention recommend to the *free people of colour* of the United States, the importance of meeting together in their respective locations on the fourth day of July. annually, for the purpose of prayer ; that addresses be delivered on those subjects connected with our peculiar situation and our moral and political improvement ; and that collections be taken up on such occasions to aid the objects of the Convention.

Mr. Olney of Canterbury, Con., was introduced to the Convention, and invited to the seat of an honorary member. Adjourned to Monday, 9 o'clock, A. M., when Mr. Van Brackle has the floor, to continue his remarks on the appointment of a committee to report on the subject of abolition.

Monday Mornimg, June 9.

The Convention met as per adjournment. The President in the chair. Prayer by Rev. Mr. Easton. The roll having been called and the Minutes of the last session read, the annual report of the Conventional Board was read and accepted.

REPORT.

The Board beg leave to Report, that they formed on the 28th of June last past, and perceiving that they were then wholly without funds, and that the funds expected to be received would not be sufficient to pay the current expenses of the year, they thought it necessary to devise some plan by which they might be increased. Having received a letter from the Rev. Charles Gardner, tendering his services to preach a discourse on the *fourth* of July, they accepted his services, and procured Zion Church at which place the address of the Convention to the people colour, with the Minutes of a former year were distributed. A collection was taken up amounting to $25. The Board likewise obtained Bethel Church, in September, and again distributed addresses and Minutes, and collected about $7. After the necessary expenses of these meetings were paid, a balance of about $16 in favour of the Board was left.

The Board would report, that for the Minutes of the last Convention, there have been no returns of moneys whatever, except from the city of New-York; from which city they received for *five hundred* copies $9 33; they likewise report that agreeably to the book of the last treasurer, Mr. Hinton there was a balance in his hands of $122 38 of which sum he remitted $88 34; stating at the same time that he retained moneys in his hands for the payment of room-hire, for the use of the Conventional Board.

The Board take pleasure in stating, that Mr. Downing and Mr. Frazer, cheerfully accommodated their sessions; and furnished refreshments to them without charge.

The Board would now lay before you their treasurer's account, hoping you will find it satisfactory; likewise the Minutes of the Conventional Board; any explanation which may be wanted, will be given by their chairman.

Signed on behalf of the Board,

WM. HAMILTON, *President.*
JAMES FIELDS, *Secretary.*

TREASURER'S ACCOUNT.

DR. *Conventional Board, in account with Jno. Robertson, Treasurer.* CR.

1834.			1834.		
June 14.			*June* 14.		
To Sundries paid for Books, Stationary, copying Minutes, &c.	$136	18¾	By Sundries received to date	$284	55½
Balance in the Treasurer's hands to date . .	148	36¾			
	$248	55½		$284	55½

Mr. Van Brackle, resumed at great length his speech on the appointment of a committee on abolition. On the question being submitted to the house, it was decided in the affirmative ; and Messrs. Barbadoes, Merriman, Hogarth, Bird, Drayton, London and Spywood, appointed as a committee to report resolutions proper to be adopted on the subject.

Dr. Atlee, the elder, of Philadelphia, was introduced by the President, and addressed the Convention ; expressing the high gratification afforded him by the interview, and the orderly manner of conducting the deliberations.

The report of the Corresponding Secretary, was read and accepted.

The committee appointed to consider the claims of the Liberator, &c., made the following report, which was adopted.

The committee appointed to consider the claims of the Liberator, and to point out the best method of sustaining its in-influence ; and also, to notice all such papers as are pledged to our cause, beg leave to report to this Convention, that the Liberator demands our special regard.

We acknowledge that that periodical has been too much neglected, and therefore would recommend the following resolutions, viz. That this Convention request all auxiliary societies connected with this Convention, to pay strict attention to the patronage and circulation of the Liberator, the Emancipator, and all other papers pledged to our interest. And, that each Delegation shall be a committee to take proper measures for their ample support and permanent continuance

Adjourned, to meet at 3 o'clock, P. M.

Afternoon Session.

President in the chair. Prayer by Rev. Mr. Drayton. The roll was called and the Minutes of the morning session were read.

On motion of Mr. Van Brackle, seconded by Mr. Merri_man, *Resolved*, that the thanks of this Convention are hereby tendered to the Conventional Board, for their zealous, discreet and faithful services during the past year.

Resolved, that the publishing committee are hereby directed to publish, in connexion with the Minutes, the proclamation of Gen. Jackson and his Aid-de-camp, addressed to the free people of colour, in September, 1814.

PROCLAMATION.

Head Quarters, Seventh Military District, Mobile, September 21, 1814. To the Free Coloured Inhabitants of Louisania.

Through a mistaken policy you have heretofore been deprived of a participation in the glorious struggle for national rights, in which our country is engaged. This no longer shall exist.

As sons of Freedom, you are now called upon to defend our most inestimable blessing. As Americans, your country looks with confidence to her adopted children, for a valourous support, as a faithful return for the advantages enjoyed under her mild and equitable government. As fathers, husbands, and brothers, you are summoned to rally round the standard of the Eagle, to defend all which is dear in existence.

Your country, although calling for your exertions, does not wish you to engage in her cause, without remunerating you for the services rendered. Your intelligent minds are not to be led away by false representations—your love of honour would cause you to despise the man who should attempt to deceive you.   In the sincerity of a soldier, and the language of truth, I address you.

To every noble hearted freeman of colour, volunteering to serve during the present contest with Great Britain, and no longer, there will be paid the same bounty in money and lands, now received by the white soldiers of the United States, viz., one hundred and twenty-four dollars in money, and one hundred and sixty acres of land.   The non-commissioned officers and privates will also be entitled to the same monthly pay and daily rations and clothes, furnished to any American soldier.

On enrolling yourselves in companies, the Major General commanding,   will select officers for your government, from your white fellow citizens.   Your non-commissioned officers will be appointed from among yourselves.

Due regard will be paid to the feelings of freemen and soldiers.   You will not, by being associated with white men in the same corps, be exposed to improper comparisons or unjust sarcasm.   As a distinct, independent battalion or regiment, pursuing the path of glory, you will, undivided, receive the applause and gratitude of your countrymen.

To assure you of the sincerity of my intentions and my anxiety to engage your invaluable services to our country, I have communicated my wishes to the Governor of Louisiana, who is fully informed as to the manner of enrolments, and will give you every necessary information on the subject of this address.

ANDREW JACKSON,

Major General Commanding.

———

" *Proclamation to the Free People of Colour.*"

" Soldiers !—When on the banks of the Mobile, I called you to take up arms, inviting you to partake the perils and glory of your white fellow citizens, *I expected much from you ;* for I was not ignorant that you possessed qualities most formidable to an invading enemy. I knew with what fortitude you could endure hunger and thirst, and all the fatigues of a campaign. *I know well how you loved your native country*, and that you had as well as ourselves, to defend what man hold most dear—his parents, relations, wife, children and property. *You have done more than I expected.* In addition to the previous qualities I before knew you to possess, I found moreover, among you, a noble enthusiasm which leads to the performance of great things.

Soldiers!—The President of the United States shall hear how praiseworthy was your conduct in the hour of danger, and the representatives of the American people will, I doubt not, give you the praise your exploits entitle you to. Your General anticipates them in applauding your noble ardour.

The enemy approaches, his vessels cover our lakes, our brave citizens are united, and all contention has ceased among them. Their only dispute is, who shall win the prize of valor, or who the most glory, its noblest reward.

By Order,
THOMAS BUTLER, *Aid de Camp.*"

Adjourned till to-morrow, at 9 o'clock, A. M.

Tuesday Morning, June 10.

President in the chair. Prayer by the Rev. Mr. Jackson. The roll was called and the Minutes of the last session were read.

Resolved, that the Convention adjourn at half past 2 P. M. on Thursday. On motion of Mr. Whipper, seconded by Mr. Hutchins, *Resolved,* that this Convention make *a positive and formal declaration* to the world, of their sentiments on those subjects which now engage the attention of the people of the United States, with respect to the future condition of the coloured population ; including a definite expression of the course they feel *morally bound* to pursue, that they may successfully aid in the prosecution of the objects contemplated.

Resolved, that the President appoint a committee of *three* to report on the above resolution. Messrs. Whipper, Hamilton and Stewart were appointed, with instructions to report on Wednesday morning.

The committee appointed to consider and report on the subject of abolition, submitted the following report, which was adopted, and ordered to be published in connexion with preamble and constitution of the New England Anti-Slavery Society.

REPORT.

" Whereas we believe that Slavery is contrary to the precepts of Christianity, dangerous to the liberties of the country, and ought immediately to be abolished ; and whereas, we believe that the citizens of New-England not only have the right to protest against it, but are under the highest obligation to seek its removal by a moral influence ; and whereas, we believe that the free people of colour are unrighteously oppressed, and stand in need of our sympathy and benevolent co-operation ; therefore, recognizing the inspired declaration that God ' hath made of one blood all nations of men for to dwell on all the face of the earth,' and in obedience to our Saviour's golden rule, ' all things whatsoever ye would that men should do to you, do ye even so to them ;' we agree to form ourselves into a society, and to be governed by the following principles.

" The objects of the society shall be, to endeavour, by all means sanctioned by law, humanity and religion, to effect the abolition of slavery in the United States; to improve the character and condition of the free people of colour, to inform ond correct public opinion in relation to their situation and rights, and obtain for them equal civil and political rights and privileges with the whites."

Whereas the principles of the Anti-Slavery Societies embrace all the objects of ¡benevolence, and advocate the rights of the bond as well as the free.

Resolved, that they merit the expression of our warmest gratitude, and cheerful support, individually or collectively.

Resolved, that it is expedient that this Convention, or its members individually co-operate with the Anti-Slavery advocates to the utmost of our ability, in the onward march of prosperity, or in the adverse frowns of the opponents of the glorious cause which they have espoused.

On motion of Mr. Merriman, seconded by Mr. Spywood, *Resolved,* that this Convention deem it the duty of all persons of colour, to discountenance all Boarding houses where gaming is tolerated and practised Adjourned to meet to-morrow, at 9 o'clock, A. M.

Wednesday Morning, June 11.

President in the Chair. Prayer by Rev. Mr. Dennison. The roll having been called and the minutes of the last session read, the Committee appointed to condense the reports of the several delegations submitted the following

REPORT.

THE Committee appointed to condense the reports of delegations have had under consideration *twenty-five* reports. From these, they have derived very satisfactory information on the state of the *free* coloured population generally. They are gratified to learn that not only have the institutions for moral, religious and literary improvement throughout the non-slave holding states increased in numbers, but that they have during the past year assumed a character of decided superiority. *In moral reform*, the people appear to have made rapid advancement. Temperance societies are being made the order of the day; gaming and extravagance are being superseded by a judicious husbandry of finances; and idleness and levity are yielding precedence to industry and reflection. Day and Sabbath Schools of an acknowledged reputable character have been multiplied; teachers of colour, have been introduced to public patronage: literary societies and libraries have been established; lectures have been instituted and contributions levied for their support. And, notwithstanding the malevolence of the Colonization Society, the friends of the coloured man are evidently increasing. Seminaries of learning are being made accessible to our youth upon equal terms; Manual Labour Schools for the promiscuous admission of white and coloured lads upon liberal conditions are being organized; and facilities for travelling with comfort are, through our untiring friends of the Anti-Slavery Societies, every day increasing.—On the whole, your Committee think that we have great cause of gratulation to ourselves; of high esteem for our benefactors; and of deep heartfelt reliance on the Almighty Disposer of human events.

The Committee to whom was referred the inquiry, Whether any laws affecting the interests, &c. of people of colour have been enacted during the past year by State Legislatures, reported that so far as their inquiries have extended, no law of oppressive tendency has been enacted during the past year.

But that a memorial is now pending before the Legislature of Connecticut praying the passage of a law prohibiting the influx of coloured persons into that State. And that a remonstrance to the same has been made by the coloured Citizens of New-Haven ; the result was not promulged when the Delegates from that quarter set out for this City.

The Committee appointed to frame a Constitution for the government of the contemplated society, presented their report, which was made the order of the day, for three o'clock this afternoon.

On motion of Mr. Luca, seconded by Mr. Hogarth,' *Resolved*, That whereas the government of the Hartford Literary and Religious Institute contemplate the support of a High School in the City of Hartford, for the benefit of coloured youth ; and whereas public aid must be necessarily elicited for the support of said School ; that this Convention recommend the object as a praiseworthy one, fully entitled to liberal public patronage.

Adjourned, to meet at 3 o'clock, P. M.

Afternoon Session.

President in the Chair. Prayer by Rev. Mr. Todd. The roll having been called and the minutes of the morning session read, the report of Committee on constitution was called for, taken up by sections and discussed, when, on motion, *Resolved*, that this Report be referred back to the same Committee ; and that the Committee be enlarged by the addition of two to the original number. Messrs Gardner and Closson were appointed.

The President introduced Dr. Abm. L. Cox to the Convention.

The Committee to whom was referred the subject of the exclusion of coloured citizens from acquiring knowledge in the Mechanic Arts, reported that they deplore the existence of a formidable prejudice existing among the Mechanics of the country generally, against the instruction of coloured youth ; and also that a determined opposition to the employment of coloured workmen, on the part of Masters, and extreme reluctance on the part of journeymen mechanics, to work in the same shop with coloured men, prevails to great extent, In view of these facts, however, they feel incompetent to devise such means as might be efficient to counteract the evil.

Resolved, That it be recommended by this Convention to the coloured people in the United States, that they avoid any uncalled for interference or participation in the public discussions or public meetings of Colonization or Anti-Slavery Societies.

Resolved, That the Clergymen of the coloured Churches be requested to aid the delegates in their respective regions of country, in promoting the objects of this Convention.

Adjourned till to-morrow, 9 o'clock.

Thursday Morning, June 12.

Convention met pursuant to adjournment. President in the Chair. Prayer by Rev. Hoshea Easton. The roll was called and the minutes of the last session were read.

The Committee appointed to prepare a Declaration of Sentiment, reported and their Report was accepted as follows.

———

Declaration of Sentiment.

That this Convention earnestly deplore the depressed condition of the coloured population of the United States ; and they have in vain searched the history of nations to find a parallel.

They claim to be the offspring of a parentage, that once, for their excellence of attainment in the arts, literature and science, stood before the world unrivalled. We have mournfully observed the fall of those institutions that shed lustre on our mother country, and extended to Greece and Rome those refinements that made them objects of admiration to the cultivators of science.

We have observed, that in no country under Heaven have the descendants of an *ancestry* once enrolled in the history of fame ; whose glittering monuments stood forth as beacons, disseminating light and knowledge to the uttermost parts of the earth, reduced to such degrading servitude as that under which we labour from the effect of *American slavery* and *American prejudice.*

The separation of our fathers from the land of their birth, earthly ties and early affections, was not only sinful in its nature and tendency, but it led to a system of robbery, bribery and persecution, offensive to the laws of nature and of justice.

Therefore, under whatever pretext or authority laws have been promulgated or executed, whether under parliamentary, colonial, or American legislation, *we declare* them in the sight of Heaven wholly *null* and *void,* and should be *immediately abrogated.*

That we find ourselves, after the lapse of three centuries, on the American continent, the remnants of a nation amounting to three millions of people, whose country has been pillaged, parents stolen, nine generations of which have been wasted by the oppressive cruelty of this nation, standing in the presence of the Supreme Ruler of the Universe, and the civilized world, appealing to the God of nations for deliverance.

Surely there is no people on earth whose patriotic appeals for *liberty* and *justice,* possess more hallowed claims on the just interposition of Divine Providence, to aid them in removing the unqualified system of tyranny and oppression, under which human beings ever groaned.

We rejoice that it is our lot to be the inhabitants of a country blest by nature, with a genial climate and fruitful soil, and where the liberty of speech and the press are protected by law.

We rejoice that we are thrown into a revolution where the contest is not for landed territory, but for freedom ; the weapons not carnal, but spiritual ; where struggle is not for blood, but for right; and where the bow is the power of God, and the arrow the instrument of divine justice ; while the victims are the devices of *reason,* and the prejudice of the human heart. It is in this glorious struggle for civil and religious liberty, for the establishment of peace on earth and good will to men, that we are morally bound by all the relative ties we owe to the author of our being to enter the arena, and boldly contend for victory.

Our reliance and only hope is in God. If success attend the effort, the downfal of Africa from her ancient pride and splendour, will have been more than glorious to the establishment of *religion;* every drop of blood spilt by her descendants under the dominion of prejudice and persecution, will have produced peaceful rivers that shall wash from the soil of the human heart, the mountains of vice and corruption, under which this nation has long withered.

And if our presence in this country will aid in producing such a desirable reform, although we have been reared under a most debasing system of tyranny and oppression, we shall have been born under the most favourable auspices to promote the redemption of the world ; for our very sighs and groans, like the blood of martyrs, will prove to have been the seed of the church ; for they will freight the air with their voluminous ejaculations, will be borne upwards by the power of virtue to the great Ruler of Israel, for deliverance from this yoke of merciless bondage. Let us not lament, that under the present constituted powers of this government, we are disfranchised ; better far than to be partakers of its guilt. Let us refuse to be allured by the glittering endowments of official stations, or enchanted with the robe of American citizenship. But let us choose like true patriots, rather to be the victims of oppression, than the administrators of injustice.

Let no man remove from his native country, for our principles are drawn from the book of divine revelation, and are incorporated in the Declaration of Independence, " that all men are born equal, and endowed by their Creator with certain inalienable rights ; that among these are life, liberty and the pursuit of happiness." Therefore, our only trust is in the agency of divine truth, and the spirit of American liberty; our cause is glorious and must finally triumph. Though the blighting hand of time, should sweep us from the stage of action ; though other generations should pass away, our principles will live for ever ; we will teach our children, and our children's children, to hand them down to unborn generations, and to the latest posterity ; not merely for the release of the bondman from his chains, nor for the elevation of the free coloured man to the privileges of citizenship ; nor for the restoration of the world from infidelity and superstition ; but from the more fatal doctrine of *expediency,* without which the true principles of religion can never be established, liberty never secure, or the sacred rights of man remain inviolate.

It is our fortune to live in an era, where the moral power of this nation is waking up to the evils of slavery, and the cause of our oppressed brethren throughout this country. We see two *rival* institutions* invoking the benevolence of nations to aid in changing our condition. The former proposes an indirect action on the sin of slavery, by removing the free, to the land of their fathers. The latter, a direct action on the subject of slavery by denouncing its guilt, while it pleads for the elevation of the free coloured man in the land of his nativity.

The former we reject. *First,* Because it is unnecessary, there being sufficient amount of territory on this continent to contain ten times the number of its present inhabitants. *Secondly,* Because it is anti-republican in its nature and tendency; for if our country were now overflowing with a redundant population, we should deny the right of any one class of men to designate those that should be first removed. *Thirdly,* Because if the few be removed, we have no security that slavery would be abolished ; besides, if that were achieved, the victims of prejudice could scarcely be removed in a *century,* while the prejudice itself would still exist. Therefore we, as ardent lovers of our country's welfare, would be guilty of leaving it to writhe under the dominion of a prejudice inimical to the principles of morality, religion and virtue, while on the contrary we might have aided its removal. Therefore we believe and affirm that the duty we owe to the land of our birth, the interest of our suffering brethren, the cause of justice, virtue and religion, appeal to us in the most emphatic strains to remain on our soil, and see the salvation of God and the true principles of *freedom.*

Therefore we do not desire to see our numbers decreased, but we pray God that we may lawfully multiply in numbers,

* The Am. Co. So. and A. A. S. S.

in moral and intellectual endowments, and that our visages may be as so many Bibles, that shall warn this guilty nation of her injustice and cruelty to the descendants of Africa, until righteousness, justice and truth, shall rise in their might and majesty, and proclaim from the halls of legislation that the chains of the bondsman have fallen, that the soil is sacred to liberty, and that without distinction of nation or complexion she disseminates alike her blessings of *freedom to all mankind.*

Then let us rally around her *standard* and aid in cementing and perpetuating that bond of union, but not till then.

As it regards the latter institution, we believe that it is preparing the way for that desirable event. With them we will make one common cause, satisfied to await the same issue.

With them we are willing to labour for its achievement, and terminate our lives as martyrs, in support of its principles. We will raise our moral flag, bearing for its inscription, " do unto others, as you would have them do unto you ;" under this banner we will rally our countrymen without distinction of caste or complexion.

We therefore declare to the world, that our object is to extend the principles of universal peace and good will to all mankind, by promoting sound morality, by the influence of education, temperance, economy, and all those virtues that alone can render man acceptable in the eyes of God or the civilized world.

We therefore consider it due to our friends, and our enemies, nay, to the world, that previous to our taking this decided stand, we should make this just exposition of our *sentiments.*—We have drawn our principles of human rights from an authority above human legislation.—Therefore we cheerfully enter on this moral warfare in defence of *liberty, justice,* and *humanity,* conscious that whether we live to witness its completion, or die in anticipation of its glorious results, that it has already been committed to the friends of liberty and christianity throughout the world, and to them we look for its final consummation.—We therefore mutually pledge ourselves to these principles, the cause and the world, to do all that in our power lies, to hasten the period when *justice and universal liberty shall sway the sceptre of nations.*

The Committee on Constitution submitted their Report in form of a Constitution to govern each successive Convention.

Adjourned to 3 o'clock, P. M.

Afternoon Session.

President in the Chair. Prayer by Rev. Mr. Easton. The roll was called and the minutes of the morning session were read.

The Constitution for the government of the successive Conventions was taken up by sections for adoption. The merits of each section having been discussed, the Constitution was adopted with the exclusion of the second section of Art. second.

CONSTITUTION.

Whereas, the people of colour in these United States have signified their approbation of an "Annual Convention for the improvement of the free people of colour in these United States," by their choosing and sending Delegates to represent them in said Conventions for the last four years. And whereas, it is considered necessary for the stability and duration of the policy of such annual meetings, that written articles of a compact between the said people and their representatives should be established; and whereas, the former mode of government by precedents, being vacillating and unstable, it is considered politic to establish a constitution. Therefore, we, the Delegates assembled in this fourth annual convention, held in the City of New-York in the month of June, year 1834, do conclude that the following articles shall be a constitution to govern the said conventions.

ARTICLE I.

SECTION. I. This Association shall be known as "The National Convention of the people of colour," and shall consist of such number of Delegates as may be selected and sent by the people of colour, in the manner hereinafter prescribed.

SECT. II. The Convention shall hold its sittings annually, alternately in the cities of Philadelphia and New-York, on the first Monday in the month of June.

SECT. III. The Delegates shall be coloured men, over the age of twenty-one years, and who shall have resided in the state from which he shall be returned at least six months previous to his election.

SECT. IV. Each and every village, town, city, or county, in the different states of the union in which a society is or may be formed, auxiliary to the Convention, shall be entitled to send Delegates, with or without the participation of persons not members; but under no pretence whatever shall any other body or society be allowed to send Delegates from such village, town, city, or county, where a Society shall or may exist, without the sanction of the senior society, in their participating in the selecting and electing such Delegates. But provided, that in any village, town, city, or county, where no such society shall exist, the people of such village, town, city, or county, may by public meeting, send Delegates; and, to prevent difficulties, there shall be a regular return of each Delegate, signed by the President or Chairman and Secretary of every society or public meeting of any village, town, city, or county, at least two weeks previous to the sitting fo the Convention, forwarded to the President of the Conventional Board, who shall keep a record of and present the same at the opening of the Convention.

SECT. V. Each convention shall be the judge of the qualification of its own members; appoint its own officers, and make rules for its own government, during its sitting.

ARTICLE II.

SECT. I. The convention shall declare the number of Delegates to be sent by each county, according to the number of its coloured inhabitants, and the amount of money to be contributed by each Delegation to the Treasury of the convention, on presenting their credentials; provided, however, that if any county shall possess a less number of inhabitants than the ratio of representation that may be determined on such county, shall be deemed to have possessed the right of sending one representative; and provided that any county having an auxiliary society should, within the year preceding the sitting of the convention, have contributed to the Treasury of the convention a sum equal to the amount to be paid by the number of its delegation, such delegations shall be exempted from the tax imposed on each Delegation. And, in order to ascertain the number of Delegates to be returned from each county, it shall be necessary that the credentials of each Delegate shall contain a statement of the number of coloured inhabitants such county contained, at the last census of the inhabitants of said county, taken before the return of such delegation.

ARTICLE III.

SECT. I. There shall be an executive committee, to be called "The Conventional Board," whose duty it shall be to transact the business of the Convention in its recess. This Board shall consist of a President, Vice-President, Recording Secretary, Corresponding Secretary, Treasurer, and a Sub-Committee of seven members; all of whom shall be elected annually by the convention, which election shall be by ballot.

SECT. II. The President shall preside at each meeting of the Conventional Board, and also preside at the opening of the annual convention, until the same is organized by the appointment of its own officers. It shall also be his duty to prepare and send a message to the convention at the opening of each session, depicting the condition of our people and suggesting for the consideration of the convention such matters as he shall deem worthy of their consideration.

The Vice-President shall, in case of the death, absence or resignation of the President, do and perform all the duties of the office of President.

The Corresponding Secretary shall notify the persons appointed to office by the convention, and correspond with the committees and agents appointed to advance the interest of our people ; such correspondence being subject to the inspection of the president.

The Recording Secretary shall keep accurate minutes of the proceedings of the Conventional Board, which shall be laid before the convention at its opening, and shall act as Secretary until the convention is organized.

The Treasurer shall receive all moneys collected for the Treasury of the convention, and pay all drafts made on him by the President and Secretary of the Conventional Board, at any of its meetings. But, before he enters upon the duties of his office, he shall give to the Committee of seven of the Board, who is hereby authorized to act as trustees to this association, such a bond or obligation, and in such penalties as they may require, which bond or obligation shall be cancelled on the surrender of all moneys and securities in his possession belonging to the Convention.

SECT. III. The Conventional Board shall have power to fill all vacancies in their Board, at any meeting at which a majority of the members shall be present, they shall pay all moneys appropriated by the Convention, and the expenses incurred at each sitting. They shall present to the convention, after the organization of each sitting, a regular account with its Treasurer ; and, when a new Conventional Board is appointed, pay over all moneys, and deliver over all documents and papers belonging to the Convention, to the new board.

ARTICLE IV.

SECT. I. When the Treasury of the Convention shall contain a larger sum than five hundred dollars, it shall be invested in United States securities; the script for which to be held by the Conventional Board as Trustees of the convention.

ARTICLE V.

Until the present Constitution shall go into effect, the precedent of all former Conventions shall continue in force, but no alteration shall be made to this Constitution at the session the alteration is proposed ; but the proposition may be discussed and published in the Minutes, and the question decided at the next sitting of the Convention.

PETER VOGELSANG.
WM HAMILTON.
SAMUEL VAN BRACKLE.
JAMES BIRD.
JOHN D. CLOSSON.

Resolved, that the hour of adjournment be suspended to the close of the day.

On motion of Mr. Whipper, seconded by Mr. Jackson, Resolved, That this Convention recommend the establishment of Societies on the principle of *Moral Reform*, as set forth in the declaration of sentiment.

Resolved, that the President appoint a Committee of *five* to nominate the Conventional Board, Messrs. Hutchins, Bird, Butler, Gardner and Van Brackle were appointed.

The Committee to nominate the Conventional Board, reported as follows and their report was accepted—viz.

JNO. P. BURR *President*,
DANIEL B. BROWNHILL, *Vice President*,
SAMUEL VAN BRACKLE, *Recording Secretary*,
WILLIAM WHIPPER, *Corresponding Secretary*,
JOHN BOWERS, Sen. *Treasurer*.

COMMITTEE.

JAMES Mc CRUMMELL.	JUNIUS C. MORELL,
JOSHUA BROWN,	JAMES CORNISH,
SAMUEL C. HUTCHINS,	ROBERT C. GORDON, Jr.

JACOB WHITE.

MAINE.

Mr. MANUEL, *Vice-President*, Portland.
REUBEN REUBEN, *Corresponding Secretary*, Portland.

MASSACHUSETTS.

RICHARD JOHNSON, *Vice-President*, New-Bedford.
JAMES G. BARBADOES, *Corresponding Secretary*, Boston.

RHODE ISLAND.

GEORGE C. WILLIS, *Vice-President*.
ALFRED NIGER, *Corresponding Secretary*.

CONNECTICUT.

J. W. CREED, *Vice-President*.
LUKE LATHROP, *Corresponding Secretary*.

NEW-YORK.

THOMAS L. JINNINGS, *Vice-President*.
HENRY SIPKINS, *Corresponding Secretary*.

NEW-JERSEY.

JOHN D. CLOSSON, *Vice-President*.
ABNER H. FRANCIS, *Corresponding Secretary*.

PENSYLVANIA.

JAMES BIRD, *Vice-President*.
JAMES NEEDHAM, *Corresponding Secretary*.

MARYLAND.
JAMES HINER, *Vice-President*
ROBERT COOLEY, *Corresponding Secretary.*
DELAWARE.
ISRAEL JEFFRIES, *Vice-President.*
PETER HUBBARD, *Corresponding Secretary.*
DIST. COLUMBIA.
ARTHUR WARING, *Vice-President.*
JNO. COOK, *Corresponding Secretary.*
OHIO.
JNO. LIVERPOOL, *Vice-President.*
OWEN T. B. NICKEN, *Corresponding Secretary.*

On motion of Mr. Whipper, seconded by Mr. Jackson,

Resolved, That this convention again earnestly recommend the subject of Temperance to our people generally *on* the principle of total abstinence.

On motion of Mr. Jackson, seconded by Mr. Easton,

Resolved, That this Convention earnestly recommend to all its constituents their abstinence, as much as possible, from goods contaminated with the blood and tears of the slave.

On motion of Mr. Barbadoes, seconded by Mr. Scarlett,

Resolved, That this Convention duly appreciate the magnanimity of the British Public, and the Anti-Slavery Societies of Great Britain in the missions of Messrs. Stewart and Thompson, advocates of our cause. And that the unanimous thanks of this Convention be presented through Mr. Charles Stewart, whom we welcome to these shores as a messenger of truth, benevolence and philanthropy; and whom we recognize as our friend and brother.

Resolved, that the thanks of this Convention be tendered to the President for the patient and impartial manner in which he has presided at this Convention.

Resolved, that the thanks of this Convention be tendered to the Vice-Presidents for their assistance given to the President in maintaining order.

Resolved, that the thanks of this Convention be tendered to the Secretaries, for the able manner in which they have performed the duties of their office.

Resolved, that this Convention adjourn, and that another Convention be summoned to meet in the City of Philadelphia on the first Monday in June 1835. The Rev. Mr. Todd then addressed the Convention and concluded with Prayer.

HENRY SIPKINS, *President.*
B. F. HUGHES, *Secretary.*
ABNER H. FRANCIS, *Asst. Secretary.*

MINUTES

OF THE

FIFTH ANNUAL CONVENTION

FOR THE IMPROVEMENT

OF

THE FREE PEOPLE OF COLOUR

In the United States,

HELD BY ADJOURNMENTS,

IN THE WESLEY CHURCH, PHILADELPHIA,

FROM THE FIRST TO THE FIFTH OF JUNE, INCLUSIVE,

1835.

———••••———

PHILADELPHIA:
PRINTED BY WILLIAM P. GIBBONS,
Sixth and Cherry sts.
————
1835.

MINUTES.

———◆———

AGREEABLY to public notice, the delegates appointed to attend the Fifth Annual Convention met at Wesley church at 10 o'clock A. M. John P. Burr, President of the Conventional Board took his seat as chairman of the meeting, and Samuel Vanbrakle and Junius C. Morell, officiated as secretaries. Prayer was offered by the Rev. Edward Crosby of New York, and after some preliminary remarks by the chairman, it was on motion *Resolved*, That this meeting adjourn till 3 o'clock.

Monday afternoon, June 1, 3 o'clock.

The delegates again assembled, and the president of the Conventional Board called the house to order, and a prayer was offered up in behalf of the objects of the Convention, by the Rev. Stephen Smith. It was then on motion *Resolved*, that a committee of five be appointed to nominate officers for the Convention.

The committee reported as follows, which was unanimously adopted.

REUBEN RUBY, President,

JAMES H. FLEET, }
NATHAN JOHNSON, } Vice Presidents,

John F. Cook, Secretary,

Samuel Van Brakle, }
Henry Ogden, } Assistant Secretaries,

On motion of Robert Purvis, *Resolved*, That a committee of one member from each state be appointed by the chair, to lay before this Convention, such business as may be necessary to be acted upon, and report to-morrow morning. The president appointed Stephen Smith, Columbia; Augustus Price, Washington City, D. C.; Francis Lippins, Easton; Nathan Johnson, New Bedford; George A. Black, Portland; and Robert Purvis, Philadelphia.

Tuesday Morning, June 2d, 9 A. M.

A quorum being present, prayer was offered by the Rev. Stephen Smith. The minutes of the previous sittings were read and the roll called.

Mr. Purvis of the committee appointed to report business necessary for the action of the Convention arose and stated, "That the limited time allotted the committee had deprived them of extending their investigation as far as they desired, but they had arrived to the conclusion, that they could not better execute the important trust committed to their care, than by recommending to their consideration and attention, the business that engaged the attention of the Convention last year." The report was received, and committees were appointed on the several subjects, brought forward by the committee of inquiry last year, for which the reader is referred to the minutes of 1834. As but few of the committees reported we shall omit their notice at present, together with the rules and regulations, they being the same as those used on former occasions.

3 o'clock, P. M.

President in the chair, the meeting was opened by a prayer from the Rev. Mr. Rhoads. On motion of F. A. Hinton, seconded by R. Purvis, *Resolved*, That a committee of five be appointed, to inquire into andreport in writing, whether we ought, and how far, to countenance, aid, and coöperate with the measures of the American Anti-slavery Society. The resolution was adopted and referred to the committee.

On motion of Augustus Price, seconded by Stephen Smith, *Resolved*, That this Convention do now proceed to organize an association to be known by the name of the *American Moral Reform Society*, for improving the condition of mankind, embracing for its creed, the principles contained in the declaration of sentiment published in the minutes of the Convention of last year.

Here J. C. Morell called for the reading of the declaration of sentiment which was read by the secretary. He then requested the mover to make some explanations, in support of the resolution.

Here F. A. Hinton introduced Edwin P. Atlee of Philadelphia, who addressed the convention with much fervour and good feeling concerning our condition. A. H. Price's resolution was again read, upon which a warm and animated discussion arose; after which it was withdrawn by Mr. Price, and the following substituted by F. A. Hinton, seconded by S. Smith :

Resolved, That it is the sense of this convention, that we do form a National Moral Reform Society.

Which, after much debate, was adopted.

On motion of J. C. Morell, seconded by J. H. Fleet,

Resolved, That a committee be appointed, to inquire into the expediency of devising ways and means by which colored students of medicine may obtain a regular and legal diploma.

Adopted and referred to Messrs. Morell, Fleet and Hinton.

On motion of W. Whipper, Resolved, That a committee of five be appointed to prepare a constitution for a National Moral Reform Society.

Whereupon Messrs. Whipper, Smith, Price, Crosby and Powell were appointed.

Resolved, That a committee be appointed to condense the reports of the several delegations.

Whereupon Messrs. Purvis, Whipper and Closson were appointed.

On motion of J. P. B. Eddy, seconded by Mr. F. C. Lippins,

Resolved, That hereafter delegates to our National Convention be elected by the people in general meeting assembled.

Which, after much discussion was laid over, the hour of adjournment having arrived.

Wednesday morning, June 3d.

After prayer by the Rev. E. Crosby, the house proceeded to business. Alfred Niger of Providence, Rhode Island, Benjamin Clark of York, Pennsylvania, and Joshua Woodlin of Burlington, N. Jersey, appeared and took their seats. A report of the situation of the people of colour, in Burlington, was read and received, also one from York, Pennsylvania. Mr. Purvis of the committee appointed to consider the claims of the presses in our favour presented the following report.

Report.

The committee to consider the claims of such papers as are devoted to the cause of human rights, in this country, do respectfully report that they have duly considered the importance of the subject, referred to them. Your committee believe that it is only through the instrumentality of that most potent reformer of public sentiment the public press, that any certain, speedy and radical change will be effected in the moral and political relation which we, as a people, hold in this country. And we beg leave to recommend the adoption of the following resolution.

Resolved, That this Convention deem it obligatory upon every Christian, philanthropist, and patriot, of whatever hue or condition, to give his aid and support to those presses devoted to the great and holy cause of human rights.

Robert Purvis,
James H. Fleet, } Committee.
Frederick A. Hinton.

A communication was then read by the secretary of the convention, from the Baltimore Phœnix Society, which on motion of Mr. Morell, was referred to a select committee of three; whereupon Messrs. Whipper, Van Brakle and Price were chosen, to report on Friday afternoon next.

It was moved by J. P. B. Eddy, seconded by Joshua Woodlin,

Resolved, That this convention when assembled shall have power to elect any abolitionist as an honorary member in the convention, being from any city or place where there are no delegates to represent the colored people.

Mr. Shipley and Mr. Buffum were introduced, and admitted as honorary members in this convention.

On motion of Mr. Ogden, seconded by R. Purvis, it was

Resolved, That a committee of two be appointed to correspond with gentlemen in Liberia, and endeavour to ascertain the situation of those of our brethren who may have considered themselves deluded by the American Colonization Society, with a request that they publish their correspondence from time to time.

Messrs. Purvis and Hinton were appointed.

On motion of Mr. Van Brakle, seconded by Mr. Johnson, it was unanimously

Resolved, That Mr. Henry Ogden be, and is hereby requested to act as an assistant secretary to this convention.

Mr. Arnold Buffum then advanced and addressed the meeting, and was followed by Mrs. Moore; both of whom spoke in a very feeling manner.

On motion of Mr. Powell, seconded by Mr. Smith, it was unanimously Resolved, That the thanks of this convention be tendered to Mrs. Moore, Dr. E. P. Atlee, and Mr. A. Buffum, for their congratulatory remarks offered at the present session.

On motion of Mr. Morell, seconded by Mr. Lippins, it was unanimously Resolved, That the thanks of this convention be tendered through the president and secretary, to the members of the Pennsylvania Society, for Promoting the Abolition of Slavery, for their praiseworthy exertions in behalf of suffering humanity.

On motion of Mr. Powell, seconded by S. Van Brakle, it was Resolved, That the house go into a committee of the whole, to consider the state of the union, and report this afternoon, at 5 o'clock.

On motion of Mr. Clark, seconded by Mr. Morell, it was Resolved, that the thanks of this convention be tendered to that veteran in the cause of immediate emancipation, Benj. Lundy—that we sympathize with him in his sufferings for the cause of abolition, and the welfare of colored Americans.

On motion of Mr. Price, it was unanimously Resolved, That Mr. E. Hambleton, of the Clarkson Anti-Slavery Society of Pennsylvania, be permitted to address this convention. Also, that Mr. Eli Hambleton be admitted as an honorary member in this convention.

Adjourned by prayer, by the Rev. J. Todd, to meet at three o'clock this afternoon.

Wednesday afternoon, June 3.

Prayer by the Rev. Mr. Rhoads. President in the chair. Roll called by the secretary, minutes of the preceding meeting read. On motion of Mr. Samuel Van Brakle, seconded by Nathan Johnson, it was unanimously

Resolved, That the members of this convention return their sincere thanks to the theological students of Lane Seminary, in the state of Ohio, for their spirit of philanthropy, and their zeal in the cause of abolition; with the hope that they may be laden in the day of Eternity, with an everlasting trophy of glory.

On motion of Mr. Ogden, seconded by Mr. Van Brakle, it was

Resolved, That the Rev. Mr. Rhoads be and is hereby appointed chaplain of this convention.

W. Whipper, of the committee to whom was referred the resolution in relation to the formation of a National Reform Society, submitted a constitution as their report, which was received, taken up by sections, and adopted.

On motion of Mr. Price, seconded by Mr. Closson, it was unanimously Resolved, That this convention do adjourn on Friday evening next, *sine die.*

On motion of Benjamin Clark, seconded by John D. Closson, it was unanimously

Resolved, That the thanks of this Convention be tendered, through the President and Secretary, to the Hon. John Evans, of York, Pa., for his noble defence in the case of the wife of John Williams, of Middletown, Pa., and the rescue from the jaws of slavery, of his two infant children.

On motion of William P. Powel, seconded by Mr. J. P. B. Eddy, it was Resolved, That the Conventional Board bring in the report of their proceedings of last year, a statement of the funds, and all other business left in their hands to transact, on Friday morning next.

On motion of W. Whipper, seconded by A. Price, it was unanimously Resolved, That a committee of three be appointed to prepare an address to the people of the United States, giving an exposition of the principles of our society, and the wants of our people.

Whereupon Messrs. Whipper, Price, and Niger were appointed.

On motion of Mr. W. P. Powell, seconded by Mr. Crosby, it was Resolved, That a committee of three be appointed to prepare the minutes of this (the Fifth) Annual Convention of the Free People of Color, for publication.

Messrs. Whipper, Hinton and Fleet were appointed that committee.

On motion of Mr. Benjamin Clark, seconded by Mr. Lippins, it was unanimously Resolved, That this Convention hail with joy the progress of the temperance reformation among the colored, as well the white inhabitants of our country ; and as intemperance and slavery are closely allied, this convention recommend to our people the formation of temperance societies, which we believe will facilitate the cause of immediate and universal emancipation.

On motion of Mr. Price, seconded by Mr. Smith, it was unanimously Resolved, That a committee of three be appointed to inquire into the expediency of promoting the science of medicine among our people in the United States.

Which resolution was afterward referred to a committee already appointed on a similar subject.

On motion the convention then adjourned.

Thursday morning June 4th.

President in the chair. Prayer by Mr. Rhoades. Roll called, and minutes of the preceding meeting read by the secretary.

On motion of Mr. W. Whipper, seconded by J. F. Cook, it was unanimously

Resolved, that this convention recommend the formation of auxiliary societies to the American Moral Reform Society, in all the cities, towns, and villages, in the U. States where our people are located, and they are hereby requested to send delegates to anniversary meetings of the parent institution.

The following resolution moved by the same gentlemen was also after much discussion adopted :

Resolved, that each society formed auxiliary to the American Moral Reform Society, contribute at least five dollars, at each annual meeting to aid in promoting the objects of the said society.

The following resolutions presented by Mr. James H. Fleet and seconded by John F. Cook were unanimously passed.

Resolved, that this convention recommend to the free people of colour throughout the U. States, the propriety of petitioning congress and their respective state legislatures to be admitted to the rights and privileges of American citizens, and that we be protected in the same.

Resolved, that this convention recommend to the free young men of colour throughout the U. States, the propriety of forming and promoting societies for their improvement in moral and literary knowledge.

Mr. Price, of the committee to whom was referred the suggestion in relation to manual labour schools, offered the following as their

Report.

The committee to whom was referred the duty to ascertain how many manual labour schools are established in the U. States for the instruction of coloured youths, beg leave to state, that as far as the committee have been able to learn, there is but one, which is located in the village of Peterborough, Madison County, N. York State, founded by Gerritt Smith, Esq. The number of scholars is limited to eighteen : at present there are but nine : this school has been in operation one year. In conclusion, your committee beg leave to offer the following resolution for your consideration and adoption.

Resolved, that this convention recommend to their auxiliaries and to the free people of colour throughout the United States, the propriety of taking up collections, and opening books, and receiving subscriptions to aid in erecting a manual labour college, to be located in some place hereafter named by the American Moral Reform Society of the free people of colour. Furthermore, that each auxiliary society or delegation shall transmit to each annual meeting of the American Moral Reform Society, a report of the amount subscribed and collected ; and when a sufficient amount shall have been obtained, the annual meeting of the Moral Reform Society, of the free people of colour, shall then proceed to the location and erection of a manual labour college.

Those who voted in favour of the above report as amended, are Messrs. Downing, Closson, Ogden, Woodlin, Smith, Clark, Whipper, Cook, Fleet, and Reuben Ruby, *President.* The gentlemen voting on the contrary, are Messrs. Johnson, Niger, Eddy, Gordon, Morell, Cornish, Van Brakle, Price, and Lippins.

On motion of Mr. Morell, seconded by Mr. Eddy, it was

Resolved, that this convention do recommend to our people annually to assemble in conventions, by delegates for the purpose of devising ways and means for our future elevation.

On motion of Mr. Whipper, seconded by Mr. Downing, it was

Resolved, that this convention, request the board of managers of the American Moral Reform Society, to establish as soon as possible a press, to be the organ through which the principles of our institution, shall be made known to the world. And be it further Resolved, that the delegates to this convention do, immediately on their return home, use their efforts to obtain subscriptions for the same,

On motion of Mr. Morell seconded by Mr. Van Brakle, it was
Resolved, that all delegates to our conventions, from the city and
county of Philadelphia, shall be elected by the people.

On motion the meeting then adjourned.

Thursday afternoon, June 4th.

Prayer by the chaplain. President in the chair, the roll being
called. A report from the committee appointed on the exclusion
of our people from church privileges and travelling by steam boats,
was received and laid upon the table.

A very fervent and affectionate letter from the Rev. Charles W.
Denison, expressing his hearty coöperation in the objects of the
convention, and his regret at being unable to be present at their deliberations, was presented by W. Whipper, and read by the secretary. He informed the convention " that his projected *History of
the People of Colour*, was in a good state of progress, and would be
put to press as soon as all the materials for which he had made extensive arrangements could be obtained.

On motion of B. Clark, seconded by J. P. B. Eddy, it was
Resolved, That a committee of three be appointed to ascertain
the number of High Schools in the United States, that have accepted colored students upon the same footing with other persons, and
that the thanks of this body be presented to the directors and professors, if any there be of such high schools, for their benevolence
and philanthropy, in thus recognizing our rights and those of our
children, as American citizens.

Messrs. Clarke, Eddy and Downing were appointed.

On motion of Mr. Morell, seconded by Mr. Clarke, it was
Resolved, That the thanks of this convention be tendered, through
the president and secretary, to the different Anti Slavery Societies
in the United States, for their untiring zeal in the cause of human
liberty.

At the suggestion of W. Whipper, seconded by R. Purvis, it was
Resolved, That it is the duty of every *lover of freedom*, to abstain from using the products of slave labour, as far as practicable.

On motion of S. Smith, seconded by T. Downing, it was

Resolved, That when this Convention adjourn, it adjourn to meet in the city of New York, on the first Monday in June, 1836.

On motion of R. Purvis, seconded by W. Whipper, it was

Resolved, That we do most heartily welcome that distinguished philanthropist and friend of the human race, Mr. George Thompson, to our shores, and most ardently desire that the blessing of Heaven may crown his illustrious mission to this country.

On motion of W. Whipper, seconded by S. Smith, it was

Resolved, that the free people of colour are requested by this convention, to petition those state legislatures that have adopted the Colonization Society, to abolish it.

The hour of six having arrived, the convention was prolonged by motion to half past six o'clock.

On motion of W. Whipper, seconded by R. Purvis, it was

Resolved, That we regard with heartfelt admiration, the high and holy stand taken by many ministers of the Gospel and Christian churches, in favour of Immediate Emancipation, and do sincerely request our colored churches, to exert themselves equally to promote the cause of Moral Reform.

On motion of Mr. Clark, seconded by Mr. Purvis, it was

Resolved, As we have been informed that sugar is manufactured in France, from the beet root, therefore be it Resolved, That we recommend to our people the practicability of making an effort some where in this state, to produce sugar from that root, and if successful, to report to the next convention, the result of their efforts.

On motion of F. C. Lippins, seconded by S. Smith,

Resolved, That this Convention appoint a committee of five, to nominate officers for the government of the American Moral Reform Society, instituted by this Convention.

Which motion was under consideration when the meeting adjourned.

June 5th, Friday morning.

President in the chair. Prayer by the chaplain. Roll was called. Minutes of the preceding meeting read.

The resolution of the previous meeting, in relation to appointing officers was then called up and after much debate was adopted, and the house proceeded to the choice of the committee, which resulted as follows ; viz. Messrs. Whipper, Smith, Purvis, Van Brakle, and Lippins.

On motion of Mr. Morell, seconded by Mr. Van Brakle, it was

Resolved, that a committee of five be appointed to report to the next annual convention, as near as practicable, the actual number of coloured slave holders in the U. States, with their names and location, and the number of slaves held by them : as well as any incidents connected therewith, and also to suggest such measures, as may be in their opinion best calculated to remedy the evil complained of.

Messrs. Morell, Price, Woodlin, Smith, and Van Brakle, were appointed.

On motion of Mr. Purvis, seconded by Mr. Frederick A. Hinton, it was unanimously

Resolved, that this convention recommend the Liberator, a weekly paper published by our devoted friends Garrison and Knapp, in Boston, as eminently deserving of the support of every free coloured citizen in these U. States.

Resolved, that it is further especially recommended to all who subscribe for papers devoted to our cause, to bear in mind, that patronage includes a punctual compliance with the terms of subscription.

Mr. Whipper, of the committee to report proper officers for the government of the American Moral Reform Society, reported the following citizens of Philadelphia as its officers, which was unanimously received and adopted.

JOHN P. BURR, President,

REV. MORRIS BROWN,
FREDERICK A. HINTON,

John B. Roberts,
Stephen H. Gloucester,

Joshua Brown,
Thomas Butler.

The report of the New York delegation in relation to the improvement of their people, was received, read, and on motion of John F. Cook, referred to the committee on condensing reports.

The credentials and report of J. Peck of Carlisle, Penn. was received and read. J. Peck was admitted as a delegate.

A petition from Providence, R. I., was received and read, and on motion referred to the committee on condensing reports.

The report on the condition of the people in Essex county, New Jersey, was received, read, and referred to the committee as above.

The report of the committee on distinctions in travelling, and associating in churches with the whites, was taken up, and on motion adopted as amended.

Report.

Your committee have had under consideration the subject assigned to them, and beg leave to report the following as the conclusion of their investigations.

First, that this Convention request ministers of the Gospel, in the different sections of our country, to use their influence in their several churches, to extinguish the prejudice, if any there exists, which debars colored members from equal rights and privileges in the same. And also, do recommend to our people and the friends of our race, to patronize those lines of stages and steamboats, which make little or no distinction among their passengers.

On motion of W. Whipper, seconded by R. Purvis,

Resolved, That we recommend as far as possible, to our people to abandon the use of the word " colored," when either speaking or writing concerning themselves ; and especially to remove the title of African from their institutions, the marbles of churches &c.

Which motion was under consideration when the Convention adjourned.

Friday afternoon, June 5th, 1835.

Prayer by the chaplain, President in the chair ; roll called ; minutes of previous meeting read.

William Whipper's resolution in relation to us, using the words "colored" and "Africans," was called up, and after an animated and interesting discussion, it was unanimously adopted.

On motion of J. F. Cook, seconded by Robert Purvis, it was unanimously Resolved, that each delegation in this Convention be a committee to promote the objects of the American Moral Reform Society, in their respective communities.

On motion of William Whipper, seconded by Robert Purvis, it was Resolved, that a committee of five be appointed to nominate the Conventional Board.

Messrs. Hardenberger, Downing, Whipper, Morell and Purvis were chosen.

On motion of Henry Ogden, seconded by John D. Closson, it was Resolved, that the thanks of this Convention be tendered to the colored schools of Philadelphia, for their liberal donation and praiseworthy exertions for the encouragement of our schools.

The committee appointed to nominate a Conventional Board, report the following, which was adopted :

WILLIAM HAMILTON, President.

SAMUEL HARDENBERGER, Vice-President.

Thomas L. Jennings, Rec. Secretary.

Henry Lippins, Cor. Secretary.

Thomas Downing, Treasurer.

Committee—James R. Hicks, Theo. S. Wright, Leaven Williams, Philip A. Bell, John Robertson, Samuel E. Cornish and Christopher Rush.

On motion of Mr. Hinton, Resolved, that the Declaration of Sentiment be printed with the minutes of this Convention. Carried.

On motion of J. D. Closson, seconded by Mr. Niger, Resolved, that the committee on publication cause to be printed 2000 copies of the minutes of the Convention, and each delegation be presented with 100 copies gratis. Adopted.

On motion of Mr. Morell, seconded by Mr. J. F. Cook, it was Resolved, that each delegation be a committee to nominate the Vice-Presidents and Corresponding Secretaries for their respective places.

The committee on the exclusion of colored youths from mechanical employment made the following report:

The committee to whom was referred the resolution to point out the most efficient means of promoting a general knowledge of those mechanical arts from the acquirement of which colored youths are excluded, beg leave most respectfully to report:

That their knowledge of the extent of this great barrier to our elevation, beyond the boundaries of the state of Pennsylvania, is very limited. And while they with pleasure acknowledge that there are several trades in this state accessible to colored youths, such as shoe makers, sail makers, carpenters, tailors &c., they regret at the same time, to say, that after acquiring these arts, they are with few exceptions, excluded from any patronage, except that given to them by those with whom they acquire the trade, who are mostly colored men ; consequently, the chance of pursuing their respective occupations, is very limited. They also state, that there are many of the most important, lucrative arts, from which they are wholly excluded : such as jewellers, watch makers, machinists, and many others too tedious to mention. And as a remedy for this great evil they would recommend that this Convention instruct the several delegates to enforce on the minds of their constituents the necessity of encouraging manual labour schools, where our youths may acquire the necessary arts, and afterwards become proprietors of establishments, and impart encouragement and instruction to others. They would also have this Convention appeal, through its minutes, to abolitionists throughout the country, who are mechanics, to take colored youths, and teach them their respective trades, and encourage them in their pursuit.

> *Stephen Smith,*
> *James Cornish,* } Committee.
> *Francis C. Lippins.*

The Committee on High Schools made the following report:

The committee to whom was referred the resolution relative to the number of High Schools in the United States that admit colored students upon an equal footing with the rest of the community, beg leave to report, that, so far as they have been enabled to ascertain there are within the several states, six Colleges, or High Schools, viz.: Oneida Institute, in the state of New York, of which the Rev. Beriah Green is the President; Mount Pleasant, in Amherst, Mass. Mr. Hubbard principal; Canaan in the state of New Hampshire, the Rev. Mr. Kimball, principal, one in Ohio, viz. the Western Reserve; one in Gettysburg in the state of Pennsylvania, and one in the city of Philadelphia, of which Miss Buffum is principal.

Your committee now suggest the propriety of the following resolution :

Resolved, that this Convention recommend the youth of our people speedily to embrace the present opportunity to procure a classical education, and that the thanks of this Convention be tendered to the Directors and Professors of all such institutions, for their generous philanthrophy and liberal patriotism in thus acknowledging the imperishable rights of man.

BENJAMIN CLARK.
JOSHUA P. B. EDDY,
THOMAS DOWNING.

On motion of William Whipper, seconded by A. Price, it was unanimously Resolved, that this convention do most heartily congratulate the friends of religion, morality and equal rights on the happy termination of slavery in the West India colonies, and do rely with the utmost confidence, that the operation of those principles will bring forth the same happy result to our *much favored*, yet GUILTY country.

On motion of R. Purvis, seconded by F. A. Hinton, it was unanimously Resolved, that, in proportion as we find the spirit of Colonization dying, prejudice diminishes. Therefore, we desire the friends of human liberty never to cease smiting the monster until its ghost has ceased to delude the philanthrophy of the nation.

On motion of Mr. Morell, seconded by Mr. Clark, it was Resolved, that this Convention recommend to our people to discountenance and refrain from witnessing the pro-slavery farces and ape-like exhibitions, commonly known as Colonization meetings.

On motion of Mr. Powell, seconded by Mr. Purvis, it was

Resolved, that this Convention place no confidence in a society recently formed in Boston, called " the American Union," believ-

3

ing it to be only Colonization in a new dress, or a wolf in sheep's clothing.

On motion of Wm. Whipper, seconded by Robert Purvis, it was

Resolved, that our duty to God, and to the principles of human rights, so far exceeds our allegiance to those laws that return the slave again to his master, (from the free states,) that we recommend our people to peaceably bear the punishment those inflict, rather than aid in returning their brethren again to slavery.

On motion of J. Cornish, seconded by Mr. Morell, it was

Resolved, that this Convention, in the name of the people it represents, present its special thanks to the Ladies constituting the Female Anti-slavery Society throughout this country, believing their untiring exertions and irresistible influence to be a most powerful auxiliary in the great cause of emancipation.

On motion of J. F. Cook, seconded by Mr. Morell, it was

Resolved, that this Convention recommend to their auxiliary Society at Baltimore, to grant free citizens of color to participate in selecting and electing delegates to our Convention by paying a sum not less than twenty-five cents per annum.

The following persons were appointed Vice-Presidents and Corresponding Secretaries in the following places, as agents for the Annual Convention of the Free People of Colour.

MAINE—PORTLAND.
C. C. MANUEL, V. P.   J. M. JOHNSON, C. S.

RHODE ISLAND—PROVIDENCE.
GEORGE C. WILLIS, V. P.   Wm. J. BROWN, C. S.

MASSACHUSETTS—NEW BEDFORD.
RICHARD G. OVERING, V. P.   RICHARD C. JOHNSON, C. S,

NEW JERSEY—NEWARK.
J. D. CLOSSON, V. P.   HENRY OGDEN, C. S.

PENNSYLVANIA—PHILADELPHIA.
DANIEL B. BROWNHILL, V. P.   JAMES NEEDHAM, C. S,

MARYLAND—BALTIMORE.
NATHANIEL PECK, V. P.   ROBERT COWLEY, C. S,

DISTRICT OF COLUMBIA—WASHINGTON.
AUGUSTUS PRICE, V. P.   JOHN F. COOK, C. S,

On motion of Wm. Whipper, seconded by S. Smith, it was

Resolved, that the delegates present pledge themselves to furnish a sufficient amount of money to pay for the printing of the minutes, as soon as they can be prepared for the press.

On motion of George H. Black, seconded by S. Smith,

Resolved, That we recommend to our people the 25th day of June, to be kept as a day of fasting and prayer, in behalf of our suffering brethren in slavery.

On motion of W. Whipper, seconded by R. Purvis,

Resolved, That the Christian forbearance practised by our people during their persecution by those mob riots of 1834, merits the praise and respect of the whole Christian world; and is a most successful refutation of the pro-slavery arguments advanced in this country, by men who are governed by inveterate and warlike dispositions.

Resolved, That their peace, quietude and humility, during that period of excitement, have, in point of civilization and Christian kindness, placed them far above the agitators, abettors, or actors of that humiliating and degrading persecution.

The committee to whom was submitted the various reports on the condition of the free colored population, respectfully report, that the various documents submitted to their charge, possess much interesting and useful matter, and exhibit the most flattering prospects of our people, throughout the various sections of our country. They have found them too numerous to admit of publication in the minutes, but do most respectfully suggest, that they may be placed in the hands of the Executive Committee of the American Moral Reform Society, together with all other documents that may be committed to their charge, for publication in the anti-slavery periodicals.

On motion of Mr. Morell, it was Resolved, that all the former appointments of Vice-Presidents and Corresponding Secretaries, except those where we have made especial appointments at this session, be continued.

On motion of Robert Purvis, seconded by Wm. Whipper, it was unanimously Resolved, that the thanks of this Convention be, and are hereby tendered to the President, Vice-President and Secretaries, for the dignified manner in which they have discharged their arduous duties.

On motion, Resolved, that the President and Trustees of this Church receive the thanks of this Convention, for accommodating us with this house.

REUBEN RUBY, President.

JAMES H. FLEET, } V. Presidents.
NATHAN JOHNSON, }

JOHN F. COOK, Secretary.

SAMUEL VAN BRAKLE, } Assistant Secretaries.
HENRY OGDEN, }

DELEGATES.

MAINE.
Portland.

Reuben Ruby,   George H. Black.

MASSACHUSETTS.
New Bedford.

William P. Powell,   Nathan Johnson.

RHODE ISLAND.
Providence.

Alfred Niger,   Nathan Gilbert.

NEW YORK.
City.

Thomas L. Jennings,   Thomas Downing,
Edward Crosby,   Samuel Hardenberger.
Philip A. Bell,

Troy, N. Y.

Wm. Rich,   Wm. M. Livezeley,   Clarence Seldon.

NEW JERSEY.
Newark.

John D. Closson,   Henry Ogden,   John A. King.

Burlington.
Joshua Woodlin.

PENNSYLVANIA.
Philadelphia.

Junius C. Morell,   Robert Purvis,
James Cornish,   James Newman,
Samuel Van Brakle.

Columbia.

Rev. Stephen Smith,   William Whipper.

Lancaster.

Rev. J. P. B. Eddy,   F. A. Hinton.

Easton.

Francis C. Lippins.

York.

Benjamin Clarke.

Chester.

William H. Chapman,   Andrew J. Gordon.

Carlisle.

John Peck.

WASHINGTON, D. C.

John F. Cook,   Dr. James H. Fleet,   Augustus Price.

N. B. Each delegation paid in five dollars, to carry out the objects of the Convention.

———◦+◦———

Declaration of Sentiment.

That this Convention earnestly deplore the depressed condition of the coloured population of the United States; and they have in vain searched the history of nations to find a parallel.

They claim to be the offspring of a parentage, that once, for their excellence of attainment in the arts, literature and science, stood before the world unrivalled. We have mournfully observed the fall of those institutions that shed lustre on our mother country, and extended to Greece and Rome those refinements that made them objects of admiration to the cultivators of science.

We have observed, that in no country under Heaven have the decendants of an *ancestry* once enrolled in the history of fame, whose glittering monuments stood forth as beacons, disseminating light and knowledge to the uttermost parts of the earth, been reduced to such degrading servitude as that under which we labour from the effect of *American slavery* and *American prejudice.*

The separation of our fathers from the land of their birth, earthly ties and early affections, was not only sinful in its nature and tendency, but it led to a system of robbery, bribery and persecution offensive to the laws of nature and of justice.

Therefore, under whatever pretext or authority these laws have been promulgated or executed, whether under parliamentary, colonial, or American legislation, *we declare* them in the sight of Heaven wholly *null* and *void*, and should be *immediately abrogated.*

That we find ourselves, after the lapse of two centuries, on the American continent, the remnants of a nation amounting to three millions of people, whose country has been pillaged, parents stolen, nine generations of which have been wasted by the oppressive cruelty of this nation, standing in the presence of the Supreme Ruler of the Universe, and the civilized world, appealing to the God of nations for deliverance.

Surely there is no people on earth whose patriotic appeals for *liberty* and *justice* possess more hallowed claims on the just interposition of Divine Providence, to aid them in removing the most unqualified system of tyranny and oppression, under which human beings ever groaned.

We rejoice that it is our lot to be the inhabitants of a country blest by nature, with a genial climate and fruitful soil, and where the liberty of speech and the press is protected by law.

We rejoice that we are thrown into a revolution where the contest is not for landed territory, but for freedom ; the weapons not carnal, but spiritual ; where struggle is not for blood, but for right ; and where the bow is the power of God, and the arrow the instrument of divine justice ; while the victims are the devices of *reason*, and the prejudice of the human heart. It is in this glorious struggle for civil and religious liberty, for the establishment of peace on earth and good will to men, that we are morally bound by all the relative ties we owe to the author of our being, to enter the arena and boldly contend for victory.

Our reliance and only hope is in God. If success attend the effort, the downfall of Africa from her ancient pride and splendour, will have been more than glorious to the establishment of *religion;* every drop of blood spilt by her descendants under the dominion of prejudice and persecution, will have produced peaceful rivers, that shall wash from the soil of the human heart, the mountains of vice and corruption, under which this nation has long withered.

And if our presence in this country will aid in producing such a desirable reform, although we have been reared under a most debasing system of tyranny and oppression, we shall have been born under the most favourable auspices to promote the redemption of the world ; for our very sighs and groans, like the blood of martyrs, will prove to have been the seed of the church ; for they will freight

the air with their voluminous ejaculations, and will be borne upwards by the power of virtue to the great Ruler of Israel, for deliverance from this yoke of merciless bondage. Let us not lament,
that under the present constituted powers of this government, we
are disfranchised ; better far than to be partakers of its guilt. Let
us refuse to be allured by the glittering endowments of official stations, or enchanted with the robe of American citizenship. But
let us choose like true patriots, rather to be the victims of oppression
than the administrators of injustice.

Let no man remove from his native country, for our principles
are drawn from the book of divine revelation, and are incorporated
in the Declaration of Independence, " that all men are born equal,
and endowed by their Creator with certain inalienable rights ; that
among these are life, liberty, and the pursuit of happiness." Therefore, our only trust is in the agency of divine truth, and the spirit
of American liberty ; our cause is glorious and must finally triumph.
Though the blighting hand of time should sweep us from the stage
of action ; though other generations should pass away, our principles will live forever ; we will teach our children, and our children's
children, to hand them down to unborn generations, and to the latest posterity ; not merely for the release of the bondman from his
chains, nor for the elevation of the free coloured man to the privil-
leges of citizenship ; nor for the restoration of the world from infidelity and superstition ; but from the more fatal doctrine of *expediency*, without which the true principles of religion can never be
established, liberty never secure, or the sacred rights of man remain
inviolate.

It is our fortune to live in an era, where the moral power of this
nation is waking up to the evils of slavery, and the cause of our oppressed brethren throughout this country. We see two *rival* institutions* invoking the benevolence of nations to aid in changing our
condition. The former proposes an indirect action on the sin of
slavery, by removing the free, to the land of their fathers. The latter, a direct action on the subject of slavery by denouncing its guilt,
while it pleads for the elevation of the free coloured man in the land
of his nativity.

The former we reject. *First*, because it is unnecessary, there
being sufficient amount of territory on this continent to contain ten
times the number of its present inhabitants. *Secondly*, Because it
is anti-republican in its nature and tendency ; for if our country
were now overflowing with a redundant population, we should deny

* The Am. Co. So. and A. A. S. S.

the right of any one class of men to designate those that should be first removed. *Thirdly*, Because if the few be removed, we have no security that slavery would be abolished ; besides, if that were achieved, the victims of prejudice would scarcely be removed in a *century*, while the prejudice itself would still exist. Therefore we, as ardent lovers of our country's welfare, would be guilty of leaving it to writhe under the dominion of a prejudice inimical to the principles of morality, religion and virtue, while on the contrary we might have aided its removal. Therefore we believe and affirm that the duty we owe to the land of our birth, the interest of our suffering brethren, the cause of justice, virtue and religion, appeal to us in the most emphatic strains to remain on our soil, and see the salvation of God and the true principles of *freedom*.

Therefore we do not desire to see our numbers decreased, but we pray God that we may lawfully multiply in numbers, in moral and intellectual endowments, and that our visages may be as so many Bibles, that shall warn this guilty nation of her injustice and cruelty to the descendants of Africa, until righteousness, justice and truth, shall rise in their might and majesty, and proclaim from the halls of legislation that the chains of the bondsman have fallen, that the soil is sacred to liberty, and that without distinction of nation or complexion she disseminates alike her blessings of *freedom to all mankind.*

Then let us rally around her *standard* and aid in cementing and perpetuating that bond of union.

As it regards the latter institution, we believe that it is preparing the way for that desirable event. With them we will make one common cause, satisfied to await the same issue.

With them we are willing to labour for its achievement, and terminate our lives as martyrs, in support of its principles. We will raise our moral flag, bearing for its inscription, " do unto others as you would have them do unto you ;" under this banner we will rally our countrymen without distinction of caste or complexion.

We therefore declare to the world, that our object is to extend the principles of universal peace and good will to all mankind, by promoting sound morality, by the influence of education, temperance, economy, and all those virtues that alone can render man acceptable in the eyes of God or the civilized world.

We therefore consider it due to our friends, and our enemies, nay, to the world, that previous to our taking this decided stand, we should make this just exposition of our *sentiments.*—We have drawn out principles of human rights from an authority above human legislation.—Therefore we cheerfully enter on this moral warfare in defence of *liberty*, *justice*, and *humanity*, conscious that whether we live to witness its completion, or die in anticipation of its glorious results, that it has already been committed to the friends of liberty and christianity throughout the world, and to them we look for its final consummation.—We therefore mutually pledge ourselves to these principles, the cause and the world, to do all that in our power lies, to hasten the period when *justice and universal liberty shall sway the sceptre of nations.*

———————

To the American People.

Fellow Citizens—We form a portion of the people of this continent, on whom an unmeasurable amount of obloquy, and scorn, and contempt have been poured, on account of the depravity of our morals ; and who have been educated under the influence of a system, that impairs the mental vigour, blights with its blasting influence the only successful hope on which the mind can be reared, that keeps from our grasp the fruits of knowledge, the favour of just and equitable laws, and presents a formidable barrier to the prosecution of arts and sciences of civilized life. The lucrative avocations, mechanic arts, and civil associations by which men acquire a knowledge of government, and the nature of human affairs, have been almost wholly reserved as a dignified reward, suited only to the interest and use of the fairer complexion. Yet, in despite of all these, when all the avenues of privileged life have been closed against us, our hands bound with stationary fetters, our minds left to grope in the prison cell of impenetrable gloom, and our whole action regulated by constitutional law and a perverse public sentiment, we have been tauntingly required to prove the dignity of our human nature, by disrobing ourselves of inferiority, and exhibiting to the world our profound Scholars, distinguished Philosophers, learned Jurists, and distinguished Statesmen. The very expectation on which such a requisition is founded, to say the least, is unreasonable, for it is only when the seed is sown that we can justly hope to reap. If amidst all the difficulties with which we have been surrounded, and the privations which we have suffered, we presented an equal amount of intelligence with that class of Americans that have been so peculiarly favoured, a *very grave* and *dangerous* question would present itself to the world, on the natural equality of man, and the best rule of logic would place those who have oppressed us, in the scale of inferiority. This we do not desire ; we love the appellation that records the natural and universal rights of man, (to enjoy all the attributes of human happiness,) too well, to deprive a single being on earth of such an heavenly inheritance. We can never consent to degrade the creation of man by even attempting to defend the impartiality of his Author. If there be those who doubt that we are made in the image of God, and are endowed with those attributes which the Deity has given to man, we will exhibit them our " hands and side."

The general assertion that superiority of mind is the natural offspring of a fair complexion, arrays itself against the experience of the past and present age, and both natural and physiological science. The ignorance that exists on this subject we are not accountable for, nor are we willing to admit a theory alike irreconcilable with philosophy and common sense.

It is in view of these mighty evils that exist in our country, which are truly national, that has caused us to meet in annual convention for six successive years to take into consideration the best method of remedying our present situation by contributing to their removal ; during which period we have associated the collected wisdom of our people, in their representative character, from half the states of this Union, extending from Maine to Washington, southernly, and from thence westwardly to Cincinnati, Ohio, and have come to the conclusion to form a National Moral Reform Society, as a means best calculated to reach the wants and improve the condition of our people.

We have selected four valuable subjects for rallying points, viz.: Education, Temperance, Economy, and Universal Liberty. We hope to make our people, in theory and practice, thoroughly acquainted with these subjects, as a method of future action. Having placed our institution on the high and indisputable ground of natural laws and human rights, and being guided and actuated by the law of universal love to our fellow men, we have buried in the bosom of Christian benevolence all those national distinctions, complexional variations, geographical lines, and sectional bounds that have hitherto marked the history, character and operations of men; and now boldly plead for the Christian and moral elevation of the human race. To aid us in its completion, we shall endeavour to enlist the sympathies and benevolence of the Christian, moral and political world. Without regard to creeds, we shall only ask for the fulfilment of Christian duty, as the surest method of extending righteousness and justice. We shall aim to procure the abolition of those hateful and unnecessary distinctions by which the human family has hitherto been recognized, and only desire that they may be distinguished by their virtues and vices.

We hope to unite the colored population in those principles of Moral Reform. 1st. As a measure necessary to be practiced by all rational and intelligent beings, for the promotion of peace, harmony and concord in society. 2d. As a measure necessary to aid in effecting the total abolition of slavery. And 3d. As having a tendency to effect the destruction of vice universally.

In order to this, we will appoint agents to disseminate these truths among our people, and establish auxiliaries wherever practicable, that the same leaven of righteousness and justice may animate the body politic. We will establish a press, and through it make known to the world our progress in the arts, science, and civilization. For aid in the prosecution of our undertaking we shall appeal to the benevolence of nations, but more particularly to our own. For, as God has so abundantly blessed her with internal resources as a means of gratifying her spiritual and temporal wants, so we believe she should employ them to his honour and glory, in disseminating the blessings of education, peace, happiness and prosperity to her own fellow citizens. And if America is to be instrumental through the providence of Almighty God in blessing other portions of the peopled earth, by extending to the heathen and Pagan idolater the knowledge of the true God, a pure science, an unadulterated religion, an exalted and benevolent philanthrophy, how necessary is it that she should first purify her own dominions, by extending to all her children those divine and precious gifts; so when she shall have joined other nations in rearing the standard for the redemption of the world, every ray of light that may reach those benighted regions will, when falling on the prism of truth, present one pure, unmixed stream of Christian love, and cease to becloud the horizon of everlasting justice. We will first appeal to the Christian churches to take the lead in establishing the principles of supreme love to God, and universal love to man. We will do all in our power to aid her in forming a moral structure against which " the gates of hell cannot prevail."

We plead for the extension of those principles on which our government was formed, that it in turn may become purified from those iniquitous inconsistencies into which she has fallen by her aberration from first principles ; that the laws of our country may cease to conflict with the spirit of that sacred instrument, the Declaration of American Independence. We believe in a pure, unmixed republicanism, as a form of government best suited to the condition of man, by its promoting equality, virtue, and happiness to all within its jurisdiction. We love our country, and pray for the perpetuation of its government, that it may yet stand illustrious before the nations of the earth, both for the purity of its precepts, and the mildness and equableness of its laws.

We shall advocate the cause of peace, believing that whatever tends to the destruction of human life, is at variance with the precepts of the Gospel, and at enmity with the well being of individuals as well as of society. We shall endeavour to promote education, with sound morality, not that we shall become " learned and mighty," but "great and good." We shall advocate temperance in all things, and total abstinence from all alcoholic liquors. We shall advocate a system of *economy*, not only because luxury is injurious to individuals, but because its practice exercises an influence on society, which in its very nature is sinful. We shall advocate universal liberty, as the inalienable right of every individual born in the world, and a right which cannot be taken away by government itself, without an unjust exercise of power. We shall exhibit our sympathy for our suffering brethren, by petitioning congress to procure the immediate abolition of slavery in the District of Columbia, and her territories. We shall endeavour to strengthen public sentiment against slavery, so long as a slave treads the soil of these United States. We shall aim at the extinction of mental thraldom ; an evil much more dangerous, and exceeding the former, both in extent and power. We shall persuade our brethren from using the products of slave labour, both as a moral and Christian duty, and as a means by which the slave system may be successfully abrogated,

We shall appeal to the coloured churches to take decisive measures to rid themselves of the sin of slavery and immorality. We shall endeavour to pledge all the ministers and elders of our churches to the cause of Moral Reform. We hope to train the undisciplined youth in moral pursuits, and we shall anxiously endeavour to impress on our people everywhere, that in moral elevation true happiness consists. We feel bound to pursue the present course as a duty we owe to ourselves, our God, our common country, and the interests of suffering humanity. The free coloured population of the United States now amount to about 400,000, and are constantly increasing by a double process, and we believe that the philanthropic exertions that are now making in our country for the abolition of slavery, will shortly remove the fetters from thousands annually, and these will be continually adding to our number. We are unable to conceive of any better method by which we can aid the cause of human liberty, than by improving our general character, and embracing within our grasp the liberated slave for moral and mental culture. By pursuing this course we shall certainly remove many of the objections to immediate emancipation. And we further believe, that all who have either thought or felt deeply on this subject will not only sanction such an organization, but will feel bound to aid in promoting its objects. We shall intreat those that are constantly persecuting and calumniating our general character, to cease with their vituperations, and suffer a people already bowed to the dust, to breathe out their existence in peace and quietude. We will intreat our brethren to bear with Christian fortitude the scoffs and indignation that may be cast on them on account of their complexion, and pity the source from whence it emanates, knowing it is the offspring of wickedness and ignorance.

In the present state of society, we must expect to endure many difficulties, until the world improves in wisdom, and a polite education, and a more liberal and enlightened philosophy supplants the present system of national education. If we but fully rest ourselves on the dignity of human nature, and maintain a bold, enduring front against all opposition, the monster, prejudice, will fall humbly at our feet. Prejudice, like slavery, cannot stand the omnipotence of Truth. It is as impossible for a bold, clear and discriminating mind that can calmly and dispassionately survey the structure upon which prejudice is founded, and the materials of which it is composed, to be chained within its grasp, as it is for the puny arm of rebellious man to control the operations of the universe.

We will endeavour to establish in our people a correct knowledge of their own immortal worth, their high derivation as rational, moral and intelligent beings. We shall appeal to them to abandon their prejudice against all complexion and bury them in oblivion, and endeavour to live in the same country as children of one common father, and as, brethren possessing the same holy, religious faith, and with a zeal determined on the promotion of great and glorious objects. We shall endeavour to impress on them, at all times, to maintain in every station of life that affability of manner, meekness, humility and gentleness, that ornaments the Christian character; and finally, we will appeal to Heaven for the purity of our motives, and the rectitude of our intentions, and to men for the means of prosecuting them; to Christians, philanthropists and patriots, without regard to creed, profession, or party. In short, we shall aim to whatever seemeth good, consistent with these principles, for the promotion and welfare of our people.

Having now stated the most prominent objects that will command our attention and support, there are others, that from mere *custom* and usage, many might suppose it were our duty to vindicate. From these we must respectfully dissent, viz.: We will not stoop to contend with those who style us inferior beings. And as we know of no earthly tribunal of sufficient competency and impartiality to decide on a question, involving the natural superiority of individuals and nations, we shall not submit so grave a decision to creatures like ourselves, and especially to our enemies. In the preamble of our constitution, we claim to be American citizens, and we will not waste our time by holding converse with those who deny us this privilege, unless they first prove that a man is not a citizen of that country in which he was born and reared. Those that desire to discuss with us the propriety of remaining in this country, or of the method of our operations, must first admit us as a cardinal point, their equals by nature, possessing like themselves, from God, all those inalienable rights, that are universally admitted to be the property of his creatures. We will not admit that strength of mind lies concealed in the complexion of the body. Having now performed a duty we owed to the people of these United States, in explaining the whole course of action, of an Institution for the improvement of the morals, bearing the broad and illustrious title of American, we view in anticipation, the most happy results to our beloved country, and will most heartily rejoice, if that in an hour of danger, we shall have been fortunate enough to have aided in rescuing her from the evils into which she has fallen ; and we do most cordially hope that a moral fabric may be reared, that will promote the cause of righteousness and justice throughout the universe.

WILLIAM WHIPPER,
ALFRED NIGER,
AUGUSTUS PRICE.

The American Moral Reform Society.

In view of the most mighty consideration that ever engaged the attention of man, and resting our hopes of a triumphant success on the great Author of all good, we, the subscribers, citizens of the United States of America, in Convention assembled, believing that the successful resuscitation of our country from moral degeneracy depends upon a vigilant prosecution of the holy cause of Moral Reform, as in its promotion is involved the interest, happiness and prosperity of the great Republic, and also that the moral elevation of this nation will accellerate the extension of righteousness, justice, truth, and evangelical principles throughout the world: Therefore, in accordance with the recommendation of the fourth annual Convention, held in the city of New York, we do agree to form ourselves into a National Society, based on the principles set forth in the Declaration of Sentiment.

ART. I. This Society shall be called THE AMERICAN MORAL REFORM SOCIETY.

ART. II. Any person may become a member of this Institution who shall pledge himself to practice and sustain the general principles of Moral Reform as advocated in our country, especially those of Education, Temperance, Economy, and Universal Liberty, by contributing to its objects.

ART. III. The annual meeting of this Society shall be on the second Monday in June, in each year, in the city of Philadelphia.

Art. IV. The officers of this Society shall consist of one President, four Vice-Presidents, three Secretaries, (Foreign, Home and Recording,) a Treasurer, and a Board of Managers of seven persons.

Art. V. It shall be the duty of the Board to supervise and direct the action and operation of the Society, as well as its financial concerns.

Section 1st. All candidates for membership must apply to the Board of Directors, whose duty it shall be to admit all who subscribe to the principles contained in this Constitution.

Art. VI. Any member violating the principles set forth in this Constitution will be disqualified for membership, and shall be subject as the Board may direct.

Art. VII. The funds of this Society shall be appropriated to the diffusion of light on the subject advocated, and its Constitution may be altered from time to time, so as to keep pace with the great object of Moral Reform.

Signed on behalf of the officers of this Society.

JAMES FORTEN, Sen., President.

Vice Presidents.

Reuben Ruby, Maine.   Walter Proctor, Penn.
Samuel E. Cornish, N. York.   Jacob C. White.

Treasurer.

Joseph Cassey.

Secretaries.

Robert Purvis, Foreign Corresponding Secretary,
William Whipper, Home Corresponding Secretary,
James Forten, Jr., Recording Secretary.

Board of Managers—*John P. Burr*, Chairman, *Rev. Morris Brown, John B. Roberts, Thomas Butler, F. A. Hinton, Joshua Brown, Stephen H. Gloucester*, Secretary.

The Conventions
of the 1840's

WHEN THE NATIONAL CONVENTION MET IN 1843, IT WAS confronted with a much different set of circumstances than those of the 1830's. Lines had hardened between black and white in general and between various factions of antislavery advocates. While the conventions of the 1830's had examined the possibilities of providing a better education for the younger generation, that younger generation had been subjected at first hand to the abuses attendant upon both segregated and attempted desegregated education. Better educated than their elders, but building upon the foundation laid by them, the new generation was more self-confident, far more inclined to speak for themselves without consulting Boston or any other center from whence white friends had extended friendly, but paternalistic hands to the Negro.

The convention of 1843 made it clear that they would think and act for themselves. An attempted reestablishment of Boston influence in 1847 was far from successful. The convention of 1848, drawing heavily from self-made men of the newer areas of the country, had no intention of returning to the old ways. It was at the convention of 1843 that Henry Highland Garnet, only a few years out of college, came close to making a call for a slave uprising. He repeated the challenge in 1847 and by the end of the decade he had a sympathetic hearing from many in the black community. When challenged from Boston on his advocacy of using the ballot instead of refusing to participate in the government, Garnet gave as much as he took—and he did it publicly.

The black man during the 1840's remained interested in temperance, peace, education, moral reform, and in all the other areas of concern to the conventions of the 1830's, but he was no longer willing to turn the other cheek. Now force should be met by force. Manstealers were not to be dealt with any more gently than the highwayman. Militancy, mental and physical, was on the upswing.

Where the conventions of the 1830's had felt little inclination to challenge the establishment in any other way than by remonstrance and petition, the younger generation aligned the conventions with the liberals of the era—the Liberty party and Free Soil party. Even Frederick Douglass, still a Garrisonian at the time, was unable to head off the new trend, and it was not long before Douglass, too, had joined the political activists.

Nor were the men of these years willing to stand by merely to watch while the slave was being delivered from his chains. Better to demonstrate the blessings of self-made enterprise. Some condemned what they referred to as menial tasks, but if they went too far in this direction and made some people ashamed of what they had to do to make a living, they had the purest of motives in doing so. They wanted to see the black man in a position of respect. Some began to reexamine their stance on emigration. Could it be that a respected and industrious Negro nation beyond the bounds of the United States could help to destroy slavery and the cotton South? Most of these men were convinced that the open country had certain blessings for mankind not to be found in crowded city areas, so they advocated getting onto the farm as a means of uplift. The men of the 1840's lacked nothing in vigor and determination, nor was there any evidence of lack of the optimism so characteristic of America in the age when Manifest Destiny was so visibly with us.

MINUTES

OF THE

NATIONAL CONVENTION

OF

COLORED CITIZENS:

HELD AT BUFFALO,

On the 15th, 16th, 17th, 18th and 19th of August, 1843.

FOR THE PURPOSE OF

CONSIDERING THEIR MORAL AND POLITICAL CONDITION

AS AMERICAN CITIZENS.

NEW-YORK:

PIERCY & REED, PRINTERS, 9 SPRUCE-STREET.

1843.

"Ours is not the tented field—
  We no earthly weapons wield—
  Light and love our sword and shield—
    Truth our panoply."

*   *   *   *   *   *

"Onward, then, ye fearless band—
  Heart to heart and hand to hand—
  Ours shall be the Christian's stand,
    Or the martyr's grave."

PRELIMINARY MEETING.

At a meeting of colored citizens held in the city of New York, May 9th and 10th, 1843, to consider the subject of holding a National Convention, the Rev. Theo. S. Wright was appointed chairman, and A. J. Gorden, secretary. The following States were represented in said meeting, viz: Massachusetts, Connecticut, New York, New Jersey, Pennsylvania, and Ohio. The following resolutions were, after mature deliberation, adopted :

Resolved, That we deem it necessary that a National Convention of the colored citizens of the United States of America be held this year.

Resolved, That this meeting recommend that a National Convention of the colored citizens of this country be held in the city of Buffalo, on the 3d Tuesday in August, 1843.

Resolved, That a committee of three be appointed to prepare a Call, and that we, the members of this meeting, sign it and solemnly pledge ourselves in the name of God, and bleeding humanity and posterity, to Organize, ORGANIZE, ORGANIZE, until Liberty and Equality shall embrace each other, and shall scatter their blessings throughout the whole land.

The committee reported the following call, which was adopted :

THE CALL.

Fellow Citizens : At a meeting held in the city of New York on the 9th and 10th of May, 1843, composed of colored citizens from several States of this Union, for the purpose of considering the propriety of holding a National Convention of the oppressed citizens of the United States—after mature deliberation, it was decided that, by the permission of Divine Providence, a *National Convention of the Colored Citizens of the United States* be held in the city of Buffalo, to commence its sessions on the 3d Tuesday in August, 1843, at ten o'clock, A. M.

Dear Brethren : In presenting this call and soliciting your co-operation, we will mention a few of the reasons that have conspired to urge us to make this exceedingly important movement.

The oppressed in all ages of the world have emerged from their condition of degradation and servitude in proportion as they have exerted themselves in their *own cause*, and have convinced the world and their oppressors that they were determined to be free.

The history of the present and the past establish the great truth that it is as much impossible for any people to secure the enjoyment of their inalienable rights without organization, as it is to reach an end without means. Acting in accordance with this truth, the oppressed people of England, Ireland and Scotland, have banded themselves together in their respective nations to wage unceasing war against the green-eyed monster, tyranny.

Since we have ceased to meet together in National Convention, we have become ignorant of the moral and intellectual strength of our people. We have also been deprived of the councils of our fathers, who have borne the burden and heat of the day—the spirit of virtuous ambition and emulation has died in the bosoms of the young men, and in a great degree we have become divided, and the bright rising stars that once shone in our skies, have become partially obscured.

Then, brethren, shall we not meet once more ! Yes, let us assemble. We will assemble, God being willing. Come and rally under the banner of freedom—come from the east, north, south, and west. Come in the strength of the Lord, and prepared to take a *bold stand* for truth and suffering humanity, which shall prove to be unprecedented in the history of our people. We hope that every city, town, hamlet, and village will be represented as well as Literary and Benevolent Societies. (Signed.)

The above call was signed by about fifty persons, representing seven different States of the Union.

PROCEEDINGS.

In accordance with the preceding call, issued to the colored people of the several States, through the United States Clarion, a paper published at Troy, N. Y., inviting them to assemble in convention at Buffalo, on the third Tuesday in August, being the 15th of the month. At an early hour on said morning, about forty persons assembled, at a large public hall on the corner of Washington and Seneca streets in said city; and the hour for opening the Convention, agreeably to the call, having arrived, Henry Highland Garnit, Chairman of the Committee of Correspondence, called the meeting to order by reading the call of the Convention, and subsequently moving the appointment of Mr. Samuel H. Davis, of Buffalo, as Chairman, *pro tem.* The Rev. James Fountain, of Utica, N. Y., was called upon to address the throne of grace, who offered fervent prayer to God. Mr. Davis then arose and delivered to the friends assembled an excellent Address, from which the following extracts are copied :*

ADDRESS.

GENTLEMEN :

I consider this a most happy period in our history,—when we, as a people, are in some degree awake to a sense of our condition ; and are determined no longer to submit tamely and silently to wear the galling yoke of oppression, under which we have so long suffered ; oppression riveted upon us, as well by an unholy and cruel prejudice, as by unjust and unequal legislation. More particularly do I consider it ominous of good, when I see here collected, so much of wisdom and talent, from different parts of this great nation, collected here to deliberate upon the wisest and best methods by which we may seek a redress of those grievances which must sorely oppress us as a people.

Gentlemen, in behalf of my fellow-citizens of Buffalo, I bid you welcome, from the East and West, the North and South, to our city. Among you are the men who are lately from that part of our country, where they see our brethren, bound and manacled, suffering and bleeding, under the hand of the tyrant, who holds in one hand the Constitution of the United States, which guarantees freedom and equal rights to every citizen, and in the other "the scourge dripping with human gore," drawn from the veins of his fellow-man. Here also are those who live in my native New England, among the "descendants of the pilgrims," whose laws are more in accordance with the principles of freedom and equal rights ; so that but few laws are found recorded on their statute books, of which we need complain. But though their laws are not marked with such palpable and flagrant injustice towards the colored man, as those of the South ; yet there we are proscribed, by a fixed and cruel prejudice, little less oppressive. Our grievances are many and great ; but it is not my intention to enumerate or to enlarge upon them. I will simply say, however, that we wish to secure for ourselves, in common with other citizens, the privilege of seeking our own happiness in any part of the country we may choose, which right is now unjustly, and, we believe, unconstitutionally denied us in a part of this Union. We wish also to secure the elective franchise in those

* The Address, though excellent, is, in the judgment of the publishing committee, of too great length to be admitted entire.

States where it is denied us,—where our rights are legislated away, and our voice neither heard nor regarded. We also wish to secure, for our children *especially*, the benefits of education, which in several States are entirely denied us, and in others are enjoyed only in name These, and many other things, of which we justly complain, bear most heavily upon us as a people; and it is our right and our duty to seek for redress, in that way which will be most likely to secure the desired end.

In your wisdom, you will, I doubt not, take into consideration these and the many other grievances which we suffer, and form such organizations, and recommend such measures, as shall, in your wisdom, seem most likely to secure our enfranchisement—the benefits of education to our children, and all our rights in common with other citizens of this republic.

Two objects should distinctly and constantly be borne in mind, in all our deliberations. One is the diffusion of truth, and the other the elevation of our own people. By the diffusion of truth, I mean that we must take a bold and elevated stand for the truth. We must determine, in the strength of God, to do every thing that will advance the great and holy cause of freedom, and nothing that will in the least retard its progress. We must, by every means in our power, strive to persuade the white people to act with more confidence in their own principles of liberty—to make laws, just and equal for all the people.

But while the color of the skin is made the criterion of the law, it is our right, our duty, and, I hope I may say, our fixed determination, to make known our wrongs to the world, and to our oppressors ; to cease not day nor night to

"Tell, in burning words, our tale of woe,"

and pour a flood of living light on the minds and consciences of the oppressor ; till we change their thoughts, feelings, and actions towards us as men and citizens of this land. We must convince our fellow-men that slavery is unprofitable ; that it is for the well-being and prosperity of this nation ; the peace and happiness of our common country, that slavery and oppression be abolished within its borders ; and that laws be enacted equal and just for all its citizens.

Proscription is not in accordance with equal rights, no more than is oppression with holy freedom, or slavery with the spirit of free institutions. The present system of laws, in this our country, enacted in reference to us, the oppressed and down-trodden descendants of Africa, do, and will continue to operate like the cankerworm in the root of the tree of liberty, preventing its growth, and ultimately destroying its vitality. We may well say, in the language of a distinguished statesman and patriot of our own land, " We tremble for our country when we reflect that God is just, and that his justice will not always sleep." By the example of other nations, who have gone before, whose history should be a warning to this people, we learn that slavery and oppression has nowhere prospered long ;— it blasts a nation's glory and prosperity—divides her power—weakens her strength, and grows like a corroding consumption in her very vitals. · " God's judgments will not sleep forever, but he will visit the nations of the earth in justice." We love our common country—

"With all her faults, we love her still."

This is the land where we all drew our first breath ; where we have grown up to strength and manhood ; " here is deposited the ashes of our fathers ;" here we have contracted the most sacred engagements, the dearest relations of life ; here we have found the companions of our childhood, the friends of our youth, the gentle partners of our lives ; here are the haunts of our infancy, the scenes of every endearing hour :—in a word, this is our own native land I repeat it, then, we love our country, we love our fellow-citizens,—but *we love liberty more*

We, as a people, are called upon to raise our voice in our own behalf, and plead our own rights, because so few are found to plead for us. The oppressed of every other land, no matter how distant their location, no matter what their complexion, when the fact is known that any people are oppressed, and are seeking their freedom, the friends of liberty are ready to espouse their cause, with all the talent and eloquence which this great nation possesses. Men of every rank can plead the cause of freedom. Even the slaveholders, who hold their iron grasp, like the grasp of death, on the necks of their fellow-men ; yes, who rule this nation too, with more than a tyrant's sway, can talk very earnestly in freedom's cause, and plead with their potent eloquence for the rights of men. What was it, a few years since, that caused so much excitement in this nation, and among the friends of liberty through-out the world, in behalf of the patriotic Greeks ! Was it not the fact, that they were oppressed and were seeking their freedom ! Money, as well as arms and am-munition, were sent out from our own land. And not only these, many of freedom's noblest sons eagerly volunteered their own services, risking their lives and for-tunes to the dangerous chances of war with the infidel, tyrant Turks, to secure the liberty and independence of the unconquerable Greeks.

D. voted Poland also, in her severe but vain struggle to throw off the Russian yoke, shared in the warmest sympathies and ardent prayers of freedom's votaries. They were expressed in our halls of legislation and literature, and in the temples of God, with all the force and charms with which high-wrought eloquence and soul-stirring poetry could invest them.

These things ought to encourage us When we show to this nation and the world that we are properly awake to our own interests, and by wise, persevering, and determined measures, are seeking our rights, we too shall have the sympathy and assistance of the lovers of freedom, wherever freedom's friends are found.

How is it in regard to Irish liberty ! Behold how the leaders of each political party seem to vie with each other, which shall be foremost in the cause of Irish repeal, and who can plead most for the liberty of that unhappy people.

These things should encourage us to seek our own liberty and the liberty of our brethren in bonds, by every means in our power ; to make known the multitude and insufferable wrongs, imposed on us by arbitrary and oppressive laws, bearing us down to the earth, here in our own native land ; enacted, too, by the very people who bid eternal defiance to tyranny, and declare, in the most broad and unrestricted terms, for universal freedom and equal rights, and claim to themselves alone the honor of waving, untarnished, the banner of liberty among the nations of the earth.

It is time that we were more awake to our own interests, more united in our efforts, and more efficient in our measures. We must profit by the example of our oppressors. We must act on their principles in resisting tyranny. We must adopt their resolutions in favor of liberty. "They have taught us a lesson, in their strug-gle for independence, that should never be forgotten. They have taught the world emphatically, that a people, united in the cause of liberty, are invincible to those who would enslave them ; and that heaven will ever frown on the cause of injus-tice, and ultimately grant success to those who oppose it." Shall we, then, longer submit in silence to our accumulated wrongs! Forbid it, heaven ! that we should longer stand in silence, "hugging the delusive phantom of hope," when every gale that sweeps from the South, bears on its wings, to our ears, the dismal sound of slavery's clanking chains, now rivetted on three millions of our brethren, and we ourselves are aliens and outcasts in our native land.

Is the question asked, what we shall do ! Shall we petition for our rights! I do not pretend to dictate the course that should be pursued ; but I have very little hope in petitioning longer. We have petitioned again and again, and what has been the result! Our humblest prayers have not been permitted a hearing. We could not even state our grievances. Our petitions were disregarded ; our supplications slighted, and we spurned from the mercy-seat, insulted, abused, and slandered ; and this day finds us in the same unhappy and hopeless condition in which we have been for our whole lives—no other hope is left us, but in our own exertions, and an "appeal to the God of armies !" From what other source can we expect that help will come ! Shall we appeal to the Christian community—to the church of our own land! What is her position! Behold her gigantic form, with hands upraised to heaven! See her increased and made rich by the toil, and sweat, and blood of slaves! View her arrayed in her pontifical robes, screening the horrid monster, slavery, with her very bosom—within her most sacred enclosures ; that the world may not gaze on its distorted visage, or view its hellish form! Yes, throwing around this accursed system, the very drapery of heaven, to cover this damning sin and give it character and respectability in the eyes of the country, and in the eyes of the world. We cannot, therefore, look to her for help, for she has taken sides against us, and on the side of slavery. Shall we turn to either of the great political parties of the day! What are our prospects there! Is there any hope of help! No, they are but the slaves of slavery, too, contending which shall be most faithful in supporting the foul system of slavery, that they may secure the vote of the slave-holder himself, and of his scores of human cattle. Shall we then look to the aboli-tionists, and wait for them to give us our rights? I would not say a word that would have a tendency to discourage them in their noble efforts in behalf of the poor slave, or their exertions to advance the cause of truth and humanity. Some of them have made great sacrifices, and have labored with a zeal and fidelity that justly entitle them to our confidence and gratitude. But if we sit down in idleness and sloth, waiting for them, or any other class of men to do our own work, I fear it will never be done. If we are not willing to rise up and assert our rightful claims, and plead our own cause, we have no reason to look for success. We, ourselves, must be willing to contend for the rich boon of freedom and equal rights, or we shall never enjoy that boon. It is found only of them that seek.

In regard to the elevation of our own people   On this subject I cannot now en-large, nor need I, for we all know, and see, and feel its need. We know that any people wanting in intelligence and moral worth, cannot long be free. In the lan-guage of one of our most distinguished orators, " For ourselves and in ourselves there is a mighty work to be accomplished,—an influence to be exerted, which can come from no other source. We must learn to act in harmony with the principles of God's moral government, or permanent prosperity can never be ours."

Mr. Davis having concluded his address, it was,

On motion, Resolved, that Messrs. Henry Thomas and A. H. Fran-cis, of Buffalo, be appointed Secretaries pro. tem.

It was then moved that the delegates present their credentials.— About forty persons answered to the motion.

It was then moved that a committee of seven, to nominate officers for the Convention, be appointed by the chair. The chair appointed the following persons, viz: J. H. Townsend, of Albany, N. Y.; R. Allen, of Detroit, Mich.; Geo. Ware, of Buffalo, N. Y.; J. W. Duffin, of Geneva, N. Y.; Robert Banks, of Detroit, Mich.; F. Douglass, of Boston, Mass.; and D. Lewis, of Toledo, Ohio.

On motion, the chair appointed the following persons a committee to make a roll of the delegates, viz.: Robert Banks, of Detroit, Mich.; N. W. Jones, of Chicago, Ill.; and W. W. Brown, of Buffalo, N. Y.

Moved by Chas. B. Ray, that all gentlemen present, from places from which there is no regular deputed delegation, be considered as delegates from those places, and that all other gentlemen be considered as corres-ponding members.

This motion was opposed by Messrs. H. H. Garnit, D. Lewis, A. H. Francis, R. Francis, and others ; and advocated by Messrs. Charles B. Ray, Frederic Douglass, C. L. Remond, and A. G. Beman. The gentlemen in the opposition took the ground, that thus to open the door to the con-vention, would give a decided advantage to places near by over places more remote, the tendency of which might be to give a local rather than a general character to the business ; and some feared also that it might bring into the convention persons of discordant or local views, the ten-dency of which would also be to protract discussion, and unnecessarily consume the time of the Convention, and that it were best now to adopt a preventive. The gentlemen in the affirmative of the question consid-ered the reasons advanced by the opposition as not valid, and their fears as groundless—that as nearly all the persons who would be enrolled in the Convention by that vote would be honorary members, and while it would give them a right to discuss questions, it would give them no right to vote upon them, and that while they had a right to discuss questions, yet as they were but honorary members their better judgment would teach them that the time of the Convention belonged to the delegates proper. The gentlemen in the affirmative further contended, that there were many persons present who had not been favored with having been sent as delegates; but their interest in the Convention had brought them here, and that they thought with us, and felt with us, and doubtless had many thoughts in their mind, which, if made known, might be of service to the Convention, and which they would like to express; and as the Convention was as vital to them as to us, it being a common cause, they ought to have the right to express their views—besides, we had come here to assert principles embracing the largest liberty to all, and to take broad ground in favor of the free expression of opinion; and to reject the motion now before us, would be subversive of the very spirit which has brought us together. Upon taking the question, the motion was lost. The Convention now adjourned to meet at 2 o'clock, P. M.

Afternoon Session.—The Convention met according to adjournment. The Chairman pro tem. not being present, Robert Banks, of Detroit, Mich., was appointed Chairman. Prayer by Rev. Theo. S. Wright.

The committee on nominations reported the following list of officers for the Convention :—For

PRESIDENT,
AMOS G. BEMAN, of New Haven, Conn.

VICE PRESIDENTS,

F. Piere, of Maine,	A. M. Summer, of Ohio,
F. Douglass, of Mass.	H. Johnson, of Michigan,
W. W. Matthews, of Conn.	and
Jas. Sharp. of New-York,	N. W. Jones, of Illinois.

SECRETARIES,
Chas. B. Ray, of New-York, | Jas. W. Duffin, of Geneva, N.Y.
A. H. Francis, of Buffalo, N. Y.

The motion respecting the admission of honorary members and persons as delegates who had not been delegated to this body, was on motion of H. H. Garnit. who voted with the majority, reconsidered. Upon the question being taken it was again lost. Whereupon Chas. B. Ray arose and submitted the following resolution:

Resolved, That all gentlemen present, who have come from places from which there is no regularly appointed delegation to the Convention, be considered as delegates from those places, and that all other gentlemen be requested to take seats as honorary members.

The mover urged the adoption of this resolution from a few serious and weighty considerations, and regarded it as vital to the harmony and success of the Convention. The President vacated the chair to one of the Vice Presidents, and urged in a short but masterly speech the adoption of the resolution. The question was now called for, and the resolution adopted by a large majority.

It was moved that a committee of nine persons to bring forward business for the Convention be appointed by the chair. The chair appointed the following persons, viz.: H. H. Garnit; Chairman; Robert Banks, David Lewis, Theo. S. Wright, C. Lennox Remond, M. C. Munro, J. H. Townsend, N. W. Jones, and Geo. Weir.

It was moved that a committee of three persons, to draft rules to govern the Convention, be appointed by the chair. The chair appointed the following persons, viz.: A. H. Francis, W. W. Brown, and J. P. Morris.

The Committee reported the following list of Rules, which were taken up separately and adopted :

RULES.

1st. Resolved, That each session of this Convention be opened by addressing the Throne of Grace.

2d. Upon the appearance of a quorum, the President shall take the chair and call the Convention to order.

3d. The minutes of the preceding session shall be read at the opening of each session, at which time mistakes, if there be any, shall be corrected.

4th. The President shall decide all questions of order, subject to an appeal of the Convention.

5th. All motions and addresses shall be made to the President, the member rising from his seat.

6th. All motions, except those of reference, shall be submitted in writing.

7th. All committees shall be appointed by the Chair, unless otherwise ordered by the Convention.

8th. The previous question shall be always in order, and, until decided, shall preclude all amendment and debate of the main question, and shall be put in this form : Shall the main question be now put ?

9th. No member shall be interrupted while speaking, except when out of order, when he shall be called to order by, or through the Chair.

10th. A motion to adjourn shall be always in order, and shall be decided without debate.

11th. No member shall speak more than twice on the same question, without the consent of the Convention, nor more than fifteen minutes at each time.

12th. No motion shall be reconsidered during the same session at which it was passed.

13th. No resolution, except of reference, shall be offered to the Convention, except it come through the business committee ; but all resolutions rejected by the committee may be presented directly to the Convention, if the maker of the resolution wishes to do so.

14th. The sessions of the Convention shall commence at 9 o'clock A. M., and at 2 o'clock P. M., and shall close at 12 o'clock at noon, and at 6 o'clock P. M.

15th. The roll shall be called at each session immediately after prayer.

The business committee reported, in part, a series of resolutions, numbered 1, 2, 3, 4, which were accepted and laid on the table, to be called up in due order for further action.*

A committee was appointed to select speakers and make preparations for the evening meeting.

The Convention now adjourned to meet at the Park Presbyterian Church, at 8 o'clock P. M., which had been kindly tendered to the Convention for evening public meetings, and to meet in regular session, as per rule No. 14.

The meeting in the Park Church was largely attended by the citizens generally, without regard to class or rank, and was addressed by H. H. Garnit, C. B. Ray, F. Douglass, and C. L. Remond.

---

* Each series of resolutions, as they were reported from the business committee appear in the minutes, just where the last of the series was adopted.—page 15.

Wednesday, August 16th, 1843.

Morning Session.—The Convention met pursuant to adjournment, The President in the chair. Prayer by the Rev. James N. Gloucester, of New York. The Convention then united in singing a liberty song. The minutes of the previous meeting were read, and after some slight corrections, approved.

The committee on business reported a series of resolutions numbered 5, 6, 7, 8, 9, 10. The report was accepted and laid upon the table, to be called up in course.

The Committee on the roll submitted the following list of delegates, which was, on motion, accepted:

ROLL OF DELEGATES.

MAINE.
F. Pierc.

MASSACHUSETTS.
C. L. Remond, *Salem.*
Fred. Douglass, *Boston,*

CONNECTICUT.
A. G. Beman, *N. Haven.*
W. W. Matthews, *do.*

NEW YORK.
Theo. S. Wright, *N. Y. City,*
Charles B. Ray, *do.*
James N. Gloucester, *do.*
J. H. Townsend, *Albany.*
Wm. P. McIntire, *do,*
H. H. Garnit, *Troy,*
John Wendall, *Schenectady,*
T. Woodson, *Utica.*
B. S. Anderson, *do.*
James Fountain, *do.*
James W. Duffin, *Geneva.*
Jason Jeffrey, *do.*
Noah Palk, *do.*
H. W. Johnson, *Canandaigua,*
James Sharpe, *Rochester.*
Ralph Francis, *do.*
J. P. Morris, *do.*
R. H. Johnson, *do.*
Wm. Sanders, *do.*
David Wycoff, *do.*
Harrison Powell, *do.*
James P. Jackson, *do.*
John Granbia, *Phelps.*
Wm. Johnson, *Batavia.*
A. Peek, *Brockport.*

Albert Outley, *Lockport.*
Sampson Talbot, *do.*
E. B. Dunlap, *Niagara Falls,*
J. F. Platt, *Penn Yan.*
Uriah Lett, *do.*
George Weir, *Buffalo.*
Wm. Hall, *do.*
W. W. Brown, *do.*
Abner H. Francis, *do.*
S. H. Davis, *do.*
Jermin W. Loguen, *Bath,*

OHIO.
J. H. Malvin, *Cleveland.*
R. Robinson, *do.*
David Lewis, *Toledo.*
David Jenkins, *Columbus.*
J. M. Cordozer, *do.*
A. M. Sumner, *Cincinnati.*
W. H. Yancy, *do.*
Wm. Watson, *do.*

MICHIGAN.
R. Banks, *Detroit.*
W. C. Munro, *do.*
Robert Allen, *do.*
Henry Jackson, *do.*
G. W. Tucker, *do.*

ILLINOIS.
Nimrod W. Jones, *Chicago.*

VIRGINIA.
Luke Dod.

NORTH CAROLINA.
Thomas Pollock, *Raleigh.*

GEORGIA.
Joseph Roxbury, *Augusta.*

Resolution No. 1, previously reported by the committee, was called up and read. Frederic Douglass proposed to amend it by inserting the word " Christian" before the term church. The amendment, after some discussion, in which several gentlemen participated, was withdrawn. The motion then recurred upon the original resolution, upon which a spirited and somewhat lengthy discussion ensued, in which the following gentlemen participated: In the affirmative, H. H. Garnit, R. H. Johnson, F. Douglass, W. C. Munro, C. L. Remond, C. B. Ray, and J. H. Townsend; in the negative, Theo. S. Wright, E. B. Dunlap, P. Harris, and J. Sharpe.

The brethren in the affirmative all agreed in the existence of the church, but a difference of opinion existed as to what constituted the true church. They all agreed that the existing church in this country was corrupt—was wedded strongly to slavery, and was a pro-slavery church; that the passage of anti-slavery resolutions, as indicated on the face of them, was no evidence of their not being pro-slavery, while they keep what is called the negro-pew, and made a distinction at the communion-table on the ground of color; this with them was slavery in another form, its very spirit. And with respect to the leading ecclesiastical bodies, the gentlemen in the affirmative contended, that in their judgment, there was no hope of reforming them, they were so wedded to public opinion, so popularity-seeking, that they were past reforming, and that no true friend of liberty, especially no man of color, could, to be consistent, longer remain in church fellowship with them, and that they ought forthwith to withdraw from them. The brethren on the other side of the question took the old ground, that if they withdrew church fellowship, they would by that act, cut off all the influence they had, with which to reform them. Some of them did little more than to define their position as members of churches in affiliation with the great ecclesiastical bodies; they referred to acts of these bodies, to show an improvement in anti-slavery action, and which to them was great ground of hope; they thought, should they withdraw from them, they would have withdrawn from a body which soon would be as much anti-slavery as could be desired, and they felt called upon to remain and help bring about that end. This was the ground taken, especially by Mr. Wright, of New York.

While this discussion was pending, the business committee came in and asked leave to present the following report, and upon which they asked immediate action:

Resolved, That a weekly newspaper be established in some large city, which shall be the organ of the colored people and their friends, and that each member of this Convention pledge himself to procure subscribers for it, and that an executive committee be appointed by this Convention, under whose management the paper shall be published.

Resolved, That a financial committee of three be appointed, to attend to the financial affairs of the Convention.

Resolved, That a committee be appointed to collect statistical information from the delegates present, and to make out a report upon the condition of our people.

On motion, the report was accepted.

On motion, so much of the report as referred to the establishment of a weekly newspaper was referred to the following committee for them to consider the subject and report thereon, viz., Charles B. Ray, of New York; R. Banks, of Detroit; Wm. P. McIntire, of Albany; N. W.

Jones, of Chicago; H. H. Garnit, of Troy; T. Woodson, of Utica; S. H. Davis, of Buffalo.

The chairman appointed the following a committee on finance, viz., W. W. Brown, J. H. Platt, and J. Jeffrey.

The chair also announced the following persons a committee on the condition of the colored people, viz., J. N. Gloucester, of New York, chairman; Theo. S. Wright, of do; W. C. Munro, of Detroit; A. H. Francis, of Buffalo; W. H. Yancy, of Cincinnati; and S. Talbot, of Lockport.

The hour for adjournment having arrived, the Convention adjourned to meet at the hour appointed.

———

Afternoon Session.—The Convention met as per adjournment. The President in the chair. Prayer by the Rev. Mr. Davis, of Canada. The Convention united in singing a liberty song.

The roll was then called and the minutes of the previous meeting were read and approved.

The chairman of the committee on finance reported the following resolution:

Resolved, That a collection be taken up during each session, also at the evening meetings, for the purpose of defraying the expenses of the Convention; the deficiency, whatever it may be, to be made up by the members.

The resolution was adopted.

The resolution pending at the hour of adjournment was called up, and a motion made for its reference to a select committee. The motion was lost. Charles Lennox Remond then obtained the floor, and proceeded to discuss the original resolution, taking the same view of the question as above stated. The previous question was then called for and sustained, when the question was put and the vote ordered to be taken by the yeas and nays. The resolution was adopted by the following vote: *Yeas*—C. L. Remond, F. Douglass, C. B. Ray, J. H. Townsend, W. P. McIntire, H. H. Garnit, T. Woodson, B. S. Anderson, J. Fountain, J. W. Duffin, J. Jeffrey, R. H. Johnson, W. Sanders, W. Johnson, A. Peck, A. Outley, S. Talbot, E. B. Dunlap, J. F. Platt, U. Lett, W. Hall, W. W. Brown, S. H. Davis, J. W. Loguen, D. Lewis, W. C. Munro, R. Banks, R. Allen, H. Jackson—23. *Nays*—J. N. Gloucester, J. Wandall, J. Sharpe, J. P. Morris, E. B. Dunlap, G. Weir, G. W. Tucker, N. W. Jones, J. Malvin, D. Jenkins—10.

The following persons were excused from voting, some on the ground that not having heard but partially the discussions, they were not prepared to decide; others on the ground that the discussions had produced conviction in their minds for and against the question, and they wished to be excused from voting, viz., T. S. Wright, N. Polk, H. W. Johnson, H. Powell, J. P. Jackson, J. Granbia, R. Francis, A. H. Francis, R. Robertson, A. M. Sumner, W. Watson, and W. H. Yancy—13.

The business committee reported, by their chairman, H. H. Garnit, an address to the slaves of this land, prepared for the occasion, which was read and accepted.

C. B. Ray moved its reference to a select committee of five, of which he hoped Mr. Garnit, whose production the address was, would be the chairman. Mr. Ray remarked, that his object in moving its reference to a committee was, that it might pass through a close and critical examination, and perceiving some points in it that might in print appear objectionable, to have it somewhat modified, and also that it might proceed forth from a special committee, of which the author should be the chairman, and thus receive the usual credit due to, chairmen of committees presenting documents to public bodies.

H. H. Garnit arose to oppose the motion of reference, and anticipating more than was contemplated by the mover, and fearing the fate of the address, if the motion prevailed, proceeded to give his reasons why the motion should not prevail, and why the address should be adopted by the Convention, and sent out with its sanction ; in doing which Mr. Garnit went into the whole merits of the case. He reviewed the abominable system of slavery, showed its mighty workings, its deeds of darkness and of death—how it robbed parents of children, and children of parents, husbands of wives ; how it prostituted the daughters of the slaves ; how it murdered the colored man. He referred to the fate of Denmark Vesey and his accomplices—of Nat Turner ; to the burning of McIntosh, to the case of Madison Washington, as well as to many other cases—to what had been done to move the slaveholders to let go their grasp, and asked what more could be done—if we have not waited long enough—if it were not time to speak louder and longer—to take higher ground and other steps. Mr Garnit, in this speech, occupied nearly one hour and a half, the rule having been suspended to allow him to proceed. It was a masterly effort, and the whole Convention, full as it was, was literally infused with tears. Mr. Garnit concluded amidst great applause.

Frederic Douglass, not concurring with certain points in the address, nor with the sentiments advanced by Mr. Garnit, arose to advocate its reference to the committee, and also to reply to Mr. Garnit. Mr. Douglass remarked, that there was too much physical force, both in the address and the remarks of the speaker last up. He was for trying the moral means a little longer ; that the address, could it reach the slaves, and the advice, either of the address or the gentleman, be followed, while it might not lead the slaves to rise in insurrection for liberty, would, nevertheless, and necessarily be the occasion of an insurrection ; and that was what he wished in no way to have any agency in bringing about, and what we were called upon to avoid ; and therefore, he hoped the motion to refer would prevail.

Mr. Garnit arose to reply, and said that the most the address said in sentiment, with what the gentleman excepted to, was, that it advised the slaves to go to their masters and tell them they wanted their liberty, and had come to ask for it; and if the master refused it, to tell them, then we shall take it, let the consequence be what it may.

Mr. Douglass said, that would lead to an insurrection, and we were called upon to avoid such a catastrophy. He wanted emancipation in a better way, as he expected to have it.

The question of reference was further discussed by James N. Gloucester, taking the same view of the case with Mr. Douglass ; and by Wm. C. Munro, who opposed its reference, concurring fully in the views expressed by Mr. Garnit.

The hour for adjournment, as fixed upon by the rules, having come, the Convention adjourned to meet at 9 o'clock Thursday morning.

Thursday August, 27th, 1843.

Morning Session.—The Convention met pursuant to adjournment—the President in the chair—prayer by the Rev. James Sharpe of Rochester, N. Y. The members then united in singing a liberty song—the roll of the Convention was called—the minutes of the previous meeting were read and approved.

The address to the slaves and its reference, being the subject of discussion at the hour of adjournment, the discussion was resumed, and Mr. Sharpe of Rochester, having obtained the floor, proceeded to speak in opposition to the address—the discussion under the motion having taken this wide range, Mr. Sharpe having occupied the time prescribed by the rules, asked for a suspension of them to allow him to proceed—the rules were not suspended. E. B. Dunlap of Niagara, rose to reply to Mr. Sharpe, but from the ground he took in the debate was pronounced out of order. C. B. Ray having obtained the floor, pressed his motion of reference, giving his reasons for so doing. The question was called for and put, and the motion prevailed by a large majority. The chair announced the following as the committee on the address. H. H. Garnit, chairman, F. Douglass, A. M. Sumner, S. N. Davis, and R. Banks.

The Resolution No. 2, upon the church, was then called up, and after its second reading was adopted without debate.

Resolution No. 3, upon church relations, was then called up. F. Douglass moved an amendment—the amendment was lost. C. B. Ray moved to insert the words—"and all other existing evils," after the words—"sin of slavery"—the amendment prevailed—the resolution was then adopted.

Resolution No. 4 was called up and warmly discussed in the affirmative of the question by Theo. S. Wright, F. Douglass, Wm. Watson, R. H. Johnson, C. L. Remond, and C. B. Ray; in opposition to it Geo. Weir. The friends in favor of the resolution took the ground that, a church that discriminated between its members on account of color, or graduated privileges upon such a principle, merely, took positive anti-christian ground, and was not a true church of Christ, and that persons so proscribed and treated, ought not longer to remain in such a church or fellowship such a body of men as christians, and as christians themselves they could not consistently do so, and ought to come out from among them. Mr. Weir in opposing the resolution, supposed cases in which only such churches existed, and enquired to know where persons coming out from such churches would go. The brethren on the other side of the question replied, that where they were solitary and alone, let each set up divine worship in his own house ; this were decidedly preferable to remaining in fellowship with such churches, with no hope of changing their character. Frederic Douglass moved an amendment that all after the words "equality," be stricken out ; the amendment prevailed. The previous question was called for, and upon being put was lost—the motion then returned upon the resolution as amended—it was adopted.

1. *Resolved*, That we believe in the true Church of Christ, and that it will stand while time endures, and that it will evince its spirit by its opposition to all sins, and especially to the sin of slavery, which is a compound of all others, and that the great mass of American sects, falsely called churches, which apologize for slavery and prejudice, or practice slaveholding, are in truth no churches, but Synagogues of Satan.

2. *Resolved*, That we solemnly believe that slaveholding and prejudice sustaining ministers and churches (falsely so called), are the greatest enemies to Christ and to civil and religious liberty in the world.

3. *Resolved*, That the colored people in the free States who belong to pro-slavery sects that will not pray for the oppressed—nor preach the truth in regard to the sin of slavery and all other existing evils, nor publish anti-slavery meetings, nor act for the entire immediate abolition of slavery, are guilty of enslaving themselves and others, and their blood, and the blood of perishing millions will be upon their heads.

4. *Resolved*, That it is the bounden duty of every person to come out from among those religious organizations in which they are not permitted to enjoy equality.

The Convention then adjourned to meet at the hour fixed upon by the rules.

Afternoon Session.—The Convention met according to adjournment—the President in the chair—prayer by the Rev. J. H. Townsend of Albany. The members united in singing a liberty song—the roll was then called and the minutes of the previous meeting were read and approved. Mr. T. T. Tatum of Buffalo, now rose and announced that a gentleman of Pittsburgh, Pa., had forwarded to the friends of the slave nine fugitive slaves, and that one of the number was now in the house—(great cheering). The person was called to show himself, also to give his name, and where from; this being done, H. H. Garnit arose and moved that Mr. Dod be a delegate to this Convention from Virginia—the motion was carried with cheers. C. B. Ray arose and moved that Thomas Pollock from Raleigh, N. C., being present under similar circumstances, be considered a member from North Carolina; the motion was unanimously carried.

The next business in order was a series of resolutions from the business committee previously reported, numbering 5, 6, 7, 8 and 9.

Resolution No. 5 was called up and read, and upon motion to adopt, Frederic Douglass arose and spoke in opposition to the resolution. W. W. Brown, C. L. Remond, R. Francis and P. Harris, also opposed its adoption. The resolution was advocated by H. H. Garnit, Wm. C. Munro, J. N. Gloucester, Theo. S. Wright, David Lewis and C. B. Ray. The brethren on the opposition contended, that this was decidedly a Liberty party resolution, that they did not come here to adopt the Liberty party —that they were opposed to that party—some of them said they were opposed to all parties, believed them verily and necessarily corrupt, and our friends from Mass., said they would not except the Liberty party. Some of the brethren on the other side of the question, said that, as this resolution did not mention party, it could not be said that we were adopting any party; others of them contended that this did adopt the Liberty party, for that reason they went for it, if it did not they would go against the resolution and so amend it, as to make it take still stronger ground, and they considered that the question of the Liberty party was now fairly before the Convention, and they felt bound to go for it. The question was fully and fairly discussed warmly on both sides, and the resolution was adopted with but 7 dissenting voices.

Resolution No. 6 was called up, read and adopted without debate.

Resolution No. 7 upon Agriculture, was read, and on motion referred to a committee of five to consider which and report as early as possible. The chair announced the following gentlemen on said committee. Charles B. Ray, of New York, chairman, A. M. Sumner, and W. H. Yancy of Cincinnati, O., D. Jenkins, of Columbus, O., and Sampson Talbot, of Lockport, N. Y.

Resolution No. 8, upon the mechanic arts was read, and on motion referred to a committee of three to consider which, and report at the earliest possible period. The chair announced the following gentlemen on said committee. Robert Banks, of Detroit, Mich., Geo. Weir, of Buffalo, and James Fountain, Utica, N. Y.

Resolution No. 9 on Temperance, was called up, and after a few remarks from several gentlemen, setting forth the glorious influence, and happy effects of the Temperance movements upon the community, and urging upon the Convention the importance of practically holding up those principles in our several communities, the resolution was adopted.

Resolution No. 10, offered to the Convention under rule 13, by Wm. C. Munro, was on motion laid upon the table, to be made the order of the day immediately after the opening of the evening session.*

The hour for adjournment having come, the Convention adjourned to meet at half past 7 o'clock.

5. *Resolved*, That it is the duty of every lover of liberty to vote the Liberty ticket so long as they are consistent to their *principles.*

6. *Resolved*, That we believe that it is possible for human governments to be righteous as it is for human beings to be righteous, and that God-fearing men can make the government of our country well pleasing in his right, and that slavery can be abolished by its instrumentality.

7. *R solved*, That this Convention recommend and encourage agricultural pursuits among our people generally, as the surest and speadiest road to wealth, influence and respectability.

8. *Resolved*, That this Convention recommend to our people the importance of aspiring to a knowledge of all the Mechanic arts of the age.

9. *Resolved*, That among the various and important measures for the improvement of our people, this Convention view the principles of Temperance as of vital import, and we urge the hearty adoption of them by our whole people.

Evening Session.—The Convention met as per adjournment. Henry Johnson, one of the Vice Presidents in the chair. Prayer by the Rev. Geo. Weir, of Buffalo—the roll of the Convention was called—the minutes of the previous meeting were read and approved. The resolution of Wm. C. Munro being the order of the day, was called up and Mr. Munro proceeded to discuss the subject matter of the resolution, which he did in a very forcible manner. He endeavored to show the absurdity of several decisions having been made in inferior courts, that colored men though native and free born were not citizens. Mr. Munro thought it high time for us to speak out upon this subject, and that the present was the time. The resolution was opposed by R. H. Johnson. While this question was pending, the committee to whom had been re-

---

* This resolution after having been called up and discussed two several times, was indefinitely postponed and finally voted to be expunged from the minutes.

ferrod the address to the slaves, came in and announced that they were ready to report. Frederic Douglass claimed the privilege of speaking to the resolution pending—the house voted that Mr. Douglass proceed: —he opposed the resolution, and stated that the constitution of this country was a slaveholding instrument, and as such denied *all* rights to the colored man. Others who opposed the resolution, said that its sentiments were self-evident—that nothing could be plainer, than that native free born men must be citizens, and that the converse of this was palbably absurd—it was for this reason that they were opposed to the resolution; it was too plain and self-evident, to be entertained by the Convention for a moment, and they were opposed to bringing it in, and now that it was before us, to entertain it for a moment. While this subject was pending, a motion was made that the report of the committee on the address (the report of the committee being in order), be the first thing in order to-morrow morning—the motion was lost—the committee then presented the address with some very slight alterations: they also reported the following resolution.

Resolved, That each member of this Convention who is friendly to the sentiments contained in this address, come forward and sign it in the name of the ever living God, and that measures be taken to print 1000 copies for circulation—The report was accepted.

A motion was made that to-morrow at 10 o'clock be the order of the day to collect reports and statistical information from the delegates upon the state and condition of our people.

A motion was made by Mr. Sumner of Cincinnati, that the further consideration of the address to the slaves, be laid over until to-morrow at 2 o'clock P. M. Mr. Wright of New York, proposed an amendment —to fix the time at 9 o'clock A. M., instead of 2 P. M.—While this motion was pending, the hour for adjournment having come, the Convention adjourned to meet as per the rules.

Friday, August 18th, 1843.

Morning Session.—The Convention met according to adjournment. The president in the chair—prayer by the Rev. Mr. Malvin, of Cleveland, O.—The roll of the Convention was then called, and the minutes of the previous meeting read and approved. C. L. Remond moved a reconsideration of the vote by which the minutes had been approved— the motion did not prevail.

C. B. Ray moved, that one of the assistant secretaries having left the city, and the other being detained on business, that two persons be appointed to fill their places protempore—whereupon Messrs. W, P. Mc Intire and W. H. Yancy were on motion appointed.

The address to the slaves, with the resolution attached, being under consideration at the hour of adjournment, now being the order of the day, was called up, and Mr. Sharpe, of Rochester, obtained the floor to speak in opposition to it. The subject was further discussed on the same side by Mr. W. Watson of Cincinnati, and by Mr. Malvin of Cleveland, O. The president then announced that the order of the day had arrived, it being to hear reports and to collect statistics upon the condition of our people.

3

On motion of Charles B. Ray, it was resolved that we do adjourn sine die on, or before 12 o'clock to-night.

On motion of Mr. A. M. Sumner, it was Resolved, That the order of the day be suspended that we may proceed to consider the address to the slaves, and the resolution attached. Mr. Sumner proceeded to oppose the address. He remarked that the adoption of that address by the Convention would be fatal to the safety of the free people of color of the slave States, but especially so to those who lived on the borders of the free States ; and living in Cincinnati as he did, he thought he was fully prepared to anticipate very properly what might be the result thereabouts, and he felt bound on behalf of himself and his constituents, to oppose its passage. Mr. Sumner said, that we of Cincinnati were prepared to meet any thing that may come upon us unprovoked, but we were not ready injudiciously to provoke difficulty; he entreated the Convention to pause before they adopted the address.

Mr. Munro moved that no person who had before spoken on this subject, be permitted to speak more than ten minutes—it was carried.

Messrs. Watson of Cincinnati, and Jenkins of Columbus, O., and Malvin of Cleveland, O., took the same view of the question with Mr. Sumner. The subject was further opposed by Messrs. Outley of Lockport, N. Y., Remond of Salem, Mass., and Brown of Buffalo. The subject was advocated by Messrs. Johnson of Rochester, and Lewis of Toledo, O.; they concurred with Mr. Garnit, and thought it was time to speak the sentiments of this address.

Mr. Garnit then rose and spoke at length, he being allowed by vote an additional ten minutes, urging the adoption of this address. He took much the same view of the subject that he had before taken, excepting that he reviewed the objections of the brethren who thought it would be fatal to the free people of the slave states, and to those also on the borders of the free states.

C. B. Ray, chairman of the committee to whom had been referred, the subject of the Press, announced on behalf of the committee, that they were ready to report—the report was accepted and laid on the table to be called up at the next session. The hour for adjournment having arrived, the Convention adjourned.

Afternoon Session.—The Convention met pursuant to adjournment—the president in the chair—prayer by the Rev. Mr. Watson of O. The members united in singing a liberty song. The roll of the Convention was called—the minutes of the previous meeting were read and approved.

The committee to whom had been referred the subject of the Mechanic Arts, reported by their chairman Robert Banks—the report was accepted and on motion adopted. For the report see page 26.

The address to the slaves now being the order of the day, Frederic Douglass rose and made some forcible remarks against its adoption. Mr. Townsend of Albany, moved that the question upon the address be now taken—it was carried. Mr. Remond moved that the question be taken by the yeas and nays—carried. The question being taken was lost by the following vote. Yeas—Theo. S. Wright, J. H. Townsend, W. P. McIntire, H. H. Garnit, John Wandall, T. Woodson, James Fountain,

Jason Jeffrey, H. W. Johnson, A. Peek, R. H. Johnson, S. Talbot, E. B. Dunlap, U. Lett, D. Lewis, W. C. Munro, R. Banks, R. Allen—18. *Nays*—C. Lennox Remond, F. Douglass, James Sharpe, J. P. Morris, R. Francis, W. Johnson, A. Outley, J. F. Platt, G. Weir, W. W. Brown, S. H. Davis, A. M. Sumner, W. Watson, W. H. Yancy, D. Jenkins, G. W. Tucker, H. Jackson, N. W. Jones, Joseph Roxbury —19.

On motion it was resolved that all persons having statistical information respecting our people, report the same to the committee on the condition of the colored people.

The business committee reported a series of resolutions on colonization—the report was accepted.

It was on motion resolved, that the resolutions be taken up separately.

Resolution No. 11 was called up, and after a few remarks explanatory of the resolution was adopted.

Resolution No. 12 was read and adopted without debate.

Resolution No. 13 was then taken up and supported by Mr. Munro, of Mich.—R. H. Johnson rose to reply. Mr. Wright of New York, moved the previous question—the motion was carried—the motion then recurred upon the resolution—it was adopted.

Resolution No. 14 was called up, read and adopted without debate.

Resolution No. 15 was also adopted without debate.

Resolution No. 16 upon Colonization Missionaries was called up and read; this resolution elicited remarks from several gentlemen.—Some of them enquired if the Colonization Society as such, had in fact any Missionaries proper under their control—if they had not, we ought not to infer that they had, and say so as did this resolution ; if they had, then the resolution ought to pass in its present form—they further said that there were Missionary operations in and about Liberia, to which this resolution would in truth apply, and they were for so applying it—but they believed those Missionaries were not under the auspices of the Colonization Society. The brethren on the other side said that whether these Missionaries were, or were not directly under the auspices of the Colonization Society, they supported and encouraged it, and threw themselves upon it for protection; and it encouraged—supported, and in some form protected them; and if they were not one in form, they were in fact, and the resolution fitly applied to them. The brethren on the other side admitted that the resolution did apply to them in spirit, all they wanted was that it might be so worded as to apply to them strictly in letter.

Resolution No. 17 was taken up, and adopted without debate.

11. *Resolved*, That it *may* be possible that the scheme of American Colonization was originally established upon pure motives ; but if it were, its subsequent operations show that it has been fostered and sustained by the *murderous spirit of slavery* and prejudice.

12 *Resolved*, That such being the character of the institution, it has neither the confidence or respect of the free people of color of the United States.

13 *Resolved*, That the manner in which the American Colonization Society secures its victims—to wit, by begging slaveholders to emancipate their slaves, only on condition that they will go to Liberia, shows in what low estimation it should be held by the common sense, and philanthropy of the nation.

14. *Resolved*, That those professed ministers of the gospel, and professing christians, who believe and declare that the pure gospel cannot elevate our race in this

part of the world, are blind guides and shamefully ignorant, and that they libel pure religion and undefiled, which is able to exalt man from his lowest estate, to companionship with God and angels.

15. *Resolved*, That inasmuch as this is our native land, and as our sweat and blood have been poured out in it, that neither persuasion, intrigue or physical force shall drive us from it.

16 *Resolved*, That we entertain but a very poor opinion of the Missionary efforts of the American Colonization Society, and that we have formed our opinions from the facts elicited from some of the Missionaries themselves, wherein they have stated that they had shot down some of the natives to whom they were sent to preach the gospel.

17. *Resolved*, That we believe that the American Colonization Society has done incalculable injury to Africa, by swallowing up all the good that was intended for that unfortunate and much abused country.*

The report upon the Press which had been laid upon the table, was now called up and read, and on motion was adopted—with the resolutions accompanying it. See page 27.

The business committee reported the following resolution: the report was accepted and on motion adopted.

18 *Resolved*, That this Convention appoint a Corresponding Committee, consisting of two from each state, whose business it shall be to issue a call for another National Convention whenever they shall deem it expedient, and that said committee be appointed by the house.

19. *Resolved*, That this Convention designate the place for the meeting of the next National Convention.

It was moved that the house do now proceed to appoint said Committee, and to designate the place for the holding of the next Convention.

The house appointed the following corresponding committee,—for the State of Maine, Rev. A. N. Freeman, and H. G. Piere; N. H., Rev. J. W. Lewis; Mass., J. T. Hilton and Wm. C. Nell; R. I., J. E. Crawford and A. Nigers; Conn., Rev. J. W. C. Pennington and A. G. Beman; New York, Rev. H. H. Garnit and James W. Duffin; New Jersey, L. P. Rogers and J. C. Morel; Penn., John Lewis and J B. Vashon; Ohio, A. M. Sumner and D. Jenkins; Mich., Rev. W. C. Munro and Mr. Freeman of Ann Arbor, Indiana; A. Duncan of Madison; J. G. M. Britton of Indianapolis, Illinois; N. W. Jones of Chicago; M. Robinson of Alton.

On motion it was unanimously resolved, that the city of Troy, N. Y., be the place in which to hold the next Convention.

A resolution on the subject of travelling on the public highway was presented and laid on the table.

The committee to whom had been referred the subject of Agriculture announced through their chairman, C. B. Ray, that they were ready to report—the report was called for, read and accepted. It was moved that it be adopted—upon the motion to adopt Mr. Townsend of Albany, wished to make a few remarks; he said he thanked the committee for bringing in that report—it was just what we wanted; just what this Convention ought to send out to the world; he believed that

---

* It is proper to state that this series of resolutions elicited but very little debate, as there was but one sentiment in the Convention upon that subject, and that sentiment had been so often and so fully expressed.

our people would have to turn their attention to Agriculture before they would ever be an elevated people; he spoke of the great evil in our people's clustering about the large cities, and picking up just what they could get to do, and never having any thing permanent; he had lived in some of those cities, and had seen much to convince him of the bad policy of so clustering about them; he said he hoped, as he doubted not, the report would be unanimously adopted. Mr. Weir of Buffalo also spoke in favor of the report; he advanced about the same train of thought with Mr. Townsend, he hoped the report would be adopted—the report was adopted. See page 30.

The committee on the condition of the colored people announced through their chairman, J. N. Gloucester, that they were ready to report, upon which several members rose and said that they had in their possession statistical information, which they had not handed to the committee—they were requested to do so, to enable the committee to complete their report.

The business committee reported a series of resolutions upon various subjects, which report was accepted.

It was on motion resolved, that the resolutions be taken up separately.

Resolution No. 20 upon the success of the abolition cause was called for, and its adoption was moved, when Mr. Wright of New York rose and proceeded to make some remarks upon the resolution—he referred to the self-denying spirit of the anti-slavery men of this country, and briefly reviewed the history and progress of the cause, and remarked that its triumph thus far was a matter that called for thankfulness to the God of the oppressed. The resolution was then unanimously adopted.

Resolution No. 21 was read and adopted without debate.

Resolution No. 22, also upon slavery, was read and adopted without remark.

Resolution No. 23, upon State Conventions of our people, was then read and adopted without debate.

Resolution No. 24, with the preamble attached upon education, and the moral training of our youth was read, and after a few remarks from several gentlemen approving highly of its subject matter, in the course of whose remarks one gentleman took occasion also to express his regret that the subject of education had not been brought forward at an earlier day, so that it could have been referred to a committee in time for them to have considered and reported ably upon the subject*—it was then adopted.

Resolution No. 25, upon the formation of the Freeman's Party, was read, and its adoption being called for, was opposed by F. Douglass, C. L. Remond, and W. W. Brown : and warmly advocated by H. H. Garnit, W. C. Munro, and others. The gentlemen in the opposition said, that the Freeman's Party, to which the resolution referred, they took for granted was the Liberty Party so called,—if so, they did not hail it at all, much less did they hail it with pleasure—they neither believed in the party, nor in the leading men of the party, and as a matter of course could not, and would not enroll themselves under its broad banner, nor encourage others to do so; and they remarked that they

---

* It is proper here to state, that this resolution had, in the hurry of matters, been overlooked, until it was too late for a Committee to report upon it, and do the subject justice, as was intended.

were opposed to the resolution for the same reasons that they were opposed to the resolution previously adopted approving of the Liberty Party, and as that had already beed adopted, and the Convention in their judgment had shown itself a Liberty Party Convention, it mattered less to them as to what disposition was made of this resolution.

The gentlemen on the affirmative side of the question remarked, in substance, that by the Freeman's Party the Liberty Party was meant, and that believing most heartily in the principles of the party, in its measures and in its object, having confidence in its leaders, and believing, further, that the cause of human liberty in this country demanded the existence of such a party, that they hailed it with peculiar pleasure, and were not only ready, but believed it to be their duty to enlist under its broad banner. They sincerely believed that the cause of the slave demanded it of them, and also that they should encourage and persuade all others to do so likewise ; and they therefore urged the adoption of the resolution. The resolution was adopted.

Resolution No. 26 was then read, and without debate adopted.

20th. *Resolved*, That we return devout thanks to the God of the oppressed for the signal success which has followed the self-denying efforts of the abolition host of these United States.

21st. *Resolved*, That in the opinion of this Convention, the disabilities of the nominally free people of this country flow from slavery, and that while that heaven-daring system continues, our entire enfranchisement will be retarded—and hence we are loudly called upon to labor, in connection with the friends of impartial liberty, for the entire destruction of this destructive system.

22d. *Resolved*, That notwithstanding the numerous obstacles before us, and the great opposition to our cause, having our faith in God and in his truth, we will gird on the panoply of heaven, and pledge ourselves anew to the slave, to his master, and to the God of all, that the sword of truth, by us unsheathed, shall never return to its scabbard, till slavery is dead, till lamentation and mourning ceases, and righteousness exalts the nation.

23d. *Resolved*, That this Convention view, with feelings of satisfaction and hope, the spirit evinced by the State Conventions of our people, which have been held for the consideration of their moral and political interests, and do recommend this mode of action to all of our brethren who are oppressed with State legal disabilities.

24th. Believing that the possession of moral and intellectual worth are the legitimate sources of power, and that just in proportion as an individual or people possess these qualities, they will have the respect of all good men. Therefore

Resolved, That we urge upon our people everywhere, especially upon parents, the all-engrossing subject of the education and moral training of the young and rising generation, as an essentially important means of bettering the condition, and of elevating our whole people.

25th. *Resolved*, That we hail with pleasure the organization of the Freeman's Party, based upon the great principles contained in the Declaration of Independence, that all men are created equal, and that we cheerfully enroll ourselves under its broad banner, and hereby pledge to each other and to the world, our sacred honor, never to disband until liberty shall be proclaimed throughout all the land, unto all the inhabitants thereof.

26th. *Resolved*, That we recommend to the Freemen of this nation immediately to organize Liberty Associations in their respective counties, where they have not already done so, and nominate tried friends of liberty for all the offices for which they will be called to vote.

The hour for adjournment having come, the Convention adjourned to meet at half-past 7 o'clock.

Evening Session.—The Convention met as per adjournment, the President in the chair. Prayer by the Rev. Charles B. Ray. The roll of the Convention was called, and the minutes of the previous meeting read and approved. The Convention united in singing a liberty song. The business committee reported complete. The report was accepted.

J. N. Gloucester, chairman of the committee upon the condition of the colored people, announced that the committee were ready to report. The report was read, and, on motion, adopted. (See *last Report.*

R. Francis, having voted with the majority upon the address to the slaves, now moved a reconsideration of that vote.

Mr. Ray, of New York, rose and opposed the reconsideration of the vote, and gave his reasons, among others, that that subject had already occupied too much of the time of the Convention, and they had fixed upon the hour for the final adjournment of the Convention ; that they had as much business before them as could be attended to in the interim, and if this subject should now come up again, it would consume all the time to the hour of adjournment; for himself, with many others who had not yet spoken upon the subject, and had intended not to, would feel called upon to express their views upon the subject.

Mr. Sumner, of Ohio, objected to reconsider the vote, on the ground that several persons having remained to ·the Convention longer than they had at first intended, expressly to vote upon that subject and see it finally disposed of, had left the Convention, and he feared, that fact being known, that advantage had been taken of it ; and he was, for this reason, as well as for many others, opposed to reconsider the vote.

Mr. Banks, of Michigan, said, though having voted with the majority, he was, nevertheless opposed to reconsider the vote, for the same reasons, among others, as stated by Mr. Sumner. He thought that justice demanded that it should not be reconsidered.

Upon the question being taken, the vote was reconsidered.

Mr. Francis, of Rochester, then rose and advocated the adoption of the address, and stated, that since the adjournment he had changed his mind in respect to it, and should the question be taken, should change his vote.

Mr. Morris, of Rochester, said he had also changed his mind in respect to the merit of the address, and should also change his vote.

The President now evacuated the chair to one of the Vice Presidents, and took the floor to speak in opposition to the address. He said that he should probably want one hour to express his views upon the subject before us, whereupon the Convention suspended the rules to give him time. Mr. Beman took a moral view of the subject, and opposed it principally upon moral grounds. He said that he objected to it because it had too much of the physical, and not enough of the moral weapon about it. The remarks of Mr. Beman were of great force, and produced effect upon the audience.

Mr. Garnit rose and replied to Mr. Beman ; he endeavored to meet the objections raised by the President.

Mr. Douglass spoke forcibly in opposition to the address.

Mr. Remond spoke upon the same side of the question.

Mr. Ray rose and proceeded to speak in opposition to the address, but owing to the lateness of the hour, and the time having nearly come to adjourn, he did not proceed to give his views.

Several voices were for taking the question. The President announced that we had but a few minutes before the time would come for us to adjourn, and we had business yet to do. Some were for continuing in session until we had finished our business; others were for adjourning until to-morrow morning at six o'clock. The President announced that the time when we were to adjourn had about expired, and he should have to consider the Convention adjourned unless some action to the contrary was taken; that what was done must be done *now.*

Mr. Sumner, of Ohio, moved that we now adjourn to meet to-morrow at nine o'clock, and that the final vote upon the address be taken at half-past nine o'clock.

The motion was carried, and the Convention adjourned as per the vote.

Saturday, August 19th, 1843.

Morning Session.—The Convention met according to adjournment. The President in the chair. Prayer by the Rev. Mr. Wright, of New York.

It was on motion, resolved that we adjourn, without day, at eleven o'clock, A. M.

It was moved that we dispense with the reading of the roll, singing, &c. The minutes of the previous meeting were read and approved.

The hour having come when the final vote upon the address was to be taken, it was moved that the vote be taken by the yeas and nays—carried. Upon the question being taken, it was again rejected by the following vote:

Yeas.—J. H. Townsend, W. P. McIntire, H. H. Garnit, J. Wandall, E. B. Dunlap, W. C. Munro, R. Allen, N. W. Jones, J. Roxburg—9.

Nays.—C. L. Remond, F. Douglass, A. G. Beman, T. S. Wright, C. B. Ray, B. S. Anderson, J. Fountain, J. Sharpe, G. Weir, A. M. Sumner, W. H. Yancy, D. Jenkins, G. W. Tucker, T. Pollock.—14.

On motion of Mr. Wright, of New York, it was resolved that we now take up the resolution of Wm. C. Munro, upon the rights of citizenship under the Constitution.

On motion of Mr. Sumner, of Ohio, it was indefinitely postponed.

On motion of Mr. Sumner, it was expunged from the minutes.

It was on motion resolved, that we take up the remainder of the report from the business committee.

The following plan of operations, submitted by the committee on business, was read, and on motion adopted:

PLAN OF OPERATIONS.

The committee would respectfully recommend that at least one lecturer be employed to travel through each of the free States of this Union, to present to the people the disabilities and claims of the oppressed colored people of this land.

That such persons only shall be employed who are well informed in regard to the condition, sentiments, wants, and wishes of the colored people.

The lecturers be instructed, especially, to urge the following subjects upon the consideration of our people, viz., education—associations for improvement in science and literature—temperance—practical abolitionism—Sabbath-schools and an intelligent ministry, and an application to the mechanic arts.

That the lecturers also acquaint themselves with the advantages of agriculture, and recommend to our people in the cities and large towns, to remove to the country, and become the owners and cultivators of the soil.

That a paper be established in some large city, to be the organ of the colored people, and that in such a case, the lecturers be appointed as agents, to lay its claims before the people, and urge the importance of subscribing for it, and rendering to it a hearty support.

Resolution No. 27, upon the exercise of the suffrage, was taken up, and on motion adopted.

Resolution No. 28, upon the character of the two leading political parties, was read, and on motion adopted without remark.

27th. *Resolved*, That those who enjoy free suffrage, and who use it to elevate slaveholders and their apologists to office, are practical opposers of the basest kind, and that those who, having the power to redeem their fellow-men, by their votes, and who refuse to do it, are in effect the same.

28th. *Resolved*, That it is evident that the two great political parties, (the Whig and Democratic,) must of course be pro-slavery, while they rule, and slavery exists; and therefore we recommend our brethren, who are qualified to vote, to give their suffrage to the Liberty Party, which has the abolition of slavery for its main object.

James H. Gloucester, of New York, offered the following resolution, which was on motion adopted:

29th. *Resolved*, That we hail with great emotions of joy the recent sitting of the World's Convention, in the city of London, for the entire overthrow of slavery throughout the world; and we pray God that it may never cease its triennial assemblings until the great object be consummated.

The following resolution was offered by H. H. Garnit, and on motion adopted unanimously:

30th. *Resolved*, That we hail with joy the progress which the people of Ireland are making in the cause of liberty, and tender them our hearty sympathy.

The chair then announced the following persons as the committee to take measures to establish a press, to be the organ of the colored people of this country, as recommended in the report on the press, viz: C. B. Ray, P. A. Bell, and Theo. S. Wright, of New York; J. W C. Pennington, of Hartford, Conn.; A. G. Beman, of New Haven, Conn.; H. H. Garnit, of Troy, N. Y.; S. E. Cornish, of Newark, N. J. The committees for the several States, to be the same persons constituting the committee upon the call of another Convention.

The chair also announced the following named persons to constitute the committee to publish the proceedings of this Convention, viz., C. B. Ray, H. H. Garnit, T. S. Wright, and W. P. McIntosh.

On motion, the President was added to the committee on publication.

On motion, it was resolved that the minutes be published in pamphlet form.

Upon this motion, the Secretary arose and stated to the Convention that it would take upwards of $50 to meet the expense of issuing them in pamphlet form. He suggested, that if the delegates present were not prepared to furnish that amount of money down, that each delegation present, subscribe for as many copies as they would take, and forward the money to the committee, immediately upon their return home, as the committee would not feel warranted to publish the proceedings until sufficient money to cover the expense should be furnished them. This proposition was accepted.

The finance committee then reported, that the money collected during the sessions of the body had been more than sufficient to cover the expense, by the sum of eight dollars.

It was moved that the balance be placed in the hands of the publishing committee to aid in publishing the proceedings. Carried.

The President then announced that there was no more business before us.

The following resolutions were then offered, and on motion adopted:

Resolved, That we tender a vote of thanks to our friends in Buffalo, who have so kindly entertained us during our stay among them.

Resolved, That we present our sincere thanks to the citizens of Buffalo, for their attendance at our meetings, for the interest they have manifested, and the attention given to our deliberations during our session.

Resolved, That a vote of thanks be tendered to the trustees of this Hall for the free use of it, and especially to the officers of the Park Street Church for opening their doors for the public meetings of this Convention.

Resolved, That a vote of thanks be tendered to the President for the impartial manner with which he has presided over our deliberations, and to the other officers of the Convention, and also to the Chairman of the Business Committee, for his faithfulness in furnishing business for the Convention.

Resolved, That we adjourn sine die, by rendering thanksgiving and praise to Almighty God, who has spread his shield of protection over us, and has favored us with his approving smile.

The Rev. Theo. S. Wright then led the Convention in devout thanksgiving to Almighty God. The Convention then united in singing a hymn of praise, after which we parted to meet each other again, we hope, in Convention, if need be, either by representation or in person ; if not, to meet, we hope, where there will be no occasion to deliberate upon measures to deliver from slavery and wrongs imposed; but where all shall be equals and free in the highest and most glorious sense.

Thus ended our Convention, after a pleasant but laborious session of four days and a half.

REPORT OF COMMITTEE UPON THE MECHANIC ARTS.

The committee would have been glad to have drawn up a more full report, and gone more into detail, but time would not permit. We cannot too earnestly recommend to our people the importance of the mechanic arts. In almost every age of the world, this has been a subject of deep importance to the people; and the nearer the mechanical arts have been carried to perfection, the higher have the people risen in wealth and intellect. It is a branch of industry which naturally expands the mind; and every country where proper attention is paid to education, the mechanics form a powerful and influential body. Many of the ablest statesmen, divines, and philanthropists of this country, and in other countries, have arisen from this class. Our duty to ourselves and our posterity should impell us into all those avenues which will influence and elevate our characters. Our destiny is upward and onward. Every thing around us is on the move, and pressing forward to greater perfection. We again earnestly entreat our people to improve every opportunity in which they or their children can learn the mechanical arts.

ROBERT BANKS,
GEORGE WEIR,   } *Committee.*
JAMES H. FOUNTAIN,

REPORT OF COMMITTEE UPON THE PRESS.

Your committee, to whom had been referred the subject of a press, having, in the brief time allotted to them, considered the subject, beg leave now to report.

Your committee entertain the common views entertained of the power and influence of the press, for good or for evil; they believe that much of the existing good, as well as of the evil in the world, owes itself to the press as an instrumentality, and that most of the peculiar evils to which we of this country are subjected, if not brought into existence, are now sustained by the power and influence of the press; that slaveholding, in this country, finds now, as it ever has found, support and a grand means of defence, in the influence of the newspaper press; that that peculiar and unhallowed sensibility, so prevalent in this country, called prejudice against color, has become wider spread, and firmer fixed, by the views and sentiments which sustain it, having been taken up and palmed off upon the reading public by the press.

Your committee also are of the opinion that, if the press, with its almost mysterious influence, is so productive of mischief to us, as they really believe it has been, and as proof of which they would say, let all the mobs of the land answer, that the same power, in proper hands, but especially in our own, would be exerted, or at least might be, not only merely to counteract the influences against us, but be made an instrumentality to promote positive good, the tendency of which would be to elevate the people ; in other words, a press in our own hands would be wielded to disabuse the public mind in respect to us, and correct the false views and sentiments entertained of us, and of questions necessary to our general welfare, and would be the means of promoting correct views and sentiments in reference to the same objects.

The press takes hold of the public mind, and gets at the public heart ; its influence reaches the spot to form and influence public opinion ; and to what do the disabilities of the colored people and the slavery of this country owe their existence, more than to public opinion ? What is a more fruitful source of evil than public opinion, when wrongly formed ? This, then, once corrected, and formed as it should be, and our work, so far as the influences from without are concerned, is done. If one class of the people ought to have a press absolutely under their control, it is that class who are the proscribed, and whose rights are cloven down.

Your committee believe that the press may not, and will not only be wielded successfully in combatting and turning away the influences which are without, but it will be exceedingly useful in the influence it may and will exert within, or among ourselves. 1st.—A paper emanating from, and circulating among us, will bring us almost as it were in contact ; will make us better acquainted with each other, and with the doings of each other. It will also have the tendency to unite us in a stronger bond, by teaching us that our cause and our interests are one and common, and that what is for the interest of the one, or a point gained in our common cause in one section of the country, is for the interest of all, or a point gained by all. Besides, being the organ of the whole, it would necessarily chronicle the public measures of the whole, and thus become a medium to enable us to learn about, as well as from each other.

A paper such as it should be, necessarily conveys general information, and becomes a means of knowledge : no instrumentality is more efficient in conveying information upon general subjects than the newspaper press. If it be a means of knowledge, then it aids in the formation of character, and every family, especially where there are children, ought to take a newspaper for the information it contains. But if papers tend to the formation of character, then ought we to see to it that papers only of correct sentiments come into the hands of our children.

Your committee, while they see evidently the necessity of having established amongst us a good newspaper, find many difficulties in the way of establishing one in the present state of things, and hardly have known to what conclusion to come. They admit that we are enough in numbers to sustain three or four papers ; that there are men and women enough among us searching for useful information, and whose love of improvement lead them to feel the necessity of, and most heartily desire to have a paper, to sustain one ; but to get properly at these, is a work of time, of labor, and expense.

A paper to be well sustained must have at least *two thousand punc-*

tually paying subscribers, and if these subscribers are to be obtained, and continued, as experience has taught us they must be, by travelling agents who must receive a compensation for their services, then it must have three thousand or more punctually paying subscribers. If a paper cannot be well sustained with less than two thousand well paying subscribers, and as much time must necessarily elapse before such a number could be obtained, they therefore conceive here a difficulty in the way of establishing one, unless a few hundred dollars, with which to carry it through the first year, can be procured, either by loan or by contribution, the latter of which may, and ought to be done.

Finally, your committee are of the opinion, in view of the necessities of the case, and that something ought to be done, that this Convention ought to take measures, notwithstanding the difficulties in the way, to establish a paper of their own, as an organ for the people ; or in the event that one should be established, by any individual enterprise, of a proper character, to pledge itself to its support, by now appointing a committee whose business it shall be either to get up a paper, or in the event that one should be got up of a proper character, to adopt it as the organ of the people, and to recommend it to their patronage and support.

They would further recommend, that a committee of two from each State be appointed as a standing committee of correspondence upon the subject of the paper, whose business it shall be to appoint an agent, or agents, as the case may require, to canvass their respective States—to lay the claims of the paper before the people of those States—to procure subscribers for it, and otherwise to solicit funds in its behalf; to lecture also upon thé general condition of our people, upon the various subjects that interest and concern them—to urge them also to form lyceums for improvement in literature—and temperance and benevolent societies. Such agent shall be accountable to the State committees, and said committees shall be accountable to them for their salaries, which, however, shall be a fixed percentage upon the moneys they may raise, and shall come out of said moneys; provided, however, that said salary shall not exceed 33 1-3 per cent on the moneys raised, the balance to be paid directly to the proprietor of the paper ; or, should the Convention establish one, to the person or persons they may appoint to manage it.

Should the Convention take measures to establish a paper, your committee believe that it ought to be published in the city of New-York, it being the great commercial mart of this nation, as well as the centre of all the great benevolent operations of the country. The foregoing is the only favorable plan the committee, from the circumstances of the case, have been able to light upon. They would recommend the following resolutions :—

Resolved, That a committee of seven be appointed by this Convention to take measures, as soon as may be, to establish a weekly paper, devoted impartially to the welfare of our whole people, without regard to condition, and to the welfare of humanity universally—to appoint an editor and publisher, and to fix their salaries ; or in the event they should not establish a paper, and one should be commenced as an individual enterprise, of a proper character, to recommend said paper as entitled to the patronage and support of the people.

Resolved, That this Convention appoint a committee of two from each State, with power to increase their numbers, whose business it shall be to carry out the recommendations in the foregoing report, which refers to State committees upon the subject of a newspaper.

All which is respectfully submitted.

CHARLES B. RAY,
R. BANKS,
WM. P. McINTIRE,
N. W. JONES,   } *Committee.*
H. H. GARNIT,
T. WOODSON,
S. H. DAVIS,

REPORT OF COMMITTEE UPON AGRICULTURE.

Your committee, to whom had been referred the subject of Agriculture, regret that they have not had time to consider the subject so fully as its nature and importance demands. They beg leave, however, to submit the following as the result of their deliberations.

Among the variety of things, as well in our own country, as in all civilized countries, which tend to elevate man, or at least to bring him into more favorable notice, wealth is among the most prominent.— Whether this ought so to be is another question; but such is the state of society, that nothing is more notorious than that such is the fact. And to become wealthy, or to place one in easy circumstances, is, after all, the great aim, the absorbing thing with all people, and no less so with our own people.

Your committee admit, that there are various standards of wealth, varying according to circumstances and habits of country, and of place; but we believe, that to be independent, or in circumstances where we have a competency of the necessary things of life, is to be wealthy— and that the farmer alone, who is the owner of the soil he cultivates, can in reality be in such circumstances of independency. We admit, that there can be no absolute independence—that mankind are more or less dependant upon one another; but such a state of independence as may, in the nature of things exist, the farmer alone possesses.

Your committee would further say, that there is, and can be no real wealth, but in the possession of the soil. The soil alone possesses a real value—all other things have only a relative value: their value is to be computed from the amount of land they will purchase. Money and all other things are only creatures of exchange—representatives of a real value—that is only a real value which can be made to serve the real purposes of life, the demands of our physical being; money and all other commodities are of real value, or are useless only, as they do, or do not answer this purpose; for this alone are they really wanted, and that which will directly serve this purpose, is not only really wealth, but the only wealth which is needed. The committee avow, that the soil alone is absolutely capable of doing this, all other things being but creatures of exchange; and however much they may be used towards contributing to this purpose, are but means to that end, of which the soil is the real source of supply. Money, ships, houses, merchandise, the professions, the mechanic arts, all these, however much to be appreciated in their proper use, are valueless, unless mother earth shall have first opened her hands, and supplied us of her bounty; they cannot meet the demands of our nature, and with all the pearls of the ocean in possession, and the real wants of our nature unsupplied, would that be wealth?

Your committee insist upon it, that the man who owns his farm unencumbered, with the necessary accompaniments, with no other possessions, is independent and wealthy; and how can he be otherwise? for with a congenial sun, and the congenial showers, and both of which he is sure to have, they are unavoidable, and come of a natural necessity; with these the earth will, as she ever has done, yield her increase, food for man, and food for beast. In the language of another we would say, "If we take good care of old mother earth (cultivate her,) she will take good care of us." Besides, the products for food, from the same natural causes, will come the necessary products for clothing; hemp and flax; wool will grow upon the sheep's back, and the worm will spin our silk, and the wheel, the distaff and the loom will convert them into the convenient state for the back, and this the farmers can do in and among themselves; as to the luxuries of life, the beet and the maple tree, will, where the cane cannot be cultivated, furnish one of the most needful. Is not such a man independent? who is more so? nay more, who as much so? for who can live without the things which he grows? and where shall he who does not produce them, and must have them, go for a supply, but to the farmer—he is the farmer's dependent, how much gold soever he may have, or however many ships, or houses, or other things he may possess, these are nothing to him, unless he be supplied with what the agriculturist has, without money, and as it were without price.

Besides being independent, he is also wealthy. His farm may have cost him in its present state of cultivation, not to exceed *three hundred dollars*—that sum in money or in merchandise, commercial, or in most mechanical business, would be a capital insufficient from which to hope, even, for an ordinary living—in most cases, in most of the business operations, with a capital so small, despair would attend at every step; such a sum is but a fractional part of the value of the wardrobe of persons in some circumstances in life, yet in the more preferable countries for agriculture, it will buy a farm quite large enough, build an house, furnish the necessary implements, and make other improvements sufficient to produce a happy living. And if he is not wealthy at the commencement, as wealth may be estimated in the older countries, or the popular cities, or even in the neighborhood where he lives, he is so prospectively according to their standard, and having enough, he is so really. Still further, his farm produces, or yields him all that is necessary to live upon; he need not go in debt; at the same time, his farm is improving, and his land increasing in value, and every new crop he reaps, or new acre he cultivates, his wealth is increasing, and a few years finds him prepared to add farm to farm, and to give presently to one son a farm here, and to another a farm yonder, and himself living as he always has done, independently all the time.

This kind of independence, itself, leads to, and makes respectability. It seems to be man's true element to cultivate the soil; he was made to be a shepherd, to have flocks and herds, and to till the land—it is after God's arrangement. It seems better adapted to his moral condition, and moral susceptibilities than to plunge himself into commercial affairs.

Farming is no longer regarded in the light of drudgery and as a menial calling—that age has past—now it has got to be a scientific business, and becomes a proper subject for the vastest minds of the age. The Chemist, the Botanist, the Geologist, and the Mineralogist all find their professions very useful in farming; still farming can be successfully done, as it has been, and the farmer not theoretically learned in these sciences—but he who is a faithful farmer is now regarded as engaged in the first, and most honorable pursuits of the age.

Your committee are of the opinion, that the business of farming heartily entered into is the shortest, surest road to respectability and influence; especially would it be to a people reproached, and maligned as are our people. The business itself is respectable, and gives character, besides it puts the one farmer, be he whom he may, upon the same level with his neighbors—their occupation is one, their hopes and interests are one; his neighbors see him now, not as in other situations they may have done as a servant; but an independent man; they see him in the same position in society with themselves; they are not above him nor he above them; they are all alike upon a level; farmers, they respect their own calling, feel themselves independent—they must, and will respect his, and feel that he is alike independent; and as it is only by placing men in the same position in society, that all casts are lost sight of; all cast in his case, were he previously of the proscribed class, will fade away and be forgotten. In proof of which your committee would refer you to a statement from a body of colored farmers in Mercer Co., Ohio. They say, "In our present residence in this county, we have never in any manner been injured by our white neighbors; but on the contrary we have been treated in a kind and friendly manner. They attend our meetings, come to our mill, employ our mechanics, and day laborers, buy our provisions, and we do the same by them. That is we all seek our own convenience and interest without regard to color."

Your committee are of the opinion also, that while farming renders the man independent and makes him wealthy, that it is the only possible way to wealth now open to our people—that by turning our attention to this mode of life, we may become wealthy. We have not the capital to engage successfully in other business, which, with a large amount of capital, and fortune's smile might soon lead to wealth; but there are tens of thousands of us in different parts of the country, of almost all ages, and each having capital enough to engage in the business of Agriculture, and all of whom in a few years might become a wealthy people, and thus change the whole face of society around us decidedly for the better. In proof that such might be the fact, we would again refer you to another extract from the letter of our friends in Mercer Co., O. It is proper also to say, that these brethren only left the cities of the west in 1837, for the country, most of whom with but moderate means, to turn their attention to farming. They say, "We then agreeably to the advice of our abolition friends, resolved to save our money and move into the country, and try by labor, and economy, and honesty, and temperance, to earn for our people a better name than they had heretofore enjoyed. We have found by experiment, that the same money which paid our rent and marketing in the city, will purchase new land and improve it in the country. 'Tis true our undertaking was for us a new one. But the result is several hundred of us left our former occupations in the cities, and are now living on our own land. It was new timbered land when we bought it, and the nearest place we could purchase provisions was thirty miles distant. But we struggled along through the hardest of it. We own many thousands of acres of land. We have built comfortable houses to live in. Our land is cleared. We raise our own provisions and manufacture most of our own clothing. We have horses, and hogs, and cattle, and sheep. We have meeting houses and a school house. We have had a good school most of the time for six years. Our children have learned to read, and write, and cypher. We have Sunday schools where they are taught the principles of morality and religion. We have a saw mill and grist mill. We are striving to lead a quiet and orderly life. We wish to have our character plead for us." They further say, "We have cleared 1000 acres of wild land; made and laid up 350,000 rails, and built at least 200 different houses, to say nothing of some $10,000 which individuals of us have paid for our freedom."

They proceed to appeal to our brethren generally in very proper strains, and say, "And now, our colored brethren, we appeal to those of you who live in towns and follow those precarious occupations for a livelihood which prejudice has assigned to you; would you not be serving your country and your race to more purpose, if you were to leave your present residences and employments, and go out into the country and become a part of the bone and sinew of the land?" They proceed and say, "We the colored people must become more valuable to the State. We must help it to raise a revenue and increase its wealth, by throwing our labor into profitable employment. . . . Our employment must be of that character that people can see how we obtain a livelihood, and that we are useful. . . . But on the other hand, if our labor is all honorable and profitable, both to ourselves and the State, we shall have the increased satisfaction of a good living, and a good name, besides something to show as the fruits of our labor, and something to leave as an inheritance to our children."

The above testimony from our brethren in Carthagenia, is a case fully in point; it shows how decidedly those brethren in the short space of six years, though at first altogether unaccustomed to the business they are now following, have bettered their condition, how much more useful in all their relations, in their present circumstances they now may be than they could have been in their former ones; how much more full of hope and promise for the future for themselves and their children, are the circumstances in which they are now placed, than could have been the circumstances in which they formerly were. They have settled themselves down permanently, as well as usefully to themselves and others, and are not subject to those fluctuations and changes peculiar to a city life.

Besides the foregoing extracts, your committee would refer you to other cases of our brethren in the State of Ohio. In Jackson Co., in that State, there is a settlement of about 50 colored families, mostly farmers, and all of whom own their own farms, and in a high state of cultivation. These friends went to that country many years since, when that whole country was comparatively a new one, and that age a dark age ; and all along they have had to contend with a variety of trying obstacles. They have, however, risen above all that obstructed their pathway, and in spite of all, they have ever maintained a good reputation, have comfortably supported their families from their own produce, have educated well their children, have lived to see the wilderness become a plain, and the desert blossom as the rose, and are now in ease and comfort, with produce annually above supplying their own wants, abundantly to export.

Your committee might also refer you to other settlements of our people in the counties of Brown, Shelby and Warren, in the State of Ohio, all of which are in a flourishing state, and the people living within their own resources—independently, respectably and usefully, and in some of which, where prejudice once was rampart, is so far overcome, and lived down, that the white children and the colored children in the most friendly feeling are educated in the same school, although that is against both the laws and the spirit of that State, and the other settlements where the same is not the case, the people are educating well their own children.

Your committee without the facts above stated, and but few of which have they had the time to collect, or the room to embody, are of the settled opinion that it is time that the mass of our people in the big cities, and large towns of the East, and South, yea, and of the West too, turned their attention to this subject. As they now live, they have nothing permanently to depend upon for a support ; their occupations are precarious, as fluctuating as the wind, subject to all the changes of fortune and of circumstances to which those who employ them are subjected, as well as to all the vexatious changes in the business affairs of the country. Your committee believe that in their present occupations, if they do not on the whole exert an influence against their own highest good, and the highest good of their brethren, that they are less useful to themselves, and of little or no use to their brethren at large ; and that the comfort of their families, the future good of their children, and their whole interest, as well as the general good of our cause demands, that with their means, and their influence, and large numbers of whom have the means, they should emigrate to those countries where land is cheap, and settle themselves down as freemen, and become at once independent, useful and happy.

Many of our people in the cities have money loaned at interest, and which netts them but 5 per cent, and themselves are, as they ever have been, following the dependent occupations peculiar to the same class in large cities, and large numbers are engaged in the unpleasant business of the sea, with no hope of promotion to office ; when that money invested in a farm even in the new countries of the West, would yield at least 25 per cent from the commencement, and after a few years, from the improvements that would be made, and the increase in the valuation of the land, as the result of such improvements, it would be found to have yielded him many hundred per cent, besides himself with his family having all the time had absolute command of their time, at no one's bidding nor call, and having lived independently, and been growing in influence and respectability, and as they might, in intelligence and usefulness continually. Your committee believe that these opinions of theirs, are no airy phantoms, no heated imaginations of the brain, no wild groundless assertions, but a fair statement of what in such emergencies in thousands of instances have been—what are the occurrences of every year, and what again will be—just what the nature of the case admits of, and with a judicious selection and proper management, cannot be otherwise. And we would further say, that a person, or persons, having but a few hundred dollars beforehand, as is the case with most of our people, cannot invest it half so advantageously, as to settle themselves with it upon a farm of their own; and if such are to be the advantages of an agricultural life, who are the people in the whole land, whose position, viewed in all possible relations, and whose circumstances so demand, that they should at once avail themselves of those advantages, so much as the free colored population of this country?

Your committee would recommend, as the place towards which they who may emigrate should look as their future homes, the States of Michigan, Ohio, Indiana, Illinois, and the Territories of Wiskonson and Iowa. With respect to the States, some of them, it is true, are, or may be, objectionable on account of their laws; but these laws are not like the laws of the Medes and Persians, unchangeable. They are subject to change, and time and the growing intelligence of the people, and their better understanding of the great laws of humanity, are destined to make those laws obnoxious to the people themselves; and if they be not rescinded, they are destined to become a dead letter; and these States and Territories, but especially the latter, seem to spread themselves out in their grandeur, with their proud rivers, their noble prairies, their tall trees, their mountains and vales; all imprinted with the glory of an Almighty hand, and say to the colored population, why stay ye clustered in those big cities, the servants of all? why do ye not come out here and settle down, and cultivate my face, and turn to your account my rivers, and with the proper self moral training, I will make you all you ought, or all that man can be. The Territories have yet no constitutions; now, equal laws prevail there—the right of preemption is open to all, another great advantage, and your committee believe that no time is to be lost on our part, for us to strike for that region, that we may be found there forming acquaintances with the people, and making the people acquainted with us; and, by such contact, becoming identified with each other's interest, and interested in each other's case—that we may be on the spot, with our influence, to aid in giving character to their constitution and laws, when the time shall have come for those Territories to become States.

Your committee would submit the following plan of emigration, viz: let twenty families, more or less, with health, habits of industry, and economy, with intelligence, a sound moral and religious character, with respect for and confidence and interest in each other, who agree, as far as can be, on all great questions of fundamental morality unite together, not to form a community of interests, have things common, but to settle, each adjoining the other, on his own purchased farm, and thus form one neighborhood; and let them unite together in all matters of public interest that are for the good of the whole; such as schools, and churches, roads and bridges, if need be, and flouring mills and saw mills, the two latter of which would doubtless net a profit; and let them share that profit according to the amount of stock each had advanced; and where it can be, we would not object to a few white families in such a company; only where there is known to exist a harmony of views and feelings, where all are willing to identify themselves with each other's interests, and to care for each other's welfare, and to share alike in the sorrows and the joys, in the privileges and the privations, and to seek the one, to build up the other as he would himself; when such an arrangement can be made, we believe it will be found to be, to all concerned, in all respects essentially useful; and let them have their minister, who goes as the rest do, save only to teach them the way of life, and also their school teacher.

We further wish to say, that one of your committee, on his way to this Convention, spent some hours with a friend, a colored gentleman, who is deeply interested in this subject, who has at his command to dispose of thousands of acres of excellent land in the southern part of the State of Michigan, on one of her best rivers; and who will soon be ready to join an interesting and proper company, and go and settle upon this land, and give them all the advantages that his possession of the land will afford; he was exceedingly anxious that this subject should be brought before the Convention. Your committee would further recommend the following resolution;

Resolved, That this Convention recommend to our people, especially those in our large cities and seaport towns, to emigrate into the agricultural districts of the country, and invest their money in the purchase of the soil, and become farmers, as a positive road to wealth, influence, and usefulness.

All which is respectfully submitted.

CHARLES B. RAY,
A. M. SUMNER,
W. H. YANCY, } *Committee.*
D. JENKINS,
S. TALBOT,

REPORT OF COMMITTEE UPON THE CONDITION OF THE COLORED PEOPLE.

The committee to whom had been referred the subject of the condition of the colored people beg leave to report. They would respectfully say that their report is necessarily lean to what it should be, in view of our numerous, wide-spread, and growing population. But it must be remembered that, with the exception of three slave States, and those only from one single borough in each, that only the free States are represented in this Convention, and also but barely a majority of them; and again, that only the principal cities or larger towns of those have sent delegates ; that from some of them, but one place is here represented, and still further, that some of the delegates have brought with them no statistics, as they should have done, and are now so unable to furnish verbally any information that can be relied upon, that they do not attempt it. In view of these things, your committee do not presume that they are presenting to you the true state of the condition of our people—it is a bird's eye view merely—being confined to but very few places. It is such, however, as we have been able to glean from the scanty records that have been presented to us, and the hurried manner in which they have been obliged to gather and embody what they could. They think, however, that there is sufficient in it to wake up some interest on the part of the Convention, upon this feature of its business ; and also of all others who may read it, after it shall have suffered the will of the Convention should that will be to adopt it, and publish it with the rest of its proceedings.

ALBANY, N. Y.

Colored inhabitants 700—real estate 70,000 dollars—mechanics and persons in mercantile business 28—churches 2, Baptist and Methodist, with 300 members inclusive—Sabbath-schools 2, with 100 members inclusive—common schools 2, with 90 members inclusive—literary societies 2, with 40 members inclusive; and one semi-monthly periodical.

BUFFALO, N. Y.

Colored inhabitants 700—churches 2, Methodist and Baptist—1 Sabbath-school, with 60 members—mechanics 20—merchants 2—1 common school with 80 members—1 total abstinence society, with upwards of 300 members.

ROCHESTER, N. Y.

Colored inhabitants 500—real estate 47,000 dollars—churches 2, Methodist, with about 200 members—1 Sabbath-school with 40 members—benevolent societies 3—1 debating society—mechanics 12—a district school with 40 members.

GENEVA, N. Y.

Colored inhabitants 311—real estate 10,000 dollars—common schools 1, with 50 scholars—1 female benevolent society—public property 1500 dollars.

LOCKPORT, N. Y.

Colored inhabitants 200—real estate $10,000, 1 common school, with 30 members—churches 1, Methodist, with 30 members—one Sabbath-school, with 20 members—mechanics 10.

NIAGARA FALLS, N. Y.

Colored inhabitants 50—professors of religion 20—real estate 300 dollars.

PENN YAN, N. Y.

Colored inhabitants 30—professors of religion 20—real estate 8,000 dollars—mechanics 3—merchants 2—and 1 agriculturist.

BATH, N. Y.

Colored inhabitants 150—churches 1—1 district school—1 female benevolent society—real estate 12,500 dollars.

SCHENECTADY, N. Y.

Colored inhabitants 250—1 church—3 female benevolent societies —1 male do.—Sabbath-school 1—debating society 1—1 temperance society, with 100 members—real estate 15,000 dollars—mechanics 3.

NEWTOWN, N. Y.

Colored inhabitants 100—churches 1—1 district school—1 temperance society—real estate 2,000 dollars.

NEW YORK CITY.

Colored inhabitants 16,000—churches 10 ; Methodist 6 ; Presbyterian 1; Baptist 2 ; Episcopalian 1—communicants 3000, including those attached to other churches—Sabbath-schools 13—district schools 5, one of which embraces 4 departments, and another 2 departments, with 12 colored teachers—select schools 2—benevolent societies, male 13, female 15—temperance societies 4—literary societies, male 3. female 1—education societies 2—1 public library, with ——— volumes—public property, including churches, burying-grounds, and one public hall, 120,000 dollars—real estate difficult to estimate.

CINCINNATI, OHIO.

Colored inhabitants 4,500—churches 6, of different denominations, containing 900 members inclusive—Sabbath-schools 5, with 478 members inclusive—day schools, with four colored teachers, 200 scholars inclusive—benevolent societies, female, 5, with 340 members—temperance societies 2, adult 750 members, juvenile 350 members—literary society 1, with 40 members—real estate 350,000 dollars—mechanics 130.

COLUMBUS, OHIO.

Colored inhabitants 1000—churches 2, with 350 members—schools 3, with 75 members—temperance societies 1, with 220 members—Sabbath-schools 1, 30 members—mechanics 12--literary societies 1, with 25 members—2 female benevolent societies, with 40 members—real estate 35,000 dollars—6 agriculturists.

NEW BEDFORD, MASS.

The following letter from Mr. Johnson, of that place, will speak for itself :

NEW BEDFORD, Aug. 12th, 1843.

Gentlemen,—It would afford me much pleasure to be present at the

Convention to assemble in Buffalo on the 15th inst., but present engagements deprive me of that pleasure. I must be content by giving you the following statistical information of our people:

We have 1,100 inhabitants; 2 churches, with 200 members inclusive; one a Christian Baptist, the other an Independent Methodist; both are under the pastoral charge of colored ministers; 2 literary societies, with 50 members; 6 benevolent societies, with 160 members; 1 Sabbath-school, with 40 members—a considerable number attend the white schools and churches.

We have but few mechanics, as many of our people follow the sea in the whaling business. We have 3 merchants, 5 house carpenters, 5 tailors, 4 blacksmiths, 3 coopers, 2 painters, 1 boot maker, 1 harness maker, 1 caulker, 1 whaling captain, 1 first mate, 2 second mates, 6 third mates, and a number of under officers. The ships generally carry from 25 to 30 men. The property owned by colored people, which is principally in real estate, amounts to upwards of 100,000 dollars, and gradually increasing. We have few in affluent circumstances.

EZRA R. JOHNSON.

All which is respectfully submitted.

JAS. N. GLOUCESTER,
THEO. S. WRIGHT,
WM. C. MUNRO,
A. H. FRANCIS,
W. H. YANCY,
S. TALBOT,
} *Committee.*

☞ The subscriber would here say, on behalf of the committee of publication, that the great delay in getting these proceedings before the public, has been wholly beyond their control. We were instructed to publish them so soon as the delegates should have furnished us with the money to meet the expense of publication; and we have been waiting for them to do so; but finally have had to issue them with but part of the money necessary to cover such expense. C. B. R.

PROCEEDINGS

OF THE

NATIONAL CONVENTION

OF

COLORED PEOPLE,

AND

THEIR FRIENDS,

HELD

IN TROY, N. Y.,

ON THE

6th, 7th, 8th and 9th OCTOBER, 1847.

———◆———

TROY, N. Y.
STEAM PRESS OF J. C. KNEELAND AND CO.
1847.

PROCEEDINGS.

THE Convention was called to order by H. H. Garnet, who read the call for the Convention, and moved that Peyton Harris, of Buffalo, be chosen President, pro tem. Wm. C. Nell, of Boston, and Charles Seth of Springfield, were appointed Secretaries.

The following list embraces the names of the Delegates appointed to the Convention :

New York—Henry H. Garnet, John Spence, Henry Morton, William Rich, James H. Gardner, L. Harper, Geo. W. Gordon, James H. Davis, William S. Baltimore, Littleton Becket, William G. Allen, Henry Brister, James McCune Smith, Charles B. Ray, Griffin Griffins, Enoch Moore, William H. Topp, Stephen Woods, John Harrison, George B. Wilson, Stephen Myers, Benjamin Cutter, Abraham Caldwell, A. Hooper, P. Farnum, Wm. Warren, James H. Henderson, H. W. Johnson, George Haggimore, Francis Thompson, Samuel Van Wranken, John Lyle, George H. Baltimore, Peyton Harris, Willis A. Hodges, Thomas Van Rensselaer, Alexander Crummell, R. H. Johnson, Moses A. Jackson, Wm. P. McIntyre, Lewis Jackson, William Meads, R. D. Kenny, Eli Hall, James Blair Webb, Charles Van Hoosen.

Massachusetts—William C. Nell, Frederick Douglass, Nathan Johnson, Benjamin Weeden, William W. Brown, Henry Watson, Leonard Collins, Charles C. Seth, James Mars, Othello Burghard, Samuel Smith, P. I. Schuyler, Thomas Thomas, Martin Thomas.

Pennsylvania—Z. P. Purnell.

Connecticut—J. W. C. Pennington, Amos G. Beman.

Vermont—Peter G. Smith.

Michigan—Lewis Hayden.

New Hampshire—J. Billings.

New Jersey—Samuel B. Hyers.

Kentucky—Andrew Jackson.

On motion of Alexander Crummell, a committee of five was nominated to report a list of officers of the Convention, viz:—Benjamin Weeden, Wm. W. Brown, Willis Hodges, Stephen Myers, Alex. Crummell.

At this stage of the proceedings, the question as to admitting persons as delegates, was debated. Some were in favor of the "largest liberty," others were for making restrictions ; the question was subsequently settled by the adoption of the following :—

Resolved, That all gentlemen present, who have come from places from which there is no regular appointed delegation to the Convention, be considered as delegates from those places, and that all other gentlemen be requested to take seats as honorary members.

On motion, the following committee was then appointed to draft rules for the Convention : H. H. Garnet, R. D. Kenny, William H. Topp.

The nominating committee reported as follows :

President—NATHAN JOHNSON, of New Bedford, Mass.

Vice-Presidents—J. W. C. Pennington, Hartford, Conn.,J. McCune Smith, New York, Peyton Harris, Buffalo, N. Y.

Secretaries—Wm. H. Topp, Albany, Wm. C. Nell, Boston, Mass., Chas. B. Ray, New York.

Which list was accepted and unanimously adopted.

The President elect took his seat, and the Convention joined in prayer, offered by Leonard Collins, of Springfield, Mass.

Mr. Garnet, from Committee on Rules, reported the following, for the government of the Convention.

RULES.

1. *Resolved,* That each session of the Convention be opened by addressing the Throne of Grace.

2. Upon the appearance of a quorum the President shall take the chair and call the Convention to order,

3. The minutes of the preceeding session shall be read at the opening of each session, at which time mistakes, if there be any, shall be corrected.

4. The President shall decide all questions of order subject to an appeal of the Convention.

5. All Motions and addresses shall be made to the President, the member rising from his seat.

6. All motions, except those of reference, shall be submitted in writing.

7. All Committees shall be appointed by the chair unless otherwise ordered by the Convention.

8. The previous question shall always be in order, and until decided shall preclude all amendment and debate, of the main question and shall be put in this form, "Shall the main question be now put."

9. No member shall be interrupted while speaking except when out of order, when he shall be called to order by or through the chair.

10. A motion to adjourn shall always be in order, and shall be decided without debate.

11. No member shall speak more than twice on the same question without the consent of the Convention, nor more than 15 minutes at each time.

12. No Resolution, except of reference, shall be offered to the Convention, except it come through the business Committee; but all resolutions rejected by the Committee may be presented directly to the Convention if the maker of such wishes to do so.

13. Sessions of the Convention shall commence at 9 o'clock, A. M., and 2 o'clock, P. M., and shall close at 1 o'clock, P. M., and at 6 o'clock P. M.

The Report accepted and the Rules adopted.

On motion, the following persons were appointed a committee, to prepare and report business for the Convention :—H. H. Garnet, C. B. Ray, Leonard Collins, Lewis Hayden, Willis Hodges.

On motion of C. B. Ray, a Roll committee was appointed by the chair, viz : Wm. P. McIntyre, Stephen Myers.

H. H. Garnet, on behalf of the business committee, presented a series of resolutions, Nos. 1, 2, 3, 4, 5, 6, 7, 8, 9, 10, which were accepted and Resolution No. 1 adopted, and a committee of two, on Agriculture, was accordingly appointed, viz :—C. B. Ray, Willis Hodges.

Resolution No. 2 was taken up and adopted, and a committee of three on Temperance, was appointed, viz :—S. Myers, J. W. C. Pennington, L. Collins.

Resolution No. 3, on "Universal Freedom" was taken up and warmly discussed by several; and an amendment by J. McCune Smith, viz : On the best means of abolishing Slavery and Caste in the United States, was adopted, and the following committee appointed :—Fred'k Douglass, Thos. Van Rensselaer, John Lyle, R. D. Kenny, Alex. Crummell.

Here Thos. Van Rensselaer moved that no members be designated by titles. Amended by J. Mc. Smith, " That the Secretaries obtain names of delegates in full, and omit titles."

On motion of W. W. Brown, to appoint a Finance Committee, the chair nominated W. W. Brown, Stephen Myers, Wm. S. Baltimore.

Resolution No. 4, on Commerce, was taken up and adopted, and the following were appointed a committee :—J. W. C. Pennington, W. C. Nell, R. D. Kenny, Peyton Harris, Chas. Seth.

Resolution No. 5, on Printing Press, &c., was taken up and adopted, and a committee of three was appointed, viz :—J. McCune Smith, Wm. H. Topp, G. B. Wilson.

Resolution No. 6, on Education, was also adopted, and a committee of three appointed, viz :—Alex. Crummell, J. McCune Smith, P. G. Smith.

Alex. Crummell here obtained leave to read a series of resolutions which was connected with the report subsequently submitted by him. The resolutions were received, and laid over for further consideration, and the Convention adjourned to 2 o'clock, P. M.

Convention called to order by the President   Prayer by H. H. Garnet.

The minutes not being ready to read, Thos. Van Rensselaer, of N. Y., in a few brief remarks laid the subject of a Bank before the Convention, to be established for the benefit of the colored people.

The minutes of the Morning Session were now read, corrected and adopted.

J. McCune Smith, on behalf of the committee upon the Printing Press, made a report, which was accepted, and on motion to adopt it, Thos. Van Rensselaer spoke at length against the adoption of the report, expressing fears that the undertaking was too great to be carried into successful operation.

C. B. Ray advocated the adoption of the report. Stephen Myers opposed the measure, if it contemplated establishing a new paper, to the embarrassment of those now in existence, but was in favor of merging the "Ram's Horn" and "National Watchman" in one, to be the National paper.

Andrew Jackson of Kentucky warmly advocated the adoption of the report as an organ of the Colored Americans.

Peyton Harris of Buffalo spoke in favor of Press, &c.

George Wilson advocated the report, was in favor of a National Paper established upon a firm basis.

Lewis Hayden doubted the propriety of establishing a National Press,—and wanted more light upon the subject before the report should be adopted.

H. H. Garnet advocated the adoption of the Report, and said, that the cause of freedom had so far advanced, that some method hitherto untried, needed to be resorted to   He believed that the most successful means which can be used for the overthrow of Slavery and Caste in this country, would be found in an able and well-conducted Press, solely under the control of the people of color.— He believed most religiously in the doctrine of self-help.   One of the poets had truly said,

> " Hereditary bondmen, know ye not,
> Who would be free, themselves must strike the blow ?"

The establishment of a National Printing Press would send terror into the ranks of our enemies, and encourage all our friends, whose friendship is greater than their selfishness. He had listened carefully to argument, in opposition to the measure, and was surprised to see the greatest amount of it came from editors, who are, or are to be. Of course there was nothing of selfishness in all this. With or without the sanction of the Convention, a Press would be established, by the help of God.

Frederick Douglass was opposed to the adoption of the Report, was in favor of a Press, but a National Press he was satisfied could not well be sustained. A Paper started as a National organ, would soon dwindle down to be the organ of a clique; it would in his opinion require a creed for the government of the Editor, in order to sustain a National Press. He was in favor of sustaining the "Ram's Horn, National Watchman, and Northern Star."

J. Mc. Cune Smith rose to support the Report and urged the necessity of having a Press, through which at any and all times the voice of the Colored People may be heard, and that a Press established upon the basis designed in the Report would prove an incalculable benefit in promoting our interest ; he instanced the fact, that in the recent struggle in Connecticut to obtain equal suffrage, the colored people of that State, were without the necessary means through which to make known and urge their claims,—whereas if this National Press were established—papers speaking forth our sentiments, making known the wrongs we suffer, and demanding the rights due to manhood could then be issued by *thousands*, where now there is none.

Willis Hodges spoke against the Report—to his mind it was clear that a National Press was not needed.

Mr. Collins was in favor of a National Organ—and wanted the combined influence of the leading men in New York, Philadelphia, and other chief Cities and towns, to be brought into action to sustain said organ.

Mr. Lyall advocated the adoption of the Report.

W. W. Brown doubted the practicability of sustaining a National Press. A National Press established by the colored people should be supported by them, and as reference had been made to the manner in which the "Liberator" was kept afloat, he asked, Would the colored people do by the National Press as well as the friends or supporters of the Liberator ? They put their hands into their pockets and give their *hundreds* of dollars; now he doubted the like being done by the colored people.

Mr. Alexander Crummell rose to enquire if the Report contemplated establishing a paper. Mr. Ray said the object of the Report did contemplate printing a paper, to be the National Organ, but it did not preclude the probability of making those papers now published that Organ. No war upon any paper need grow out of the Report. Mr. C. thought much " mist" had been thrown about the Report, and would like a few minutes to clear it up. Mr. C. obtained the floor. On motion the Convention, adjourned to hold an Evening Session, at 7 o'olock, at Morris Place Hall.

————

EVENING SESSION.

Convention called to order by Vice Pres't Pennington. Prayer by Mr. Schuyler, of Worcester. Singing a Liberty song. Minutes of the afternoon session were then read and approved.

On motion of W. W. Brown, it was resolved that at the hour of half-past eight o'clock all business of the Convention be suspended to allow the Finance Committee to use means to raise funds.

Mr. Crummell not being present to claim the floor, Thomas Van Rensselaer spoke at length in opposition to the Report. Having consumed his time an additional 10 minutes was allowed him by vote. F. Douglass again opposed the adoption of the Report. J. McCune Smith spoke at length in favor of the Report and was also voted an additional 10 minutes. Here the debate was suspended, the Chair having notified the Convention that the hour had arrived for the Finance Committee to act, and W. W. Brown made an appeal to the Convention and audience generally to aid in defraying the expenses of the Convention, and subsequently reported Eighteen Dollars collected.

Debate upon the Report resumed, and Willis Hodges opposed its adoption.

Alex. Crummell advocated its adoption; Leonard Collins in favor. R. H. Johnson spoke against the Report, asking the question, " Are we ready for a National Press?"

On motion of H. H. Garnet, the Convention adjourned to Thursday Morning, 9 o'clock, at Liberty street church.

SECOND DAY.

Thursday Morning, *Oct. 7th.*

Convention called to order by the President—Prayer by E. N. Hall. Minutes of last evening were read and approved. Discussion resumed on the "National Press," by Stephen Myers, who favored the Press, but not a National paper at present. Peyton Harris followed, in favor of the adoption of the Report. H. H. Garnet moved to lay the Report on the table until eleven o'clock—adopted.

Leonard Collins moved a re-consideration of the vote to lie over, and the motion prevailed, and A. G. Beman moved the previous question on the whole matter.

The Report being called for by several members, it was read by J. M. C. Smith. On motion of R. D. Kenney, the yeas and nays were called for, and the Report was adopted.

YEAS.

New York—H H Garnet, John C Spence, L Harper, Geo W Gordon, Wm S Baltimore, Littleton Becket, James H Henderson, Geo Haggimore, Samuel Van Wranken, John Lyle, Geo H Baltimore, Peyton Harris, Henry Brister, James McCune Smith, Alexander Crummell, Griffen Griffin—16.

Massachusetts—Henry Watson, Leonard Collins, Chas C Seth, James Mars, Othello Burghard, Samuel Smith, P J Schuyler, Martin Thomas, Thomas Thomas—9.

Connecticut—J W Pennington.—1.

New Jersey—Samuel B Hyers,—1. Total, 27.

NAYS.

New York—Willis A Hodges, Thos Van Rensselaer, Moses A Jackson, R H Johnson,—4.

Massachusetts—Wm C Nell, Benjamin Weeden—2.

Connecticut—Amos Gerry Beman,—1.

Michigan—Lewis Hayden—1. Total 9.

A. G. Beman was here appointed Secretary. A discussion arose relative to the appointing a " Home Agent," by A. Crummell and R. Johnson, and on motion, H. H. Garnet was elected Agent.

It was moved by James Mars, that one from each State be appointed to nominate a committee to establish said Press.

On this question an animated discussion occurred ; closed by J. McCune Smith offering the following : Whereas, the Convention has sanctioned the project of establishing a National Press, and that part of the Report which refers to the appointment of a National Press—Therefore,

Resolved, That so much of the Report on the Press as refers to the appointment of a Committee, (Sec. 2, 3, 4,) be referred to a Committee of seven, with power and authority to carry out the intention of the Convention in adopting said Report. Adopted, and the following were appointed the Committee, viz : J. M. C. Smith, N. Y., Z. P. Purnell, Pa., James Mars, Mass,, J. W. C. Pennington, Conn., Andrew Jackson, Ky., Leonard Collins, Mass., A. G. Beman, Conn.

W. W. Brown moved that each Delegate be taxed Twenty-five Cents, to meet the expenses of the Convention, and J. M. C. Smith called for a statement of the exact sum needed, and the receipts, &c., and offered the following as an amendment : *Resolved,* That each member be taxed the sum of One Dollar, to meet the expenses of the Convention, and for the printing the minutes thereof— and all members who desire, shall receive a sufficient number of copies, the sale of which may pay back said dollar.

H. H. Garnet stated the voluntary efforts of the Committee of Arrangements for the Convention, &c.

The amendment of Dr. Smith was, after some debate, adopted.

Alex. Crummell, from the committee on Education, reported, and on motion of B. Weeden the report was accepted, and the Convention adjourned to 2 o'-clock.

———

AFTERNOON SESSION.

Convention called to order by the President. Prayer by Mr. Schuyler. Proceedings of Morning Session were read and approved.

Thos. Van Rensselaer called for the reading of a portion of the Report on Education, which was complied with by A. Crummell, when the discussion was resumed—J. M. C. Smith and Mr. Van Rensselaer, in favor. H. H. Garnet in favor of Colored Academies, but did not see the necessity of Colored Colleges, because there were those to which colored youth could be admitted. Leonard Collins, Alex. Crummell, Z. P. Purnell and Peyton Harris, advocated the report, and Mr. Johnson opposed ; and on call for the yeas and nays, the report was a-dopted—yeas 26, nays 17, and the following committee was nominated to report the committee of Twenty-five: Alex. Crummell, S. Myers, T. Van Rensselaer, L. Collins, F. Douglass.

YEAS.

New York—John C Spence, William S Baltimore, Littleton Becket, James H Henderson, Geo Haggimore, Peyton Harris, Chas B Ray, Alexander Crummell, Griffen Griffins, William H Topp, Stephen Woods, Lewis Jackson, John Harrison, William Meads, Geo B Wilson, Eli N Hall, James Blair Webb, Abraham Caldwell, James McCune Smith—19.

Massachusetts—Leonard Collins, James Mars, Stephen Smith, Martin Thomas, P I Schuyler, Thomas Thomas.—6.

Pennsylvania—Z P Purnell—1.   Total 26.

NAYS.

New York—Henry H Garnet, H W Johnson, John Lyles, Thos Van Renselaer, R H Johnson, M A Jackson, R D Kenny, Stephen Myers, Chas Van Hoosen,—9.

Massachusetts—Wm C Nell, Frederick Douglass, Benjamin Weeden, Wm W. Brown, Henry Watson, Chas C Seth—6.

Connecticut—Amos G Beman—1.

Michigan—Lewis Hayden—1.   Total, 17.

The Business Committee reported the following:

Moved, That a committee of Five be appointed to report on the propriety, the mode, and the places of holding Annual National Conventions of the Colored People and their friends of these United States; amended by adding two in addition, and adopted by appointing R. D. Kenny, Benj. Weeden, Mass., L. Hayden, J. W. C. Pennington, Conn., F. Douglass, O., —— Henderson, N. Y., —— Hyers, N. J.

W. W. Brown moved that a committee of three be appointed to nominate persons to speak in the evening at Morris Hall, viz: S. Myers, Weeden, Johnson, who subsequently reported the following; Henry Highland Garnet, Fred. Douglass, Thos. Van Rensselaer, A. G. Beman, Alex. Crummell, J. W. C. Pennington. Adjourned to 7 o'clock, P. M.

EVENING MEETING.

Per announcement, a large audience assembled at Morris Hall. Commenced by singing the "Fugitive." Prayer by Leonard Collins. The Chairman invited attention to H. H. Garnet, who read an eloquent and impressive address to the Slaves of the United States. He was followed by other speakers, viz: A. G. Beman, Fred. Douglass and Alex. Crummell, whose several speeches were received with enthusiastic admiration.

W. W. Brown of the Finance Committee made an appeal and obtained a contribution.

Alex. Crummell moved the acceptance of the committee of Twenty-five on the "College," which motion was carried, viz: *Troy*—William Rich, *Albany*—Will.

liam H. Topp, Stephen Myers, Moses Jackson. *New York*—William A. Tyson, Charles L. Reason, James McCune Smith, George T. Downing, John J. Zuille, Albro Lyons, Samuel E. Cornish, Charles B. Ray, Alexander Crummell, Patrick H. Reason, N. B. Vidal, Christopher Rush, E. V. Clark. *Philadelphia*—Joseph Cassey, William Douglass, James J. G. Bias, Stephen Smith.

Adjourned to 9 o'clock, Friday, A. M.

THIRD DAY.

FRIDAY MORNING, *Oct.* 8*th*, 1847.

Convention called to order by the President. Prayer by A. G. Beman. Proceedings of last meeting were read and approved.

J. W. C. Pennington and Chas. Seth, urged the presentation of the report on Commerce.

H. H. Garnet moved that the Committee on Commerce now report, and that at 11 o'clock, A. M., the Committee on Convention submit their report—adopted.

J. W. C. Pennington, from the Committee on Commerce, reported, and spoke explanatory of objects therein suggested. Lewis Hayden moved acceptance—carried.

Here the President vacated his seat in favor of J. W. C. Pennington, Vice President, whereupon a vote of thanks, &c., was passed.

A. G. Beman moved to appoint a Committee of five, to report as suggested in the resolutions of Committee on Commerce—carried.

R. D. Kenney gave some commercial statistics, and the above Committee was augmented as follows, viz: J. W. C. Pennington, Nathan Johnson, Peyton Harris, W. C. Nell, R. D. Kenny, M. A. Jackson, A. G. Beman, Thos. Van Rensselaer, A. M. Sumner, H. H. Garnet, Alex. Thuey, Robert Barks.

Thomas Van Rensselaer called for the Report on Agriculture, which, with several Resolutions, was submitted by C. B. Ray for the Committee, and on motion was accepted.

S. Myers, from the Committee on Temperance, submitted the following as their Report: *Resolved*, That the subject of Temperance be referred to the Convention which is to be held at Great Barrington, July 7th, 1848, which was accepted.

R. D. Kenny, from Committee on Convention, reported *Cleveland, Ohio*, or *Newark, N. J.* Benj. Weeden moved that Newark be designated, which motion was discussed for and against by Stephen Myers, H. H. Garnet, R. D. Kenny, F. Douglass, Alex. Crummell and T. Van Rensselaer. R. H. Johnson moved that Rochester be substituted as an amendment. Several members claimed the floor, and calls for question were made. Leonard Collins obtained the right to speak, and moved PITTSBURGH as an amendment to the amendment. The vote was called for on the previous question, and resulted in the call for the amendment, Rochester, which was decided by Yeas, 12, Nays, 29—lost.

YEAS.

New York.—L. Harper, T. H. Henderson, George Haggimore, John Lyles, R H Johnson, L Jackson, C Van Hoosen,—7

Massachusetts—Wm H Brown, Henry Watson, P I Schuyler—3.

Michigan—Lewis Hayden—1.

Kentucky—Andrew Jackson—Total 12.

NAYS.

New York—Henry H Garnet, H Morton, Geo W Gorden, J H Davis, S Van Wranken, Peyton Harris, W A Hodges, Thos Van Rensselaer, Alex Crummell, E Moore, M A Jackson, Wm Meads, G B Wilson, R D Kenney, S Myers, B Cutter, J B Webb, John Spence—18.

Massachusetts—F Douglass, W C Nell, Nathan Johnson, Benj Wheeden, Chas C Seth, Saml Smith, Thos Thomas, Martin Thomas—8.

Connecticut—J W C Pennington, Amos G Beman—2.

New Jersey—S B Hyers—1. Total 29.

F. Douglass moved Cleveland as an amendment, and also called the previous question, which was decided by Yeas 18, Nays 19.

YEAS.

New York—Geo Haggimore, S Van Wranken, John Lyles, Peyton Harris, W N Hodges, Thos Van Rensselaer, M A Jackson, Lewis Jackson, Wm Meads, R D Kenney, B Cutter, J Spence—12.

Massachusetts—Frederick Douglass, Wm W Brown, Henry Watson, Thos Thomas, Martin Thomas—5.

Connecticut—A G Beman.

Michigan—Lewis Hayden. Total 19.

NAYS.

New York—H H Garnet, H Morton, Geo W Gordon, W S Baltimore, J H Henderson, Chas B Ray, Alex Crummell, R H Johnson, E Moore, Geo B Wilson, S Myers, J B Webb, C Van Hoosen—13.

Massachusetts—Nathan Johnson, Benj Wheeden, Wm C Nell, Leonard Collins, Saml Smith, P I Schuyler—6.

New Jersey—S B Hyers. Total 20.

The original motion on Newark, N. J., was then put and resulted thus: Ayes 25, Nays 14, and was decided to be the place for the next Convention

YEAS.

New York—H H Garnet, H Morton, L Harper, G W Gordon, W S Baltimore, J H Henderson, S Van Wranken, W A Hodges, Chas B Ray, Alexander Crummell, Wm Meads, Geo B Wilson, Stephen Myers, B Cutter, J B Webb, J Spence, E Moore—17.

Massachusetts—N Johnson, W C Nell, B Wheeden, Chas C Seth, Samuel Smith, P I Schuyler, Thos Thomas—7.

Connecticut—J W C Pennington. Total 25.

NAYS.

New York—Geo Haggimore, John Lyles, P Harris, Thos Van Rensselaer, R H Johnson, L Jackson, R D Kenny, C Van Hoosen—8.

Massachusetts—F Douglass, H Watson, M Thomas, W W Brown, L Collins—5

Michigan--L Hayden.

Kentucky—A Jackson. Total 15. And was decided to be the place for the next Convention; and Alexander Crummell moved that the 3rd Wednesday of September, 1848, be the time for said Convention, which motion prevailed.

A. G. Beman moved to appoint an Executive Committee of five, to be appointed by the President, to call said Convention. Adjourned to 9 o'clock, A. M.

AFTERNOON SESSION.

Convention called to order by the President. Prayer by C. B. Ray.

Minutes of morning session were read and approved.

On motion of A. G. Beman the report on Agriculture was taken up, and on motion for adoption, Stephen Myers, of Albany, advocated its adoption with the Resolutions.

C. B. Ray, of New York, spoke in favor of the recommendations embodied in the report.

Mr. Lyall was in favor of the third resolution attached to the report.

F. Douglass was fearful that the munificence of Mr. Smith would operate as an injury unless the lands bestowed by him be occupied, &c.; was in favor of immigration, and thought the best eulogium bestowed on Mr. Smith for his liberal donation would be by the owner of a lot going upon it and occupying it.

H. H. Garnet was also in favor of immigration, and urged all to go. The previous question being called for, the main question was put and the report adopted.

F. Douglass, on behalf of the committee upon the " Best means to Abolish Slavery and Caste in the United States," read the report, and was accepted and on motion for adoption, H. H. Garnet took exceptions to the phraseology in the report, " Sanctity of Religion," " Shedding of blood," " Moral Suasion."

Willis Hodges was opposed to the portion of the report relative to " Moral Suasion."

John C. Spence followed, giving his views as agreeing with the remarks of Mr. Garnet.

James H. Gardner, was opposed to moral suasion.

Mr. Beman moved to have the report referred back to the committee for modification. The report being called for was again read by Mr. Douglass, who gave some explanation.

Andrew Jackson rose to speak in favor of the report. It was here resolved to hold a meeting for business in the evening.

H. H. Garnet having the floor, the Chair announced the Committee to issue call for next Convention as follows: E. P. Rodgers, Newark, N. J., C. B. Ray,

New York, W. C. Nell, Boston, A. G. Beman New Haven, A. M. Sumner
Cincinnati, Ohio, and the Convention adjourned to 7 o'clock, P. M.

FRIDAY EVENING MEETING.

Called to order by V. P. Pennington. Singing Liberty song. Prayer by Mr.
Lyall. On motion, the reading the afternoon's proceedings was dispensed with,
and upon a call, the Report on Abolition &c. was again read by Mr. Douglass.

H. H. Garnet resumed his remarks, to shew the necessity of qualifying certain expressions contained in the Report, and urged so much as related to "*Religion sanctifying Slavery*," be amended by a substitute to read *Religion, falsely so called*. Another objectionable feature was the word "Moral Suasion,"
and was in favor of adding after Suasion and "Political action." His time having expired, it was voted to allow him to finish his remarks.

W. W. Brown advocated the Report and urged that Moral Suasion was needed in order to convince and convert the white people here in favor of abolishing
Slavery.

F. Douglass took the floor again to explain and advocate the Report.

A. G. Beman was in favor of adding "political action." [Mr. Beman while
on the floor made allusion to an article contained in a daily paper of Troy,
which article reflected quite severely upon the doings of the Convention, and
particularly upon some of his remarks made use of in his address the evening
previous, and appealed to the audience if such an attack was just. The response was one of indignation towards the writer of said article.]

Andrew Jackson resumed in favor of the Report, and upon call of previous
question a vote was taken and the Report was lost.

The Finance Committee reported $9 07 collected. On motion it was Re-
solved that this Convention adjourn *sine die* at 12 o'clock to-morrow (Saturday.)
Song, and adjourned to 9 o'clock A. M.

FOURTH DAY.   SATURDAY MORNING, OCT. 9.

Convention called to order by Vice Pres't Harris. Prayer by Mr. Spense, of
Troy, N. Y. Minutes of Friday afternoon and evening were read and ap-
proved, when H. H. Garnett, from the Business Committee, reported a series of
Resolutions numbering 7, 8, 9, 10; all of which were adopted.

The following Resolutions were submitted by ———— ————: "*Resolved*,
That the creation and permanent establishment of a Banking Institution by the
colored people of the United States is a measure which deserves the attention
of this Convention.

"*Resolved*, That a Committee of three be appointed by this Convention to
report on Banks and Banking Institutions."

Mr. A. Jackson moved to adopt them. Thomas Van Rensselaer spoke in
favor of a Banking Institution originating among the colored people of the U.
States, because they at present contribute to their own degradation by investing
capital in the hands of their "*enemies.*" Messrs. M. A. Jackson and W. C.

Nell were opposed to a Bank, and on motion of Thomas Van Rensselaer the resolutions were laid on the table to give way to a Reconsideration of the vote of last evening upon Mr. Douglass' Report. The vote was reconsidered, and A. G. Beman moved to a reference to a Committee of three. Messrs. Douglass, Johnson and Garnett, were appointed, and on motion two were added, Messrs. Van Rensselaer and Beman. Mr. Van Rensselaer here urged the necessity of continuing the Convention a day or two longer, that more important matters which were unfinished might be disposed of. The Bank question was now resumed. Willis Hodges was in favor of a Bank, established for the benefit of colored people. Several members here claimed the floor; the Chair decided in favor of Mr. Harris, and the decision of the Chair was appealed from, and the Chair was sustained. Mr. Peyton Harris proceeded at some length to advocate the establishment of a Bank.

On motion of A. G. Beman the vote to adjourn to-day at 12 o'clock was rescinded.

On motion of H. H. Garnett, A. G. Beman was elected a Vice President.

The Committee to whom the Report on Abolition &c. was recommitted, made the Report with corrections, which was accepted, and the Report and Resolutions were adopted unanimously, and in accordance a Committee of one, (F. Douglass) was appointed.

Mr. Lyall here spoke against the Bank Resolutions. W. C. Nell was opposed to establishing a Bank, unless it be shown that the colored people cannot have the benefit of Banks now in existence. Thos. Van Rensselaer continued in favor and was allowed 10 additional minutes. S. Myers opposed the Bank. H. H. Garnet opposed, and moved the whole matter lie on the table. Carried.

Business Committee here reported Resolutions 11, 12, 13, 14, 15, 16, 17. On motion No. 14 was adopted without debate. Nos. 11, 12 and 13 elicited quite a warm discussion by Messrs. Johnson and Myers and were adopted, and the Convention adjourned to 2½ o'clock.

AFTERNOON SESSION.

Meeting called to order by Vice Pres't Beman. Prayer by ——— ———
Proceedings of morning were read and approved.

Willis Hodges moved a reconsideration of the "Bank Question" and advocated its passage. Mr. Van Rensselaer remarked, "that we should be willing to yield to the force of circumstances and establish a Bank for the purpose of our own elevation, though it should not be exclusive," &c., &c. Samuel Smith, of Lee, and Mr. Garnet, of Troy, opposed. Upon question the Resolution was adopted and the following were appointed a Committee: Thomas Van Rensselaer, New York, Wm. H. Topp, Albany, Peyton Harris, Buffalo, to report at the next National Convention. A communication was here read by the Secretary from Lewis Putnam, Utica, N, Y.

Resolution 15 was now taken up. On motion to adopt, Lewis Hayden was in favor of the Resolution so to read as to include " the abettors of," as well as Slaveholders themselves. Mr. Spence, of Troy, opposed, on the ground that the object designed in the Resolution was not susceptible of doing any good, but rather the reverse. Peyton Harris objected to the passage of the Resolution. S. Myers was in favor. The Resolution was adopted,and a Committee of three was appointed to draft an Address to the Slaveholders, to report at the next Convention, consisting of H. H. Garnet, T. Van Rensselaer and A. G. Beman.

Resolution 17 was taken up and *lost.* M. A. Jackson moved to appoint a Committee of three to publish the Minutes of the Convention. H. H. Garnet, W. H. Topp and Thomas Van Rensselaer were appointed.

The Committee would recommend the appointment of the following Committees, to consist of as many persons as may be deemed sufficient.

    1. A Committee of 2 on Agriculture. Passed.

        A Committee of 4 on Religion. Laid over.

    2. A Committee of 3 on Temperance. Passed.

    3. A Committee of 3 on Universal Freedom. Amended, that a Committee of three be appointed to report on the best method of abolishing Slavery and Caste in the United States of America.

    4. A Committee of 5 on Commerce. Passed.

    5th *Moved,* That a Committee of three be appointed to report on the propriety of establishing a Printing Establishment and Press for the colored people of the United States. Passed.

    6. *Moved,* That a Committee of three be appointed to make a report on the state and wants of Educational privileges of the colored people in the United States. Passed.

    7. *Resolved,* That we return devout thanks to the Father of Mercies for the signal success which has followed the self-denying efforts of the friends of Freedom in the United States and throughout the civilized world.

    8. *Resolved,* That notwithstanding the numerous obstacles that lie in our upward road, and great opposition to our cause which everywhere meets us, yet, having our faith in God and his immutable truth, we solemnly pledge ourselves anew to be faithful to the interests of our enslaved brethren until death.

    9. *Resolved,* That we believe in the Church of God as established by his Son Jesus Christ, and that it never fails to evince its spirit by its opposition to all manner of sin, especially to that mother of abominations, Slavery ; and that those sects (falsely called Christian Churches) who tolerate Caste, and practice Slave holding, are nothing more than synagogues of Satan.

    10. *Resolved,* That the Declaration of American Independence is not a lie, and, if the fathers of the Revolution were not base and shameless hypocrites, it is evident that all men are created equal,and are endowed by their Creator with certain inalienable rights, among which are life, liberty and the pursuit of happiness.

11. *Resolved,* That in our judgment it is the duty of all men to abstain from the use of ardent spirits and from the traffic in it.

12. *Resolved,* That it is expedient that the friends of Temperance, without a thought of color, but as one man, unite our efforts to extend the principles of Temperance throughout the world.

13. *Resolved,* That the influence of Temperance on the intellectual elevation, the moral character, the social happiness and the future poospect of mankind, is such as ought to obtain for it the cordial approbation and the united vigorous and persevering effort of all the philanthropic and humane of every class and sex of the country.

14. *Resolved,* That this Convention earnestly urge the attention of our colored citizens and their friends to the duty of holding State Conventions in their several States, for the purpose of urging, morally and politically, upon the people of each State the duty of acknowledging and establishing all the rights which are withheld from them; likewise to consider all the local interests for their improvement or elevation.

15. *Resolved,* That this Convention make an Address to the Slaveholders in this country, and demand of them that they immediately let the slaves go free.

16. *Resolved,* That a Committee of three be appointed to carry the above Resolution into effect.

17. *Resolved,* That this Convention recommend to our people the propriety of instructing their sons in the art of war.

W. C. Nell offered the following Resolves which were passed:

Resolved, That our sincere thanks are hereby submitted to the Committee of Arrangements for having generously volunteered their efforts for the successful accommodation of Delegates to the Convention.

Resolved, That we tender our grateful acknowledgments to the friends at Troy for their agreeable contribution to our comfort while sojourning in their beautiful city.

Resolved, That we would also express our gratitude to the proprietors of Liberty Street Church for the gratuitous use of their house for the sittings of this Convention.

A Resolution was adopted recommending the "Ram's Horn," "National Watchman," "Northern Star," "Disfranchised American" and "The Mystery," as worthy the encouragement and support of the people.

The amount paid to the Publishing Committee was $34. They received the Minutes from the Secretaries on the 21st of October. The Minutes appear to be incomplete in some instances, but the Publishing Committee have strictly followed the manuscript placed in their hands.

Finance Committee reported $ collected; voted the balance, after paying Printing &c., to go to Committee on Publishing, and after a song the Convention adjourned *sine die.*

REPORT OF THE COMMITTEE ON A NATIONAL PRESS.

———

The Committee on a "*National Press and Printing Establishment for the People of Color*" made the following
REPORT,
on the importance and practicability of such an undertaking:

"It being admitted that the Colored People of the United States are pledged, before the world and in the face of Heaven, to struggle manfully for advancement in civil and social life, it is clear that our own efforts must mainly, if not entirely, produce such advancement. And if we are to advance by our own efforts, (under the Divine blessing,) we must use the means which will direct such efforts to a successful issue.

Of the means for the advancement of a people placed as we are, none are more available than a Press. We struggle against opinions. Our warfare lies in the field of thought. Glorious struggle! God-like warfare! In training our soldiers for the field, in marshaling our hosts for the fight, in leading the onset, and through the conflict, we need a Printing Press, because a printing press is the vehicle of thought—is a ruler of opinions.

Among ourselves we need a Press that shall keep us steadily alive to our responsibilities, which shall constantly point out the principles which should guide our conduct and our labors, which shall cheer us from one end of the land to the other, by recording our acts, our sufferings, our temporary defeats and our steadily approaching triumph—or rather the triumph of the glorious truth "Human Equality," whose servants and soldiers we are.

If a Press be not the most powerful means for our elevation, it is the most immediately necessary. Education of the intellect, of the will, and of character, is, doubtless, a powerful, perhaps the most powerful means for our advancement: yet a Press is needed to keep this very fact before the whole people, in order that all may constantly and unitedly labor in this, the right direction. It may be that some other means might seem even more effectual than education; even then a Press will be the more necessary, inasmuch as it will afford a field in which the relative importance of the various means may be discussed and settled in the hearing of the whole people, and to the profit of all.

The first step which will mark our certain advancement as a People, will be our Declaration of Independence from all aid except from God and our own souls. This step can only be taken when the minds of our people are thoroughly convinced of its necessity and importance. And such conviction can only be produced through a Press, which shall show that although we have labored long and earnestly, we have labored in too many directions and with too little concert of action; and that we must, as one man, bend our united efforts in the one right direction in order to advance.

We need a Press also as our Banner on the outer wall, that all who pass by may read why we struggle, how we struggle, and what we struggle for. If we convince the world that we are earnestly and resolutely striving for our own advancement, one half the battle will already be won, because well and rightly begun. Our friends will the more willingly help us ; our foes will quail, because they will have lost their best allies—our own inertness, carelessness, strifes and dependence upon others. And there is no way except through a Press—a National Press—that we can tell the world of our position in the path of Human Progress.

Let there be, then, in these United States, a Printing Press, a copious supply of type, a full and complete establishment, wholly controled by colored men; let the thinking writing-man, the compositors, pressman, printers' help, all, all be men of color;—then let there come from said establishment a weekly periodical and a quarterly periodical, edited as well as printed by colored men;—let this establishment be so well endowed as to be beyond the chances of temporary patronage; and then there will be a fixed fact, a rallying point, towards which the strong and the weak amongst us would look with confidence and hope; from which would flow a steady stream of comfort and exhortation to the weary strugglers, and of burning rebuke and overwhelming argument upon those who dare impede our way.

The time was when a great statesman exclaimed, "Give me the song-making of a people and I will rule that people." That time has passed away from our land, wherein the reason of the people must be assaulted and overcome : this can only be done through the Press. We have felt, and bitterly, the weight of odium and malignity wrought upon us by one or two prominent presses in this land: we have felt also the favorable feeling wrought in our behalf by the Anti-Slavery Press. But the amount of the hatred against us has been conventional antipathy, and of the favorable feeling has been human sympathy. Our friends sorrow with us, because, they say we are unfortunate! We must batter down those antipathies, we must command something manlier than sympathies. We must command the respect and admiration due men, who, against fearful odds, are struggling steadfastly for their rights. This can only be done through a Press of our own. It is needless to support these views with a glance at what the Press has done for the down-trodden among men; let us rather look forward with the determination of accomplishing, through this engine, an achievement more glorious than any yet accomplished. We lead the forlorn hope of Human Equality, let us tell of its onslaught on the battlements of hate and caste, let us record its triumph in a Press of our own.

In making these remarks, your Committee do not forget or underrate the good service done by the newspapers which have been, or are now, edited and published by our colored brethren. We are deeply alive to the talent, the energy and perseverance, which these papers manifest on the part of their self-sacrificing conductors. But these papers have been, and are, a matter of serious pecuniary loss to their proprietors; and as the proprietors are always poor men, their papers have been jeoparded, or stopped for the want of capital. The history of *our* newspapers is the strongest argument in favor of the establishment of a Press. These papers abundantly prove that we have all the talent and industry requisite to conduct a paper such as we need; and they prove also, that among 500,000 free people of color no one man is yet set apart with a competence for the purpose of advocating with the pen our cause and the cause of our brethren in chains. It is an imposition upon the noble-minded colored editors, it is a libel upon us as a free and thinking people, that we have hitherto made no effort to establish a Press on a foundation so broad and national that it may support one literary man of color and an office of colored compositors.

The importance and necessity of a National Press, your Committee trust, are abundantly manifest.

The following plan, adopted by the Committee of seven, appointed by the Convention with full power, is in the place of the Propositions proposed by the Committee of three.

1st. There shall be an Executive of eleven persons, to be denominated the Executive Committee on the National Press for the Free Colored People of the United States, viz:

2nd. *Massachusetts*—Leonard Collins, James Mars; *Connecticut*—Amos G. Beman, James W. C. Pennington; *Kentucky*—Andrew Jackson; *New York*—J. McCune Smith, Chas. B. Ray, Alex. Crummell; *New Jersey*—E. P.

Rogers; *Pennsylvania*—Andrew Purnell, George B. Vachon; of which Committee James McCune Smith, of New York, shall be Chairman, and Amos G. Beman, of Connecticut, Secretary.

3d. The members of this Committee residing in the city of New York shall be a Financial Committee, who shall deposite, in trust for the Executive Committee, in the "New York Seaman's Bank for Savings," all the funds received by them from the Agents.

4th. No disposition shall be made of the funds by any less than a two-thirds majority of the whole Committee.

5th. The Committee shall hold stated meetings once in six months, and shall then publish an account of their proceedings, the receipts, and from whom all sums are sent to them by the Agents.

6th. The Rev. J. W. C. Pennington, of Connecticut, shall be the Foreign Agent of the National Press; and the Agents shall always be ex-officio members of the Committee.

7th. The remuneration of the Home Agent shall be 20 per cent.; of the Foreign Agent 30 per cent., on collections made.

8th. The meetings of the Committee shall take place in the city of New York.

9th. The Agents shall report and remit to the Committee, at least once a month for the Home, and once in two months for the Foreign Agent.

10th. Members of the Committee, from any two States, may call an extra meeting thereof by giving the Chairman and Secretary thirty days notice.

Respectfully submitted,

J. Mc'CUNE SMITH,
G. B. WILSON,
WM. H. TOPP.

REPORT OF THE COMMITTEE ON COMMERCE.

The Committee on Commerce, on meeting to take into consideration the subject assigned them, found in the possession of one of their number a document which seems to them to be so immediately connected with the subject, that they agree to have it read.

By the mysterious providence of God, we find that captivity has dispersed our race far and wide. Long years of darkness, imbecility and slavery, have been our portion. But God hath appointed us unto restoration. For princes shall come out of Egypt, and Ethiopia shall soon stretch forth her hands unto God. We bless and praise Jehovah's name that he ever liveth to carry out his own counsels of judgment and mercy. To this island of Jamaica, he hath been especially gracious. He hath brought to our shores the inestimable boon of Freedom, and opened before us a career of glory that is sufficient to animate and inspire the most apathetic and deadened soul. What hath the Eternal here wrought? He hath conferred upon us the blessings of free institutions, and the gift of a country, in the most endearing sense of that term. We are the great body of the people. We have a climate which seems made for us, and we for the climate. Surely, "the lines have fallen unto us in pleasant places, and we have a goodly heritage." The price by which great things may be obtained is in our hands, and our only desire is that it may be used wisely and for the best of purposes. But to make our advantages of the best possible avail, we need encouragement and co-operation from our brethren and friends throughout the world. Lend us your prayers and your sympathies, and we *stipulate on our part, that the great experiment which is now in progress for the elevation of our long injured race, shall be thoroughly successful and satisfactory in its results.* It is our blessing, notwithstanding hitherto it has not been in our power to turn it to the best account, that we are surrounded by similar moral and political institutions, and speak a language the same as that spoken by the great body of our brethren in America, and friends in other parts of the world. In this we are afforded great facilities for correspondence. We also possess a goodly number of churches and chapels and schools, such as our present circumstances might be thought to admit of. In these institutions no caste distinctions are tolerated. Our civil and political advancement is, upon the whole, encouraging. In the jury box, in the magistracy, in the municipal corporations and the Legislature, we are rapidly filling our places. But in one respect our progress does not keep pace with our general advancement. In the Commerce of the country we have no proportionate share. Now the relation existing between us and our brethren of North America, is one of mutual sympathy and co-operation in all that pertains to the general welfare of the race, and your co-operation with us, is in nothing more demanded than in *Commercial enterprise.* In this island our people constitute phatically the market, and in America abound those commodities which are in the greatest demand amongst us. There is already commercial intercourse, existing to some extent, between the two countries. But in whose hands, whether in America, or on this island, is this important department of national prosperity? In the hands of the friends, or the foes, of the advancement of the African race? Is the influence which it gives, exerted for, or against us? We fear that with few exceptions these interrogatories must be answered in the negative. This state of things ought no longer to continue. Did we possess a body of merchants in America, and a correspondent body in Jamaica, impressed with that indelible type which is the peculiar characteristic of the African race, we cannot mistake the vast amount of good that would be accomplished on all sides. White Americans visiting our ports, and having to transact business, for the most part, with men of our hue, would be found ere long to have acquired more humane and rational views of our race. They would stand rebuked as regards the prejudice and oppression which evil minded men are ever disposed to invoke against us and to inflict upon us.— They would return from our shores with more favorable impressions, and the re-action upon North American slavery would be irresistibly great. Unite the most repulsive of mankind in enlightened commercial intercourse, and their antagonism will be found to lose its edge, and the feelings of civility and politeness succeed to its place.

Commerce is the great lever by which modern Europe has been elevated from a state of barbarism and social degradation, whose parallel is only to be found in the present condition of the African race—to the position which she now so proudly occupies. Commerce ever has been the great means by which the Jews, her ancient people, have been able to preserve their national existence. To Commerce, America owes her present importance, and we, too, if we would acquire any very great influence for good, must join in the march of Commerce. With the means which Commerce supplies, enlightenment can be carried forward, religious and philanthropic institutions sustained, and the natural resources which God has caused to be buried in the bosom of the soil, may be successfully developed, and made to contribute their quota to universal happiness, which is calculated to bind all mankind in one common brotherhood.

To our white Anti-slavery friends, we would convey our deep and abiding sense of the cordial interests which they have manifested in our advancement. We would at the same time express our regret that in their cursory visits among us, they seem to have quite overlooked the absence of commercial engagements among our class. We solicit their co-operation in rendering us at once an intelligent community, and the West Indies shall become the great nursery from which may be obtained those best suited, from their peculiar constitution, to carry the blessings of Religion, Agriculture and Commerce to the very heart of Africa. We believe the Niger Expedition to have been perfectly feasible, and failed only from the want of associating with it a sufficient number of intelligent and God-fearing men of the African race. May our Anti-slavery friends then feel the importance of engaging our people, both here and in America, in the pursuit of a healthy and vigorous Commerce. This will give us energy of character, and fit us for embarking in the most arduous enterprises for the rescue of suffering humanity. May God move their hearts to assist us in such a manner as we may best assist ourselves.

To carry out these views we have availed ourselves of the opportunity which is presented in the visit of Mr. Pennington to our island, to organize a society to be called the Jamaica Hamic Association. The object of this Society is to effect a correspondence with our brethren in America, and friends throughout the world. We solicit your hearty concurrence with us in these measures as we are anxious to engage our race, and friends, universally, in some common effort for the extinction of slavery and the elevation of our people, and engage them in Commerce throughout the wide range of our dispersion ; and Agriculture in our fatherland will place within our reach the means of successfully competing with slavery on the one hand, of disarming prejudice on the other, and at the same time of promoting that charitable feeling which everywhere and under all circumstances characterize the christian. A movement of this kind would be indeed the harbinger of better times, and a dawn of that glorious day when the lion shall lie down with the lamb, and they shall no more hurt nor harm in all the holy mountain of the Lord.

Committee—EDWARD VICARS, President ; Peter Constantine, George Ennis, Vice Presidents; Peter Jallep, James Millington, Secretaries ; George Reily, Treasurer ; Robert Duaney, Teller, &c., &c.

Kingston, Jamaica, April 28th, 1846.

Resolved, That we hail with great pleasure the courteous proposal from our brethren in the island of Jamaica to open a friendly correspondence with us.

Resolved, That we cordially respond to the sentiments contained in the address of the Jamaica Hamic Association, believing as we do that a more intimate acquaintance with our brethren in those islands will be of mutual benefit and advantage.

Resolved, That a committee of thirteen be appointed to reply to the address of the Jamaica Hamic Association, and that said committee be instructed to express to our brethren our cordial sympathy and readiness to unite with them in any proper measures for the advancement of our common cause.

Signed—J. W. C. Pennington, Randall D. Kenney, W. C. Nell, P. Harris, Charles Seth.

Resolved, That the committee of West India Correspondence be, and they are hereby, instructed to report their correspondence to the next Annual Convention.

The following committee was appointed by the Convention, in accordance with the recommendation of the Report : *Connecticut*, J. W. C. Pennington, A. G. Beman ; *New York*, R. D. Kenney, T. Van Rensselaer, George Hogarth, Peyton Harris, Henry H. Garnet, Nathan Johnson ; *Massachusetts*, Moses Jackson, Wm. C. Nell ; *Ohio*, A. M. Sumner ; *Michigan*, Robt. Banks ; *Nassau, N. P.*, Alex. Theuy.

REPORT OF THE COMMITTEE ON AGRICULTURE.

Your Committee to whom was referred the subject of Agriculture, regret that they have not had time so fully to consider the subject as its importance demands ; they beg leave, however, to submit the following reflections.

By Agriculture, is meant the cultivation and improvement of the soil, with everything intimately connected therewith, such as the cultivation of fruit, the raising of flocks, herds, &c.

This subject is beginning now to take its proper rank among the great questions of the civilized world. More than formerly, it is receiving a portion, at least, of the attention it demands, as well in Europe as in this country, from men in the first conditions of life, both as respects literature and wealth. And well it may, for it was the primitive pursuit of life, the calling of earth's first born ones, the mode of subsistence and happiness prescribed by God himself, therefore the true mode by which to live, the best mode. When God made this earth, he intended to people it with man, as well as to make it the abode of beast. It was, therefore, as necessary to provide some thing, as well as some place, upon which to subsist. God, therefore, who understood the wants of man and beast, and best how to supply them, made the earth of the composition of which it is, that it might yield food for man and food for beast. And when he said, "In the sweat of thy face shalt thou eat bread," he meant, that by man's labor should he eat bread. And it is equally evident, that that labor was to be expended in procuring from the earth a subsistence. Your Committee have made these remarks, from their convictions that an Agricultural life was *the* life intended for man to pursue. If so, then it is among the most happy and honorable of pursuits.

The great aim of the masses of mankind, in this life, is to be placed in easy circumstances, or beyond want, prospective as well as present. Towards this point they bend all their efforts, it is the great absorbing theme that engrosses all their thoughts and attention. Or if to be placed beyond want for the future, as well as the present, be not the absorbing theme with man, then what shall we eat, or what shall we drink, and wherewithal shall we be clothed, is the question. When man is thus provided for, or has the means by which, in ordinary cases, he is certain thus to be provided for; if he does not regard himself in easy circumstances, all his anxieties and cares for the future, vanish away.

The question now is, what pursuit in life is best adapted to place man in the circumstances in which it is his highest aim to be placed, viz : freedom from undue care and anxiety about the necssaries and comforts of life. Your Committee, without hesitation, reply, that the cultivation of the soil, of which man is himself the owner, is the very pursuit best adapted to accomplish this end. For the man who owns his farm and devotes his time to cultivate it, to planting and sowing, to the raising of fruits and flocks and herds, with a congenial sun and refreshing showers, will, after a few months, when cometh the harvest, reap and gather into barns, food for the supply of his own wants and the wants of his beasts. And if, at seed time, he has laid his plans accordingly, he will, in ordinary cases, have something to dispose of to meet such wants, as the products of his farm, directly, do not meet. If the earth should yield but sparingly, the producer thereof will have the first supply ; if any be in want, it must be him who produces not.

The wants of man, in most cases, are more of the imaginary than real. The imaginary wants, what men would have if they could, occupy the thoughts and the attention, much more than they pain the heart. It is the real wants that cause solicitude, anxieties and pain. Now, the pursuit of Agriculture, will, in all ordinary cases, produce wherewith to meet the real wants of life, and in most cases do even more. In fact, it is the only pursuit in which a man has so many reasons to expect that the reward of his hands will be given him. For harvest, as well as seed time, is sure to come. The liabilities also, to a failure, in this pursuit, are less than in others. The pursuit of Agriculture, then, is the surest road for man to place himself in easy circumstances, or beyond want.

The farmer is an *independent man ;* the man of no other pursuit is so much so. He may do without what men of trade and traffic have to dispose of, and upon the disposal of which, depends their very living ; but they cannot do without what he produces. To him they must come for the very things upon which human existence, under God, is absolutely dependent. Without him, they have neither house, home, food, nor clothing. They must have the bread he produces, the cotton, the flax, and the wool he grows. They must have the timber from his forest, the clay from his bed for brick, the sugar from his grove, his beet, or his cane. They must have the silk from the worm he nurses, and the covering for the feet even, from the back of the herds and the flocks he raises. Yea, the very articles in which they trade and traffic, are the fruit of the farmer's toil. If he toil not, then they trade and' traffic not. The great staples of the commerce of the world, are either directly or indirectly the products of the farm. Let the farmer cease his toil, or toil only to supply his own wants; let him produce for himself alone, and not for others, and our merchants must close their shops ; our ships must lie moored at their respective docks; our manufactories must cease the hum of the spindle, and the loom, and the millions of operatives must scatter themselves whither they will. Our cities, too, must become desolate, and the capital of the world of nothing worth. The converse of this, it is true, is the state of the civilized world ; but it is because the agriculturalist toils on, producing what he can, and the earth yields sufficiently, through his skill, for him who toils, and for him who toils not. The surplus beyond the wants of the producer is converted into articles of trade, and the merchant buys, sells, ships and gets gain, and commerce and trade flourish.

An agricultural life is productive of moral, mental and physical culture. The farmer levels the forest, shatters and cleaves the rock in sunder, and tills the soil, which God's own hands have made ; and when he climbs the mountain, even to the clouds, or enters the forest, or surveys the plain ; when his eye glances upon the waving grass and grain, upon the thrifty corn, he sees the order, the variety, the beauty, and the wonders of nature, and must be led to look from nature up to nature's God, to love and admire the wisdom, the goodness, and the power of God, as thus displayed, and be made a better man.

But an agricultural life is evidently the employment designed by God for man ; it must be adapted to his whole nature, mental and physical, as well as moral, and conduce therefore to the growth of the mind. An agricultural pursuit is peculiarly adapted to, and promotive of, scientific pursuits. It may very naturally lead to the study of the structure and composition of the various earths, rocks and minerals, of which the earth is composed, and of the vegetables which she produces. The Agriculturist may then become the better geologist, mineralogist and botanist, because aided in the study of these sciences by the very employment he follows, and that too, without interfering scarcely at all with that employment. It must, then, produce mental culture. And the very nature of the employment calls into exercise the muscles and the physical powers of the body, and must conduce to physical culture and to health.

But an Agricultural life is open to all, and the things that obstruct other modes of life do not obstruct this. And if it be the road to competency, to independence and to easy circumstances, and if, in addition thereto, it is conducive to moral, mental, and physical culture, then ought it to be resorted to by our own people. For from all, or nearly all, the other pursuits in life, which lead to easy circumstances, we are deprived, or have not the means to embark therein, to compete with those long skilled in these pursuits and having capital adapted thereto. But we live in a country yet comparatively in its infancy, and most of which is an unbroken wilderness, with a temperate climate, and where land is both cheap and productive. And there is no barrier to the purchase of the soil by our people in any part of the country where it is desirable to seek a home. And if we may not, from the peculiar circumstances in our case, be men of other pursuits, we may become, if we will, Agriculturalists, and be independent and happy. Besides, the farmer's life is adapted to our pecuniary circumstances and condition. To commence a business, in the business part of the country, which would yield, in ordinary cases, a competency, would require a capital much larger than the most of us possess. But a few dollars, comparatively, will purchase a farm sufficiently large to afford a comfortable subsistence, at the outset; will provide the necessary implements of husbandry, and at the same time be the most productive investment that can be made of small sums of money. For every stroke of the ax, every furrow of the plow, and every rod that is cultivated, while it meets the current wants, will be adding improvements and increasing the value of the farm. He may not have money as men in other pursuits have, he does not need it as they do; they are dependent upon their money for the necessaries of life, he has them without money and without price. But though he has not the money they have, the very means by which he lives adds annually to the value of his farm, and he is becoming every year a wealthier man.

An Agricultural life also tends to equality in life. The community is a community of farmers. Their occupations are the same; their hopes and interests the same; they occupy a similar position in society; the one is not above the other, whether of the proscribed or any other class, they are all alike farmers. And as it is by placing men in the same position in society that all castes fade away, all castes in this case will be forgotten, and an equality of rights, interests and privileges only exist. An Agricultural life then is the life for a proscribed class to pursue, because it tends to break down all proscriptions.

Your Committee cannot close these suggestions without refering to the beneficent act of GERRIT SMITH, Esq., which has opened the way to our people to the farmers life. They refer to it also because they wish to urge those possessed of these advantages to use them, as well from the influence it will exert upon others as for the benefit that will result to themselves. Your Committee think they see in this beneficent act of Mr. Smith's, a Divine Providence directing our people to this mode of life as well as opening the way to it. They regard this as a God-send, which, like other gifts of God, is not to be slighted, but used and not abused; and which, if used, will give to us a character, a name and a place among the people of earth, useful to ourselves, gratifying to the donor and honorable to God. For here we have put into our hands, without money and without price, the means to place us in independent and happy circumstances. And we believe that the destiny of our people now hangs upon the use to be made of this gift by those to whom it is given, as much as upon any one thing that presents itself to our consideration. That, if this land shall be settled and improved, and the wilderness made to bud and blossom as the rose, as bud and blossom it may, by its now present owners, that they will work for themselves a character and create an influence that shall command the respect for themselves and their brethren, of those who now very little respect us; that will stop the mouths of those who speak slightly of us, and will exert an influence upon our brethren who have not shared in those gifts, to turn their attention to and engage in the pursuit of Agricultural life.

Your Committee, aware that this gift of land by Mr. Smith concerns the people of the State of New York directly, have, nevertheless, referred to it here, with the hope that the Convention will pass the Resolutions in reference to this matter herewith submitted, both to evince our appreciation of those gifts, and to express our high regard for the donor, as well as to exert some influence upon those in possession of these lands to go and cultivate them. We also submit a resolution recommending our people generally to become Agriculturalists, as the life easiest of access to them.

Whereas, GERRIT SMITH, of Peterboro, has made a donation of One Hundred and Forty Thousand acres of land, to Three Thousand Colored Citizens of New York; and,

Whereas, This Convention regards the above donation as a manifestation of love on the part of the donor; a love for God, in carrying out the Divine intention to grant to all a share in the means of subsistence and happiness; a love for humanity, in seeking the down-trodden and oppressed among men as the objects of this donation, and a love of human progress in placing in the hands of the oppressed the means of self-elevation; and,

Whereas, The freedom, independence and steadiness of the farmer's life will throw among the colored people elements of character essential to happiness and progress; Therefore,

Resolved, That this Convention do express its deep thanks to Gerrit Smith, of Peterboro, for his splendid donation to the cause of God and humanity.

Resolved, That this Convention do call upon the Grantees of this land to forsake the cities and towns and settle upon this land and cultivate it, and hereby build a tower of strength for themselves.

Resolved, That we recommend to our people, also, throughout the country, to forsake the cities and their employments of dependency therein, and emigrate to those parts of the country where land is cheap, and become cultivators of the soil, as the surest road to respectability and influence.

Resolved, That a copy of the preamble and these resolutions that refer to the gift of Mr. Smith, be signed by the President and Secretary of this Convention, and transmitted to him at Peterboro.

All which is respectfully submitted,

CHARLES B. RAY,
WILLIS A. HODGES.

REPORT OF THE COMMITTEE ON ABOLITION.

The Committee appointed to draft a Report respecting the best means of abolishing Slavery and destroying Caste in the United States, beg leave most respec fully to Report : That they have had the important subjects referred to them, under consideration, and have carefully endeavored to examine all their points and bearings to the best of their ability; and from every view they have been able to take they have arrived at the conclusion that the best means of abolishing slavery is proclamation of truth. and that the best means of destroying caste is the mental, moral and industrial improvement of our people.

First, as respects Slavery. Your Committee find this monstrous crime, this stupendous iniquity. closely interwoven with all the great interests. institutions and organizato s of the country ; pervading and influencing every class and grade of society, securing their support, obtaining their approbation. and commanding their homage. Availing itself of the advantage which age gives to crime, it has perverted the judgment, blunted the moral sense, blasted the sympathies,and created in the great mass,---the overwhelming majority of the people---a moral sentiment altogether favorable to its own character, and its own continuance. Press and pulpit are alike prostituted,and made to serve the end of this infernal institution. The power of the government, and the sanctity of religion. church and state,are joined with the guilty oppressor against the oppressed---and the voice of this great nation is thundering in the ear of our enslaved fellow countrymen the terrible fiat, *you shall be slaves or die !* The slave is in the minority, a small minority. The oppressors are an overwhelming majority. The oppressed are three millions. their oppressors are seventeen millions. The one is weak, the other is strong ; the one is without arms, without means of concert, and without government ; the other possess every advantage in these respects; and the deadly aim of their million of musketry, and loud-mouthed cannon tells the down-trodden slave in unmistakable language, *he must be a slave or die.* In these circumstances, your committee are called upon to report as to the best means of abolishing slavery. And without pretending to discuss all the ways which have been suggested from time to time by various parties. and factions, though did time permit. they would gladly do so, they beg at once to state their entire disapprobation of any plan of emancipation involving a resort to bloodshed. With the facts of our condition before us. it is impossible for us to con emplate any appeal to the slave to take vengence on his guilty master, but with the utmost reprobation Your Committee regard any counsel of this sort as the perfection of folly, suicidal in the extreme, and abominably wicked. We should utterly frown down and wholly discountenance any attempt to lead our people to confide in brute force as a reformatory instrumentality. All argument put forth in favor of insurrection and bloodshed. however well intended, is either the result of an unpardonable impatience or an atheistic want of faith in the power of truth as a means of regenerating and reforming the world. Again we repeat, let us set our faces against all such absurd. unavailing, dangerous and mischievous ravings. emanating from what source they may. The voice of God and of common sense, equally point out a more excellent way, and that way is a faithful, earnest, and persevering enforcement of the great principles of justice and morality,religion and humanity. These are the only invincible and infallible means within our reach with which to overthrow this foul system of blood and ruin. Your Committee deem it susceptible of the clearest demonstration, that slavery exists in this country, because the people of this country WILL its existence. And they deem it equally clear, that no system or institution can exist for an hour against the earnestly-expressed WILL of the people. It were quite easy to bring to the support of the foregoing proposition powerful and conclusive illustrations from the history of reform in all ages, and especially in our own. But the palpable truths of the propositions, as well as the familiarity of the facts illustrating them, entirely obviate such a necessity.

Our age is an age of great discoveries; and one of the greatest is that which revealed that this world is to be ruled, shaped and guided by the *marvelous might of mind*. The human voice must supersede the roar of cannon. Truth alone is the legitimate antidote of falsehood. Liberty is always sufficient to grapple with tyranny. Free speech—free discussion—peaceful agitation,—the foolishness of preaching these, under God, will subvert this giant crime, and send it reeling to its grave, as if smitten by a voice from the throne of God. Slavery exists because it is popular. It will cease to exist when it is made unpopular. Whatever therefore tends to make Slavery unpopular tends to its destruction. This every Slaveholder knows full well, and hence his opposition to all discussion of the subject. It is an evidence of intense feeling of alarm, when John C. Calhoun calls upon the North to put down what he is pleased to term "this plundering agitation." Let us give the Slaveholder what he most dislikes. Let us expose his crimes and his foul abominations. He is reputable and must be made disreputable. He must be regarded as a moral leper—shunned as a loathsome wretch—outlawed from Christian communion, and from social respectability—an enemy of God and man, to be execrated by the community till he shall repent of his foul crimes, and give proof of his sincerity by breaking every chain and letting the oppressed go free. Let us invoke the Press and appeal to the pulpit to deal out the righteous denunciations of heaven against oppression, fraud and wrong, and the desire of our hearts will soon be given us in the triumph of Liberty throughout all the land.

As to the second topic upon which the Committee have been instructed to report, the Committee think the subject worthy of a far wider range of discussion than the limited time at present allotted to them will allow. The importance of the subject, the peculiar position of our people, the variety of interests involved with questions growing out of it, all serve to make this subject one of great complexity as well as solemn interest.

Your Committee would therefore respectfully recommend the appointment of a Committee of one, whose duty it shall be to draft a full Report on this subject, and report at the next National Convention.

Your Committee would further recommend the adoption of the following Resolutions as embodying the sentiments of the foregoing Report:

Resolved, That our only hope for peaceful Emancipation in this land is based on a firm, devoted, and unceasing assertion of our rights, and a full, free and determined exposure of our multiplied wrongs.

Resolved, That, in the language of inspired wisdom, there shall be no peace to the wicked, and that this guilty nation shall have no peace, and that we will do all that we can to *agitate!* AGITATE !! AGITATE !!! till our rights are restored and our Brethren are redeemed from their cruel chains.

All of which is respectfully submitted,
FREDERICK DOUGLASS,   JOHN LYLE,
ALEXANDER CRUMMELL.   THOS. VAN RENSSELAER.

REPORT

OF

THE PROCEEDINGS

OF THE

COLORED NATIONAL CONVENTION,

HELD AT CLEVELAND, OHIO,

On WEDNESDAY, SEPTEMBER 6, 1848.

ROCHESTER:

PRINTED BY JOHN DICK, AT THE NORTH STAR OFFICE.

1848.

REPORT

~~~~~

The Delegates of the National Convention of Colored Free-men, met in the Court House, Cleveland, O., Wednesday, September 6th, 1848, 10 o'clock, A. M.

On motion of D. Jenkins of Ohio, Abner H. Francis of N. Y., was called to the chair, and William H. Burnham, of Ohio, appointed Secretary.

. The enrolling of Delegates was here gone through with, and on motion, a committee of five on organization was appointed by the Chair, viz :—J. Jones, of Ill., F. Douglass, of N. Y., Henry Bibb, of Mich., C. H. Langston and J. L. Watson, of Ohio. The Committee reported :

For President,

FREDERICK DOUGLASS, of New York.

For Vice President,

J. JONES, of Illinois.

For Secretary,

WILLIAM H. DAY, of Ohio.

The report of the Committee was adopted, and the Convention added as Vice Presidents, one from each State represented, viz:—Allen Jones, of Ohio, Thomas Johnson, of Michigan, and Abner H. Francis, of New York.

For Assistant Secretaries,

William H. Burnham and Justin Holland, of Ohio.

A Business Committee of seven was hen appointed. A point of order was here raised by A. H. Francis, of N. Y., as to appointing and rejecting gentlemen from the Committee who were not regular delegates, which was settled by passing a resolution, saying, that all colored persons present or who might be present were delegates, and were expected to participate as such.

The Business Committee, consisted of the following persons:—Chairman, M. R. Delany, M. D., New York; C. H. Langston, and D. Jenkins, Ohio; H. Bibb, and G. W. Tucker,

Mich; W. H. Topp, New York, and Thomas Brown, Ohio; and on motion two were added to that Committee, viz:—J. L. Watson, and J. Malvin, of Ohio.

On motion, a Committee on Rules for the government of the Convention was appointed—D. Jenkins, of Ohio, Chairman.

Also, Committee on Finance, G. W. Tucker, of Michigan, Chairman.

The President was conducted to the chair by A. H. Francis, and after an able address from the President and the appointing of the above Committees, the Convention adjourned to 2 1-2 o'clock, P. M.

Wednesday, 2 1-2 o'clock, P. M., Second Session.

The Convention met, President in the Chair. After some remarks of the President as to the requisites to good order, the Business Committee not being ready to report, opportunity was given for a volunteer speech or song. The time not being taken up, the President sang with applause, a liberty song.— Mr. Allan Jones, of Ohio, spoke of the object of the Convention, and followed with a narrative of his slave-life. He said he had earned for his master $10,000, and after he had paid for his liberty, $360, and yet some people would say he was " not able to take care of himself."

The Committee on Rules here reported, and after the discussion of proposed amendment, the Report as 'a whole was adopted. Messrs. Cox and Day, were here called out to sing a Liberty song.

F. Douglass then offered the following resolution: — That this Convention commends the conduct of Capt. Sayres and Mr. Dayton, in their noble attempt to rescue from cruel bondage 76 of our brethren in the Capital of this Republic, and that we deeply sympathise with them in their present unjust and atrocious imprisonment. F. Douglass made a few remarks in its support. A. H. Francis, of N. Y., made a few remarks on an article in the " Cleveland Plaindealer,"abusive of Bibb and the Buffalo Convention, asserting that the article was false in fact and cringing to prejudice in principle. Henry Lott supported the resolution. Frederick Douglass followed, speaking of the principle involved, namely, the morality of running away. After remarks in accordance with the invitation of the President by Messrs. Patterson, Fitzgerald, Lewis, J. M. Langston, Watson, of Oberlin, and Jones, of Ill., the Business Committee reported a portion of the Declaration of Principles [See Resolutions 1, 5.]

The Pledge to sustain, was changed in its position so as to come after the Resolutions, and the Preamble laid on the table for the purpose of first considering the Resolutions, of which the 1st was passed. The 2d, was taken up and earnestly sustained by Dr. Delany. W. H. Day, here obtained the floor, when the President announced that the hour of adjournment had arrived, whereupon the Convention adjourned.

A crowded public meeting was held in the evening at the Court House. The exercises were conducted by Messrs. Douglass, Bibb, and Delany, and the enthusiastic cheering showed how well the sentiments were received.

Thursday, 9 o'clock, A. M.   Third Session.

Convention was called to order by the President. Prayer by the Rev, John, Lyle of N. Y.

The names of Delegates not present and who had not been present in person but by credentials, were on motion struck out from the Roll. The minutes of the previous Session were then approved.

William H. Day having the floor, offered an amendment to the 2d, Resolution, namely, to insert the words, "and professional"—which amendment was adopted.

J. D. Patterson, here obtained the floor to object to some expressions used by M. R. Delany in discussing the 2d, Resolution. He argued that those who were in the editorial chair and others, not in places of servants, must not cast slurs upon those, who were in such places from necessity. He said, we know our position and feel it; but when he heard the Doctor say, that he would rather receive a telegraphic despatch that his wife and two children had fallen victims to a loathsome disease, than to hear that they had become the servants of any man, he thought that he must speak.

Dr. Delany replied: He meant not, nor did the Resolution mean to cast a slur upon any individual, and presenting in a strong light the Resolution and its reasonableness, closed with a hope, that his brother (Patterson,) had been convinced, as he took him to be a minister, or student for the ministry—and ministers exert great influence.

John L. Watson, of Cleveland, O., remarked that we were aiming at the same thing, but he had a different way of getting at it. He understood Dr. Delany, as having, the day before, said, that if we became the boot-blacks, the white mechanics would look down on us, but if we became mechanics, etc., they would respect us. To this he took exceptions.

The President suggested that the discussion had taken a desultory turn, and that it would be best to keep to the question.

After remarks by several gentlemen, D. Jenkins moved the previous question, was sustained, and the 2d Resolution adopted. The 3d Resolution adopted also.

The 4th Resolution was read, and J. L. Watson remarked upon it. A. H. Francis, of N. Y., heartily supported the Resolution. He might, he said, relate an experience. He had been in nearly all the avocations named in the Resolution; he had been waiter, etc., and he had been in a mercantile business of $20,000 or $30,000 a year, and was in mercantile business now. He felt that we ought to take a stand in favor of the Resolution.

David Jenkins, of Ohio, was in favor of the Resolution.— He was a painter in the city of Columbus, and although, when first he went there he was not employed by others, he went to work and employed himself, and was there yet. He had succeeded in obtaining contracts from the State and County in which he resides.

Frederick Douglass took the floor. He thought that as far as speakers intimated that any useful labor was degrading, they were wrong. He would suggest a Resolution so as to suit both parties, which he thought might be done. He had been a chimney-sweep, and was probably the first that had ever made the announcement from the public stand. He had been a wood-sawyer. He wished not that it should stand thus: — White Lawyer—Black Chimney-sweep; but White Lawyer, Black Lawyer, as in Massachusetts; White Domestic, Black Domestic. He said: Let us say what is necessary to be done, is honorable to do; and leave situations in which we are considered degraded, as soon as necessity ceases.

He was followed by several gentlemen, when Messrs. Patterson, Copeland and Douglass, severally proposed amendments, which were on motion rejected.

The 4th Resolution was adopted with but one dissenting vote.

The Business Committee reported the remainder of the Declaration of Principles. [See Resolutions 6, 10.] The 5th Resolution unanimously adopted.

The 6th Resolution was referred to a Committee of five— Henry Bibb, Chairman. The 7th Resolution was adopted. The 8th Resolution was under discussion when the Convention's hour of adjournment arrived.

Thursday, 2 1-2 o'clock P. M. Fourth Session.

Convention met, President Douglass in the Chair. Prayer by J. D. Patterson. Report of morning session read, corrected and approved, and Convention resumed the consideration of the 8th Resolution.

William H. Topp, of N. Y., was opposed to this Resolution passing, for the reason, first, that he wished to do nothing that would commit himself against the Buffalo nomination, for he intended to give his support and influence to Mr. Van Buren, but all who voted in favor of the Resolution would, to be consistent, be compelled to oppose the Buffalo nominees.

Henry Bibb defended the entire equality position of the Buffalo Convention. J. D. Patterson agreed with Mr. Bibb.

Mr. Day, of Ohio, rose to a point of order, as to the propriety of discussing the merits of the Buffalo Platform, under this Resolution.

The President decided that strictly the point of order would obtain, but as he supposed gentlemen to be giving reasons for not supporting the Resolution, as they were in favor of the Van Buren Platform, he thought they might proceed. Mr. Patterson proceeded, and was soon called to order by the President for not speaking to the Resolution under consideration.

While this was pending, and after earnest remarks by various gentlemen, the Business Committee presented Resolutions 13—23 for the consideration of the Convention.

Resolution No. 8 was then adopted; Nos. 9 and 10 adopted.

A Committee of five was here appointed to prepare an Address to the Colored People of the United States—that Committee to report to this Convention.

Eleventh resolution taken up and adopted. F. Douglass was appointed the Committee to carry out the spirit of the 11th resolution. Resolution No. 21, with reference to time of final adjournment, was on motion here taken up and adopted.

Twelfth resolution taken up, and after earnest remarks in its favor, adopted.

The 13th Resolution, referring to the Buffalo nominations, was on motion laid over till morning. 14th adopted. Resolution 15th was read, and the word "necessary" was substituted for the word "justifiable," and the Resolution as amended was adopted; when the Convention adjourned.

Thusday evening, the Public Meeting was held in the Tabernacle, which was more than filled at an early hour; and when at the close the audience joined in singing "Come join the Abolitionists," and sent up three hearty cheers for "Liberty — Equality — Fraternity, " the slaveocrat must have trembled.

Friday, 9 o'clock A. M.   Fifth Session.

Convention was called to order by Vice-President Jones, of Illinois.   Prayer by Rev. Mr. Kenyon, of Cleveland.

The 13th Resolution was then taken up.   Messrs. Francis, of N. Y , Brown and Jenkins, of Ohio, and Lightfoot, of Mich., spoke in its favor.   C. H. Langston thought the 8th and 13th Resolutions conflicted, and was opposed to this Convention's saying that the Buffalo Convention had for its object entire equality.   He was in favor of the new movement, but would not be so inconsistent as to pass this while the other was on the records.   The 13th, on motion, was laid on the table, for the sake of rescinding the 8th,   The 8th was rescinded, and the 13th again taken up.   After remarks by many gentlemen, the Committee on the Address reported that they had met, and each had proposed a written abstract of what such an address should be, and that the Committee had appointed one of their number from the various abstracts to put together an address.   F. Douglass here read the substance of the different abstracts, that the Convention might know the substance of the address.   The action of the Committee was approved.

M. R. Delany here proposed a substitute for the 8th Resolution, as follows:

Resolved, That we recommend to our brethren throughout the several States, to support such persons and parties alone as have a tendency to enhance the liberty of the colored people of the United States.

This substitute was adopted, and on motion the 13th Resolution was adopted also.

William H. Day, Frederick Douglass, John Lyle, Sabram Cox, Richard Copeland, and W. B. Depp, asked permission to enter their dissent from the vote endorsing the 13th Resolution on the minutes.

The 14th resolution was so amended as to read, " to obtain their liberty," instead of the words, " effecting their escape," as it was thought that the slave *might* need to use some other means for liberty than running away.

Resolution 16 adopted.   The 17th Resolution was read, when F. Douglass took the floor in opposition to the preamble, inasmuch as it intimated that slavery could not be abolished by moral means alone.   Henry Bibb sustained the preamble and resolutions at length.   Frederick Douglass replied.

J. Jones, of Ill., here proposed nn amendment to the preamble, as follows:

Whereas, American slavery is politically, as well as morally, an evil of which this country stands guilty; and whereas, the two great political parties of the Union have, by their acts and nominations, betrayed the sacred cause of human freedom; and "whereas a Convention," &c., which was accepted, and the preamble, as amended, prefixed to the 13th Resolution.

The Secretaries were instructed to prepare a synopsis of the proceedings of the Convention, and forward it to Mr. Harris, Editor of the Cleveland Herald, and to the Editors of the North Star, as they had said they would be happy to publish them free of charge. H. G. Turner, Editor of the Cleveland True Democrat made a similar proposal.

It was also resolved to print 500 copies of the proceedings in pamphlet form, and the Secretaries were appointed a Committee of publication.

Convention then adjourned.

Friday, P. M., 2 1-2 o'clock. Sixth Session.

Convention assembled, Vice-President Jones in the Chair.

Prayer by Rev. William Ruth, of Colchester, C. W.

The 11th Rule was suspended, and 5 minutes voted as the allotted time for speakers. No. 19 was called up for reading.

When Frederick Douglass appeared and Dr. Delany asked that the President might now have the attention of the Convention as he was to leave at three o'clock, and had a few parting words to give.

The President's valedictory was able, eloquent and earnest, and a vote of thanks was passed by acclamation. [See Resolution, No. 20.]

No. 49, on motion, was recommended to the consideration of the people of the United States.

22d Resolution being the next in order, was on motion laid on the table. The 23d Resolution was about to be amended so as to pass a vote of thanks to the Sheriff having charge of the Court House, and to all the citizens of Cleveland for their hospitality, etc., as well as to Judge Andrews and the Cleveland Bar, when A. H. Francis, who with his lady had just returned from the Steamboat Saratoga, and had brought back with him Frederick Douglass, proposed that the resolution should read, "to all the citizens of Cleveland *excepting one!*" He proceeded to state a fact. He went on the steamboat Saratoga, was asking for a cabin passage, was refused by the Clerk, whon a gentleman, (God forbid, he would not say gentleman,) a —— some one in the audience said —— thing —— in the shape of a colored man, interfered, telling him that it was of no use for him to try to obtain a cabin passage on those boats, and intimating that colored men had no business in the cabin.

The Resolution as amended was adopted, and another as follows :

That Alexander Bowman of the Steamboat Saratoga and resident of Cleveland, receive the burning reprobation of this Convention, until he repents.

And he did receive it, if a unanimous shout against him is any evidence of it. He was fairly ostracised.

Messrs. J. L. Watson, J. Malvin and J. Lott, were appointed committee to inform the parties in each resolution, of the action of the Convention.

Dr. Delany, from the Business Committee reported on Nos. 23, 24, 25, 26, 28, and 28. Nos. 24 and 25 passed.

The Rules were then suspended, to hear two resolutions presented by Elder Kenyon in behalf of the citizens of Cleveland, and moved their adoption by O. D. O'Brien. They were adopted, as follows, the citizens of Cleveland only voting on them:

Resolved, That we hail as an omen of vast good to the colored people of this entire nation, the present Convention held in this city; and that with such examples of intelligence, eloquence, wit, and power of argument, as have been presented before us in the sentiments and speeches of the various members of said Convention, we are confident of the ultimate elevation of the colored population, to all the social, intellectual, civil and religious rights and immunities, of a republican and Christian country.

Resolved, That we bid a hearty God-speed to these our brethren, the sons of Africa, and citizens of America, in all well-directed and legitimate efforts to secure for themselves an honorable and elevated position amongst men.

No. 26, as amended, adopted; 27 adopted also. No. 28 taken up, but was almost immediately laid on the table. No. 30 adopted.

No. 29 as amended was adopted, as also Nos. 31 and 32.— The preamble to the Declaration of Principles was here taken from the table and adopted.

On motion of G. W. Tucker, No. 22 was taken up, and after earnest discussion indefinitely postponed. No. 3 was here presented by M. R. Delany, as it had been rejected by the committee. G. W. Tucker moved its indefinite postponement.

The Rule was here suspended, and the time of adjournment extended to 7 o'clock. After an animated discussion upon the indefinite postponement, the Rules were suspended to hear remarks from a lady who wished to say something on the subject of the Rights of Woman. The President then introduced to the audience, Mrs. Sanford, who made some eloquent remarks, of which the following is a specimen:

"From the birth-day of Eve, the then prototype of woman's destiny, to the flash of the star of Bethlehem, she had been the slave of power and passion. If raised by courage and ambition to the proud trial of heroism, she was still the marred model of her first innocence; if thrown by beauty into the ordeal of temptation, man lost his own dignity in contemning her intellectual weight, and refusing the right to exercise her moral powers; if led by inclination to the penitential life of a recluse, the celestial effulgence of a virtuous innocence was lost, and she only lived out woman's degradation!

"But the day of her regeneration dawned. The Son of God had chosen a mother from among the daughters of Eve! A Saviour, who could have come into this a God-man, ready to act, to suffer, and be crucified, came in the helplessness of infancy, for woman to cherish and direct. Her *exaltation was consummated!* * * * * * * *

"True, we ask for the Elective Franchise; for right of property in the marriage covenant, whether earned or bequeathed. True, we pray to co-operate in making the laws we obey; but it is not to domineer, to dictate or assume. We ask it, for it is a right granted by a higher disposer of human events than man. We pray for it now, for there are duties around us, and we weep at our inability.

"And to the delegates, officers, people and spirit of this Convention, I would say, God speed you in your efforts for elevation and freedom; stop not; shrink not; look not back, till you have justly secured an *unqualified citizenship of the United States, and those inalienable rights granted you by an impartial Creator.*"

Convention passed a vote of thanks to Mrs. Sanford, and also requested a synopsis of her, from which the above are extracts.

A vote of thanks was here passed to John M. Sterling, Esq., of Cleveland, for the presentation of a bundle of books entitled "Slavery as it is."

Discussion was resumed on the indefinite postponement of the Resolution as to Woman's Right. Objection was made to the resolution, and in favor of its postponement, by Messrs. Langston and Day, on the ground that we had passed one similar, making all colored persons present, delegates to this Convention, and they considered *women persons.*

Frederick Douglass moved to amend the 33d Resolution, by saying that the word persons used in the resolution designating delegates, be understood to include *woman*. On the call for the previous question, the Resolution was not indefinitely postponed. Mr. Douglass' amendment was seconded and carried, with three cheers for woman's rights.

No. 34 was passed.

The whole of the 6th Resolution was referred to the next National Convention.

The National Central Committee appointed was—

FREDERICK DOUGLASS, N. Y.   CHARLES H. LANGSTON, O.
J. JONES, Illinois,   HENRY BIBB, Michigan,
J. G. BRITTON, Indiana,   JOHN PECK, Pennsylvania,
GEORGE DAY, Wisconsin,   J. P. HILTON, Mass.,
            JOSIAH CONVILLE, New Jersey.

On inquiry, it was found that the Convention was composed of Printers, Carpenters, Blacksmiths, Shoemakers, Engineer, Dentist, Gunsmiths, Editors, Tailors, Merchants, Wheelrights, Painters, Farmers, Physicians, Plasterers, Masons, Students, Clergymen, Barbers and Hair Dressers, Laborers, Coopers, Livery Stable Keepers, Bath House Keepers, Grocery Keepers.

At 7 o'clock, the Convention adjourned *sine die*, with three cheers for Elevation—Liberty—Equality, and Fraternity.

Resolutions, &c., presented to the National Convention of Colored Freemen by the Business Committee.

DECLARATION OF SENTIMENTS.

Whereas, in the present position of the Colored people in the United States of North America, they, as a class, are known to the country and the intelligent world alone as menials and domestics or servants ; and

Whereas, it is apparent, as the history of the world, both ancient and modern, will testify, that no people thus conditioned, from the Conventional order of society, can attain an equality with the dominant class ; and

Whereas, an equality of persons cannot be claimed, where there is not an equality of attainments,—attainments establishing character, and character being that which is essentially necessary to make us equal to our white fellow-countrymen;—

Resolved, That the following Declaration of Principles we pledge ourselves to maintain and carry out among the colored people of the United States to the best of our ability.

1. Resolved, That we shall forever oppose every action, emanating from what source it may, whether civil, political, social or religious, in any manner derogatory to the universal equality of man.—Adopted.

2. Resolved, That whatever is necessary for the elevation of one class is necessary for the elevation of another; the respectable industrial occupations, as mechanical trades, farming or agriculture, mercantile and professional business, wealth and education, being necessary for the elevation of the whites; therefore those attainments are necessary for the elevation of us. Adopted.

3. Resolved, That we impressively recommend to our brethren throughout the country, the necessity of obtaining a knowledge of mechanical trade, farming, mercantile business, the learned professions, as well as the accumulation of wealth,—as the essential means of elevating us as a class.—Adopted.

4. Resolved, That the occupation of domestics and servants among our people is degrading to us as a class, and we deem it our bounden duty to discountenance such pursuits, except where necessity compels the person to resort thereto as a means of livelihood.

5. Resolved, That as Education is necessary in all departments, we recommend to our people, as far as in their power lies, to give their children especially, a business Education.

6. Resolved, That the better to unite and concentrate our efforts as a people, we recommend the formation of an association, to be known as the——. [Referred to a Committee, and subsequently the whole Resolution referred to the next Convention.]

7. Resolved, That while our efforts shall be entirely moral in their tendency, it is no less the duty of this Convention to take Cognizance of the Political action of our brethren, and recommend to them that course which shall best promote the cause of Liberty and Humanity.

8. Resolved, That we recommend to our brethren throughout the several states, to support no person or party, let the name or pretensions be what they may, that shall not have for their object the establishment of equal rights and privileges, without distinction of color, clime or condition.

9. Resolved, That holding Liberty paramount to all earthly considerations, we pledge ourselves, to resist properly, every attempt to infringe upon our rights.

10. Resolved, That Slavery is the greatest curse ever inflicted on man, being of hellish origin, the legitimate offspring of the Devil, and we therefore pledge ourselves, individually, to use all justifiable means for its speedy and immediate overthrow.

11. Whereas a knowledge of the real moral, social, and political condition of our people is not only desirable but absolutely essential to the intelligent prosecution of measures for our elevation and improvement, and whereas our present isolated condition makes the attainment of such knowledge exceedingly difficult, Therefore
Resolved, That this National Convention does hereby request the colored ministers and others persons throughout the Northern States, to collect, or cause to be collected accurate

statistics of the condition of our people, during the coming year, in the various stations and circuits in which they may find themselves located, and that they be, and hereby are requested to prepare lists, stating—

1st. The number of colored persons in the localities where they may be stationed; their general moral and social condition; and especially how many are farmers and mechanics, how many are merchants or storekeepers, how many are teachers, lawyers, doctors, ministers, and editors; how many are known to take and pay for newspapers; how many literary, debating, and other societies, for moral, mental, and social improvement; and that said ministers be, and hereby are, respectfully requested to forward all such information to a Committee of one, who shall be appointed for this purpose, and that the said Committee of one be requested to make out a synopsis of such information and to report the same to the next colored National Convention.

12. Resolved, That Temperance is another great lever for Elevation, which we would urge upon our people and all others to use, and earnestly recommend the formation of societies for its promotion.

13. Resolved, That while we heartily engage in recommending to our people the Free Soil movement, and the support of the Buffalo Convention, nevertheless we claim and are determined to maintain the higher standard and more liberal views which have heretofore characterized us as abolitionists.

14. Resolved, That as Liberty is a right inherent in man, and cannot be arrested without the most flagrant outrage, we recommend to our brethren in bonds, to embrace every favorable opportunity of effecting their escape,

15. Resolved, that we pledge ourselves individually, to use all justifiable means in aiding our enslaved brethren in escaping from the Southern Prison House of Bondage.

16. Resolved, that we recommend to the colored people every where, to use every just effort in getting their children into schools, in common with others in their several locations.

17. Whereas, American Slavery is politically and morally an evil of which this country stands guilty, and cannot be abolished alone through the instrumentality of moral suasion and whereas the two great political parties of the Union have by their acts and nominations betrayed the sacred cause of human freedom, and

Whereas, a Convention recently assembled in the city of Buffalo having for its object the establishment of a party in support of free soil for a free people, and Whereas said Convention adopted for its platform the following noble expression, viz; " Free Soil, Free Speech, Free Labor and Free Men," and believing these expressions well calculated to increase the interest now felt in behalf of the down-trodden and oppressed of this land; therefore,

Resolved, That we recommend to all colored persons in possession of the right of the elective Franchise, the nominees of that body for their suffrages, and earnestly request all good citizens to use their united efforts to secure their election to the chief offices in the gift of the people.

Resolved, that the great Free Soil Party of the United States, is bound together by a common sentiment expressing the wish of a large portion of the people of this Union, and that we hail with delight this great movement as the dawn of a bright and more auspicious day. [The Resolutions were rejected, but the Preamble prefixed to the 13th Resolution.]

18. Resolved, That Love to God and man, and Fidelity to ourselves ought to be the great motto which we will urge upon our people.

19. To the honorable members of the Convention of citizens of color of the United States of America, greeting. I beg leave to report for your consideration the result of my labors as an Agent to promote a project of home emigration to the State of Michigan. * * * I was appointed on October the 24th, in the year 1845 by an organization of gentlemen of color in the Vicinity of Lewis, Ohio. * * The object of my agency was to explore wild unsettled territory. * * I found large and fertile tracts of government land, in Kent and other counties, but in Oceana and Mason counties there are peculiar facilities, which do not present themselves in any of the other parts of the State which I have visited. Oceana and Mason are lake counties, with about sixty miles seaboard. There are navigable rivers emptying into Lake Michigan and affording at their mouths good harbors, delightful sites for cities and villages, also with hydraulic powers of every magnitude. Plenty of land ready for the plow at $1,25 per acre. Valuable Timber may be had here in abundance. Grass is now to be found from knee-high to the height of a man. The surface of the meadows is a deep vegetable mould, below which in many places are found beds of Lime. Fruit, Fish, and Game in abundance. Also, Salt Springs. Plaster of Paris has been discovered there. During the last spring a constant trade was kept up between these lands and Chicago, Milwaukee, and the ports on Lake Michigan. There are four sawmills in the two counties. Lumber is wanted at $7 per thousand on the lake shore. Shingles, shingle-bolts, staves, tan-bark, cedar posts, &c., all bring a liberal price, and demand Gold and Silver, and provisions during the season of navigation. I now submit the subject, &c., hoping that you will adopt some feasible plan to arouse our people to consider the importance of the same.
JEFFERSON FITZGERALD."

20. Resolved, That the thanks of this Convention be tendered to the President for the able and impartial manner in which he has presided over its deliberations.

21. Resolved, That this Convention adjourn *sine die* on Friday, Sept. 8th, 6 o'clock P. M.

22. Whereas, we find ourselves far behind the military tactics of the civilized world, therefore,

Resolved, That this Convention recommend to the Colored Freemen of North America to use every means in their power to obtain that science, so as to enable them to measure arms with assailants *without* and invaders within; therefore,

Resolved, That this Convention appoint Committees in the different States as Vigilant Committees, to organize as such where the same may be deemed practicable.

23. Resolved, That this Convention return their sincere thanks to Judge Andrews and the Bar of Cleveland, in adjourning the Court and tendering to us the use of the Court House for the sittings of the Convention. [See minutes.]

Resolved, That among the means instrumental in the elevation of a people there is none more effectual than a well-conducted and efficient newspaper; and believing the North Star, published and edited by Frederick Douglass and M. R. Delany at Rochester, fully to answer all the ends and puroses of a national press, we therefore recommend its support to the colored people throughout North America.

24. Resolved, That the Convention recommend to the colored citizens of the several Free States, to assemble in Mass State Conventions annually, and petition the Legislatures thereof to repeal the Black Laws, or all laws militating against the interests of colored people.

25. Whereas, we firmly believe with the Fathers of '76, that "taxation and representation ought to go together;" therefore,

Resolved, That we are very much in doubt as to the propriety of our paying any tax upon which representation is based, until we are permitted to be represented.

26. Resolved, That, as a body, the professed Christian American Chruches generally, by their support, defence, and participation in the damning sin of American Slavery, as well as cruel prejudice and proscription of the nominally free colored people, have forfeited every claim of confidence on our part, and therefore merit our severest reprobation.

27. Resolved, That Conventions of a similar character to this are well calculated to enhance the interests of suffering humanity, and the colored people generally, and that we recommend such assemblages to the favorable consideraion of our people.

28. Resolved, That the next National Convention of Colored Freemen shall be held in Detroit, Michigan, or at Pittsburgh, Pa., some time in the year 1850.

29. Resolved, That among the many oppressive schemes against the colored people in the United States, we view the American Colonization Society as the most deceptive and hypocritical—"clothed with the livery of heaven to serve the devil in, " with President Roberts, of Liberia, a colored man, for its leader.

30. Resolved, That we tender to the citizens of Cleveland our unfeigned thanks for the noble resolution passed by them in approval of the doings of this Convention.

31. Resolved, That the prejudice against color, so called,

is vulgar, unnatural, and wicked in the sight of God, and wholly unknown in any country where slavery does not exist.

32. Resolved, That while we are engaged in the elevation of our people, we claim it to be our duty to inquire of our public lecturers and agents an explanation in reference to the disbursement of funds they may have collected from time to time for public purposes.

33. Whereas, we fully believe in the equality of the sexes, therefore,

Resolved, That we hereby invite females hereafter to take part in our deliberations.

34. Whereas, a portion of those of our colored citizens called barbers, by refusing to treat colored men on equality with the whites, do encourage prejudice among the whites of the several States; therefore,

Resolved, That we recommend to this class of men a change in their course of action relative to us; and if this change is not immediately made, we consider them base serviles, worthy only of the condemnation, censure, and defamation of all lovers of liberty, equality, and right.

AN ADDRESS TO THE COLORED PEOPLE OF THE UNITED STATES.

FELLOW COUNTRYMEN :—

Under a solemn sense of duty, inspired by our relation to you as fellow sufferers under the multiplied and grievous wrongs to which we, as a people, are universally subjected,—we, a portion of your brethren, assembled in National Convention, at Cleveland, Ohio, take the liberty to address you on the subject of our mutual improvement and social elevation.

The condition of our variety of the human family, has long been cheerless, if not hopeless, in this country. The doctrine perseveringly proclaimed in high places in church and state, that it is impossible for colored men to rise from ignorance and debasement, to intelligence and respectability in this country, has made a deep impression upon the public mind generally, and is not without its effect upon us. Under this gloomy doctrine, many of us have sunk under the pall of despondency, and are making no effort to relieve ourselves, and have no heart to assist others. It is from this despond that we would deliver you. It is from this slumber we would rouse you. The present, is a period of activity and hope. The heavens above us are bright, and much of the darkness that overshadowed us has passed away. We can deal in the language of brilliant encouragement, and speak of success with certainty. That our condition has been gradually improving, is evident to all, and that we shall yet stand on a common platform with our fellow-countrymen, in respect to political and social rights, is certain. The spirit of the age—the voice of inspiration—the deep longings of the human soul—the conflict of right with wrong—the upward tendency of the oppressed throughout the world, abound with evidence, complete and ample, of the final triumph of right over wrong, of freedom over slavery, and equality over caste. To doubt this, is to forget the past, and blind our eyes to the present, as well as to deny and oppose the great law of progress, written out by the hand of God on the human soul.

Great changes for the better have taken place and are still taking place. The last ten years have witnessed a mighty change in the estimate in which we as a people are regarded, both in this and other lands. England has given liberty to nearly one million, and France has emancipated three hundred thousand of our brethren, and our own country shakes with the agitation of our rights. Ten or twelve years ago, an educated colored man was regarded as a curiosity, and the thought of a colored man as an author, editor, lawyer or doctor, had scarce been conceived.— Such, thank Heaven, is no longer the case. There are now those among us, whom we are not ashamed to regard as gentlemen and scholars, and who are acknowledged to be such, by many of the most learned and respectable in our land. Mountains of prejudice have been removed, and truth and light are dispelling the error and darkness of ages. The time was, when we trembled in the presence of a white man, and dared not assert, or even ask for our rights, but would be guided, directed, and governed. in any way we were demanded, without ever stopping to inquire whether we were right or wrong. We were not only slaves, but our ignorance made us willing slaves. Many of us uttered complaints against the faithful abolitionists, for the broad assertion of our rights; thought they went too far, and were only making our condition worse. This sentiment has nearly ceased to reign in the dark abodes of our hearts ; we begin to see our wrongs as clearly, and comprehend our rights as fully, and as well as our white countrymen. This is a sign of progress ; and evidence which cannot be gainsaid. It would be easy to present in this connection, a glowing comparison of our past with our present condition, showing that while the former was dark and dreary, the present is full of light and hope. It would be easy to draw a picture of our present achievements, and erect upon it a glorious future.

But, fellow-countrymen, it is not so much our purpose to cheer you by the progress we have already made, as it is to stimulate you to still higher attainments. We have done much, but there is much more to be done. While we have undoubtedly great cause to thank God, and take courage for the hopeful changes which have taken place in our condition, we are not without cause to mourn over the sad condition which we yet occupy. We are yet the most oppressed people in the world. In the Southern States of this Union, we are held as slaves. All over that wide region our paths are marked with blood. Our backs are yet scarred by the lash, and our souls are yet dark under the pall of slavery. Our sisters are sold for purposes of pollution, and our brethren are sold in the market, with beasts of burden. Shut up in the prison-house of bondage— denied all rights, and deprived of all privileges, we are blotted from the page of human existence, and placed beyond the limits of human regard. DEATH, moral DEATH, has palsied our souls in that quarter, and we are a murdered people.

In the Northern states, we are not slaves to individuals, not personal slaves, yet in many respects we are the slaves of the community. We are, howeve ', far enough removed from the actual condition of the slave to make us largely responsible for their continued enslavement, or their speedy deliverance from chains. For in the proportion which we shall rise in the scale of human improvement, in that proportion do we augment the probabilities of a speedy emancipation of our enslaved fellow-countrymen. It is more than a mere figure of speech to say, that we are as a people, chained together. We are one people—one in general complexion, one in a common degradation, one in popular estimation.— As one rises, all must rise, and as one falls all must fall. Having now, our feet on the rock of freedom, we must drag our brethren from the slimy depths of slavery, ignorance, and ruin. Every one of us should be ashamed to consider himself free, while his brother is a slave. The wrongs of our brethren, should be our constant theme. There should be no time too precious, no calling too holy, no place too sacred, to make room for this cause. We should not only feel it to be the cause of humanity, but the cause of christianity, and fit work for men and angels. We ask you to devote yourselves to this cause, as one of the first, and most successful means of self improvement. In the careful study of it, you will learn your own rights, and comprehend your own responsibilities, and, scan through the vista of coming time, your high, and God-appointed destiny. Many of the brightest and best of our number, have become such by their devotion to this cause, and the society of white abolitionists. The latter have been willing to make themselves of no reputation for our sake, and in return, let us show ourselves worthy of their zeal and devotion. Attend Anti-slavery meetings, show that you are interested in the subject, that you hate slavery, and love those who are laboring for its overthrow. Act with white Abolition societies wherever you can, and where you cannot, get up societies among yourselves, but without exclusiveness. It will be a long time before we gain all our rights ; and although it may seem to conflict with our views of human brotherhood, we shall undoubtedly for many years be compelled to have institutions of a complexional character, in order to attain this very idea of human brotherhood. We would, however, advise our brethren to occupy memberships and stations among white persons, and in white institutions, just so fast as our rights are secured to us.

Never refuse to act with a white society or institution because it is white, or a black one, because it is black ; but act with all men without distinction of color. By so acting, we shall find many opportunities for removing prejudices and establishing the rights of all men.— We say, avail yourselves of *white* institutions, not because they are white, but because they afford a more convenient means of improvement. But we pass from these suggestions, to others which may be deemed more important. In the Convention that now addresses you, there has been much said on the subject of labor, and especially those departments of it, with which we as a class have been long identified. You will see by the resolutions there adopted on that subject, that the Convention regarded those employments, though right in themselves, as being, nevertheless, degrading to us as a class, and therefore, counsel you to abandon them as speedily as possible, and to seek what are called the more respectable employments. While the Convention do not inculcate the doctrine that any kind of needful toil is in itself dishonorable, or that colored persons are to be exempt from what are called menial employments, they do mean to say that such employments have been so long and universally filled by colored men, as to become a badge of degradation, in that it has established the conviction that colored men are only fit for such employments. We therefore advise you, by all means, to cease from such employments, as far as practicable, by pressing into others. Try to get your sons into mechanical trades ; press them into the blacksmith's shop, the machine shop, the joiner's shop, the wheelwright's shop, the cooper's shop, and the tailor's shop.

Every blow of the sledge-hammer, wielded by a sable arm, is a powerful blow in support of our cause. Every colored mechanic, is by virtue of circumstances, an elevator of his race. Every house built by black men, is a strong tower against the allied hosts of prejudice. It is impossible for us to attach too much importance to this aspect of the subject. Trades are important. Wherever a man may be thrown by misfortune, if he has in his hands a useful trade, he is useful to his fellow-man, and will be esteemed accordingly; and of all men in the world who need trades, we are the most needy.

Understand this, that independence is an essential condition of respectability. To be dependent, is to be degraded. Men may indeed pity us, but they cannot respect us. We do not mean that we can become entirely independent of all men ; that would be absurd and impossible, in the social state. But we mean that we must become equally independent with other members of the community. That other members of the community shall be as dependent upon us, as we upon them. That such is not now the case, is too plain to need an argument. The houses we live in are built by white men—the clothes we wear are made by white tailors—the hats on our heads are made by white hatters, and the shoes on our feet are made by white shoe-makers, and the food that we eat, is raised and cultivated by white men. Now it is impossible that we should ever be respected as a people, while we are so universally and completely dependent upon white men for the necessaries of life. We must make white persons as dependent upon us, as we are upon them.— This cannot be done while we are found only in two or three kinds of employments, and those employments have their foundation chiefly, if not entirely, in the pride and indolence of the white people. Sterner necessities, will bring higher respect.

The fact is, we must not merely make the white man dependent upon us to shave him, but to feed him; not merely dependent upon us to black his boots, but to make them. A man is only in a small degree dependent on us, when he only needs his boots blacked, or his carpet-bag carried; as a little less pride, and a little more industry on his part, may enable him to dispense with our services entirely. As wise men it becomes us to look forward to a state of things, which appears inevitable.— The time will come, when those menial employments will afford less means of living than they now do. What shall a large class of our fellow-countrymen do, when white men find it economical to black their own boots, and shave themselves? What will they do when white men learn to wait on themselves? We warn you brethren, to seek other and more enduring vocations.

Let us entreat you to turn your attention to agriculture. Go to farming. Be tillers of the soil. On this point we could say much, but the time and space will not permit. Our cities are overrun with menial laborers, while the country is eloquently pleading for the hand of industry to till her soil, and reap the reward of honest labor. We beg and intreat you, to save your money—live economically—dispense with finery, and the gaities which have rendered us proverbial. and save your money. Not for the senseless purpose of being better off than your neighbor, but that you may be able to educate your children, and render your share to the common stock of prosperity and happiness around you. It is plain that the equality which we aim to accomplish, can only be achieved by us, when we can do for others, just what others can do for us. We should therefore, press into all the trades, professions and callings into which honorable white men press.

We would in this connection, direct your attention to the means by which we have been oppressed and degraded. Chief among those means, we may mention the press. This engine has brought to the aid of prejudice, a thousand stings. Wit, ridicule, false philosophy, and an impure theology, with a flood of low black-guardism, come through this channel into the public mind; constantly feeding and keeping alive against us, the bitterest hate. The pulpit too, has been arrayed against us. Men with sanctimonious face, have talked of our being descendants of Ham — that we are under a curse, and to try to improve our condition, is virtually to counteract the purposes of God!

It is easy to see that the means which have been used to destroy us, must be used to save us. The press must be used in our behalf: aye! we must use it ourselves; we must take and read newspapers; we must read books, improve our minds, and put to silence and to shame, our opposers.

Dear Brethren, we have extended these remarks beyond the length which we had allotted to ourselves, and must now close, though we have but hinted at the subject. Trusting that our words may fall like good seed upon good ground; and hoping that we may all be found in the path of improvement and progres.

We are your friends and servants,
(Signed by the Committee, in behalf
of the Convention)   FREDERICK DOUGLASS,
H. BIBB,   W. L. DAY,
D. H. JENKINS, A. H. FRANCIS.

The Conventions
of the 1850's

THE DECADE OF THE 1850's IS PERHAPS THE MOST interesting of the periods covered in this collection of documents. Unfortunately, the national conventions do not reflect as fully as might be desired the variations in the thinking of Negro Americans as black togetherness began to influence the thinking of the man in the street and the man who attended the conventions. As the decade progressed, this togetherness became a Negro Nationalism with two branches, those who preferred staying at home, always in the majority, and those who sought a home beyond the seas, a very vocal minority.

The majority, under the leadership of Frederick Douglass, who was ably supported by James McCune Smith, George T. Downing, and William J. Watkins, to name but a few, developed a plan for a Negro-directed community which would bypass white controls to the extent possible, run its own library-museum-propaganda agency, and above all, operate an institution of higher education for the Negro, under Negro control.

The minority, led by Martin R. Delany, Henry Highland Garnet and others, made elaborate schemes to colonize Africa or areas in the American semitropics where they hoped to compete with cotton and sugar production in the American South. Henry Bibb and Samuel R. Ward died as emigrants to foreign lands, as did many other men who had staked their all on building a Negro nation beyond the borders, or who had emigrated for personal or monetary reasons. During this decade it was not uncommon to find sons of earlier anti-colonization, anti-emigration leaders venturing their future on foreign soil, or penetrating the United States Far West. The men of the 1850's had more than one alternative. Unfortunately, the running dispute between the stay-at-homes and the emigrationists is not well documented in the records of the national conventions, but much of the action of the great convention at Rochester in 1853 was with the emigrationist competition in mind. Had there been a national convention in 1860, emigration would have had to be a major issue.

During the 1850's too, the Negro formalized his interpretation of the Constitution of the United States. It was, by his decision at the national convention of 1855, an antislavery document. It would be supported. The black man had not followed—would not follow—the "no participation in government" vagaries of the Garrisonians. As in the 1840's, when the youthful Henry Highland Garnet had had his tiff with Boston over political affiliations, so in 1855 the Negro once again contended, this time in formal convention, that ballots were in order and that the Constitution was sufficient authority to rid the nation of slavery.

PROCEEDINGS

OF THE

COLORED

NATIONAL CONVENTION,

HELD IN

ROCHESTER, JULY 6TH, 7TH AND 8TH,

1 8 5 3 .

———~~~———

ROCHESTER:
PRINTED AT THE OFFICE OF FREDERICK DOUGLASS' PAPER.
1853.

CALL FOR A

COLORED NATIONAL CONVENTION.

FELLOW CITIZENS :—In the exercise of a liberty which we hope, you will not deem unwarrantable, and which is given us, in virtue of our connection and identity with you, the undersigned do hereby, most earnestly and affectionately, invite you, by your appropriate and chosen representatives, to assemble at ROCHESTER, N. Y., on the 6th of July, 1853 under the form and title of a National Convention of the free people of color of the United States.

After due thought and reflection upon the subject, in which has entered a profound desire to serve a common cause, we have arrived at the conclusion, that the time has now fully come when the free colored people from all parts of the United States, should meet together, to confer and deliberate upon their present condition, and upon principles and measures important to their welfare, progress and general improvement.

The aspects of our cause, whether viewed as being hostile or friendly, are alike full of argument in favor of such a Convention. Both reason and feeling have assigned to us a place in the conflict now going on in our land between liberty and equality on the one hand, and slavery and caste on the other—a place which we cannot fail to occupy without branding ourselves as unworthy of our natural post, and recreant to the cause we profess to love.—Under the whole heavens, there is not to be found a people which can show better cause for assembling in such a Convention than we.

Our fellow-countrymen now in chains, to whom we are united in a common destiny demand it ; and a wise solicitude for our own honor, and that of our children, impels us to this course of action. We have gross and flagrant wrongs against which, if we are men of spirit we are bound to protest. We have high and holy rights, which every instinct of human nature and every sentiment of manly virtue bid us to preserve and protect to the full extent of our ability. We have opportunities to improve—difficulties peculiar to our condition to meet—mistakes and errors of our own to correct—and therefore we need the accumulated knowledge, the united character, and the combined wisdom of our people to make us (under God) sufficient for these things.— The Fugitive Slave Act, the most cruel, unconstitutional and scandalous outrage of modern times—the proscriptive legislation of several States with a view to drive our people from their borders—the exclusion of our children from schools supported by our money—the prohibition of the exercise of the franchise—the exclusion of colored citizens from the jury box—the social barriers erected against our learning trades—the wily and vigorous efforts of the American Colonization Society to employ the arm of government to expel us from our native land—and withal the propitious awakening to the fact of our condition at home and abroad, which has followed the publication of "Uncle Tom's Cabin"—call trumpet-tongued for our union, co-operation and action in the premises.

Convinced that the number amongst us must be small, who so far miscalculate and undervalue the importance of united and intelligent moral action, as to regard it as useless, the undersigned do not feel called upon here for an argument in its favor. Our warfare is not one where force can be employed ; we battle against false and hurtful customs, and against the great errors opinion which support such customs. Nations are more and more guided by the enlightened and energetically expressed judgment of mankind. On the subject of our own condition and welfare, we may safely and properly appeal to that judgment. Let us meet, then near the anniversary of this nation's independence, and enforce anew the great principles and self-evident truths which were proclaimed at the beginning of the Republic.

Among the matters which will engage the attention of the Convention will be a proposition to establish a NATIONAL COUNCIL of our people with a view to permanent existence. This subject is one of vast importance, and should only be disposed of in the light of a wise deliberation. There will come before the Convention matters touching the disposition of such funds as our friends abroad, through Mrs. Harriet Beecher Stowe may appropriate to the cause of our progress and improvement. In a word, the whole field of our interests will be opened to enquiry, investigation and determination,

That this may be done successfully, it is desirable that each delegate to the Convention should bring with him an accurate statement as to the number of colored inhabitants in his town or neighborhood—the amount of property owned by them—their business or occupation—the state of education—the extent of their school privileges and the number of children in attendance, and any other information which may serve the great purposes of the Convention.

In order that no community shall be represented beyond its due proportion, it is intended that the Convention shall only be composed of regularly chosen delegates, appointed by public meetings, and bearing credentials signed by the President of said meetings.

It is recommended that all colored churches, literary and other societies, banded together for laudable purposes, proceed at once to the appointment of at least one, and not more than three, delegates to attend the National Convention. Such persons as come from towns, villages or counties, where no regular delegate may have been chosen, shall be received and enrolled as honorary members of the Convention.

JAMES W. C. PENNINGTON,
HENRY M. WILSON,
CHARLES B. RAY,
JAMES McCUNE SMITH,
EDWARD V. CLARK, } *N. Y. City*

Wm. J. WILSON,
JUNIUS C. MORELL,
JOHN N. STILL,
AMOS N. FREEMAN, } *Brooklyn, N. Y.*

JACOB P. MORRIS,
FREDERICK DOUGLASS, } *Rochester N. Y.*

Wm. H. TOPP,
STEPHEN MYRES, } *Albany N. Y.*

J. W. LOGUEN,
Geo. B. VASHON, } *Syracuse N. Y.*

GEORGE T. DOWNING,
Wm. JOESON,
JOHN N. SMITH, } *Providence R. I.*

JOHM MERCER LANGSTON,
Wm. H. DAY,
DAVID JENKINS,
JOHN I. GAINES, } *Ohio.*

CHARLES H. REASON,
J. J. G. BIAS,
J. B. VASHON,
ROBERT PURVIS, } *Pennsylvania.*

DAVID RUGGLES,
L. KELLY,
ROBERT MORRIS,
C. L. REMOND, } *Mass.*

H. O. WAGONER, *Illinois.*
E. P. ROGERS, *Newark, N. J.*
GEO. De BAPTIST, *Detroit Mich.*
BENJAMIN LYNCH,
S. S. BALTIMORE, } *Troy N, Y.*

ISAAC CROSS,
GEO. GARRISON,
AMOS GERRY BEMAN,
JEHIEL C. BEMAN,
GEORGE W. FRANCIS,
JOHN E. BURR,
LEVERETT C. BEMAN, } *Connecticut.*

PROCEEDINGS OF THE
NATIONAL CONVENTION,
HELD IN ROCHESTER ON THE 6TH, 7TH AND 8TH OF JULY, 1853.

FIRST DAY--MORNING SESSION.

Pursuant to the Call, the Convention assembled in Corinthian Hall on Wednesday, July 6th, 1853, and was called to order by Rev. Amos G. Beman of Connecticut.

On motion of Rev. Charles B. Ray, of New York, the Rev. John Peck, of Pittsburgh, Pa., was appointed President pro tem.; and Wm. Whipper, of Pennsylvania, and Wm. C. Nell, of Massachusetts, were appointed Secretaries pro tem. James McCune Smith, M. D., then read the Call for the Convention.

On motion of David Jenkings, of Ohio, the delegates were called upon by States, to present their credentials.

Moved by James McCune Smith, that the signers of the Call be considered members *de facto* of this body, whether elected or not. After some discussion, on motion of Wm. H. Day, it was amended so as to read that the signers to the Call of this Convention be, and are hereby constituted members of this Convention. The amendment was carried, and the motions as amended was then adopted.

It was moved that a Committee of eight be appointed by the Chair to nominate officers for the convention. The Chair appointed the following, named persons said Committee : James McCune Smith, Rev. L. A. Grimes, Rev. Stephen Smith, Wm. H. Day, T. G. Campbell, Rev. Byrd Parker, Rev. A. G. Beman, Rev. Wm. C. Munroe.

On motion, the Convention adjourned to meet at 2½ P. M.

AFTERNOON SESSION.

Convention met at 2½ P. M. Rev. John Peck, President, pro tem., in the Chair. Prayer by Rev. Jehial C. Beman. The Committee on nominations reported by their Chairman, James McCune Smith, the following named persons as officers of this Convention :

President—James W. C. Pennington, D. D., of New York ; *Vice President*—Wm. H. Day, of Ohio ; Amos G. Beman, Connecticut ; Wm. C. Nell, Massachusetts ; Frederick Douglass, New York ; James C. McCrumbell, and John B. Vashon, Pennsylvania ; John Jones, Illinois.

Secretaries-. Peter H. Clarke, Ohio ; Chas. B. Ray and Wm. J. Wilson, New York ; Charles L. Reason, Pennsylvania.

The President, on taking the Chair, made a short address. The officers were invited to their respective seats.

Moved that a business Committee of 9 be appointed. J. C. McCrummell, moved an amendment that the Committee consist of 12. Carried. The motion as amended was then adopted. The Chair appointed the following named persons said Committee, viz. : James McCune Smith, Wm. Whipper, C. H. Langston, H. O. Wagoner, J. C. Beman, Wm. H. Topp, Wm. C. Nell, Wm. C. Munroe, John J. Gaines, Stephen Smith, Horace B. Smith, Geo. T. Downing.

Moved that a Committee of 3 be appointed on Finance. Carried. Edward V. Clarke, David Jenkins and T. G. Campbell, were appointed said Committee

Moved that a Committee of 5 be appointed on a Declaration of Sentiments Frederick Douglass, H. O. Wagoner, Rev. A. N. Freeman, J. M. Whitfield, G. B. Vashon.

The Business Committee reported in part, a resolution recommending days of fasting and prayer, which were accepted.

Moved that they be taken up in sections. Carried.

The Preamble and resolution were read.

Moved that the 1st Resolution be adopted.

The question was discussed ; pending which, it was by motion laid on the table, to receive a Report from the Finance Committee. The Report provided that each member be assessed in the sum of 75 cents, and that a collection be taken up each evening.

Moved by Stephen Smith that the sum of one dollar be substituted for 75 cents, and that the provision for collections be stricken out. Carried.

Frederick Douglass, Chairman of Committee on Declaration of Sentiments made the following Report :

ADDRESS,

OF THE

COLORED NATIONAL CONVENTION,

TO THE PEOPLE OF THE UNITED STATES.

—

FELLOW-CITIZENS : Met in convention as delegates, representing the Free Colored people of the United States ; charged with the responsibility of inquiring into the general condition of our people, and of devising measures which may, with the blessing of God, tend to our mutual improvement and elevation ; conscious of entertaining no motives, ideas, or aspirations, but such as are in accordance with truth and justice, and are compatible with the highest good of our country and the world, with a cause as vital and worthy as that for which (nearly eighty years ago) your fathers and our fathers bravely contended, and in which they gloriously triumphed—we deem it proper, on this occasion, as one method of promoting the honorable ends for which we have met, and of discharging our duty to those in whose name we speak, to present the claims of our common cause to your candid, earnest, and favorable consideration.

As an apology for addressing you, fellow-citizens! we cannot announce the discovery of any new principle adapted to ameliorate the condition of mankind. The great truths of moral and political science, upon which we rely, and which we press upon your consideration, have been evolved and ennunciated by you. We point to your principles, your wisdom, and to your great example as the full justification of our course this day. That " ALL MEN ARE CREATED EQUAL : that " LIFE, LIBERTY, AND THE PURSUIT OF HAPPINESS " ARE THE RIGHT OF ALL ; that " TAXATION AND REPRESENTATION " SHOULD GO TOGETHER ; that GOVERNMENTS ARE TO PROTECT, NOT TO DESTROY, THE RIGHTS OF MANKIND ; that THE CONSTITUTION OF THE UNITED STATES WAS FORMED TO ESTABLISH JUSTICE, PROMOTE THE GENERAL WELFARE, AND SECURE THE BLESSING OF LIBERTY TO ALL THE PEOPLE OF THIS COUNTRY ; THAT RESISTANCE TO TYRANTS IS OBEDIENCE TO GOD—are American principles and maxims, and together they form and constitute the constructive elements of the American government. From this elevated platform, provided by the Republic for us, and for all the children of men, we address you. In doing so, we would have our spirit properly discerned. On this point we would gladly free ourselves and our cause from all misconception. We shall affect no especial timidity, nor can we pretend to any great boldness. We know our poverty and weakness, and your wealth and greatness. Yet we will not attempt to repress the spirit of liberty within us, or to conceal, in any wise, our sense of the justice and the dignity of our cause.

We are Americans, and as Americans, we would speak to Americans. We address you not as aliens nor as exiles, humbly asking to be permitted to dwell among you in peace ; but we address you as American citizens asserting their rights on their own native soil. Neither do we address you as enemies, (although the recipients of innumerable wrongs ;) but in the spirit of patriotic good will. In assembling together as we have done, our object is not to excite pity for ourselves, but to command respect for our cause, and to obtain justice for our people. We are not malefactors imploring mercy ; but we trust we are honest men, honestly appealing for righteous judgment, and ready to stand or fall by that judgment. We do not solicit unusual favor, but will be content with roughhanded " fair play." We are neither lame or blind, that we should seek to throw off the responsibility of our own existence, or to cast ourselves upon public charity for support. We would not lay our burdens upon other men's shoulders ; but we do ask, in the name of all that is just and magnanimous among men, to be freed from all the unnatural burdens and impediments with which American customs and American legislation have hindered our progress and improvement. We ask to be disencumbered of the load of popular reproach heaped upon us—for no better cause than that we wear the complexion given us by our God and our Creator.

We ask that in our native land, we shall not be treated as strangers, and worse than strangers.

We ask that, being friends of America, we should not be treated as enemies of America.

We ask that, speaking the same language and being of the same religion, worshipping the same God, owing our redemption to the same Savior, and learning our duties from the same Bible, we shall not be treated as barbarians.

We ask that, having the same physical, moral, mental, and spiritual wants, common to other members of the human family, we shall also have the same means which are granted and secured to others, to supply those wants.

We ask that the doors of the school-house, the work-shop, the church, the college, shall be thrown open as freely to our children as to the children of other members of the community.

We ask that the American government shall be so administered as that beneath the broad shield of the Constitution, the colored American seaman, shall be secure in his life, liberty and property, in every State in the Union.

We ask that as justice knows no rich, no poor, no black, no white, but, like the government of God, renders alike to every man reward or punishment, according as his works shall be—the white and black man may stand upon an equal footing before the laws of the land.

We ask that (since the right of trial by jury is a safeguard to liberty, against the encroachments of power, only as it is a trial by impartial men, drawn indiscriminately from the country) colored men shall not, in every instance, be tried by white persons ; and that colored men shall not be either by custom or enactment excluded from the jury-box.

We ask that (inasmuch as we are, in common with other American citizens, supporters of the State, subject to its laws, interested in its welfare liable to be called upon to defend it in time of war, contributors to its wealth in time of peace) the complete and unrestricted right of suffrage, which is essential to the dignity even of the white man, be extended to the Free Colored man also.

Whereas the colored people of the United States have too long been retarded and impeded in the development and improvement of their natural faculties and powers, ever to become dangerous rivals to white men, in the honorable pursuits of life, liberty and happiness ; and whereas, the proud Anglo-Saxon can need no arbitrary protection from open and equal competition with any variety of the human family ; and whereas, laws have been encted limiting the aspirations of colored men, as against white men—we respectfully submit that such laws are flagrantly unjust to the man of color, and plainly discreditable to white men ; and for these and other reasons, such laws ought to be repealed.

We especially urge that all laws and usages which preclude the enrollment of colored men in the militia, and prohibit their bearing arms in the navy, disallow their rising, agreeable to their merits and attainments—are unconstitutional—the constitution knowing no color—are anti-Democratic, since Democracy respects men as equals—are unmagnanimous, since such laws are made by the many, against the few, and by the strong against the weak.

We ask that all those cruel and oppressive laws, whether enacted at the South or the North, which aim at the expatriation of the free people of color, shall be stamped with national reprobation, denounced as contrary to the humanity of the American people, and as au outrage upon the Christianity and civilization of the nineteenth century.

We ask that the right of pre-emption, enjoyed by all white settlers upon the public lands, shall also be enjoyed by colored settlers ; and that the word *"white"* be struck from the pre-emption act. We ask that no appropriations whatever, state or national, shall be granted to the colonization scheme ; and we would have our right to leave or to remain in the United States placed above legislative interference.

We ask that the Fugitive Slave Law of 1850, that legislative monster of modern times, by whose atrocious provisions the writ of *"habeas corpus,"* the " right of trial by jury," have been virtually abolished, shall be repealed.

We ask, that the law of 1793 be so construed as to apply only to apprentices, and others really owing service or labor ; and not to slaves, who can *owe* nothing. Finally, we ask that slavery in the United States shall be immediately, unconditionally, and forever abolished,

To accomplish these just and reasonable ends, we solemnly pledge ourselves to God, to each other, to our country, and to the world, to use all and every means consistent with the just rights of our fellow men, and with the precepts of Christianity.

We shall speak, write and publish, organize and combine to accomplish them.

We shall invoke the aid of the pulpit and the press to gain them.

We shall appeal to the church and to the government to gain them.

We shall vote, and expend our money to gain them.

We shall send eloquent men of our own condition to plead our cause before the people.

We shall invite the co-operation of good men in this country and throughout the world—and above all, we shall look to God, the Father and Creator of all men, for wisdom to direct us and strength to support us in the holy cause to which we this day solemnly pledge ourselves.

Such, fellow-citizens are our aims, ends, aspirations and determinations. We place them before you, with the earnest hope, that upon further investigation, they will meet your cordial and active approval.

And yet, again, we would free ourselves from the charge of unreasonableness and self-sufficiency.

In numbers we are few and feeble ; but in the goodness of our cause, in the rectitude of our motives, and in the abundance of argument on our side, we are many and strong.

We count our friends in the heavens above, in the earth beneath, among good men and holy angels. The subtle and mysterious cords of human sympathy have connected us with philanthropic hearts throughout the civilized world. The number in our own land who already recognize the justice of our cause, and are laboring to promote it, is great and increasing.

It is also a source of encouragement, that the genuine American, brave and independent himself, will respect bravery and independence in others. He spurns servility and meanness, whether they be manifested by nations or by individuals. We submit, therefore, that there is neither necessity for, nor disposition on our part to assume a tone of excessive humility. While we would be respectful, we must address you as men, as citizens, as brothers, as dwellers in a common country, equally interested with you for its welfare, its honor and for its prosperity.

To be still more explicit: we would, first of all, be understood to range ourselves no lower among our fellow-countrymen than is implied in the high appellation of "*citizen.*"

Notwithstanding the impositions and deprivations which have fettered us—notwithstanding the disabilities and liabilities, pending and impending—notwithstanding the cunning, cruel, and scandalous efforts to blot out that right, we declare that we are, and of right we ought to be *American citizens.* We claim this right, and we claim all the rights and privileges, and duties which, properly, attach to it.

It may, and it will, probably, be disputed that we are citizens. We may, and, probably, shall be denounced for this declaration, as making an inconsiderate, impertinent and absurd claim to citizenship; but a very little reflection will vindicate the position we have assumed, from so unfavorable a judgment. Justice is never inconsiderate; truth is never impertinent; right is never absurd. If the claim we set up be just, true and right, it will not be deemed improper or ridiculous in us so to declare it. Nor is it disrespectful to our fellow-citizens, who repudiate the aristocratic notions of the old world that we range ourselves with them in respect to all the rights and prerogatives belonging to American citizens. Indeed, we believe, when you have duly considered this subject, you will commend us for the mildness and modesty with which we have taken our ground.

By birth, we are American citizens; by the principles of the Declaration of Independence, we are American citizens; within the meaning of the United States Constitution, we are American citizens; by the facts of history, and the admissions of American statesmen, we are American citizens; by the hardships and trials endured; by the courage and fidelity displayed by our ancestors in defending the liberties and in achieving the independence of our land, we are American citizens. In proof of the justice of this primary claim, we might cite numerous authorities, facts and testimonies,—a few only must suffice.

In the Convention of New York, held for amending the Constitution of that State, in the year 1821, an interesting discussion took place, upon a proposition to prefix the word "*white*" to male citizens. Nathan Sandford, then late Chancellor of the State, said:

"Here there is but one estate—*the people*—and to me the only qualification seems to be their virtue and morality. If they may be safely trusted to vote for one class of rulers, why not for all? The principle of the scheme is, that those who bear the burdens of the State, shall choose those that rule it."

Dr. Robert Clark, in the same debate, said:

"I am unwilling to retain the word '*white*,' because it is repugnant to all the principles and notions of liberty, to which we have heretofore professed to adhere, and to our 'Declaration of Independence,' which is a concise and just expose of those principles." He said "it had been appropriatly observed by the Hon. gentleman from Westchester, (Mr. Jay,) that by retaining this word, you violate the Constitution of the United States."

Chancellor Kent supported the motion of Mr. Jay to strike out the word "*white.*"

"He did not come to this Convention," said he, "to disfranchise any portion of the community."

Peter A. Jay, on the same occasion, said, "It is insisted that this Convention, clothed with all the powers of the sovereign people of the State, have a right to construct the government in a manner they think most conducive to the general good. If, Sir, right and power be equivalent terms, then I am far from disputing the rights of this assembly. We have power, Sir, I acknowledge, not only to disfranchise every black family, but as many white families also, as we may think expedient. We may place the whole government in the hands of a few and thus construct an aristocracy. * * * * * * But, Sir, right and power are not convertible terms. No man, no body of men, however powerful, have a right to do wrong."

In the same Convention, Martin Van Buren said:

"There were two words which has come into common use with our revolutionary struggle—words which contained an abridgment of our political rights—words which, at that day, had a talismanic effect—which led our fathers from the bosom of their families to the tented field—which for seven long years of toil and suffering, had kept them to their arms, and which, finally conducted them to a glorious triumph. They were '*Taxation and Representation.*' Nor did they lose their influence with the close of the struggle. They were never heard in our halls of legislation without bringing to our recollection the consecrated feelings of those who won our liberties, or, reminding us of everything that was sacred in principle."

Ogden Edwards without, said "he considered it no better than robbery to demand the contributions of colored people towards defraying the public expenses, and at the same time to disfranchise them."

But we must close our quotations from these debates. Much more could be cited, to show that colored men are not only citizens, but that they have a right to the exercise of the elective franchise in the State of New York. If the right of citizenship is established in the State of New York, it is in consequence of the same facts which exist at least in every free State of the Union. We turn from the debates in the State of New York to the nation; and here we find testimony abundant and incontestible, that Free Colored people are esteemed as citizens, by the highest authorities in the United States.

The Constitution of the United States declares "that the citizens of each State shall be entitled to all the privileges and immunities of citizens in the "United States."

There is in this clause of the Constitution, nothing whatever, of that watchful malignity which has manifested itself lately in the insertion of the word "*white,*" before the term "*citizen.*" The word "*white*" was unknown to the framers of the Constitution of the United States in such connections—unknown to the signers of the Declaration of Independence—unknown to the brave men at *Bunker Hill, Ticonderoga* and at *Red Bank.* It is a modern word, brought into use by modern legislators, despised in revolutionary times. The question of our citizenship came up as a national question, and was settled during the pendency of the Missouri question, in 1820.

It will be remembered that that State presented herself for admission into the Union, with a clause in her Constitution prohibiting the settlement of colored citizens within her borders. Resistance was made to her admission into the Union, upon that very ground ; and it was not until that State receded from her unconstitutional position, that President Monroe declared the admission of Missouri into the Union to be complete.

According to Nile's Register, August 18th, vol. 20, page 338-339, the refusal to admit Missouri into the Union was not withdrawn until the General Assembly of that State, in conformity to a fundamental condition imposed by Congress, had, by an act passed for that purpose, solemnly enacted and declared:

" That this State [Missouri] has assented, and does assent, that the fourth clause of the 26th section of the third article of their Constitution should never be construed to authorize the passage of any law, and that no law shall be passed in conformity thereto, by which any citizen of either of the United States shall be excluded from the enjoyment of any of the privileges and immunities to which such citizens are entitled, under the Constitution of the United States."

Upon this action by the State of Missouri, President Monroe proclaimed the admission of Missouri into the Union.

Here, fellow-citizens, we have a recognition of our citizenship by the highest authority of the United States ; and here we might rest our claim to citizenship. But there have been services performed, hardships endured, courage displayed by our fathers, which modern American historians forget to record— a knowledge of which is essential to an intelligent judgment of the merits of our people. Thirty years ago, slavery was less powerful than it is now ; American statesmen were more independent then, than now; and as a consequence, the black man's patriotism and bravery were more readily recognized. The age of slave-hunting had not then come on. In the memorable debate on the Missouri question, the meritorious deeds of our fathers obtained respectful mention. The Hon. Wm. Eustis, who had himself been a soldier of the revolution, and Governor of the State of Massachusetts, made a speech in the Congress of the United States, 12th December, and said :

" The question to be determined is, whether the article in the Constitution of Missouri, requiring the legislature to provide by law, ' that free negroes and mulattoes shall not be admitted into that State,' is, or is not repugnant to that clause of the Constitution of the United States which declares ' that the citizens of each State shall be entitled to all the privileges and immunities of citizens in the several States ?' This is the question. Those who contend that the article is not repugnant to the Constitution of the United States, take the position that free blacks and mulattoes are not citizens. *Now I invite the gentlemen who maintain this to go with me and examine this question to its root.* At the early part of the revolutionary war, there were found in the middle and northern States, many blacks and other people of color, capable of bearing arms, a part of them free, and a greater part of them slaves. The freemen entered our ranks with the whites. The time of those who were slaves were purchased by the State, and they were induced to enter the service in consequence of a law, by which, on condition of their serving in the ranks during the war, they were made freemen. In Rhode Island, where their numbers were more considerable, they were formed under the same considerations into a regiment, commanded by white officers ; and it is required in justice to to them, to add that they discharged their duty with zeal and fidelity, The gallant defence of Red Bank, in which the black regiment bore a part, is among the proofs of their valor."

14

" Not only the rights but the character of those men do not seem to be understood ; nor is it to me at all extraordinary that gentlemen from other States, in which the condition, character, the moral facilities, and the rights of men of color differ so widely, should entertain opinions so varient from ours. In Massachusets, Sir, there are among them who possess all the virtues which are deemed estimable in civil and social life. They have their public teachers of religion and morality—their schools and other snstitutions. On anniversaries which they consider interesting to them, they have their public processions, in all of which they conduct themselves with order and decorum. Now, we ask only, that in a disposition to accommodate others, their avowed rights and privileges be not taken from them. If their number be small, and they are feebly represented, we, to whom they are known, are proportionately bound to protect them. But their defence is not founded on their numbers ; it rests on the immutable principles of justice. If there be only one family, or a solitary individual who has rights guaranteed to him by the Constitution, whatever may be his color or complexion, it is not in the power, nor can it be the inclination of Congress to deprive him of them. And I trust, Sir, that the decision on this occassion will show that we will extend good faith even to the blacks."—*National Intelligencer, Jan. 2, 1821.*

The following is an extract from a speech of the Hon. Mr. Morrill, of New Hampshire, delivered in the United States Senate in the same month, and reported in the *National Intelligencer,* Jan 11th, 1821 :

" Sir, you excluded, not only the citizens from their constitutional privileges and immunities, but also your soldiers of color, to whom you have given patents of land. You had a company of this description. They have fought your battles. They have defended your country. They have preserved your privileges ; but have lost their own. What did you say to them on their enlistment ? 'We will give you a monthly compensation, and, at the end of the war, 160 acres of good land, on which you may settle, and by cultivating the soil, spend your declining years in peace and in the enjoyment of those immunities for which you have fought and bled.' Now, Sir, you restrict them, and will not allow them to enjoy the fruit of their labor. Where is the public faith in this case ? Did they suppose, with a patent in their hand, declaring their title to land in Missouri, with the seal of the nation, and the President's signature affixed thereto, it would be said unto them by any authority, you shall not possess the premises ? This could never have been anticipated ; and yet this must follow, if colored men are not citizens."

Mr. Strong, of New York, said, in the same great debate, " The federal constitution knows but two descriptions of freemen : these are citizens and aliens. Now Congress can naturalize only aliens—i. e., persons who owe allegiance to a foreign government. But a slave has no country, and owes no allegiance except to his master. How, then, is he an alien ? If restored to his liberty, and made a freeman, what is his national character ? It must be determined by the federal constitution, and without reference to policy ; for it respects liberty. Is it that of a citizen, or alien ? But it has been shown that he is not an alien. May we not, therefore, conclude—nay, are we not bound to conclude that he is a citizen of the United States ?"

Charles Pinckney, of South Carolina, speaking of the colored people, in Congress, and with reference to the same question, bore this testimony :

" They then were (during the Revolution) as they still are, as valuable a part of our population to the Union, as any other equal number of inhabitants. They were, in numerous instances, the pioneers ; and in all the labors of your armies, to their hands were owing the erection of the greatest part of the fortifications raised for the protection of our country. Fort Moultrie gave, at an early period the experience and untired valor of our citizens immortality to American arms ; and in the Northern States, numerous bodies of them were enrolled, and fought, side by side, with the whites, the battles of the Revolution."

General Jackson, in his celebrated proclamations to the free colored inhabitants of Louisiana, uses these expressions : " *Your* white fellow-citizens ;" and again : " *Our* brave *citizens are united,* and *all* contention has ceased among them."

FIRST PROCLAMATION.

EXTRACTS.

HEAD QUARTERS, 7th Military Dis't., }
Mobile, Sept. 21st, 1814. }

To the Free Colored Inhabitants of Louisiana :

Through a mistaken policy you have heretofore been deprived of a participation in the glorious struggle for national rights, in which your country if engaged.

This no longer shall exist.

As sons of freedom, you are now called on to defend our most inestimable blessings. As *Americans,* your country looks with confidence to her adopted children for a valorous support. As fathers, husbands, and brothers, you are summoned to rally round the standard of the Eagle, to defend all which is dear to existence.

Your country, although calling for your exertions, does not wish you to engage in her cause without remunerating you for the services rendered.

In the sincerity of a soldier, and in the language of truth, I address you.— To every noble-hearted free man of color, volunteering to serve during the present contest with Great Britain, and no longer, there will be paid the same bounty in money and land now received by the white soldiers of the United States, viz : $124 in money, and 160 acres of land. The non-commissioned officers and privates will also be entitled to *the same* monthly pay and daily rations, and clothes, furnished *to any American soldier.*

The Major General commanding will select officers for your government from YOUR WHITE FELLOW-CITIZENS. Your non-commissioned officers will be selected from yourselves. Due regard will be paid to the feelings of freemen and soldiers. As a distinct, independent battalion or regiment, pursuing the path of glory, you will, undivided, receive the applause and gratitude of *your* countrymen. ANDREW JACKSON,
Major Gen. Commanding.

—*Niles' Register, Dec.* 3, 1814, *Vol.* 7, *p.* 205.

SECOND PROCLAMATION.

To the Free People of Color :

Soldiers ! when on the banks of the Mobile I called you to take up arms, inviting you to partake the perils and glory of your *white* fellow-citizens, I expected much from you ; for I was not ignorant that you possessed qualities most formidable to an invading enemy. I knew with what fortitude you could endure hunger and thirst, and all the fatigues of a campaign.

I knew well how you lovedy our native country, and that you, as well as ourselves, had to defend what *man* holds most dear—his parents, wife, children, and property. You have done more than I expected. In addition to the previous qualities I before knew you to possess, I found among you a noble enthusiasm which leads to the performance of great things.

Soldiers ! the President of the United States shall hear how praiseworthy was your conduct in the hour of danger, and the representatives of the American people will give you the praise your exploits entitle you to. Your General anticipates them in applauding your noble ardor.

The enemy approaches—his vessels cover our lakes—*our brave citizens are united*, and all contention has ceased among them. Their only dispute is, who shall win the prize of valor, or who the most glory, its noblest reward.—
By order,   THOMAS BUTLER, Aid-de-Camp.

Such, fellow-citizens, is but a sample of a mass of testimony, upon which we found our claim to be American citizens. There is, we think, no flaw in the evidence. The case is made out. We and you stand upon the same broad national basis. Whether at home or abroad, we and you owe equal allegiance to the same government—have a right to look for protection on the same ground. We have been born and reared on the same soil ; we have been animated by, and have displayed the same patriotic impulses ; we have acknowledged and performed the same duty ; we have fought and bled in the same battles ; we have gained and gloried in the same victories ; and we are equally entitled to the blessings resulting therefrom.

In view of this array of evidence of services bravely rendered, how base and monstrous would be the ingratitude, should the republic disown us and drive us into exile !—how faithless and selfish, should the nation persist in degrading us ! But we will not remind you of obligations—we will not appeal to your generous feelings—a naked statement of the case is our best appeal. Having, now, upon the testimony of your own great and venerated names completely vindicated our right to be regarded and treated as American citizens, we hope you will now permit us to address you in the plainness of speech becoming the dignity of American citizens.

Fellow-citizens, we have had, and still have, great wrongs of which to complain. A heavy and cruel hand has been laid upon us.

As a people, we feel ourselves to be not only deeply injured, but grossly. misunderstood. Our white fellow-countrymen do not know us. They are strangers to our character, ignorant of our capacity, oblivious of our history and progress, and are misinformed as to the principles and ideas that control and guide us as a people. The great mass of American citizens estimate us as being a characterless and purposeless people ; and hence we hold up our heads, if at all, against the withering influence of a nation's scorn and contempt.

It will not be suprising that we are so misunderstood and misused when the motives for misrepresenting us and for degrading us are duly considered. Indeed, it will seem strange, upon such consideration, (and in view of the ten thousand channels through which malign feelings find utterance and influence,) that we have not even fallen lower in public estimation than we, have done. For, with the single exception of the Jews, under the whole heavens, there is not to be found a people pursued with a more relentless prejudice and persecution, than are the Free Colored people of the United States·

Without pretending to have exerted ourselves as we ought, in view of an intelligent understanding of our interest, to avert from us the unfavorable opinions and unfriendly action of the American people, we feel that the imputations cast upon us, for our want of intelligence, morality and exalted character, may be mainly accounted for by the injustice we have received at your hands. What stone has been left unturned to degrade us ? What hand has refused to fan the flame of popular prejudice against us ? What American artist has not caricatured us ? What wit has not laughed at us in our wretchedness ? What songster has not made merry over our depressed spirits ? What press has not ridiculed and contemned us ? What pulpit has withheld from our devoted heads its angry lightning, or its sanctimonious hate ? Few, few, very few ; and that we have borne up with it all—that we have tried to be wise, though denounced by all to be fools—that we have tried to be upright, when all around us have esteemed us as knaves—that we have striven to be gentlemen, although all around us have been teaching us its impossibility— that we have remained here, when all our neighbors have advised us to leave, proves that we possess qualities of head and heart, such as cannot but be commended by impartial men. It is believed that no other nation on the globe could have made more progress in the midst of such an universal and stringent disparagement. It would humble the proudest, crush the energies of the strongest, and retard the progress of the swiftest. In view of our circumstances, we can, without boasting, thank God, and take courage, having placed ourselves where we may fairly challenge comparison with more highly favored men.

Among the colored people, we can point, with pride and hope, to men of education and refinement, who have become such, despite of the most unfavorable influences ; we can point to mechanics, farmers, merchants, teachers, ministers, doctors, lawyers, editors, and authors, against whose progress the concentrated energies of American prejudice have proved quite unavailing.— Now, what is the motive for ignoring and discouraging our improvement in this country ? The answer is ready. The intelligent and upright free man of color is an unanswerable argument in favor of liberty, and a killing condemnation of American slavery. It is easily seen that, in proportion to the progress of the free man of color, in knowledge, temperance, industry, and righteousness, in just that proportion will he endanger the stability of slavery ; hence, all the powers of slavery are exerted to prevent the elevation of the free people of color.

The force of fifteen hundred million dollars is arrayed against us ; hence, the *press*, the pulpit, and the platform, against all the natural promptings of uncontaminated manhood, point their deadly missiles of ridicule, scorn and contempt at us ; and bid us, on pain of being pierced through and through, to remain in our degradation.

Let the same amount of money be employed against the interest of any other class of persons, however favored by nature they may be, the result could scarcely be different from that seen in our own case. Such a people would be regarded with aversion ; the money-ruled multitude would heap contumely upon them, and money-ruled institutions would proscribe them. Besides this money consideration, fellow-citizens, an explanation of the erroneous opinions prevalent concerning us is furnished in the fact, less creditable to human nature, that men are apt to hate most those whom they have injured most.— Having despised us, it is not strange that Americans should seek to render us despicable ; having enslaved us, it is natural that they should strive to prove

2

us unfit for freedom; having denounced us as indolent, it is not strange that they should cripple our enterprise; having assumed our inferiority, it would be extraordinary if they sought to surround us with circumstances which would serve to make us direct contradictions to their assumption.

In conclusion, fellow-citizens, while conscious of the immense disadvantages which beset our pathway, and fully appreciating our own weakness, we are encouraged to persevere in efforts adapted to our improvement, by a firm reliance upon God, and a settled conviction, as immovable as the everlasting hills, that all the truths in the whole universe of God are allied to our cause.

FREDERICK DOUGLASS,
J. M. WHITFIELD,
H. O. WAGONER,
REV. A. N. FREEMAN,
GEORGE B. VASHON.

The Business Committe reported through its Chairman, Dr. James McCune Smith, a plan for a National Council.

For the purpose of improving the character, developing the intelligence, maintaining the rights, and organizing a Union of the Colored People of the Free States, the National Convention does hereby ordain and institute the

"NATIONAL COUNCIL OF THE COLORED PEOPLE."

ART. 1. This Council shall consist of two members from each State, represented in this Convention, to be elected by this Convention, and two other members from each State to be elected as follows : On the 15th day of November next, and biennially thereafter, there shall be held in each State, a Poll, at which each colored inhabitant may vote who pay ten cents as a poll-tax ; and each State shall elect, at such election, delegates to State Councils, twenty in number from each State, at large. The election to be held in such places and under such conditions as the public meetings in such localities may determine. The members of the National Council in each State, shall receive, canvass and declare the result of such vote. The State Council thus elected, shall meet on the first Monday in January, 1854, and elect additional members to the National Council, in proportion of one to five thousand of colored population of such State ; and the members of Council, thus elected, to take office on the 6th day of July next, and all to hold office during two years from that date ; at the end of which time another general election by State Council shall take place of members to constitute their successors in office, in the same numbers as above. The State Council of each State shall have full power over the internal concern of said State.

ART. 2. The members of the first Council shall be elected by this Convention, which shall designate out of the number, a President, Vice-President, Secretary, Treasurer, Corresponding Secretary, and Committee of five on Manual Labor School—a Committee of five on Protective Unions—of five on Business Relations—of five on Publications.

ART. 3. The Committee on Manual Labor School, shall procure funds and organize said School in accordance with the plans adopted by this National Convention, with such modifications as experience or necessity may dictate to them. The Committee shall immediately incorporate itself as an Academy under the general Committee of the State of ———, and shall constitute the Board of Trustees of the Manual Labor School, with full power to select a location in the State designated by the National Council, to erect buildings, appoint or dismiss instructors in the literary or mechanical branches. There shall be a farm attached to the School.

ART. 4. The Committee on Protective Union, shall institute a Protective Union for the purchase and sale of articles of domestic consumption, and shall unite and aid in the formation of branches auxiliary to their own.

Art. 5. The Committee on Business Relations, shall establish an office, in which they shall keep a registry of colored mechanics, artizans and business men throughout the Union. They shall keep a registry of all persons willing to employ colored men in business, to teach colored boys mechanical trades, iberal and scientific professions, and farming; and, also, a registry of colored men and youth seeking employment or instruction. They shall also report upon any avenues of business or trade which they deem inviting to colored capital, skill, or labor. Their reports and advertisements to be in papers of the widest circulation. They shall receive for sale or exhibition, products of the skill and labor of colored people.

Art. 6. The Committee on Publication shall collect all facts, statistics and statements, all laws and historical records and biographies of the Colored People, and all books by colored authors. They shall have for the safe keeping of these documents, a Library, with a Reading Room and Museum. The Committee shall also publish replies to any assaults, worthy of note, made upon the character or condition of the Colored People.

Art. 7. Each Committee shall have absolute control over its special department; shall make its own by-laws, and in case of any vacancy occurring, shall fill up the same forthwith, subject to the confirmation of the Council. Each Committee shall meet at least once a month or as often as possible; shall keep a minute of all its proceedings, executive and financial, and shall submit a full statement of the same, with the accounts audited, at every regular meeting of the National Council.

Art. 8. The National Council shall meet at least once in six months, to receive the reports of the Committees, and to consider any new plan for the general good, for which it shall have power, at its option, to appoint a new Committee, and shall be empowered to receive and appropriate donations for the carrying out of the objects of the same. At all such meetings, eleven members shall constitute a quorum. In case any Committee neglect or refuse to send in its report, according to article 8th, then the Council shall have power to enter the bureau, examine the books and papers of such Committee; and in case the Committee shall presist in its refusal or neglect, then the Council shall declare their offices vacant, and appoint others in their stead.

Art. 9. In all cases of the meetings of the National Council, or the Committees, the travelling expenses (if any) of the members shall be paid out of their respective funds.

Art. 10. The Council shall immediately establish a bureau in the place of its meeting; and the same rooms shall, as far possible, be used by the several Committees for their various purposes. The Council shall have a clerk, at a moderate salary, who shall keep a record of their transactions, and prepare a condensed report of the Committees for publication; and also a registry of the friends of the cause.

Art. 11. The expenses of the Council shall be defrayed by the fees of membership of sub-societies or Councils, to be organized throughout the States. The membership fee shall be one cent per week.

Art. 12. A member of the Council shall be a member of only one of the Committees thereof.

Art. 13. All officers holding funds, shall give security in double the amount likely to be in their hands. This security to be given to the three first officers of the Council.

Art. 14. The Council shall have power to make such By-Laws as are necessary for their proper government.

Moved that 250 copies be printed for the use of members. Carried. Moved that a Committee of 3 be appointed to select speakers for a public meeting. Lost.

President appointed the follwing named Committees;—Committee on Agriculture, Wm. H. Day; Committee on Manual Labor School, Charles L. Reason, O. H. Langston, George B. Vashon; Committee on Social Relations, Wm. J. Wilson, Wm. Whipper, and Charles B. Ray.

President in the Chair. Prayer by Rev. Benjamin Templeton. Minutes read and approved.

Mr. Sumner moved that the roll be called, and that the members come forward and contribute one dollar towards paying the expenses of the Convention. Lost.

Letters from sundry gentleman of New Jersey read by Mr. Wm. H. Day, and on his motion, referred to the Business Committee. Report 3 from Business Committee, read and accepted. Report from Committee on Social Relations, read by the Chairman, Mr. Wm. Wilson, as follows.

REPORT OF THE COMMITTEE ON SOCIAL RELATIONS AND POLITY.

Your Committee would respectfully submit the following :

That the guarantee of our growth, strength and permanence, as a people in this country, finds its basis in the healthy, vigorous and progressive state of our *Social Relations ;* and these *relations* will find their greatest nurture, growth and strength in a wise and well directed polity.

Whether judiciously sustained to the whites, or healthy among ourselves, these relations exist.

In these relations, then, we recognize—first our *homes* surrounded by their varied appendages and influences, all operating for good or evil, and demanding the most serious deliberation and direction of this body.

We find here, the husband, wife—the parent, child—into whose performance, at least so far as pertains to the best well-being of society, the test of our severest scrutiny should pass.

Questions here arise, and should be met, in these deliberations, how far each go, or know how to go, to fulfil the measures of these obligations. What the state and condition of our homes? What the prospect of the parent ? What the culture, training, and future prospect of the child ? What the hopes, the what aspirations of each ? In a word, what the whole aspect of affairs ? In the generation of to-day looking forward to to-morrow, or beyond it, for a permanent footing, a stable home, and a happy condition in this country ?

A vigorous and searching inquiry should also be instituted between our *homes* and the *homes* of our white neighbors, and point out whatever differences that may exist for our benefit. We think it may safely be admitted, that while there have existed centuries of servitude on the one side, and the same amount of freedom on the other, the original disparity between the two classes has greatly lessened ; still we are of opinion that the proximity should have been still nearer, especially when we take into account that the one has been something more than a mere spectator to the scenes of improvement and progress of the other, most of this length of time.

And further : we are of opinion that the burthen of our disabilities, moral, social and political. finds its issue in these differences, whether they be found among ourselves, or are forced upon us by the community from without.

False ideas of natural inferiority, wicked prejudices, foul hatred, and all kindred *bars* to our progress, find their sources here.

The white American's home is free, cheerful, and surrounded [by all to make it prosperous ; ours is encumbered by *bars*, props and restraints, and shorn of most that produces prosperity.

The white American's hearth-stone finds around it a *cluster* of vigorous youth, preparing successfully for the more vigorous battle of life ; the colored American's, a few ill-trained and often worse-governed youth grouping in the gloom and mist of uncertainty. The former, a fixed reality ; the latter, since no settled purpose governs it, rather an existence in name—a mere thing of to-day. From the domicil to the active world, the white occupant has, as it were his pathway made for his entrance ; the colored occupant has yet to make his own.

How best to do it, is the question for our grave consideration.

The next point to which we would direct your attention, as having immediate connection with this, is the possession, in *"fee simple,"* of our *fire-sides*. It is lamentable to state, that not more than one in fifty of us possess our own hearth-stones ; and this is not so much from the want of means, as from ill management.

A larger number still live crowded, pent up, shoved back, and even piled up and this, too, at rates of expense, startling to contemplate ; especially is this true in larger cities.

When we add to this the feebleness and instability, the utter helplessness of a floating people, not possessing the very roofs that shelter them, having no anchorage, hold, or even footing in the soil from whence they derive their subsistence—we would earnestly call attention to this matter, hoping that in some tangible form it may be brought to bear upon our people.

All history, and our own sad experience, point with such significance to the weakness of such a class, that we ought to profit by it.

The peculiarities of our condition in this community, of which we form an integral part, render it doubly incumbent upon us to possess, hold and transmit to prosterity as much of the soil as [is] possible.

The time for this in large cities, perhaps, is gone by ; yet the country, fertile in clime and large in extent, offers abundant opportunity.

This point belonging more properly to the head of agriculture, at least in the exposition of its principles and their bearings upon our condition, we leave it to the disposition of your committee on that subject, and call attention to another point.

In thus reviewing our social state, it would be some relief if our own condition threw only its own obstacles in our way—since, then, we could easily remove them , but the difficulty does not stop here ; it goes further, and produces obstacles from without which, too, clog our way and impede our progress.

Every *bar* placed before us at the door of the hotel, the steam boat, the rail car, the stage coach, the work-shop, or the counting-room, the law court, or the Christian church, is of material of double strength, having for its composition our condition and strong prejudicial feelings generated from that condition, and is so placed as much by our own acquiescence, as by the dictate of public sentiment. With the superscription written upon each "thus far shalt thou go" these bars of separation affect us severely, producing lethargy, depression, discouragement and seeming content—prohibiting, therefore, our ready entrance, or desire to enter into the operations of business or of fields of enterprize with that commanding spirit due to ourselves, and the age in which we live. We add very little to the great aggregate of production. As a whole, we constitute, to a very large extent, a body of consumers and non-producers.

Even the intelligent foreigner, who, when cast upon our shore, is, at first, astonished at not finding us agriculturists, artisans, mediums of traffic—engaged only in few callings of an elevating character, soon settles down in the false conviction of our incapacity for these pursuits.

It is a too common opinion among us, that all the avenues to higher *social state* are closed against us, because those carved out by the whites are immeasurably closed.

We forget that we must open our own avenues, and that we must educate our own minds and the minds of our children to that end.

We forget, too, that wherever industry, tact and purpose have exhibited themselves on our part they have always been met by the same degree of favor and success from the community as any similar exhibition, as abundant evidences might be adduced to show.

We have said, that the children who cluster around the hearth stone of the co'ored American are ill-trained; we add more : they are as yet ignorant of the uses of their own faculties, to say nothing of a knowledge of their application to specific and important measures. How intimately, therefore, is their proper education connected with our dearest relations to society.

Two distinct, yet inseparable branches of education must be undergone by our youth ere they are fitted for the work of social elevation—that of the *School-Room* and that of the *Fire-Side*.

It is not our province to discuss either, briefly remarking upon each, so far only as they immedately bear upon our subject. In looking into the *school-room*, we can but approach this branch of education with some apprehensions, since the methods for the most successful culture of our children, in the opinions of many leading minds amongst us, is materially different. The two more prominent may be briefly pointed out. The one holds that no special organization for the culture of colored youth at this time are necessary ; that precisely the same species of learning imparted to white youth will best serve for colored youth , that both schools and education, as at present constituted, especially for, and wholly directed by the whites, being so far superior ; better training can be obtained therein than can be had in any that can be adapted to the especial wants of colored youth. On the other hand, it is held that colored youth is to be educated, so as to catch up in the great race we are running ; and hence, schools must be adapted to so train him ; not that he himself is so widely different from the white youth, but that the state of things which he finds around him, and which he must be qualified to change, is so widely different. The training, therefore, necessary to propel him, so that he can gain up with the whites, (as gain he must, or be utterly lost,) is to be obtained only in schools adapted to his wants; that neither schools nor educators for the whites, at present, are in full sympathy with him ; and that he must either abandon his own state of things which he finds around him, and which he is pledged to change and better, or cease to receive culture from such sources, since their whole tendency is to change him, not his condition—to educate him out of his sympathies, not to quicken and warm his sympathies, for all that is of worth to him is his elevation, and the elevation of his people.

We are fully inclined to the latter opinion. We are more than persuaded, in looking over the whole subject, that the force of circumstances compels the regulation of schools by us to supply a deficiency produced by our condition ; that it should be our special aim, to so direct instructors, regulate books and libraries ; in fine, the whole process of instruction to meet entirely our particular exigencies, continuing so long, only, as such exigencies exist.

Your Committee on Education will however place this subject fully before you.

But we go farther ; we go beyond the school-room. We would approach the *fire-side*, and would remind you that something more definite must be done there, than has yet been accomplished. With all the precepts and examples of the whites before us, it is but too apparent that we have made too little progress in the fire-side culture of our youth ; and it is equally apparent that this neglect enters too largely into all the ramifications of our social state, affecting its present and prospective advancement. With a badly fire-side trained youth, added to indifferent or objectionable school culture, such as has educated them out of their humanity, what progress, we ask, can a people expect to make, in a community like ours ? From the fire-side we must receive and teach the great lessons of self-confidence, self-dependence, perseverance, energy, and continuity. Implements such as these are more precious than rubies. They will seek for us, and make us seek for, and engage in proper callings, such as tend to elevate. They will discourage in us all such as tend to humiliate, depress, and degrade. Employments have much more to do with the moulding and stamping the character of a people than we have yet calculated for. Implements such as we have just mentioned will enable us to carve out, unaided, our own road, and walk securely in it.

The possession of means itself is but second in importance to proper employments for our youth, such as mechanism, art, commerce, agriculture, &c., since these not only produce wealth, but develop also the man. Without *agriculture*, without *mechanism*, without *art*, without commerce, without education, without knowledge or appreciation, of the *press*, what can a people do ? What power or influence can they wield ? What progress can they make ? The great gulf into which a large portion of our youth fall, and not unfrequently sink, too, beyond recovery, or even human reach, is between the school-room and their majority, (so to speak,) and this for the want mainly of such employments as we have just stated. Unsettled in purpose, and unstable in habits, not yet inured to proper labor, a large majority of our youth become enfeebled both in mind and body, and equally shackled in character. They have emerged from homes surrounded by so few attractions, that they know little of the bliss of home, and shrink from the responsibility, or even the thought of providing them for themselves. They look not forward to those happy and holy alliances, out of which issue the vitality of society, and the growth, strength, and perpetuity of the community. So far from this, we find them wasting their time, the prime of their life, and whatever of substance they may have acquired, for that which produces only disgrace, premature decay, and death. Far be it from us to overdraw this picture ; we would fain color it less gloomily, if it were not deception to do so. It is in the matter of statistics that we here so severely suffer.

Our opponents, with much boldness, we will not say with how much truth, already assert that we are fast retrograding in point of numbers, and in the vigor of our institutions. Of one thing we are certain ; comfortable homes and hearths, and correct culture and habits, tend to the increase of a people ; the reverse to their diminution. It is a matter of vital importance, then, to know whether we are in this matter really advancing ; or, it may be, receding.

We cannot dismiss this branch of our subject without briefly remarking aws which govern health and longevity, claim also a share of our attention, being intimately connected with it as well as affecting all our relations in society. In this connection, also, we can but express the hope that scientific and medical men from among us, of acknowledged ability, be fostered and encouraged ; that this point in our *social system,* hitherto too much neglected, receive due attention.

Finally, for the purpose of securing ourselves against encroachments, and making provisions for future emergencies, should they arise, our *relations* require the speedy linking together of the whole chain of enlightened mind among us, not only of the *States,* but of the whole *continent* into one *grand league,* the consideration of which should be forthwith laid before you, in the form of a well digested plan.

Since the whole object of our deliberations is to change and better our condition, rather than to laud whatever of value may be found within the pale of our *social* relations, we have preferred to bring forth in this *report* only a few, but as we deem vital points, affecting adversely these relations.— Nor have we sought to bring before you the more palpable evils, their existence among us being too apparent, and their remedy of more easy application.

In conclusion, we remark the line of our polity is clear and explicit. It must be so constructed as to produce.

First. An increased number of better regulated homes among us.

Second. Better fire-side and school culture.

Third. Such callings as will develop equally and fully ourselves and the resources around us.

Fourth. A new impetus to business operations, and an enlargement of its boundaries, by means of leagues, associations, &c., &c.

Fifth. A strict observance of, and reverence for the *marriage institution,* and obedience to those laws which secure health and longevity.

Sixth. More enlightened views of the high and holy principles of *morals* and religion.

Seventh. An intelligent and efficient clergy, fully imbued with their true mission, and ever willing and instant on performing it.

Eighth. An able, devoted, and well-sustained *press*, wielding a power and influence second to none in this, or any other country.

Ninth, and lastly. To produce among us throughout, complete Combination, Concentration, and Consolidation.

As sure and as speedily as light succeeds darkness, will such a line of *polity*, if commenced with vigor, and followed out with strictness, raise us from our present *state* to one of permanence and power in this country.

In the presence and progress of such polity, all forms of prejudice and hatred would disappear; wicked and oppressive laws become dead letters upon the pages of our statute-books; societies for our removal become extinct. In fine, all political, social, and religious disabilities would cease to exist, and be remembered only among the things that once were.

As Americans, then, [colored Americans,] for as such, only can we expect to succeed, we are called upon to throw aside all our supineness and indifference, and to act as becometh men sensible of their rights and privileges, and determined to possess, hold, and enjoy them.

WILLIAM J. WILSON, }
WILLIAM WHIPPER, } *Committee.*
CHARLES B. RAY, }

On the motion to adopt the foregoing report, considerable debate arose. J. McCune Smith opposed its adoption, because of the statement in it that the colored people of this country are not producers, for its advocacy, &c. He was followed by Rev. Lewis Woodson and Payton Harris, on the same side. Mr. Wilson replied in a short speech, denying that the Report advocated separate schools. Messrs. J. N. Still and Uriah Boston followed in support of the Report. Mr. D. B. Bowser combatted the idea that we are not producers. Mr. J. Mercer Langston moved that the Report be amended to conform to the fact, which is, that we are, to a great extent, producers.

The Chair announced the Committee on Statistics, consisting of the following gentlemen:—Lewis Woodson, M. M. Clark, A. M. Sumner. On motion, adjourned.

SECOND DAY—MORNING SESSION.

President in the chair. Prayer by Rev. M. M. Clark. Mr. Stephen Smith moved that the roll be called. Amended, that each member pay one dollar as his name is called. Not agreed to. Motion lost.

Mr. Lewis Woodson moved that the roll be corrected by striking out the names of such persons as had been elected by meetings, but were not present. Amended, that a committee on credentials be appointed. As amended, agreed to

The President announced the names of the committee: T. G. Campbell A. H. Adams, A. G. Beman, W. J. Watkins, J. N. Still, J. D. Bonner, C. H Langston, H. O. Wagoner, David H. Jackson, Horace B. Smith. Mr. A. N

Freeman moved that the President be added to the committee on Colonization. Amended, that there be an addition of two from each State, and that the Convention nominate. Agreed to. The President announced the committee on Literature : Messrs. A. M. Sumner, G. B. Vashon, J. I. Gaines. A letter from Mr. F. T. Newsome, of Cass Co., Michigan, read and referred to business committee. Report of committee on Finance taken up and discussed. Rev. W. C. Munroe thought members of the Convention should be taxed one, two or three dollars to meet expenses ; was entirely opposed to begging. Other gentlemen thought that there were friends, both able and willing to assist, who should be allowed the opportunity. Report laid over to permit Rev. A. R. Green to discuss the report on Social Relations. The gentleman argued that we are mainly consumers, and not producers. Rules suspended to allow Mr. Green to continue his remarks. Mr. J. M. Langston followed, adducing proofs that we are producers. Mr. Gloster defended the views set forth in the report. Mr. Harris rejoined. Mr. J. G. Bowers followed on the same side. Mr. Downing moved that the report be referred to the Committee, with the addition of Mr. J. M. Langston, with instructions to strike out obnoxious passages. Lost. Mr. Gordon moved its indefinite postponement. Lost. The previous question was now called for. The report, as amended by Mr. Langston, being put to the Convention, was declared doubtful. Mr. G. T. Downing called for the Ayes and Noes ; upon which the report was rejected—ayes 31, noes 63. On motion, adjourned.

AFTERNOON SESSION.

President in the chair. Prayer by Rev. Mr. Driver. Mr. Jenkins moved that to-morrow (Friday) evening be devoted to a public meeting. Amended, that this evening be devoted to that purpose ; not agreed to. Motion lost.— Report of committee on Finance taken up. Mr. Green moved that the committee be instructed to forthwith report an estimate of the probable expenses of the Convention. Agreed to. The committee reported that the probable expense would be as follows :

For rent of Hall.............................$60.00
Printing Report..................... ... . 50.00

Total.....................................$110.00

Mr. Downing moved that the roll be now called, and that delegates pay one dollar as they answer to their names. Agreed to. The roll being called, one hundred and fourteen members answered to their names. The sum collected ($114) was handed over to the committee on Finance.

The report on Colonization was made the special order of the evening.

Mr. Sumner moved that the remainder of the afternoon, or so much of it as may be necessary, be devoted to reading reports, &c. Agreed to.

Mr. George W. Clark favored the Convention with a song. The Committee on Commerce reported through their Chairman, Mr. George T. Downing, the following paper :

REPORT OF COMMITTEE ON THE IMPORTANCE OF COLORED PERSONS ENGAGING IN COMMERCIAL PURSUITS.

The subject which has been referred to your committee is a practical one—one of importance ; and we do not deem it essential to submit an extended report. Much of the time of this Convention has, and will be occupied with the consideration of other equally important matters. Our subject, being a practical business question, we hold that it will be in keeping with that practicability to be brief in our report.

The importance of our people's seeking and being found in every reputable avenue leading to wealth and respectability is so palpably manifest, that it would seem superfluous to stop and argue the point. Commerce has had a leading influence in developing intellect. Those countries which have availed themselves of its advantages, have exhibited increased regard for the arts and sciences, as well as social comforts. Commerce is the pioneer of civilization and intelligence. Commerce is expansion ; it gives a field space for essential, refined morality. But for it, half of the states and kingdoms of the world would now be unknown—would have remained the subjects of barbarism and ignorance. Commerce sought, found and benefitted them. Behold the " world-seeking" Genoese embarking on board of his sturdy barge, buffeting with unknown waves into depths and space not before traversed—not known by mortal. The mind is lost in the majestic conception which fills his comprehensive brain—a new world before him—space unmeasured ! Imagine the ravings of his mind—the probabilities which shot comet-like across his imagination, creating a glare and wonderment. What untold soarings swell the wide range of his hopes, among which is the extension of commerce. From the landing of Columbus, it may be said that the course of America has been progress. She is now considered great. The impetus which she has given to commerce is one of the leading sources of her greatness ; and the intercourse, consequent upon the business relation of the world, is to be one of the leading influences which will blot out the unfortunate stigma which now dims her progress and fair name. Let us swell the agency. Commerce leads to respectability. It is because we have not been found in this and similar avenues leading and directing, that we have been dependent and so little respected ; and is in fact the reason why we are now the proscribed class of the community. And may not your committee add, that much of the increased respect entertained for us has been brought about by the fact, that we are awakening, especially throughout the less densely settled portions of the country, to active business relations ; that we are beginning to become producers as well as consumers. The branch of commerce is almost entirely neglected, while it should receive a proportionate consideration. This avenue is open to us if we will master the perseverance and devotion necessary.—Through commerce, acquaintances and alliances are formed, and power secured. We must emerge from menial positions to the pursuit of commercial and other elevating branches of trade.

Running back a few years, we soon fall upon the time when the colored man enjoyed all that he did merely as a privilege. The entire aim of those who forced him into the country was to tax the muscle and sinew to their utmost capacity—to subject him to a state assimilating closely to that of the brute—so as best to fit him for their uses—to brutalize him into subjection and cattle ignorance.

This passed on for years, with no thought otherwise. This has been most depressing to his intellect and aspirations. But brighter times are upon us. We have sympathizers and friends. Our rights are being acknowledged. We have no longer to contend that we are men and citizens, and enjoy alike, with other citizens, the rights and immunities as such. We need now to engage in matters practicable and leading. We are becoming more and more enlightened. Our progress, in this respect, has been truly astonishing—in fact, has increased so rapidly as to have produced a kind of deformity. We have not kept pace, caught hold, or sought to lead and direct in the business pursuits commensurate with our intelligence—pursuits which tend to wealth, respectability and importance. We need combinations. We need confidence. We need to be known and referred to as business men. All of these are the immediate heirs of commerce.

The places filled in this community by our people have not involved responsibility and respect. We have been machines impelled; consequently there has not been a development of intellect in business pursuits. We have not been calculators. We have not seemed to have had any fixed end tending to our upbuilding and elevation. We have had money. We cannot be called other than industrious; but this industry, to be profitable, to serve the ends for which it is designed, must be made subservient to mind. We must husband aright our resources. What are our resources? The question is answered. The resources common to other men are energy and perseverance Have we capital? It is at our command. We have individuals possessed of the means, with combination and certainty. Where are our ships, our counting-houses, our business connection with the world? They are wanting; and only because we have never fixedly resolved to have them.

It might be expected that your Committee, in reporting upon the subject of commerce, would have given some statistics bearing thereupon; but they have not deemed it necessary. The statistics of the world might be given to establish that commerce and business enterprises tend to the greatness and consideration of nations. But in the present case, the question is, how far the engagement, on the part of our people, in business pursuits, as leaders and contractors in commercial enterprises, will tend to their upbuilding and elevation—being the proscribed portion of a nation. This point your committee have endeavored to make plain in the brief manner given above, which they most respectfully submit.

GEORGE T. DOWNING,
J. MERCER LANGSTON,
BOYD PARKER.

Report accepted. Mr. William H. Day read a report from the Committee on Agriculture. [Mr. Day has neglected to send in his report for publication. —*Committee*.] Mr. James M'Cune Smith moved that all reports brought before this Convention be published ; withdrawn. Report was received from the Business Committee, consisting of a communication from M. F. Newsome, Esq. ; Cass, Michigan ; J. Keep of Oberlin, Ohio ; J. Wilson, M. D., of Philadelphia ; Samuel Aaron, and A. Dewey, from the same place,—of resolutions by H. O. Wagener, Illinois ; L. Tillman, and A. R. Green. Mr. Josephus Fowler read a report on Temperance, &c. [This report is not among the papers handed to the *Publishing Committee*.]

On motion, adjourned.

EVENING SESSION.

Vice President, Amos G. Beman, in the chair. Prayer by W. C. Munroe Minutes read, corrected and approved.

Mr. C. B. Ray moved that each member of the Convention be furnished gratuitously with as many copies of the reports of the Convention as the number printed will allow ; agreed to. Dr. Pennington now read the report on Colonization, together with appropriate resolutions ; report received. [It is to be regretted that this report by Dr. Pennington has not been handed in for publication.] Mr. C. B. Ray moved its adoption, pending which motion, Messrs. Charles L. Remond, J. I. Gaines, J. M. Langston and Frederick Douglass took the stand, reviewing the position of the Colonization Society.

Report and resolutions accepted. Mr. Bowser, of Philadelphia, offered two resolutions, which were accepted.

On motion, adjourned.

THIRD DAY—MORNING SESSION.

Vice President, William H. Day, in the Chair. Prayer by the Rev. Mr. Wilson of New York. Minutes read and approved. On motion, the reading of the roll was dispensed with. Report from Business Committee received. Resolutions by H. O. Wagoner of Illinois, referred to Business Committee. Committee on Statistics reported that the reports came in so slowly from the various delegations, and that the subject matter was of such great importance, that they felt they would not have time to prepare such a report as its importance demanded. Report received and Committee discharged. On motion, it was agreed to appoint a Committee, consisting of one from each State, of which James M'Cune Smith shall be chairman, to digest and publish, at an early date as possible, a statistical report of the condition of the colored people of the United States. On bringing up the report on national organization, Dr. Smith made a few eloquent remarks. The report, with additions from Com. on Commerce, was read. All was agreed that it be taken up in sections. Mr. Douglass spoke, showing the necessity for such an organization. Mr. Walker, of Ohio, and Mr. L. Woodson, of Pennsylvania, both claiming the floor, the

President decided in favor of Mr. Woodson, whereupon Mr. Walker appealed. The Convention sustained the chair. Mr. Woodson then proceeded to advocate the adoption of the plan of organization. Mr. T. G. Campbell moved that the word colored be erased from the preamble. Upon which the previous question was called. Motion agreed to. Mr. Downing moved to strike out certain portions of the preamble. By leave of the Convention, Mr. Langston offered a motion to suspend debate upon the subject in hand, in order to allow Prof. C. L. Reason an opportunity to present a report from the Committee on Maual Labor Schools.

REPORT OF THE COMMITTEE ON MANUAL LABOR SCHOOL.

The aim and the end of a right culture, is primarily to develop power, and to turn that power into a proper channel. Educational Institutions ought therefore to be so modeled and so conducted as to draw out thought, incite useful inquiry, and give such aid and strength to the individual as will enable him to be something in the world, in addition to the mere scholar. Every person is here not merely to enjoy, but to work ; and schools are only valuable in their teachings, as they assist in making both thinker and worker. They may saturate men with the learning of every age—yet, except they strive to make them something more than literary flowers, they sin greatly against the individual and humanity also. The hungry world asks for grain, and those growths that give nutriment. Not by floral beauty is the physical being builded up. Not by mere word study do the races grow intellectually strong Not by eloquent abstract preaching, do the nations prove Christianity. The elements of truth, the principels of industrial advancement, of national greatness, that lie in questionable shapes amid the knowledge of the schools, must be separated from the useless materials that surround them ; and made as chyle to the human body, the givers of nutriment, the restorers of expended energy. And as in the human body, the richness of the digested food goes to make up bone, and muscle, and flesh, and the various tissues of vessels of the system— in like manner schools ought so to be fashioned, as to deposite here and there on the surface of society, artizan and merchant, mechanic and farmer, linguist and mathematician—mental power in every phase, and practical science in as many as may be. The truth of this view is virtually acknowledged in part already. Where men know beforehand what kind of knowledge their duties in life will require, they avail themselves of Institutions whose course of study is specific and well degested. Hence exist our Law-Schools, and Military Academies, and Medical Colleges. And these are necessarry, even amid a class of people whose position enables them to make the most of a *general* course of study, by the application of some of the specialities of such course, to any avocation, that, in after life, they may choose to pursue. When *we* are called upon to consider the subject of Education with reference to ourselves, and to ask what kind of an Institution would best befit *us*, the answer comes in the light of the announced doctrine, namely, one that would develop *power ;* and that kind of power most essential to our elevation. If after submitting to a general system of instruction, according to the provisions of the colleges of the land, *we* can add the store of knowledge gained to any pursuit in life *we* please, as so much starting capital, then we might not need to ask the establishing of Institutions different from those already erected. But this is not the case. We have, indeed, a few literary colleges accessible to those of us who can pay ; two Manual Labor Colleges with the system partially carried out ; besides an academy of the same kind established in Southern Ohio.

Between these two varities of schools, there need be no hesitation in deciding as to which is best adapted to our special wants. Under any circumstance, Manual Labor Establishments commend themselves to the patronage of all classes. The long entertained beliefs that mental effort may be made and continued without any reference to physical exercise, are rapidly passing away. And with them, also, those more injurious and unfriendly views of true gentility and scholarship, that hitherto have held labor in contempt. Literature has too long kept itself aloof from the furrowed field, and from the dust and bustle of the work-shop. The pale, sickly brow and emaciated form have been falsely shown to the world as the ripeness of mental discipline ; and sun-burnt and brawny muscular arms, have been among the majority of students synonymous with dulness of parts, and ignorant vulgarity. Thanks, however, to true views of the dignity of human nature, and an appreciation of the correct laws of physical development ; labor has received the anointing of the highest refinement, and healthy frames are proven to be the best accompaniment to high intellectual power.

Moreover, with regard to ourselves, a consideration of our position in this country, teaches us that our inheritance is one that can only be ameliorated by the combination of practical art, with literary preparation. Hitherto our educated youth have found no corresponding channel to their accademic equipment, and so they have failed to make their mark on society and the age. The work-shops, as a general thing, are closed to them, while at the same time they are reproached for lack of inventive or industrial talent. We know that we cannot form an equally useful part of any people without the ability to contribute our full share to the wealth, activity, social comforts, and progress of such people. If, then, the necessary education to fit us to share in these responsibilities, cannot be generally had, by reason of the prejudices of the country, where best they can be taught, namely in the work-shops and counting-houses, and the other varied establishments of the land, that have to do with the machinery of activities carried on around us ; we must needs consider the importance of making our Literary Institutions contribute by a change of form to filling up this want in our midst.

The agricultural life, standing pre-eminent, and looming in importance above all others, would demand a prominent place among the internal arrangements of such a school. Farming, as a scientific system, ought to be a part of the course of every scholar, and especially of that class of students whose highest interests would be benefitted by leaving the cities, for the freer and no less noble life in the country. No professorship in any college can claim more on the score of usefulness than that of agriculture. In none of the Institutions thus far open to us, has labor in this department been at all regulated on scientific principles. Literary preparation has absorbed most of the attention of students, because of the order and beauty infused into that phase of college life. The department of labor has ever remained crude and unseemly—subordinate in position and outline to the other, and, therefore unable to provide that extensive field for industry, as to warrant the tittle assumed by them of Manual Labor Institutions. We make no complaint against the incompleteness of any of the existing schools, in order to detract from their usefulness in other ways. We only believe it desirable, that a more thorough plan be established that will combine the literary course of the schools, scientific agricultural knowledge, theoretic mechanics and engineering, and, what is a feature we hope to see engrafted on the plan, a series of work-shops under systematic and skilful instruction. Not simply as a means of furnishing poor students with the facilities of continuing under instruction, but to remedy also as far as may be the disadvantages under which we labor in acquiring a knowledge of the mechanical arts.

To this end we advise the maturing of a plan by some other suitable Committee for erecting in some locality, central, as to population, a school of a high intellectual grade, having incorporated an Agricultural Professorship, or an equivalent thereto, a professorship to superintend the practical application of mathematics and natural philosophy to surveying, mechanics and engineering, the following branches of industry : general smithing, turning, wheelwrighting and cabinet-making ; and a general work-shop in which' may be combined such application of skill in wood, iron, and other material as to produce a variety of saleable articles,* with suitable buildings and machinery for producing the same. These superintended by competent workmen, under pay precisely as other teachers would give students a foundation for after self-support in life, and break down the distinctions that never ought to exist between the study and the work-shop. The above industrial pursuits are named, not because others more desirable perhaps, or more difficult to secure, might not have had a place given them in this imperfect report; but, because it seemed wise to choose some which are primary to most others in general usefulness, and at the same time, such as whose products have an extensive marketable demand. In establishing work-shops, it must be remembered that the introducing of any large part of the very useful or lucrative branches is an utter impossibility. All that can be aimed at in the beginning, is to elevate labor to its own true standard—vindicate the laws of physical health, and at the same time, as a repaying benefit, make the work done as intrinsic and *profitable*, a part of education as a proficiency in Latin, mathematics or medicine.

As to the *means* by which such an Institution may be erected and carried on; we advise the issuing of joint stock under proper Directors, to the amount of $50,000 in shares of $10 each, or a less number of a larger amount, if considered advisable. The Committee are of opinion that $50,000 used in the purchase of land and the erecting and fitting up of buildings, will be fully enough, to warrant the beginning of a thorough Manual Labor School, on the plan suggested.

The sale of scholarships, at judicious rates, and the contributions of the liberal and the philanthropic, ought to give an additional $100,000 as an endowment, which sum properly invested, would be a guarantee, that the liabilities and expense of the Institution would be faithfully met.

The Department of Industry for Females, the Committee cannot, in the short time given them, intelligently settle upon, except in outline. We are of opinion, that looms could be erected for the weaving of carriage and other trimmings; for bindings of various kinds; that the straw hat business in some of its branches, paper box making, and similar occupations, might from time to time be connected.

The shareholders, if such a plan be approved, would compose the college association, and would have a right to appoint the Trustees of the School, said Trustees being citizens of the State wherein such Institution shall be located.

Such is the rough outline of a plan which we think would be in judicious hands, and so modified as to conform to the proper school laws, feasible and fraught with unbounding good.

In the past, the misfortune has been that our knowledge has been much distributed. We have had educated *heads* in one large division among us, and educated *hands* in another. We do not concede in this remark, that the mind worker is not a benefactor and a creator. The inventing, the directing intellect, produces the demand for mechanical labor; but we believe, that, the instances of the marriage, so to speak, of thoroughly educated mind with manual labor, are lamentably rare among us. All over the land, our earnest youth have gone asking to be cared for by the work-shops of the country, but no acknowledgement has been made of their human relationship; their mental, and bodily fitness, have had the same contumely heaped upon them, as is received by those unfortunate beings who in social life bear upon their persons the brand of illegitimacy. As a consequence, we have grown up to too large an extent—mere scholars on one side and muscular giants on the other. We would equalize those discrepancies. We would produce a harmonious development of character. In the sweat of their brows, we would have our scholars grow powerful, and their sympathies run out for humanity everywhere. On the altar of labor, we would have every mother dedicate her child to the cause of freedom; and then, in the breeze wafted over the newly plowed field, there will come encouragement and hope; and the ringing blows of the anvil and the axe, and the keen cutting edge of the chisel and the plane,

---

*A work-shop of this kind is, we believe, now in operation in Ohio, connected with the State Penitentiary. It produces stirrups, buckles, harness-frames saw-handles, &c., &c.

will symbolize on the one hand human excellence is rough hewn by self-exertion, and on the other, fashioned into models of beauty by reflection and discipline.

Let us educate our youth in such wise, as shall give them means of success, adapted to their struggling condition, and ere long following the enterprise of the age, we may hope to see them filling everywhere positions of responsibility and trust, and, gliding on the triple tide of wealth, intelligence and virtue, reach eventually, to a sure resting place of distinction and happiness.

Respectfully submitted,

CHAS. L. REASON,
GEO. B. VASHON,   } *Committee.*
CHAS. H. LANGSTON,

Pending the motion to adopt, Mr. Douglass read a letter addressed by himself to Mrs. Stowe. This letter was read to inform the Convention what representation the writer had made to Mrs. Stowe, respecting the condition and wants of the free colored people.

ROCHESTER, March 8th, 1853.

MY DEAR MRS. STOWE:

You kindly informed me, when at your house, a fortnight ago, that you designed to do something which should permanently contribute to the improvement and elevation of the free colored people in the United States. You especially expressed an interest in such of this class as had become free by their own exertions, and desired most of all to be of service to them. In what manner, and by what means, you can assist this class most successfully, is the subject upon which you have done me the honor to ask my opinion.

Begging you to excuse the unavoidable delay, I will now most gladly comply with your request, but before doing so, I desire to express, dear Madam, my deep sense of the value of the services which you have already rendered my afflicted and persecuted people, by the publication of your inimitable book on the subject of slavery. That contribution to our bleeding cause, alone, involves us in a debt of gratitude which cannot be measured ; and your resolution to make other exertions on our behalf excites in me emotions and sentiments, which I scarcely need try to give forth in words. Suffice it to say, that I believe you to have the blessings of your enslaved countrymen and countrywomen ; and the still higher reward which comes to the soul in the smiles of our merciful Heavenly father, whose ear is ever open to the cries of the oppressed.

With such sentiments, dear Madam, I will at once proceed to lay before you, in as few words as the nature of the case will allow, my humble views in the premises. First of all, let me briefly state the nature of the disease, before I undertake to prescribe the remedy. Three things are notoriously true of us, as a people. These are POVERTY, IGNORANCE and DEGRADATION. Of course there are exceptions to this general statement ; but these are so few as only to prove its essential truthfulness. I shall not stop here to inquire minutely into the causes which have produced our present condition ; nor to denounce those whom I believe to be responsible for those causes. It is enough that we shall agree upon the character of the evil, whose existence we deplore, and upon some plan for its removal.

3

I assert then, that *poverty, ignorance* and *degradation* are the combined evils ; or, in other words, these constitute the social disease of the Free Colored people in the United States.

To deliver them from this triple malady, is to improve and elevate them, by which I mean simply to put them on an equal footing with their white fellow-countrymen in the sacred right to "*Life, Liberty* and the pursuit of happiness." I am for no fancied or artificial elevation, but only ask fair play. How shall this be obtained ? I answer, first, not by establishing for our use high schools and colleges. Such institutions are, in my judgment, beyond our immediate occasions, and are not adapted to our present most pressing wants. High schools and colleges are excellent institutions, and will, in due season, be greatly subservient to our progress ; but they are the result, as well as they are the demand of a point of progress, which we, as a people, have not yet attained. Accustomed, as we have been, to the rougher and harder modes of living, and of gaining a livelihood, we cannot, and we ought not to hope that, in a single leap from our low condition, we can reach that of *Ministers, Lawyers, Doctors, Editors, Merchants,* &c. These will, doubtless, be attained by us ; but this will only be, when we have patiently and laboriously, and I may add successfully, mastered and passed through the intermediate gradations o agriculture and the mechanic arts. Besides, there are (and perhaps this is a better reason for my view of the case) numerous institutions of learning in this country, already thrown open to colored youth. To my thinking, there are quite as many facilities now afforded to the colored people, as they can spare the time, from the sterner duties of life, to avail themselves of. In their present condition of poverty, they cannot spare their sons and daughters two or three years at boarding schools or colleges, to say nothing of finding the means to sustain them while at such institutions. I take it, therefore, that we are well provided for in this respect ; and that it may be fairly inferred from the past that the facilities for our education, so far as schools and colleges in the Free States are concerned, will increase quite in proportion with our future wants. Colleges have been open to colored youth in this country during the last dozen years. Yet few, comparatively, have acquired a classical education ; and even this few have found themselves educated far above a living condition, there being no methods by which they could turn their learning to account. Several of this latter class have entered the ministry ; but you need not be told that an educated people is needed to sustain an educated ministry. There must be a certain amount of cultivation among the people to sustain such a ministry. At present, we have not that cultivation amongst us ; and therefore, we value, in the preacher, strong lungs, rather than high learning. I do not say that educated ministers are not needed amongst us.— Far from it ! I wish there were more of them ; but to increase their number is *not* the largest benefit you can bestow upon us.

You, dear Madam, can help the masses. You can do something for the thousands ; and by lifting these from the depths of poverty and ignorance, you can make an educated ministry and an educated class possible. In the present circumstances, prejudice is a bar to the educated black minister among the whites; and ignorance is a bar to him among the blacks.

We have now two or three colored lawyers in this country; and I rejoice in the fact; for it affords very gratifying evidence of our progress. Yet it must be confessed that, in point of success, our lawyers are as great failures as are our ministers. White people will not employ them to the obvious embarrassment of their causes, and the blacks, taking their *cue* from the whites, have not sufficient confidence in their abilities to employ them. Hence, educated colored men, among the colored people, are at a very great discount. It would seem that education and emigration go together with us; for as soon as a man rises amongst us, capable, by his genius and learning, to do us great service, just so soon he finds that he can serve himself better by going elsewhere. In proof of this, I might instance the Russwurms—the Garnetts— the Wards—the Crummells and others—all men of superior ability and attainments, and capable of removing mountains of prejudice against their race, by their simple presence in the country; but these gentlemen, finding themselves embarrassed here by the peculiar disadvantages to which I have referred— disadvantages in part growing out of their education—being repelled by ignorance on the one hand, and prejudice on the other, and having no taste to continue a contest against such odds, they have sought more congenial climes, where they can live more peacable and quiet lives. I regret their election— but I cannot blame them; for, with an equal amount of education, and the hard lot which was theirs, I might follow their example.

But, again, it has been said that the colored people must become farmers— that they must go on the land, in order to their elevation. Hence, many benevolent people are contributing the necessary funds to purchase land in Canada, and elsewhere, for them. That prince of good men, Gerrit Smith, has given away thousands of acres to colored men in this State, thinking, doubtless, that in so doing he was conferring a blessing upon them. Now, while I do not undervalue the efforts which have been made, and are still being made in this direction, yet I must say that I have far less confidence in such efforts, than I have in the benevolence which prompts them. Agricultural pursuits are not, as I think, suited to our condition. The reason of this is not to be found so much in the occupation, (for it is a noble and ennobling one,) as in the people themselves. That is only a remedy, which can be applied to the case; and the difficulty in agricultural pursuits, as a remedy for the evils of poverty and ignorance amongst us, is that it cannot, for various reasons, be applied.

We cannot apply it, because it is almost impossible to get colored men to go on the land. From some cause or other, (perhaps the adage that misery loves company will explain,) colored people will congregate in the large towns and cities; and they will endure any amount of hardship and privation, rather than separate, and go into the country. Again, very few have the means to set up for themselves, or to get where they could do so.

Another consideration against expending energy in this direction is our want of self-reliance. Slavery, more than all things else, robs its victims of self-reliance. To go into the western wilderness, and there to lay the foundation of future society, requires more of that important quality than a life of slavery has left us. This may sound strange to you, coming, as it does, from a colored man ; but I am dealing with facts ; and these never accommodate themselves to the feelings or wishes of any. They don't *ask*, but *take* leave *to be*. It is a fact then, and not less so because I wish it were otherwise, that the colored people are wanting in self-reliance—too fond of society—too eager for immediate results—and too little skilled in mechanics or husbandry to attempt to overcome the wilderness ; at least, until they have overcome obstacles less formidable. Therefore, I look to other means than agricultural pursuits for the elevation and improvement of colored people. Of course, I allege this of the many. There are exceptions. Individuals among us, with commendable zeal, industry, perseverance and self-reliance, have found, and are finding, in agricultural pursuits, the means of supporting, improving and educating their amilies.

The plan which I contemplate will, (if carried into effect,) greatly increase the number of this class—since it will prepare others to meet the rugged duties which a pioneer agricultural condition must impose upon all who take it upon them. What I propose is intended simply to prepare men for the work of getting an honest living—not out of dishonest men—but out of an honest earth.

Again, there is little reason to hope that any considerable number of the free colored people will ever be induced to leave this country, even if such a thing were desirable. The black man, (*un*-like the Indian,) loves civilization He does not make very great progress in civilization himself, but he likes to be in the midst of it, and prefers to share its most galling evils, to encountering barbarism. Then the love of country—the dread of isolation—the lack of adventurous spirit—and the thought of seeming to desert their " brethren in bonds," are a powerful and perpetual check upon all schemes of colonization, which look to the removal of the colored people, without the slaves.— The truth is, dear Madam, we are *here*, and here we are likely to remain. Individuals emigrate—nations never. We have grown up with this Republic ; and I see nothing in our character, or even in the character of the American people, as yet, which compels the belief that we must leave the United States. If, then, we are to remain here, the question for the wise and good is precisely that you have submitted to me—and that which I fear I have been, perhaps, too slow in answering—namely, What can be done to improve the condition of the free colored people in the United States ? The plan which I humbly submit in answer to this inquiry, (and in the hope that it may find favor with you, dear Madam, and with the many friends of humanity who honor, love, and co-operate with you,) is the establishment in Rochester, N Y.—or in some other part of the United States, equally favorable to such an enterprise—of an INDUSTRIAL COLLEGE, in which shall be taught several important branches of the mechanic arts. This college to be open to colored youth. I will pass over, for the present, the details of such an institution as that I propose. It is not worth while that I should dwell upon these at all Once convinced that something of the sort is needed, and the organizing power will be forthcoming. It is the peculiarity of your favored race that they can always do what they think necessary to be done. I can safely trust all details to yourself, and to the wise and good people whom you represent in the interest you take in my oppressed fellow-countrymen.

Never having myself had a day's schooling in all my life, I may not be expected to be able to map out the details of a plan so comprehensive as that involved in the idea of a college. I repeat then, I leave the organization and administration to the superior wisdom of yourself and the friends that second your noble efforts. The argument in favor of an Industrial College, (a College to be conducted by the best men, and the best workmen, which the mechanic arts can afford—a College where colored youth can be instructed to use their hands, as well as their heads—where they can be put in possession of the means of getting a living—whether their lot in after life may be cast among civilized or uncivilized men—whether they choose to stay here, or prefer to return to the land of their fathers,) is briefly this—prejudice against the free colored people in the United States has shown itself nowhere so invincible as among mechanics. The farmer and the professional man cherish no feeling so bitter as that cherished by these. The latter would starve us out of the country entirely. At this moment, I can more easily get my son into a lawyer's office, to study law, than I can into a blacksmith's shop, to blow the bellows, and to wield the sledge-hammer. Denied the means of learning useful trades, we are pressed into the narrowest limits to obtain a livelihood. In times past we have been the hewers of wood and the drawers of water for American society, and we once enjoyed a monopoly in menial employments, but this is so no longer—even these employments are rapidly passing away out of our hands. The fact is, (every day begins with the lesson, and ends with the lesson,) that colored men must learn trades—must find new employments, new modes of usefulness to society—or that they must decay under the pressing wants to which their condition is rapidly bringing them. We must become mechanics—we must build, as well as live in houses —we must make, as well as use furniture—we must construct bridges, as well as pass over them—before we can properly live, or be respected by our fellow men. We need mechanics, as well as ministers. We need workers in iron' wood, clay, and in leather. We have orators, authors, and other professional men ; but these reach only a certain class, and get respect for our race in certain select circles. To live here as we ought, we must fasten ourselves to our countrymen through their every day and cardinal wants. We must not only be able to *black* boots, but to *make* them. At present, we are unknown in the Northern States, as mechanics. We give no proof of genius or skill at the County, the State, or the National Fairs. We are unknown at any of the great exhibitions of the industry of our fellow-citizens—and being unknown, we are unconsidered.

The fact that we make no show of our ability, is held conclusive of our inability to make any. Hence, all the indifference and contempt, with which incapacity is regarded, fall upon us, and that too, when we have had no means of disproving the injurious opinion of our natural inferiority. I have, during the last dozen years, denied, before the Americans, that we are an inferior race. But this has been done by arguments, based upon admitted principles, rather than by the presentation of facts. Now, firmly believing, as I do, that there are skill, invention, power, industry, and real mechanical genius among the colored people, which will bear favorable testimony for them, and which only need the means to develop them, I am decidedly in favor of the establishment of such a college as I have mentioned. The benefits of such an institution would not be confined to the Northern States, nor to the free colored people : they would extend over the whole Union. The slave, not less than the freeman, would be benefitted by such an institution. It must be confessed that the most powerful argument, now used by the Southern slave-holder —and the one most soothing to his conscience—is, that derived from the low condition of 'the free colored people at the North. I have long felt that too little attention has been given, by our truest friends, in this country, to removing this stumbling block out of the way of the slave's liberation.

The most telling, the most killing refutation of slavery, is the presentation of an industrious, enterprising, upright, thrifty and intelligent free black population. Such a population, I believe, would rise in the Northern States, under the fostering care of such a College as that supposed.

To show that we are capable of becoming mechanics, I might adduce any amount of testimony ; but dear Madam, I need not ring the changes on such a proposition. There is no question in the mind of any unprejudiced person, that the negro is capable of making a good mechanic. Indeed, even those who cherish the bitterest feelings towards us have admitted that the apprehension that negroes might be employed in their stead, dictated the policy of excluding them from trades altogether ; but I will not dwell upon this point, as I fear I have already trespassed too long upon your precious time, and written more than I ought to expect you to read. Allow me to say, in conclusion, that I believe every intelligent colored man in America will approve and rejoice at the establishment of some such institution as that now suggested. There are many respectable colored men, fathers of large families, having boys nearly grown up, whose minds are tossed by day and by night, with the anxious enquiry, what shall I do with my boys ? Such an institution would meet the wants of such persons. Then, to, the establishment of such an institution would be in character with the eminently practical philanthropy of your transatlantic friends. America could scarcely object to it, as an attempt to agitate the public mind on the subject of slavery, or to *"dissolve the Union."* It could not be tortured into a cause for hard words by the American people; but the noble and good of all classes would see in the effort an excellent motive, a benevolent object, temperately, wisely, and practically manifested.

Wishing you, dear Madam, renewed health, a pleasant passage and safe return to your native land,

I am, most truly, your grateful friend,
FREDERICK DOUGLASS.

Mrs. H. B. Stowe.

RESOLUTIONS ADOPTED.

Whereas, The social condition of the colored inhabitants of this country, in its developments, shows, beyond a question, the necessity of social reform, and a better regulation of our domestic habits ; therefore,

Resolved, That this Convention urge upon the clergy, who are not only our spiritual, but our social and moral instructors, to begin the reform, by urging upon the people who attend their preaching the neccessity of a social reform ; to use more untiring exertion than heretofore ; to induce parents to pay more attention to the domestic education of their children ; to prepare them for a better condition in society ; to instill in them a desire for their elevation in society ; to instill in them a desire for better occupations than the mass are brought up to ; to give them higher notions of what the genius and spirit of the country requires of us, than they now have ; to teach them more regular habits ; and this Convention would urge upon parents the fact, that while the mass of the people are generally employed in menial service, from necessity, while this may not, of itself, bring reproach upon a people, yet it must be admitted that, should we bring up our children to the same employment, it will, of necessity, engraft upon them unstable habits—a disregard for the mechanical branches, as well as unfit them for regular employments ; and instead of elevating their character for the future, we shall place them beneath our own position, and give them rather the downward, than the upward tendency.

Resolved, That to secure a more permanent attention to business habits than heretofore, and the acquisition of mechanical branches, it is necessary that some decisive measure be taken to open and secure the avenues of mechanical trades to our youth ; and that, as a primary measure, it is necessary that it be known to parents and youth who are willing to take colored apprentices in their workshops ; and further, that it is now expedient that intelligence offices be established, which shall register the names and places of business of such mechanics as are willing to employ colored youth ; and also the names, age, residence, &c., of such youth as are desirous of learning trades.

Resolved, That it is the duty of colored men, in any way connected with mechanical or business houses, enjoying the confidence of their employers, to use all fair and honorable means to secure for themselves business advantages, and especially, to secure the admisson of their children, or the children of others into mechanical establishments ; and in every way practicable to use their influence 'to secure and extend business advantages and business connection to those now excluded from it.

Resolved, That it is now expedient and necessary for those who have accumulated some means, to employ such means in some one or more of the general avenues of business and profit, and to make for themselves a better business character than we now possess, and thus open and secure the way for the development of new business, and right business talent.

Resolved, That the attempt to create a successful colony on the coast of Liberia is an attempt to accomplish an end in violation of the admitted laws of human civilization, and in violation of the physical laws of the human constitution.

Resolved, That, as for the American Colonization Society, we have no sympathy with it, having long since determined to plant our trees on American soil. and repose beneath their shade.

Resolved, That the several towns and cities represented in this Convention be, and are hereby advised to procure copies of Garrison's Thoughts on Colonization : and that they be advised to reiterate the resolves and addresses contained in the first part of that work, on the head of the Free People of Color.

Resolved, That in recognizing the power of the press, and the vast influence it exerts in making apparent the spirit and character of a people, we are happy in congratulating ourselves upon the fact that in *Frederick Douglass' Paper* we possess a correct exponent of the condition of our people, as well as an able, firm, and faithful advocate of their interests, and that, consequently, we cheerfully recommend it as worthy of our hearty and untiring support.

Resolved, That we welcome the newspaper recently established in Cleveland, Ohio, edited by William H. Day, as a powerful auxiliary to our cause and as an efficient lever for promoting our elevation; and that we pledge it that hearty support which its importance.

Whereas, It is not generally known to the colored citizens and others that there is, in the city of Alleghany, Pa., an institution of learning—a regularly incorporated college for the education of colored youth and others; therefore,

Resolved, That this Convention will give publicity to that institution by publishing, among the proceedings of this body, a notice of its existence.

Resolved, That a committee of one from each State represented be appointed to report an especial address to the Free People of Color of the United States; and also, that we recommend the next "National Convention" to be holden within two years, at some suitable place, which may hereafter be agreed upon.

Resolved, That the Colored People of the United States gratefully appreciate the services of the distinguished pioneer of the doctrine of universal, unconditional, and immediate emancipation, William Lloyd Garrison, and his noble co-adjutors, eliciting, as they do, our undying affection; and when we forget them, may our tongues cleave to the roof of our mouths, and our right hands forget their cunning.

Resolved, That we recommend the parents and guardians of colored children to avail themselves of every opportunity for their ingress to those schools and academies wherein there is no proscription of race or color.

Resolved. That we recognize in "Uncle Tom's Cabin" a work plainly marked by the finger of God, lifting the veil of separation which has too long divided the sympathies of one class of the American people from another; and that we feel and know that such sympathies once awake, and flowing in the proper human direction, must be the first step in that happy human brotherhood which is to be the ultimate destiny and crowning glory of our race.

Resolved, That we, as American citizens, are entitled to the right of elective franchise, in common with the white men of this country; and whenever any of our people have the use of that privilege, it is their duty to vote and vote only for such men, irrespective of party, as are known to be opposed to slavery and the Fugitive Slave Law.

Resolved, That the secrataries, in conjunction with Frederick Douglass, be appointed a Committee on Publication.

[The following resolutions have direct bearing upon the plan of organization, and in the report should be placed immediately after it:]

Resolved, That the Council shall be delegated to select its various committees.

Resolved, That the Council have power to offer a premium for prize essays on different subjects agreed on by the Council.

Resolved, That the said Council shall hear and grant petitions, and be governed by the rules of legislative bodies, and their decisions shall be final.

Resolved, That any State applying for admission into this Union, shall be admitted on such terms as may hereafter be agreed upon.

Resolved, That in establishing a National Council for our own special improvement, and a Manual Labor School for the education of our children in science, literature, and mechanical arts, this Convention do this, not to build ourselves up as a distinct and separate class in this country, but as a means to a great end, viz: the equality in political rights, and in civil and social privileges with the rest of the American people.

[The following communications were received by the Convention and deemed worthy of publication :]

LETTER FROM SAMUEL AARON.

NORRISTOWN, PA., JULY 3, 1853.

To the Rochester Convention of Colored Americans :

DEAR BRETHREN :—I feel the deepest interest in the wisdom, integrity and results of your Convention. I urged my friends here to have themselves, by all means, worthily represented ; and can say, with truth, that their delegate Mr. Augusta, is the man whom I should have preferred, had the choice been left to me. But for his solicitation, I should scarcely have penned these lines, for fear of seeming otherwise.

My strong conviction is, that my colored fellow-citizens in America should calmly and bravely breast the tide of prejudice, which I am persuaded flows more from caste than color. Let them first of all embrace the religion of the blessed Jesus ; then cultivate their mental and moral powers to the utmost ; seek each for himself, and diffuse among others, a knowledge of mechanical, commercial, agricultural, scientific and literary pursuits. See that mental capacity, and energy, and early tastes are trained for their proper career—just as judicious white men consult for the talents and predilections of their children.

Some of the brightest men in our country now are of African type. Real greatness everywhere is mostly proportioned to, and measured by the difficulties overcome ; and if so, the colored of our nation have a chance to win the true sublime—for they are abused for their degradation, and forbidden the means to rise. But, with God's help, they *can rise ;* and I look to your Convention now with a prayerful hope that you may speak to them with the power of the Prophet's voice, when he called to the bones in the valley of vision.

I not only trust that my colored brethren may yet elevate themselves, but that God may use them to save this nation from that abyss of ruin towards which its brutal pride and folly are driving it headlong. Let it see an outraged people rise to virtue and wisdom in its midst, and in spite of its malignity ; and surely prejudice itself must melt, and the blindest eye must see the glory of truth and the safety of virtue.

Our people have trampled you into ignorance, insulted your weaknesses, and nailed you on the *cross of slavery ;* but may God grant you, dear brethren, a resurrection to intelligence, and to that Christ like magnanimity that shall forgive a tyrant foe, and preach the glad tidings of man's capacity, with the Divine favor, to advance in wisdom, virtue and happiness.

Very sincerely your
Friend and brother,
SAMUEL AARON

LETTER FROM J. H. WILSON, M. D.

To the President and Members of the National Convention of Disfranchised American Citizens:

SIRS :—I exceedingly regret that it is out of my power to meet you, in consequence of a press of professional duties ; but my whole heart is with you in the advancement of the cause of our condition. I cannot but sincerely wish you God-speed ; and, that every delegate will have one ostensible object in view—a sure basis and a firm foundation, whereon you can predicate yourselves. These are peculiar times ; and I believe we are upon the eve of some great revolution, and that if ever unanimity and action is regarded of a people, it is now the whole country is concerned about *us.* Our moral and mental advancement is a subject of wonderment. Our enemies are alarmed, and they continually cry, What shall we do with them ? (us.) Let the doings of this Convention settle the question, and be the beginning of a new era in our history ; and may He who rules and superrules over destinies, guide you in all your deliberations. Respectfully yours,

J. H. WILSON.

[The following letter was not read at the Convention for want of time :]

LETTER FROM HENRY McKINNEY.

LODERSVILLE, PA., JULY 4, 1853.

To the Convention of People of Color, assembled at Rochester, State of New York:

Being an old Liberty Party man, I take the liberty, and I hope you will grant the privilege, of having this epistle read at your Convention. I have long struggled to make our people feel for your rights, and spent time and money in the struggle. I voted for Hale and Julian ; and if the Lord spares my life, my vote shall always be on the side of freedom. We expect, if our party get into power, (and we do not say when that will be,) to appoint to office in the general government only such persons as are beyond dispute thoroughly imbued with our principles ; and that the judges of the United States courts will be of different material. We expect to do away with the Fugitive Bill. We expect to abolish slavery in the District of Columbia, and in the territories, and wherever Congress has constitutional power. Then we expect to have no more slave states. We do not, as a party, propose to interfere with slavery in the slave states ; but we think then our influence, and the opinion of the world, will be such that said states will abolish slavery. We expect some of our candidates, when elected, will turn traitors under southern promises, and some from their bad inclinations. These things we dread most ; but the power we must have. When ? God only knows. Under such circumstances you may well inquire, what are our brethren, suffering under bondage, as well as this Convention assembled for the good of the whole race, to do ?—shall they sleep till the good time coming ? No ! while one being, made in the image of God, is held a slave. Can human beings be doomed to perpetual bondage ? Can human patience endure everything ? We have just read of a plot of 2,500 slaves for insurrection being discovered. Think you they feel not the heavy load ? Think you their souls are ravished with joy to see their children or their wives torn from their embrace ?—to see their homes deserted, their daughters and wives insulted, and compelled to propagate a mixed race ? This is beyond human endurance ; and the slaves will rise, or in a more shrewd and cautious course will quietly submit till they form some cool policy of poisoning the whole family of masters in a day, and take possession of the State governments—elect their Senators and Congressmen—and there having peaceable and quiet possession of the country, wil demand their representatives to be heard.

From such consequences may we be spared. Perhaps I am too timid ; but I cannot but dread *three millions* of foes, goaded to desperation by a sense of their wrongs. But in this matter you, as the free citizens of this despotic Republic, can act a great and glorious part. Let wisdom and discretion in all your councils prevail—if you will suffer me to make these remarks. Let brotherly feeling and Christian charity characterize all your acts ; and as knowledge is power, I should regard it part of the business of your Convention (if you will allow me to say it) to try to elevate the free people of color throughout the world—to inspire them with a strong feeling of self-respect and self-dependence. As a means to this end, I would recommend a general system of education, sound and practical ; and if there could be a book written upon the science of government, adapted to the use of common schools got up similar to books of Chemistry, Philosophy, Geography or Rhetoric' with questions on the margin of each leaf it would be of inestimable service Our forefathers formed this government on the principle that the people know best what they want. But, in practice, we find that party strings and factions, and slave-dealers, dictate what kind of men shall be candidates, and the people feel very proud that they are at liberty to go and vote for them.— The great trouble is, the white people, the voters, as well as the colored, in a great majority of cases, have no correct knowledge of the science of government, and never will have, in my opinion, till this science is studied in common schools. Hence we see that in our great political campaigns there is more fuss made at a "raccoon skin," a barrel of " hard cider," a filthy or a blackguard speech, or vulgar expression, than at the matters of consequence to the nation.

I hope you will excuse the length of this letter, as I intended to say but a few words—but the subject seems inexhaustible. It is my desire to see the colored people, and all races of people, enjoy their rights ; for " God created of one blood all nations to dwell upon all the face of the earth ;" and what is more contemptible than for people to boast of their race, or quarrel with another people because of a different race. We have questions enough of a personal nature, of a private nature, of self-interest, of public good, to support and educate our families, without resorting to this question—great only in meanness. I hope moderation, wisdom and discretion will guide you in your councils, and may your Convention result in harmonizing your efforts, and the general welfare of the civilized world. Yours respectfully,

HENRY McKINNEY.

Report from Finance Committee read and accepted.
On motion, adjourned.

AFTERNOON SESSION.

Vice President, Amos G. Beman, in the chair. Prayer by Rev. C. B. Ray. Minutes read and accepted. Mr. McCrummel moved that the vote rejecting the report on Social Relation be re-considered.

A resolution from the Finance Committee that each member of this Convention be taxed the additional sum of one dollar, to meet the deficiency in funds for defraying the expenses of the Convention ; and that friends present be invited to enroll their names as such ; lost. Moved, that an opportunity be given to all those who feel willing to contribute toward the defraying the expenses of the Convention, to do so ; agreed to. Moved, that the Convention adjourn to-night at eleven o'clock, *sine die;* agreed to. By Mr. McCrummel, that all reports and resolutions not already adopted by the Convention be referred to a committee of six on publication, with instructions to print them, omitting such statements or ideas as have appeared objectionable to the Convention; lost. Mr. G. M. Willis, of Jefferson, Co., N. Y., and R. D. Willis, of Oneida Co., paid one dollar and entered their names on the roll.

James M'Cune Smith moved that the Committee on Literature be allowed further time to report; withdrawn. Mr. Sumner renewed the motion, stating that the Committee had been appointed so late in the session that they could not prepare a proper report ; agreed to. Leave refused to Messrs. Gaines and Sumner to withdraw from the Committee. The preamble of the plan of organization taken up. The amendments of Mr. Downing were agreed to. Mr. J. M. Langston moved to strike out all that portion of the preamble offered by Mr. Whipper, as, in his opinion, the preamble reported from the Business Committee was sufficiently explicit upon the objects of the organization, and not liable to the objections to the others ; agreed to. First article of the plan for organization was taken up. Mr. C. B. Ray moved to strike out the word Legislature, and insert the word Council ; agreed to. Article as amended ; agreed to. Article second taken up. Mr. J. N. Still moved to amend by adding to the list of officers a Vice President and Corresponding Secretary ; agreed to. Mr. Jenkins moved that all committees consist of five members ; agreed to. Mr. Kenney, of New York, moved that three be added a Committee on Commerce ; lost. The article as amended ; agreed to. Article third taken up. Mr. A. R. Green moved that the power of selecting a location for the Manual Labor School be retained, as in the original draft, which was, that we allow the Convention to select. Mr. George T. Downing moved that we pass to the next article ; agreed to. The fourth and fifth articles read and agreed to Article sixth read. Mr. Joseph C. Holley moved to amend by inserting the words "and all books by colored authors ;" agreed ; and the article as amended agreed to. Article seventh read ; amended by the addition of the following, after the words "shall meet at least once a month," the words "or as often as possible ;" amendment and resolution agreed to. Article eighth read amended by the words "shall be empowered to receive, and appropriate donations for the carrying out of the objects of the same." Mr. Parker moved to amend that the Council meet at least once in six months ; agreed to. Article as amended agreed to. Mr. Downing moved that the delegations from the several States be requested to meet between this and the evening session, and agree upon such persons as they desire to represent them in the National Council ; agreed to. Article ninth read and agreed to. Article tenth read. Mr. Bowser proposed the following amendment : that the lyceum be located in Pittsburgh, which was amended to Cincinnati, to Chicago, to Portland, Me. After which the article was adopted. Article eleventh read and agreed to. Article twelfth read and agreed to. Article thirteenth read and agreed to. Article third again taken up. Mr. Reason's substitute laid on the table. James M'Cune Smith moved that the location of the Manual Labor School be left to the National Council ; not agreed to.

Donations of $2 from Mr. W. Whipper, of Columbia, Penn.; Mr. Bradford King, of Rochester, $2 ; Mr. T. Thomas, of Mass., paid his tax, as a member of the Convention.

Adjourned.

EVENING SESSION.

President in the chair. Prayer by the Rev. Boyd Parker. Mr. Parker moved that the Financial Committee be requested to wait upon the audience, and receive such donations as they may be willing to make ; agreed to. Third article of the plan of organization again taken up, together with the amendment, which was, "that the board of Trustees of the Manual Labor School, shall locate the school in the State designated by the Council;" amendment agreed to. On the final passage of the article, the ayes and noes being called for, the article was adopted, ayes 80 ; noes, 23. Motion to re-consider laid on the table. One dollar each was paid by Messrs. W. H. Channing and Francis Thompson, to be constituted honorary members. J. H. Hurley paid his tax as member of the Convention. Mr. Downing moved that the names presented by the various delegations be adopted by this Convention, as members of the National Council ; agreed to.

The following names were reported :

Vermont—J. W. Lewis, St. Albans ; H. O. Smith, Burlington.
Massachusetts—W. O. Nell, Boston ; J. B. Sanderson, Fairhaven.

Rhode Island—Geo. T. Downing, Providence ; Abraham C. Rice, Newport.
Connecticut—Jehiel C. Beeman, Amos G. Beeman.
New York—J. McCune Smith, New York City ; Frederick Douglass, Rochester.
Pennsylvania.—John Peck, Pittsburgh ; Stephen Smith, Philadelphia.
Ohio—Wm. H. Day, Cleveland ; John I. Gaines, Cincinnati.
Michigan—W. C. Munroe, John Freeman, Detroit
Illinois—James D. Bonner, John Jones, Chicago.
Indiana—Horace B. Smith, Indianopolis, John T. Brittain, Charlestown.

Prof. C. L. Reason offered the following resolution :

Resolved, That nothing in the provisions of the constitution of the Council just adopted shall be construed to mean that either in the Board of Instructors or in the admission of students to the contemplated manual labor schools, the principle of complexional exclusiveness is contemplated. Adopted.

Resolutions approving the purpose and character of W. H. Day's paper, the *Aliened American*, to be published at Cleveland, Ohio ; also one approving of the spirit and course of *Frederick Douglass' Paper* adopted. Mr. A. R. Green called up his resolutions recommending days of fasting and prayer. Upon them considerable discussion and confusion prevailed. Mr. Douglass moved to adjourn. Lost. Rev. W. C. Monroe spoke at length upon the resolutions. Resolutions laid on the table. J. McCune Smith moved that all reports presented to this Convention be published with minutes. The Committee on Finance reported that the receipts of the Convention had amounted to $172,-50 ; expenses $60,75 ; remaining, $111,75 ; which was paid to committee on Publication.

Resolved, That the Convention return thanks to the officers of this Convention for the able manner in which they have discharged their duty. Agreed to.

Also to the Chairman of the Business Committee. Agreed to.

Sundry resolutions were passed, which, in the hurry, could not be noted, but will be found under the head of Resolutions.

Moved that we adjourn *sine die.*

While the motion was being put and carried, Frederick Douglass advanced to the front of the stand and struck up the hymn,

> " From all that dwell beneath the skies,
> Let the Creator's praise arise,"

in which the whole Convention heartily joined.

[The following report did not come to hand in time to be printed in the order in which it was reported to the Convention.]

REPORT ON COLONIZATION.

In entering upon the duties assigned them, your committee deemed it desirable to go into the history of African Colonization, with a view to show that every system of Colonization has proved a curse to that unhappy country.

I. The first we shall notice, is that of the Dutch, which commenced in 1659. Your committee find that about that time a settlement was commenced, composed of emigrants from Holland, under the auspices of the Dutch East India Company. These settlers at first entered Africa with the most friendly intentions; and contented themselves with simply as much land as was needed for their trading establishments; subsequently, however, and at no distant period, the Dutch not only began to seize upon the best of lands in southern Africa; but furthermore reduced the natives to a most cruel state of slavery. The few traders soon enriched themselves, at the fearful expense of the natives. Holland began to pour a flood of emigrants into the country. A colony was formed; and efforts were made to subjugate the entire native population. From this time, to use the words of the Americans themselves, the white man, with gun and sword in hand, began to stride rapidly in every direction, through the whole country, taking forcible possession of the best portions of land. It soon also became a common thing for the Dutch colonist to fit out expeditions expressly to plunder the distant natives of their cattle. In 1702, about forty years after the Dutch entered the country, the governor in a despatch to the home government, confesses that he was unable to punish these intruders upon the natives, giving as a reason, that half the colony would be ruined, so great is number of the inhabitants implicated. At another time the Dutch govenor made an extensive tour into the interior, found many of his subjects, who had settled themselves far beyond the bounds of the colony; and instead of recalling them, threw out, and extended the bounds of the colony so as to take them in, and then ordered all of the natives outside of this new boundary.

"A chapter of facts from Barrow—1798—" speaking of the natives says :— " Some of their villages might have been expected to remain in this remote and not very populous part of the country. Not one, however, was to be found. There is not, in fact, in the extensive district of Graaff Reinet, a single horde of independent Hottentots; and perhaps not a score of individuals who are not actually in the service of the Dutch. These weak people the most helpless, and in their present condition perhaps the most wretched of the human race, duped out of their possessions, their country, and their liberty, have entailed upon their miserable offspring a state of existence to which that of slavery might bear the comparison of happiness. It is a condition, however, not likely to continue to a very remote posterity.

Their numbers of late years have become rapidly on the decline. It has generally been observed that where Europeans have colonized, the less civilized nations have always dwindled away, and at length totally disappeared. "There is scarcely an instance of cruelty said to have been committed against the slaves in the West India Island, that could not find a parallel from the Dutch Farmers of the remote districts of the colony towards the Hottentots in their service. Beating and cutting with thongs of the hide of the sea cow, (hippopotamus) or rhinoceros, are only gentle punishments; though these sort of whips, which they call *sjamboes*, are most horrid instruments, being tough, pliant, and heavy almost as lead. Firing small shot into the legs and thighs of a Hottentot, is a punishment not unknown to some of the monsters who inhabit the neighborhood of Camtoos river.

By a resolution of the old government, as unjust as it was inhuman, a peasant (Boor) was allowed to claim as his property, till the age of five and twenty, all the children of the Hottentots in his service, to whom he had given in their infancy a morsel of meat. At the expiration of this period the odds are ten to one that the slave is not emancipated. But should he be fortunate enough to ESCAPE at the end of this period, the best part of his life has been spent in a profitless servitude, and he is turned adrift without anything he can call his own, except a sheepskin on his back." "At that time (1798–1802) the Hottentots were a miserable, abject race of people; generally living in the service of Boors, who had so many of them that they were thought of little value as servants, and were treated more like brute beasts than human beings. Indeed, the colonists in those days scarcely considered them human; they were mostly naked; seldom was one of them to be seen with any other clothing than the sheepskin caross, together with a piece of jackall's skin for the men, and a wretched sort of leathern apron for the women, attached to a girdle of rawhide, which encircled their loins. Their food was commonly the flesh of old ewes, or any animal the Boor expected to die from age. If he was short of that, he shot a few quaggoes or other game for them. Their wages were generally a few strings of glass beads in the year, or, when the Boor returned from a journey to Cape Town, a tinder-box and knife were considered a reward of faithful services. Perhaps a very obedient man, and more than commonly industrious, got a heifer, or a couple of ewes, in a year. And if by accident any of these poor wretches happened to possess a few cattle, there was often some means fallen upon by the Boor to get rid of him, and thus his cattle became his master's. When a Hottentot offended any Boor or Booress, he was immediately tied up to the wagon wheel, and flogged in the most barbarous manner; or if the master took a serious dislike to any of these unhappy creatures, it was no uncommon practice to send out the Hottentot on some pretended message, and then to follow and *shoot him on the road;* and when thus put out of the way, his relations durst not make any inquiry about him, else they were also severely punished. Such was the condition in which we found the natives of that period."

Such were the blessings that the DUTCH conferred upon Africa by their colonization, after a lapse of nearly half a century.

II. The eighteenth century opened upon Africa, with TWO NEW SCHEMES OF COLONIZATION.

First,—The British government commenced *colonizing whites.*

Secondly.—It was about that time, the *Americans began* to turn their attention to Africa, for the purpose of *colonizing free colored persons.*

As early as 1798, an American Naval Officer, (Lieut. Stout,) being at the Cape, wrote a long letter to John Adams, then President of the United States, urging the importance of *colonizing* the free colored people in *that* part of Africa, as a counter movement of the British government, which was about to seek an opening there for portions of her population. Thus it is seen that jealousy of Great Britain had something to do with the origin of this scheme. The letter in question was published, and your committee regret they have not been able to find a copy. This they regret the more, because they have little doubt, that although no official notice was ever taken of the letter, yet, access to it in the State Department, WHERE IT IS NOW, has done much to form the opinions of Presidents, Secretaries, Senators and Representatives on this subject. It should also be kept in mind, that just about this time, an alarm began to prevail that the British Islands would soon be over-populated. The crown had just lost the thirteen colonies, and was not disposed to encourage emigration hither, no, not even to the Canadas, knowing that many would re-emigrate to the United States. The point of contest was obvious. The United States had a sufficiency of labor in the persons of free colored people, but she wanted also to rival Great Britain in population. The United States well knew that the class of population they would get from Britain would be laborers. Political economy cautioned them against over-stocking their infant Republic with labor. To get over the difficulty, this plan was adopted:—dismiss the negroes, who have hewn our wood and drawn our water, while we were preparing ourselves to become independent, and who helped us to fight our battles of independence, send them to Africa, and then we shall be in a position to receive Britain's redundant population. Your committee are serious and candid in the opinion, that these views entered fully into the original policy of *colonization.* How far they accord with that generous, and statesman-like spirit, which was due from the States, to their sable sons, they will leave you to judge. It must be added, however, that the attempt to counter-move the British crown in South Africa was an utter failure ; Britain took South Africa from the Dutch, and soon began to colonize there, whites from England, Scotland and Ireland. The Americans then turned their eyes to Western Africa.

Your committee now ask your attention to this singular coincidence, that those two schemes of *colonization* began about the same time, the British *colonizing whites ;* and the Americans *colonizing colored men* on the same continent, but from entirely opposite motives ; Britain, to relieve herself from what she believed to be over-grown population ; America, to relieve herself from what she calls obnoxious population. The influence of British *colonization* upon South Africa, and the interior and western coast, has been a curse to Africa ; the whites there have nearly exterminated several tribes, to make room for themselves. They seized on the best lands, without paying the owners. The Caffres have for forty years held them in check, without arms, ammunition, or military tactics. They have fought like men, guarding their ancestors' tombs. But the whites have paid no regard to the African's love of home or veneration for his father's grave. The white in the land of Ham has been cruel and rapacious. He has outlawed the African in his own land, he has taken from him thirty thousand square miles of maiden land, at the dash of the pen. He has robbed him of twenty-five thousand head of prime cattle, as a day's job ! This is not fiction. On the 30th day of April, 1820, five thousand whites landed on the shores of Africa, with a patronage of two hundred and fifty thousand dollars from their government ! To give a view of the motives which prompted this emigration, on the part of the persons themselves, we will make an extract from the writings of one of the best men among them. He says, "I had two objects in view, in emigrating to Africa. One was, to collect again into one social circle, and to establish in rural independence, my father's family, which untoward circumstances had broken up, and began to scatter over the world," &c. &c. Such is a specimen of the feeling with which these five thousand whites went to Africa. At that period there were seventy-five thousand others, of the same sort, demanding admission *into the land of Ham.* With all the liberality of the British people towards the African, (and we distinguish between the government and the people of the country,) your committee regret that they are not able to report any material change for the better, in the treatment of the natives by the whites, since the colony came under the control of the British crown, except relieving the remnant of the Hottentots from abject slavery. But this one good act of government seems to have been overbalanced, and more, by the unparalleled cruelty tolerated towards the Caffres. The Caffres, as a race, have generally been equal, and sometimes more than a match for the whites. Indeed, in reading the history of the Caffre war, for forty years, (the longest on record, except the second Punic—forty-seven years,) it seems that the mortal offence of that noble race is, that they consider themselves quite equal to, if not superior to white men ; and that they have done much to prove the truth of their opinion. Forty years ago, a Dutch Boor took a farm near a ford, on the banks of the great Fish River, over which the Caffres frequently drove their cattle. His fences were bad, and the Caffres' herds sometimes got into his fields. The plan he adopted, to retaliate, was to take of such trespassing cattle, one out of three, and two out of five, &c. After suffering considerable loss in this way, the Caffres became cautious ; but with their utmost care, the Boor still got his toll, in the shape of two or three fine cattle, every time a Caffre crossed with a flock. At length several Caffres combined, and set a watch over the Boor's plan of operation ; and obtaining positive knowledge that he regularly decoyed their cattle into his fields, they went and complained to their chief. That he might act upon indubitable evidence, he sent two reliable men to lie in watch, and ordered his own cattle to be driven over the river. The Boor, the rapacious old Boor, seized three of the Royal Kine. The men reported to the chief, who went with his forces, and took his cattle *vi et armis.* The Boor flew to the governor, and represented that the chief had robbed him. The matter was examined or explained, but the governor still reprimanded the chief; and ordered him to return the cattle, and then, for the sake of form, lay his complaint before him, &c. The chief refused to do so ; and the governor undertook to force him. Such is an authentic statement of the origin of a forty years' war, between the Southern Africans and the whites.

Your committee ask careful attention to the following chapter of facts collected from British writers :

" In 1811, the government undertook the forcible removal of the entire Caffre population, over the great Fish River, to make room for the whites. Hence ensued a war, of which the following will give an idea :

Sunday, January 12th, 1812.—At noon commandant Stollz went out with two companies to look for Slambie, (Islambi,) but saw nothing of him ; they met only with a few Caffres, men and women, the most of whom they shot. About sunset, five Caffres were seen at a distance, one of whom came to the camp with a message from Slambie's son, requesting permission to remain until the harvest was over, and that then he (if his father would not,) would go over the great Fish River quietly. This messenger would not give any information, respecting Slambie, but said he did not know where he was. However after having been put in irons, and fastened to a wheel, with a reim (leathern thong) about his neck, he said that if the commando went with him before daylight, he would bring them upon two hundred Caffres all asleep. Now what is to be thought of this attempt to force an envoy, by the terror of death to betray his chief into the hands of his mortal enemies ? What would be the outcry, throughout all Europe, if any flag of truce were so treated between civilized nations ? A few days afterwards, a small body of Caffres were seen at the edge of a thicket near Colonel Wilshire's camp, who made signs that they desired a parley. The Colonel, attended by another officer and myself, having moved towards them unarmed, two Caffres approached, and proved to be the one of them Islambi's, and the other Makanna's chief councellors (*pagati.*) They were, I think, as *noble looking men,* and as dignified in their demeanor, as any I have ever beheld. After a few questions and answers, relative to the disposal of Makanna, (who by this time had been sent into the colony,) and as to the prospects of an accommodation, the friend of the captive chief delivered himself in the following terms—in so manly a manner, with so graceful an attitude, and with so much feeling and animation, that the bad translation which I am able to furnish from my hasty and imperfect notes, can afford but a very faint and inadequate idea of his eloquence :—

" The war, said he, British Chiefs, is an unjust one, for you are striving to extirpate a people whom [you forced to take up arms. When our fathers and the fathers of the Boors (AMABRILU) first settled in the zureveld, they dwelt together in peace. Their flocks grazed together on the same hills, their herdsmen smoked together out of the same pipes ; they were brothers—until the herds of the Amakosa increased so as to make the hearts of the Boors sore. What these covetous men could not get from our fathers for old buttons, they took by force. Our fathers were MEN ; they loved their cattle : their wives and children lived upon milk : they fought for their property. They began to hate the colonists, who coveted their all, and aimed at their destruction. Now, their Kraals and our father's Kraals were separate. The Boors made commandoes on our fathers. Our fathers drove them out of the zureveld ; and we dwelt there ; because we had conquered it : there we were circumcised : there we were married ; and there our children were born The white men hated us but could not drive us away ; when there was war we plundered you. When there was peace some of our bad people stole, but our chiefs forbade it. Your treacherous friends Gaika, always had peace with you, yet, when his people stole, he shared in the plunder. Have your patrols ever found cattle taken in time of peace, runaway slaves, or deserters, in the Kraals of our chiefs ? Have they ever gone into Gaika's country without finding such cattle, such slaves, such deserters in Gaika's Kraals ? But he was your friend, and you wished to posses the zureveld. You came at last like locusts. We stood, we could do no more, you said, "Go over the Fish River, that is all that ew want." We yielded and came here.

"We lived in peace: some bade people stole, perhaps, but the nation was quiet—the chiefs were quiet: Gaika stole—his chiefs stole—his people stole. You sent him copper, you sent him beads, you sent him horses on which he rode to steal more. To us you sent only commandoes! We quarrelled with Gaika about grass—no business of yours; you sent a commando, you took our last cow, you left only a few calves, which died from want, along with our children; you gave half the spoil to Gaika; half you kept yourselves: without milk, our corn destroyed, we saw our wives and children perish, we saw that we must ourselves perish. We followed, therefore, the tracks of our cattle into the colony: we plundered: we fought for our lives; we found you weak: we destroyed your soldiers: we saw that we were strong: we attacked your head quarters: and if we had succeeded, our right was good, for you began the war; we failed, and you are here; we wish for peace, we wish to rest in our huts, we wish to get milk for our children, our wives wish to till the land. But your troops cover the plains, and swarm in the thickets, where they cannot distinguish the man for the woman, and shoot all. You want us to submit to Gaika. That man's face is fair to you, but his heart is false: leave him to himself; make peace with us; let him fight for himself, and we shall not call on you for help. Set Makanna at liberty, and Islambi, Dushani, Kongo and the rest will come to make peace with you at any time you fix. But if you will still make war, you may indeed kill the last man of us—but Gaika shall not rule over the followers of those who think him a woman."

This manly remonstrance, which affected some of those who heard it, even to tears, had no effect in altering the destination of Makanna, or in obtaining a reprieve for his countrymen, who were still sternly called upon to deliver up those who had been outlawed by the Cape government. All efforts to get possession of the persons of the other chiefs were unavailing. After plundering the country, therefore, of all the cattle that could be found, and leaving devastation and misery behind them, our "Christian commando" retired into the colony without gaining the object for which the war was professedly commenced, but with an additional spoil of about thirty thousand head of cattle, captured from the famishing and despairing natives. The following will show by what tenure the British crown hold the lands in Africa:—

From the "Banner," 21st January, 1852.

"MR. COBDEN ON THE CAFFRE WAR.

"At a public meeting held in Birmingham, on Tuesday week, to protest against the agressive war of South Africa, the following letter from Mr. Cobden, M. P., was read:—

'Midhurst, January 8, 1852.

"My Dear Sturge:—

I am sorry that I cannot be present at the meeting in Birmingham, respecting the Caffre war, but I rejoice that you are moving, and I trust that your resolutions, will go to the root of evil; it is not as some people would make it appear, a question of colonial office mismanagement, or of the comparative merits of one mode of warfare over another; the real question is, what title have Englishmen to the possessions of the land of the Caffres? Did we buy it and pay for it? How, when, and where was the bargain effected? There is no evidence that we ever paid one farthing of compensation to the former possessors of this land. We are paying for it now, in blood and treasure, with a vengeance, and the lesson to be inculcated on your meeting is—that God does not allow injustice to be perpetrated with impunity. As a people we have failed to respect the rights of property in weaker communities. No conqueror ever returned to our shores, after enlarging our territorial sovereignty, without a triumphant welcome, and no questions are ever asked as to our right to the conquered territories. Even an individual may engage in wars, and dispossess rulers of their sovereignty, and dub himself "Rajah" in their stead, and he will be loaded with honors, whilst we stigmatize as pirates, American adventurers. who, without a flag, and under similar circumstances, make a descent upon Cuba. Let these home truths be told us as a people. Do not let us shelter ourselves under attacks against the Colonial Office. You, the advocates of the rights of the Aborigines, constitute, I fear, but a small minority of the public; but the severe burdens which Caffre wars and other similar retributions are bringing upon the tax-payers of this country, will, sooner or later (if higher motives should fail,) bring a majority of the people to the opinion, that even in our dealings with Caffres, Dyaks, or New Zealanders, honesty and justice are the best policy.

I remain, very truly yours,
R. COBDEN.

Joseph Sturge, Esq."

"The following will show how the government is carrying on the war :—

"DOUBLE BARRELLED RIFLE CARBINES FOR THE CAPE.

" Three hundred and fifty double barrelled rifle carbines have been shipped in the Birkenhead steam troop ship for conveyance to the Cape of Good Hope. The rifle carbines, are for the use of the twelfth lancers, from the depot at Maidstone. A non-commissioned officer and privates practiced at the Royal Arsenal, Woolwich, a short time ago, to acquire a knowledge of their use, so as to be able to instruct their brother non-commissioned officers and privates on arrival at the head quarters of their regiment at the Cape of Good Hope. The non-commissioned officer and privates who were at Woolwich for the purpose stated, have embarked in the Birkenhead as part of the detachment of the twelfth lancers ordered to proceed, under the command of Cornet John Rolt, to the Cape, to join the regiment. The balls used in the double barrelled rifle carbines are of the conical description, found so effectual at long ranges by Mr. Lancaster, doing great execution at six hundred, or eight hundred, and in many instances one thousand yards range. The result of recent trials of small arms. gives reason to expect that a complete change in the arms of the British soldier will shortly take place, and it is contemplated to have rifled cannon made ready for experiments during the present year. Some beautiful self-acting machinery having been invented for grooving the cannon in the most perfect manner, it is expected that with rifle cannon and conical shape shot, the field artillery will attain a great range, far exceeding what can be obtained from small arm rifles."

The following will show, Americans are willing to make joint work of it :—

."THE CAPE MAIL.

" The general screw steamshipping company's steam-packet Propontis, Captain Glover, sailed on Thursday afternoon for St. Vincent, Sierra Leone and the Cape of Good Hope. She takes as passengers for Sierra Leone the newly appointed commandant, Major O'Conner, Lieutenants Robinson, and Rainsforth, Ensign Minty. The Propontis takes ordinance stores and despatches for the troops, officers, &c., but the most interesting part of her freight consists of a venture of four hundred and fifty patent revolving pistols, brought down by Mr. Dennett, agent for Colonel Colt, and sent to the Cape in charge of Mr. Pears, who understands thoroughly the manufacture, construction, management, and use of these formidable weapons. They are exposed, under the full cognizance of the government, for sale at a limited price, to British officers These pistols, for cavalry, weigh from three to three and a half pounds, killing at three hundred yards, and belt or navy pistols weighing less than two and a half pounds, carry a ball through a two inch plank at forty yards; they hold six balls, and are said to require less powder than the ordinary pistol.'

"LETTER FROM CAPE TOWN.

" Dates from Cape Town, S. A., to April 2nd, have been received at New London, by the arrival of the whale ship Julius Cæsar. The only matter of general interest in this intelligence relates to the conclusion of the Caffre war, or rather the view that is taken of the mode in which this war has been brought to a close. The proclamation of the Governor General, announcing the termination of hostilities, &c., &c., are spoken of as written in a "style of needless glorification ;" it is said that the Caffres are not beaten after all, that the Hottentots are not crushed ; and that the Gaikans have not been exterminated; but that the present peace is the result of the anxiety of both parties to cease from the sufferings of war. Many of the colonists seem to be complaining of General Cathcart, that he has not made better terms with the Caffres. But the Cape Town Mail seems to think that he has done the best he could, that about all that remained for him to do, was to agree with the Caffres to have hostilities on either side cease, and that about the best and only thing the colonists and others can now do, is to avoid all incitements to war, and to make the best possible arrangements for the defence of the colony, while peace continues."

Your commitee have with grief and surprise, found the following in the *British Banner*, of recent date, in regard to the Caffres :—"They have doubtless felt that, notwithstanding the advantages which casual circumstances may give them, a permanent maintainance or a successful termination of a contest with the British power is altogether out of the question."

But it is generally known that these men have fairly flogged the government forces two or three times within eighteen months, yet John Bull is remarkable for not knowing somethings. Contest with the British power is out of the question because no other nation interferes to decide points of honor between the combatants ; so old Daddy John has it all his own way. He never gets whipped, he gets fatigued once in a while, and after a feast of roast beef, and the reception of a new supply of men and guns of the most improved kind, he rests, and at it again.

Your committee have been at great pains to collect these facts, and they believe that similar facts will be found connected with the history of all the colonies, and trading stations of the whites in Africa.

III. On the general question, your committee cannot report any change in the policy and spirit of the *American Colonization Party*. That party is still our traducers, there are honorable exceptions, but what we have said is true of that party. The following from the *National Intelligencer* will show that the leaders of the scheme are still lurking about the seats of governments, both general and State, seeking influence, &c.

"COLONIZATION SCHEME.

" The Secretary of the Colonization Society has published in the official journal of that society, two arguments in favor of State appropriations, one of which is addressed to the Legislature of Virginia, and one to the Legislature of Ohio. As they represent in a certain sense the two great sections of the country, and seem to have been well received by the citizens of those States, they are deemed by the Society of sufficient importance to be fully introduced to the public at large in an article from the pen of the Secretary, Rev. W. McLain. From this introduction we gather the following particulars : The work of Colonization is now declared to be comparatively easy, the business having been reduced to a regular system. The settlements of Liberia are capable of receiving new emigrants to any extent, and more persons are now anxious to emigrate than the society can accommodate. Much is said in regard to the future enlarged operations of the society, and it is with a view of accomplishing more good that the general government and the Legislatures of the States are called upon to lend a helping hand. Upon the work already done, the society has expended nearly one million dollars, and for this it has a capital stock to show of great value. It has a territory of more than twelve thousand square miles under its control. It has a well-organized government, with all the means and appliances of civilization, whose value is not to be measured by dollars and cents. The society, according to the secretary, has a valuable and available interest in the hearts of the American people. It possesses their confidence, and the scheme of colonization is considered both desirable and practicable. It is maintained that the General and State Governments have the constitutional power to appropriate money, in the furtherance of the objects contemplated by the society, and it is thought to be their duty to take the work in hand, and carry it forward with vigor. As a nation, says Mr. McLain, we are bound to restore Africa all her children who are willing to return. We are bound to pay her the debt which centuries of patient suffering have given her the right to demand of us. Every State is bound to make provision for the welfare and happiness of the free people resident therein. If for this purpose wisdom and prudence point to their removal to Liberia, the State is bound to make the necessary appropriations for the accomplishment of the work. By way of illustrating the popularity of the society, it is stated that the Legislatures of more than half the States of the Union have passed resolutions approving of its object and operations, and that the most distinguished men in every part of the country, and in every political party and all religious denominations, have expressed their approval of the society and the scheme of colonization."

(1.) None of that party are *abolitionists*; and although some of them *profess* to be Anti-Slavery, yet they never utter one word of rebuke to slaveholders.

(2.) We do not believe, however, that the party has increased numerically. It has appeared to increase, but that is a part of its policy. There have been changes. Some who were against us, and then were for us, are again against us.

(3.) But this is accounted for in a natural way. Two causes have been at work on such minds. The seeming increase of that singular vice of Americans, negro hate, has disturbed the nerves of some good persons, and they now see no hope for the race, but in colonization in Africa. A cowardly friend will often do you more mischief than an open enemy. But only think of it. I must leave my country, because a man hates me.

Its reports still teem with their cruel slanders. Hear what they say of the free colored people of Ohio:—

Taking things therefore, as they really are, and in all probability will continue to be, in the great state of Ohio, the scheme of Colonization is not only a measure of humanity, and sound policy, but of great and overpowering necessity. It is a question, not of dollars and cents, but of high and exalted obligation, enforced by all the duties of self preservation to both races. Daily accumulating circumstances, make it more and more apparent, that the condition of the *colored people is not improving, and cannot be expected to improve!* What then is to be done? Can they remain long what they are and as they are? We think not; the voice of the State calls them to depart."

Hear how coolly they endorse the barbarous act of the State of Indiana:

"In the State of Indiana the sentiment is spreading rapidly, that it is the duty of both the State and National Governments, to adopt some general system of *colonization*. The Governor, in his late message to the Legislature, earnestly recommends the measure. His remarks on the subject, are so eminently *just* and *patriotic*, that we quote them entire :—

The subject of the colonization of the free blacks is now beginning to receive that attention which its importance demands. The circumstances which surround us. are pressing our people to look into this subject in the right, and proper light. Our Southern brethren are making rapid movements towards abridging the privileges of this class, even to banishment.— WE in the north are adopting extraordinary means for removing them; by prohibiting them from holding property, excluding them from the protection of the laws, and denying them any rights whatever. While all this is going on, OUR BETTER NATURE, the common sympathies of all men, are beginning to ask these important questions,—WHAT IS TO BE THE END OF ALL THIS? IS THERE NO REMEDY? IS THERE NO CURE FOR THIS EVIL? In the midst of all this excitement and confusion, the light breaks in upon us, which points conclusively to COLONIZATION AS THE ONLY REMEDY.'

The speeches of *colonizationists* continue to teem with the vulgar appeals to the lowest passions. Hear one of them : " Races which live in the same land, and cannot amalgamate, cannot be united in marriage, can only exist in the relation of master and slave, oppressor and oppressed. The Spaniard and the Moor, the Anglo Saxon and the North American Indian and the Norman and the Saxon, until they began to intermarry, are illustrations of the truth of the proposition, that two races which cannot amalgamate by intermarriage, can only subsist in the same land in the relation of master and slave, or oppressor and oppressed. By oppressor and oppressed, I mean the relation which now subsists between the white man and the free blackman in this country. Oppressed ! What evidence is there of it ? Is there a free colored man who can drive a hack or a dray in the city of New York ? Has there never been a riot in the free States of Ohio ? Many. Have there never been riots in Massachusetts ? Yes. In Philadelphia ? Yes. And who have been the victims of these riots ? The free black man. And why does not this occur oftener than it does ? It is because we have a mighty West, and West creates a demand for labor, which leaves no room on sea board on all the avenues of employment for the white man and the black man to travel together, in pursuit of bread, without jostling each other. But the time will come, the time is coming—and it has been referred to in one of the addresses which have been made this evening, when there will be but ONE LOAF OF BREAD, AND TWO MEN TO EAT IT : who would get it ?"

But the great point with the party, and the one upon which they claim a victory, is the fact, that the independence of the Government of Liberia, has been recognized by Great Britain, France, Prussia. This is easily met.

(1) Why does not the American government recognize the Independence of the government of Hayti, whose trade is only surpassed in value by two other nations, with whom we are connected in commerce.

(2) Why does not Britain recognize the rights of the African chiefs' government, to rule their own subjects ?

(3) Why does not France recognize the independence of Algiers ?

(4) We demur to the claim of *bonafide* independence on the part of the Republic of Liberia, because the COLONIZATION PARTY in this country, several of the slave States, and pro-slavery individuals still exert a controlling influence over its territory. The colonization party in this country is obnoxious to the colored race, because it seems to be profoundly ignorant of some important facts in the present state of Africa, or else it wilfully conceals or ignores them so as to gain its object. Is it not known to the members of the American colonization party, that some of the native African tribes, are as white as they are themselves ? HEREN, (Vol. 1, page 295,) speaking of one of the large nations of Fezzan, says " the western branch of the race is *white*." Capt. Lyon, of the British Navy, speaking of the same race, says, " they are generally *white*." Africa is inhabited by more than forty separate and distinct families of nations, speaking more than one hundred and twenty different languages. In the families are to be found all the varieties of races, that are in any other portion of the Globe. With what kind of honesty then, can the colonization party of America, teach that Africa is exclusively *our* country, when it is false, in the face of this fact drawn from the natural history of man in that land. But making all due allowances for the differences of opinion, in reference to the native population of Africa, why does the party conceal from the colored men in this country, the fact that the whites have been colonizing themselves in Africa, for nearly a century, and that they are at this moment, as they have been for nearly a half century in mortal combat with the natives, to drive them from the south, and west, across the interior, to the extreme east. Is that party aware that the Dutch Boors, the mortal haters of the Africans, have just established a Republic in Africa, with the avowed intention of incorporating into it, a large tract of the best inland. Unless all and every one of the present schemes of colonization in Africa, be utterly discarded, and a pure system of Gospel Evangelization, be adopted in the stead thereof, Africa is destined to be the theatre of bloody conflict, between her native sons, and intruding foreigners, black and white, for a century yet to come.

The British in the South and the North, the French in the south-east and the Americans on the west, speculating in lands, cheating and warring, afford little promise of a political milennium for the land of Ham.

The LIBERIANS themselves, with their government backing them, are pursuing precisely, the same policy, that other colonizers have for the last hundred years in Africa : 1. They boast that they have made their arms so often felt, that "no combination of the natives can be induced to fight them." The following extract appeared in one of the most widely circulated papers in Europe some time since, when President Roberts was negotiating funds to purchase " Gallinas." " Vast pains have been taken in the American press, and in a portion of that of this country, to eulogize the republican system of government at Liberia, but those who have aproached its shores and taken a near and impartial view of the system give a very different account of it.— They tell of *reckless wars* upon the *natives* attended with both *rapine* and *bloodshed*, of legislation framed in a spirit of jealousy and exclusiveness, not much less infamous than that of certain white slaveholding democracies , of commercial regulations most oppressive and restrictive, and that the condition of the natives is worse, rather than better, since the domination of these self-styled pioneers of African civilization. The laws published by their friends, for instance, in the appendix to the report of the Lord's committee on slave trade of last session, support these statements too well to leave doubt as to the truth of what is said of their practical application."

The Liberians justify and connive at all the encroachments of the white foreigners, even to the damage of their own dignity. The whites from other lands have taken possession of every commercial river on the west coast, preparatory to an enforcement of their policy on Africa, for untold generations yet to rise. Have we heard one word of remonstrance from these native whippers ? No. A short time since, a white foreign force was marched upon the town of Lagos, within a few degrees of President Roberts' boundary, where, after two days fighting, the town was destroyed, an immense number of natives killed, and the king deposed, &c., &c. Has any remonstrance gone forth, from the government of Liberia ? Not a word. Have the papers of the Republic condemned it ? No. Has there been a public meeting held in the Republic, to protest against such outrages ? None. The reason is obvious, men who live in glass houses cannot afford to throw stones. The truth is, the Liberians are in league with the worst enemies of Africa's dearest interest.

And that the government of Liberia has followed a similar course, with the native towns and chiefs' is shown by the facts in connexion with the recent boasted capture, trial, fine and imprisonment of King Boombo, an affair, which upon strict diplomatic review will prove the following points.

(1.) That President Roberts acted deceitful and cowardly in sending for King Boombo to meet him on the beach, as if to hold a palaver, thus inducing him to come unarmed, when he himself was armed to the very teeth.

(2.) That he has insulted the pride of the native kings of Africa, by trying one of their number, at his petty court of quarter sessions. The idea, that the ancient Kings of Africa owe allegiance to his petty government of yesterday, is perfectly ridiculous, and none but a tutelary tyrant would assume it. The fact is, Roberts is prompted by the secret worshippers of African-hating republicans in America.

(3.) That the fine and punishment inflicted upon that King, are of such an extravagant character as to show up the whole case in its own light. To whom is this fifty thousand dollars to go, that will more than pay Roberts' government debt ? Cowards always inflict unreasonable punishment. Who is to hold King Boombo's reign of government, during the two years he is imprisoned, and how is he to pay his fine ?

One other review and we have finished. We are compelled to regard the Liberians with distrust.

(1.) We have no evidence of their independence, they are evidently yet under the control of the colonization party in this country, and are not trustworthy in their judgment of matters, regarding the race of this country.— Some time since, the Liberians assembled in public meeting at the courthouse in Monrovia to address the free colored people in the United States, and here are some of the things they say :—*As much speculation and uncertainty continue to prevail among the people of color in the United States respecting our situation, &c.* "Tell us," say the Liberians in their address to the free colored people, "which is the white man, who, with a prudent regard for his own character, CAN associate with one of you on terms of equality ? Ask us which is the white man, who would decline such association with one of our number, whose intellectual and moral qualities are not an objection ? We unhesitatingly answer both these questions by saying, the white man is not to be found." But hear the Liberians in another place : "We solicit none of you to emigrate to this country, for we know not who among you, prefers rationa independence and the honest respect of his fellow men, to that mental sloth and careless poverty, which you already possess and your children will inherit after you." Once more. The address says : "Judge then, of the feelings with which we hear the motives of the colonization society traduced, and that too, by men too ignorant to know what that society has already accomplished, too weak to look through its plans and intentions, or too dishonest to acknowledge either. But without pretending to any prophetic sagacity, we can predict to that society the ultimate triumph of their HOPES and LABORS and the disappointment and defeat of those who oppose them." It is unnecessary to say that this language has never been softened or modified, and it has much the appearance of having been manufactured in America, and sent out to order.

We believe that our fathers were sagacious in their first impression' of the colonization scheme. It was well known, that at the time this scheme first came to light, the whole country went for it. There was not even a second-rate white man that stood with us. Our fathers made the first attack alone, and with fearful odds against them. We conclude with the following resolutions :

I. It is not true that the free colored people have been induced by abolitionists to oppose the colonization scheme. Our fathers set us the example, and we are more and more convinced of the wisdom of that example.

II. That the several colored communities represented in this Convention be advised to procure copies of Garrison's Thoughts on Colonization, and to re-resolve, and to confirm the several resolutions and addresses of that work, under the head of

"VOICES FROM THE COLORED PEOPLE."

In behalf of the Committee on Colonization,

J. W. C. PENNINGTON,
Chairman.

To the Committee on Publication of the Minutes of the National Convention of the Colored People :

GENTLEMEN :—I regret that it will be impossible to submit the Report on Statistics in time to be incorporated with the minutes. The facts placed in my hands in the Convention are entirely too few, in regard to the People of Color, their wealth, occupations, school privileges, churches, societies, &c , &c., to form the basis of an accurate or even proximate report. And the members of the Committee on Statistics, with two exceptions, have failed to furnish any further facts up to this date.

This is the less to be regretted, as the census of 1850 will be published in a few weeks, containing much additional matter of deep interest in this connexion.

The report, when complete, will be submitted to, and published under the direction of, the National Council or its Committee on Publications.

Very respectfully yours,

J. McCUNE SMITH,
Chairman of Com. on Statistics

NEW YORK, August 18th, 1853.

PROCEEDINGS

OF THE

Colored National Convention,

HELD IN

FRANKLIN HALL, SIXTH STREET, BELOW ARCH,

PHILADELPHIA,

OCTOBER 16th, 17th and 18th,

1855.

PRINTED BY ORDER OF THE CONVENTION.

SALEM, NEW JERSEY:
PRINTED AT THE NATIONAL STANDARD OFFICE.
1856.

A CONVENTION of the Colored People of the United States assembled in Franklin Hall, Sixth Street, below Arch, Philadelphia, pursuant to the following call, from a Committee appointed by the National Council, June 3d, 1855, to call a National Convention of the Colored People of the United States.

The Convention was called to order by Rev. STEPHEN SMITH, of Philadelphia; when on motion of Mr. STEPHEN MYERS, of Albany, Mr. SMITH was appointed temporary Chairman; and Mr. FRANKLIN TURNER, of Philadelphia, Secretary. The following call for the Convention was then read by Mr. ISAIAH C. WEARS, of Philadelphia, which was adopted:

A CALL FOR A NATIONAL CONVENTION OF COLORED AMERICANS.

FELLOW CITIZENS:—The present aspect of the *times*, and the condition of our brethren in bonds, and our own peculiar position as Freemen, require of us some well directed effort to counteract the debasing influence that holds us in our present anomalous condition in this our native country; and in obedience to the demands of stern necessity for united action, the undersigned, agreeable to appointment and by direction of the National Council at its last meeting, held in the city of New York, May 10th, 1855, do call a Convention of the People, through *their* delegated representatives, to assemble in the city of PHILADELPHIA, Pa., on the 16th DAY of OCTOBER, 1855, under the form and title of a National Convention of the Free People of Color of the United States.

After close observation, and mature deliberation, we have

arrived at the conclusion, that the *Free People of Color*, if they would disencumber themselves from whatever tends to impede their march, and remove whatever obstacles are in the way of their progress—if they would fully subserve the cause of Liberty, which is the *cause of God*, they must take upon them the responsibility of doing and acting for themselves—of laying out and directing work of their own *elevation*. That so far from being mere aids and lookers-on, the time has fully come when they must be the guides, leaders and active operators in this great Reform.

Who, it may be asked, can lay a stronger claim to a cause, and who, having the power and ability, can better promote it, than the most deeply interested; and upon whom has the elevation of the People of Color in these United States a stronger claim, and who can better direct and promote the *work*, than the People of Color themselves? In our elevation lies the freedom of our enslaved brethren ; in that elevation is centered the germ of our own high destiny, and the best well-being of the whole people.

Years of well-intended effort have been expended for the especial freedom of the slave, while the elevation of the free colored man as an *inseperable priority* to the same, has been entirely overlooked. But to every true friend of freedom it must now be too obvious, that the whole process of Operation against the huge and diabolical system of oppression and wrong, has been shorn of more than half its strength and efficacy, because of this neglect of the interests of the Free People of Color—interests so vital that we dare not longer permit them to remain in a state of neglect. If nothing else, then, these years of experience have taught every true friend of Liberty, that the elevation of the free man is inseperable from, and lies at the very threshold of the great work of the slave's restoration to freedom, and equally essential to the highest well-being of our own common country.

It is equally obvious that since the work of elevation of the Free People of Color is (so to speak) the lever by which the whole must rise, that work must now receive a vigorous and hearty support from all of those upon whom it has a claim.

The *work* thus foreshadowed for the consideration of the Convention, is various, and much of it difficult ; yet, the power of its accomplishment lies in systemization and direction of it —and while we would make no direct specifications—while we would be proscriptive in nothing, still we would recommend such a course as shall prepare us, and those to come after us, to take a manly part in all things in which we have an interest, in common with the rest of our fellow-citizens. We would have the Convention ascertain the precise point now reached in our present progress. We would call its attention to the state and character of Education and educational privileges among us, with a view to their improvement, or, if need be, change and adaptation to our demands. We would direct it to an examination of our *business relations* and *habits*, and devise such ways and means as will render them more available. We would have it give, if possible, to whatever of *mechanical* or *artistic* skill there is among us, impetus and extension.

To the department of Agriculture, also, we would have it direct its attention and encouragement; so that, in all, there will be begot in us, and in our youth especially, a strong and increasing desire for these pursuits. There are also Political and Social Rights that lie at the very foundation of our manhood, to be obtained and errors among ourselves to be corrected, and confidence to be strengthened or restored. Much of the *work* commenced in the *National Convention* at *Rochester* in '53, demands now a vigorous prosecution; other portions of it remodeled or shaped to meet our newer experiences; and the whole to receive a stimulus that will forward it towards its completion. The progress of events, too, may have given rise to exigencies that require additional agencies hitherto unforseen, but now demanding attention and direction. In all this, then, *fellow-citizens*, there is enough to concentrate our united wisdom, and enlist our most hearty co-operation.

With these views, *fellow-citizens*, we again earnestly entreat you to come together in the true spirit of men having a clear conception of our needs, a just sense of our rights, and an abiding *determination* to do our *duty*. The election for members to the Convention will be held on the third Tuesday of September, 1855. The people in the various neighborhoods, Church organizations, Benevolent or Literary societies, are respectfully urged to meet on that day, and elect delegates to the Convention to meet at Philadelphia on the 16th day of October ensuing, at —— o'clock.

WILLIAM J. WILSON, ⎫
STEPHEN SMITH,   ⎬ *Committee.*
JOHN W. LEWIS,   ⎭

The following Committee was then appointed by the Chairman to examine the credentials of the delegates: Messrs. J. F. Williams, of Harrisburg, Pa.; Stephen Myers, of Albany, N. Y.; and Rev. Amos G. Beman, of New Haven, Conn.

A fervent prayer was then offered by Rev. J. C. Beman, of Middletown, Conn. While the Committee on Credentials were preparing to report, the Convention was addressed by Rev. Stephen Smith, Rev. J. Campbell, and Rev. L. A. Grimes.

The Committee on Credentials reported delegates present from the States of Massachusetts, Connecticut, New York, and Pennsylvania.

ROLL.

MASSACHUSETTS.

Robert Morris,	Charles L. Remond,
John S. Rock,	William C. Nell,
Leonard S. Grimes,	Leo. L. Lloyd,

William Jackson.

RHODE ISLAND.—George T. Downing.

CONNECTICUT.

J. C. Beman,	Samuel T. Gray,
George H. Washington,	A. J. Morrison,

Amos G. Beman.

NEW YORK.

Stephen Myers,	J. McCune Smith,
James W. Duffin,	Peter A. Bell,
Jason Jeffries,	Edward V. Clark,
William H. Topp,	R. D. Kenny,
W. J. Hodge,	C. B. Ray,
Lewis H. Nelson,	Peter S. Porter,
Daniel Russel,	Henry Beverly,
J. J. Simons,	Charles L. Williams,
Joseph B. Smith,	J. W. Bowers,
George Le Verre,	J. J. Scott,
Janius C. Morrell,	J. W. C. Pennington,
James M. Williams,	Peter M. Gray,
W. J. Wilson,	David Rossell,
Robert Hambleton,	Charles S. Hodges,
Edward Crosberry,	Fredrick Douglass,
Jacob R. Gibbs,	William J. Watkins,
Thomas J. White,	J. R. V. Morgan.

PENNSYLVANIA.

Stephen Smith,
Robert Collins,
Adam S. Driver,
James H. Wilson,
Ulysses B. Vidal,
John C. Bowers,
Charles L. Reason,
Jesse Bolden.
James Fell,
Joseph C. Stevens,
Alfred S. Cassey,
Henry Ray,
Jacob C. White,
Francis A. Duterte,
Samuel Van Brakle,
Edward M. Thomas,
Joel Ware,
Davis D. Turner,
Benjamin B. Moore,
Franklin Turner,
Rachel Cliff,
Samuel Golden,
Elizabeth Armstrong,
J. J. Gould Bias,
Isaiah C. Wears,
Basil Macal,
Daniel Morgan,
Edward Young,
Robert Douglass.
Peter Burtou,
James McCrummill,
Grayton S. Nelson,
Jeremiah Asher,
William W. Whipper,
Addison W. Lively,

Aaron L. Still,
Charles H. Bustill,
William A. K. Smith,
William R. Decorderer,
William Parker,
Robert Purvis,
Daniel Colly,
John F. Willams,
Jabez P. Campbell,
Edmund Kelly,
Thomas C. Burton,
William P. Price,
William T. Cato,
Nathaniel W. Depee,
G. W. Reed,
Joshua Woodland,
E. J. Adams,
James Presser,
John G. Dutton,
Samuel Williams,
Jacob W. Glasgow,
Robert Jones,
Thomas Charnock,
James G. Frisby,
Jonathan Lopeman,
William Jackson,
James Needham,
William Douglass,
Thomas P. Hunt,
Samuel H. Amos,
Augustus Dorsey,
Ebenezer Black,
Thomas Gibbs,
William Moore,
John Addison,

Thomas Kennard.

NEW JERSEY.

Joseph Reeves,
E. P. Rogers.

Henry A. Thompson,
E. H. Treeman,

Robert Stewart.

CANADA.—Mary A. Shadd.

A motion was then made to adjourn until two o'clock; but after some discussion it was withdrawn.

A motion prevailed that a Committee of one from each State be appointed to nominate permanent officers for the Convention. The Committee consisted of Rev. L. A. Grimes, of Mass.; Abram J. Morrison, of Conn.; Stephen Myers, of N. Y.; and John C. Bowers, of Pa.

During the absence of the nominating Committee, the following Committee was appointed on rules: J. C. White, J. S. Rock, J. C. Morrell, G. D. Washington and J- McCrummell.

The Committee on nominations for permanent officers then made the following report:

For President—REV. AMOS G. BEMAN, of Connecticut.

Vice Presidents—JACOB C. WHITE and JOHN F. WILLIAMS, Pa.; Rev. L. A. GRIMES and WM. C. NELL, Mass.; J. W. DUFFIN and P. A. BELL, N. Y., and Rev. J. C. BEMAN of Connecticut.

Secretaries—Dr. J. S. ROCK, of Massachusetts; GEO. W. LEVERE, N. Y.; FRANCIS A. DUTERTE and ROBT. DOUGLASS, Pennsylvania.

The report was adopted.

A committee of two, consisting of Drs. J. J. G. Bias of Pennsylvania, and J. McCune Smith, N. Y., was appointed to conduct the President elect to the Chair.

On taking the Chair, the President returned his thanks for the honor conferred on him; and promised to discharge his duties in an impartial manner, and requested the aid of the members in carrying out the objects of the Convention, &c.

Mr. J. C. White was excused from acting as one of the Vice Presidents, and Dr. J. J. Gould Bias appointed to fill the vacancy.

The following committees were then appointed:

Business Committee—Professor C. L. Reason, of Pennsylvania; Dr. McCune Smith, N. Y.; C. H. Bustill, Pa.; Wm. H. Topp, N. Y.; Geo. H. Washington, Conn.; J. C. Morrell, N. Y., and Franklin Turner of Pennsylvania.

Finance Committee—Stephen Smith, of Pa.; Aaron Still, Pa.; Chas. L. Remond, Mass.; G. V. Nelson, Pa., and J. J. Simons, N. Y.

The committee on rules then made a report recommending "Cushing's Manual of Parliamentary Practice."

A motion then prevailed, after some discussion, to return the report to the committee, with instructions to report a few written rules for the government of the Convention. Whereupon all the committee resigned.

A Committee was then appointed to draw up a set of written rules. The committee consisted of Messrs. Wm. H. Topp, of N. Y.; S. Golden, Pa., and J. C. Morrell, N. Y.

Convention then adjourned for one hour.

AFTERNOON SESSION.

The Convention met according to adjournment, the President in the Chair.

Prayer was offered by Rev. Wm. T. Catts.

On motion, E. J. Marsh was appointed on the committee on credentials, in place of Beman, appointed President.

On motion, Edward Galpin, of Connecticut, was admitted a corresponding member.

Rev. Adam S. Driver and Rev. Stephen Smith, of Pennsylvania, Samuel T. Gray, Conn., and William C. Nell, Mass., were appointed a committee on statistics.

On motion, Mr. Reese, of New Jersey, was admitted a corresponding member.

The Chair then announced that he had a communication from Dr. J. W. C. Pennington, of New-York, which was referred to the business committee.

On motion, Mr. William Whipper, of Columbia, Pa., was admitted a corresponding member.

A communication from Mr. J. W. Lewis was referred to the business committee.

A motion to appoint a committee of three to read letters of correspondence, was lost.

Mr. Charles L. Remond, of Mass., moved that we admit Miss Mary A. Shadd, of Canada, a corresponding member. This question gave rise to a spirited discussion, after which the motion was passed.

Mr. F. Douglass, of N. Y., then moved a reconsideration. Carried.

The Hall being engaged for the evening; on motion, the Convention adjourned to meet at the Philadelphia Institute at half past seven o'clock.

EVENING SESSION.

The Convention met in Philadelphia Institute, pursuant adjournment. The President in the Chair, the question on the admission of Miss Shadd was discussed, affirmatively by Messrs. F. Douglass and Wm. J. Watkins, N. Y., and Samuel T. Gray; and negatively by P. A. Bell, J. C. Wears, C. S. Hodges, Lewis H. Nelson, and J. C. Bowers. The yeas and nays were called for, and resulted as follows:

Yeas, 38—Nays, 23.

The Committee on Rules then made a report, which was accepted, and after some discussion adopted.

The Business Committee, through their Chairman, Professor Charles L. Reason, then made a report of some papers received through the New York and Philadelphia delegations.

The following is from the Philadelphia delegation:

Your committee appointed to report views relative to the Industrial School, respectfully submit as a report, that having carefully considered the subject in the varied aspects which it presents, have arrived at these conclusions:—

In a report like this, it will not be expected that this subject will be handled in the detailed manner which its great weight would seem to demand. We will therefore briefly give some of the reasons for discouraging the enterprise now under consideration.

The first difficulty to be met, is the capital required to carry out instruction to a successful issue. On this point your Committee are of the opinion, that to teach even a few of the trades, much more will be required than will be easily within our reach, and for which a fair return will be received. Besides it will be conceded, that unless a youth acquire a profession congenial to his mental and physical abilities, and to his tastes, the trade thus acquired will avail him but little. For says an author of some note, "The proper choice of a profession is one of the most important steps in life." If but few trades can be taught, owing to limited capital or other causes, this institution can be of use but to few; for if within the circle of professions taught in the institution, a pupil can find none suited to his peculiar demands, it would be worse than useless, and a loss of time and means, to endeavor to acquire one in which his nature forbids he should excel.

Thus we believe that our demand for a variety of employments, is only limited by the trades themselves.

Again, the plan of an industrial school combines the mental culture with mechanical training, which we conceive to be in part going over the ground already occupied. We have institutions of learning of the first stamp open to us, where the rising generation can draw from the fountains of knowledge side by side with the most favored of the land, and at the same time by their contact and influence help materially to do away with that deep-rooted prejudice of which we so bitterly complain. The Industrial School being necessarily (if not in theory, yet in fact) a complexional institution, must foster distinctions, and help to draw more definitely (so far as educational privileges are involved) those lines of demarkation which we have labored and still are endeavoring to eradicate.

The question will also arise, is it possible in the period allotted for a collegiate course, to afford time sufficient for the acquirement of a trade in such a thorough manner as to enable the learner to compete successfully with those who have been trained by the usual method? The time generally considered necessary to learn a mechanic art, is from three to five years, working ten hours per day, and even after this there are many who have still wide room for improvement.

Considering, then, the necessity under which we labor of being at least equal, if not superior as workmen, in order to overcome the prejudice existing against us, we cannot believe that the disconnected hours applied to attaining the said trades will suffice, in the limited period, to give that proficiency of execution and workmanlike ability which we believe to be indispensably necessary to success in business, and the ultimate triumph of our enterprise.

An institution such as is now under consideration, will not be able to accomplish much for the masses. Our people are wide-spread as are the free states of this Confederacy, their wants are varied as their localities, and all demand that their requirements should be equally cared for. The great number of our people are poor, and in consequence would be unable to avail themselves of such advantages as the institution might afford, even if it was their wish so to do.

What then is to be done? What new means must we devise? From all sides we hear the demand for occupations that shall keep pace with the rising intelligence of our people. This then is the subject which is daily forced upon us, and it must be met with a determination to adopt such plans as will be most certain of success within our reach, and likely to do the greatest good to the largest number. Having objected to the plan proposed for the accomplishment of the desired object, it will of course be expected that we will suggest some substitute. This we will endeavor to do, and will present the skeleton of a plan, believing that the concentrated wisdom of the convention now about to assemble will be able to fashion it into such a "harmonious whole" as will meet the end we have so much desired.

Let the National Council, when duly organized, establish as a part of their operations a Mechanical Bureau, accumulating a fund to be employed in the promotion of the Mechanic Arts amongst colored men. They shall organize in the several

States, or any locality, Boards of Control, who, when they shall find a responsible person or persons having a knowledge of any desirable occupation, and willing for a fair remuneration as Agent or Foreman to impart the art to colored youth, shall report the same to the Bureau, giving all necessary information as to the amount of capital &c. required for carrying out the said object. The Bureau, after making such provision as may be necessary, and instituting such supervisorship as may be desirable, shall advance the amount deemed necesssary, requiring such reports from time to time as will be consistent with the prudent management of financial affairs, and all profits from such enterprise shall go into the general fund.

By following out such a plan, we may hope for success; and in a few years, we doubt not, the benefits would be plainly perceived. We could then employ our capital and direct our efforts in each and every place where a favorable opening may present; and ere many years shall have rolled away, we may be gladdened with the sight of our people employed in walks of life ennobling in their tendency, and calculated to lead still higher and higher, until we have achieved such a character as will sweep away the dark clouds of prejudice and oppression which would now o'erwhelm us.

Mr. J. C. Wears moved that so much of the report as referred to the mechanical bureaus be adopted. The motion was defended by Mr. Wears, and opposed by Dr. J. McCune Smith and Rev. T. P. Hunt. The Convention adjourned to meet on the following morning at 9½ o'clock in Franklin Hall.

SECOND DAY—MORNING SESSION.

The Convention met pursuant to adjournment. Prayer was offered by Rev. E. J. Adams, Pa. The roll was called, and 109 delegates answered their names. The minutes of Tuesday's proceedings were read by the Secretary, and after being corrected were adopted.

Professor Charles L. Reason then read the following report:

REPORT

Of the Committee on Mechanical Branches among the Colored People of the Free States.

THE development of the physical energies of man, and their control for the weal of society, is one of the prime subjects of political economy. That which God once made in his own image is among the last in the order of creation. The formation of physical proportions come first, then the removal of the darkness which surrounds the practical workings of our physical creations, until there is light, and into that which is formed as the result of first beginnings, shall be breathed the life of superior intelligence. It is the nature of man to follow the order of creation. The physical world in its beautifully enchanting proportions are first spread out before him—he looks, admires, and then tries to imitate. This practice brings the power of thinking into active ·exercise, and impresses a steady but sure conviction of the necessity of mental culture. The rude tenements brought into existence by physical necessity, are rebuilt and improved upon as time, thought, and culture suggest.

The learning of the world has never been able to keep pace with the development and enlargment of physical power. The mass in the early ages of the world saw the most beautiful arches, dwellings and temples, while the knowledge of letters even was confined to the few.

The wealth of nations commences not in learning, but in physical energies. Learning comes as a necessity of growth. The thinking minds and the energetic wills have been the rulers of the earth; the masses have toiled under the servitude of their control and direction. The spirit of freedom, however, has overcome enslavement by the few, freedom has led to more general education, and hence there is more general intelligence as the result of freedom among the masses. A knowledge of the requirements of freedom, then, in developing the physical powers, must be a part of the foundation of modern civilized society. No people may expect to escape the performance of the duties thus imposed with impunity. It is a law which must be obeyed, or the penalties of its violotions suffered. There need be no cavil as to where society is to begin. The Builder of the Universe has settled that by the necessity which he has thrown around the superstructure of human progress. There must be a basis; Learning is a part of society—it must enter into the composition of society; but the masses cannot be deeply learned, in fact only partially developed. Common School education is all that even the most enlightened countries afford the masses. These are foundation facts with all peoples, so must it be with the colored people of these United States. We must begin with the tillage of the earth and the practice of the mechanical branches, with whatever learning we may have, or the best we can now get. The observations above presented are a natural result growing out of the investigations of your Committee on Mechanical Branches among the colored people. An examination of the meagre facts which your Committee have gathered shows that while some have realized the true nature of the necessities of our position, others have wholly neglected the means first to be used, or have been driven by public prejudice and the force of circumstances, into modes of living entirely inconsistent with the principles of human progression, viz: non-productive labor.

Your Committee beg leave further to state, that having been appointed by the National Council which assembled in the City of New York, May last, to report to the National Convention to assemble in the City of Philadelphia, October 16, 1855, and accepting the appointment, availed itself of the facility of addressing circular letters to such gentlemen, as we thought would aid us in collecting such information as might be used to advantage by the Convention, and to some extent reliable for reference as to the actual state of Mechanical existence of our people; believing in the idea of producing facts rather than sophistical coloring.

The circular was responded to in a satisfactory manner by many to whom it was addressed, and your Committee feel under many obligations for assistance and suggestions from Mr. Nell, of Boston; Mr. Johnson, of New Bedford, Mass.; Peck, of Pittsburgh, Pa.; Bowers, of Philadelphia; Woodson, of Pittsburgh, Pa.

And we thank the "Herald of Freedom," edited by Mr. Peter H. Clark, of Cincinnati, Ohio, for the very liberal course pursued in endeavoring to give us facts.

Living in the midst of progressive civilization as we do, the statistics show that we are not mixing sufficiently in the elements of that progress. Your Committee take pleasure in presenting the views of some gentlemen agreeing in the views of your Committee, and of others differing widely from it, your Committee deem it in keeping with the purpose of its appointment to give them.

Mr. Johnson, of New Bedford, says, "There does not appear any great desire on the part of parents to secure trades for their children. I think the chances for them to obtain situations as apprentices, very few and difficult. There is little or no disposition to encourage colored men in business, who have means to carry it on.

We have several colored men who possess their thousands, accumulated in California, and are anxious to start in some business, but from well-grounded fear of success, either do nothing here or return to California. Our colored mechanics are principally from the south."

Mr. Nell, of Boston, says, "There is a growing disposition among parents to secure trades for their children, and the avenues are daily being opened to them. The same is true in regard to colored men in business. The past five years a spirit has been very active for real estate investments, both by individuals and land companies.

"The Equal School Rights Reform having triumphed, a brighter day will soon dawn upon the prospects of colored citizens and their children."

Mr. Woodson thinks that white tradesmen think more of a black tradesman than they do of a mere black man, and they will do more for him as a tradesman than they will as a mere man. Where colored mechanics work and live among white ones, they are more regular in their habits, and economical in their expenditures, than where they work and live alone.

Mr. J. Bonner, of Chicago, Ill., says, "Although the best class of our people in this State, are farmers, they constitute much of the wealth and respectability of Illinois. Many of them, however, I am credibly informed, are desirous of giving their sons mechanical trades. The parents in our city are generally in favor of giving their sons and daughters trades; and I am informed that the same disposition is manifested throughout our cities and towns; but we have no facilities for thus procuring these trades, and hence the few mechanics among us.

Mr. Clark says, "A very large proportion of our population were mechanics before emigrating from the Southern States, but have ceased to follow their trades for want of encouragement."

These gentlemen being in different sections of the country, hold in some degree views differing from each other ; but all showing a want of some great desideratum to advancement in this great element of national growth—and wealth and happiness. While in this connection, your Committee is willing to charge on the bulk of this nation all that guilt and wickedness entailed upon us, we would also invite your attention to the many evils among ourselves that do more to retard our movements, "crush out" our aspirations, and place higher and stronger hindrances in our way to obtaining trades, than can all the *whites* put together, notwithstanding their willingness, for circumstances of interest control them, whilst a narrow prejudice emanating from a low estate to a large extent controls us, in the general sense.

The whites taking their cue as they do from the government, we must expect it to be a kind of domestic article purely native in its proclivities, to discourage us. Even this can be removed as circumstances shall show it to be their interest to do so. All prejudice connected with the Yankee spirit is subject to moderation by the influences that might be brought to bear by a vigorous application of the trades within our reach.

We are a part of this great nation, and our interests cannot be entirely separated. We are now one inseparably by the decrees of God.

As a people we must not be dictated to by discouragement ;— if discouraged by the whites, we must learn to avail ourselves of every legitimate means to encourage our own mechanics and professional men.

This would enable us to overcome the spirit, that we have inherited from the dark prison house of slavery, casting its pall around our very vitals, and we found to dwell on the inability of our professional men and mechanics or their extravagant rates, or some other pretence too hollow and frivolous to mention.

To remedy some of the evils practiced by us, your Committee recommend that Committees of practical business men, in the large cities, say Boston, New York, Philadelphia, Buffalo, Pittsburg, Cincinnati, hold a series of conversational meetings, and endeavor to cultivate a proper and correct estimate of interest to govern purchase and sale, and inculcate the idea that to encourage our own mechanics, we create means to learn our boys trades and render them more independent of the prejudices around them.

Your Committee would recommend private residences as the most suitable places to conduct these conversations as thereby we should get better access to the minds of our females. They could enter freely into the conversations, and correct ideas would finally be inculcated in the sentiments of wives and mothers as to the important part of the great duties which they are to perform in moulding the future character of our youth for improvement, and also by association and community of ideas the wives will be prepared to introduce more of the element of the German and French character in social existence carried into our "business relations," of mutual assistance by council, clerkship, and physical labor.

As a people, we must understand that all that is not *white* is black, and all that is not *black* is white, we would recommend our clergy, our teachers, and leading men, and above all our women on whom we must depend for our future leaders to inculcate a disposition for trades, agriculture and such of the higher branches of business as are necessary and requisite to develope persistance—our requirement to do something for the advancement of Society from the cradle to the grave! that each may leave his or her foot-prints upon the earth for good—tangible evidence that each has done somewhat to destroy caste—and to destroy the opinion that we raise our children to that sweet stage of life which prepares them for business (16 years) with no other aspirations than to be a waiter, we cannot hope for much until we shall advance the premium—and hypothecate coupons, on the qualifications of our youth.

Your Committee would further suggest the necessity of raising funds in the different cities, towns, &c., to be funded to the best advantage;—not upon the plan of the Franklin fund, but that if A or B learns his trade and continues sufficiently long at work to accumulate something, that the fund, or such part of it as the Trustees thereof shall deem fit, be loaned for a series of years sufficient to guarantee a hopeful success, provided the applicants can present the legitimate discharge of agreement of apprenticeship, and devotion to business, &c. It would have the effect to build up so many practical mechanics, that young men would not be compelled to turn in disgust from the trades they love and seek the employment of steamships.

This republic is yet in its infancy, and we must grow with it —let us follow in the footsteps of the whites in this respect, as the only tangible ground—we must use similar means to reach similar ends, notwithstanding disabilities. If we can live in this country, bidding defiance to its wicked laws, we can do anything that prosperity requires at our hands.

As a further means of advancement, this Convention might recommend to the different cities, and towns, Trades Unions on a small scale, or as your Committee would call them, Co-partnerships, say from three to five in each business as the parties might prefer to engage; on the principle of division of labor and division of profits according to capability—looking to it that their financial man and book-keeper be looked up to as an index of security—and let all the partners in the Union work to make the Capital pay if possible 25 per cent.—and keep on until the investment becomes a paying one: and thus show the fallaciousness of the 6 per cent. idea of Savings Bank investments. A Thousand Dollars might in a judicious outlay in a lucrative business pay from 25 to 75 per cent.

Your Committee have seen sufficient, by clear evidence, to guarantee the opinion, that our people in Ohio, Illinois, and Michigan, in active business, (aside from Agriculture,) have $1,500,000; in Massachusetts, Maine, Rhode Island, and Connecticut, $2,000,000; in New York and Pennsylvania, $3,000,000; and California, $200,000; saying nothing of the Six Hundred Thousand Dollars invested in Savings Banks in and around New York, and its vicinity, and also similar amounts around other cities.

The youth who has the spirit of accumulation, and is intelligent with figures and the Pen, having saved something as a beginning in life, ought like the whites buy goods and venture his turn in the stream of trade and business. They would find by perseverence that in time they would receive the reward they merit, and the true principle of personal elevation brought to the common stock to destroy the barriers around our feet.

With these remarks, your Committee submit the following statistics:

MAINE.

Working at their Trades and Professions.

Carpenter 1; Engineer 1; Tailor 1; Tailoresses and Seamstresses 5; Dressmakers 6; Captains 2; School Teachers 3; Clergymen 3; Musicians 3; Farmers 16; Shipbuilder 1;— Total 41.

Not working at their Trades and Professions

Carpenters 3; Masons 3; Tailors 2; Milliners 2; Caulkers 1; Bootmakers 3; Bakers 3; Dressmakers 3;—Total 23.

NEW HAMPSHIRE,—No Returns.

VERMONT.

Working at their Trades, &c.

Dressmakers 3; Engineer 1; Machinists 2; Blacksmiths 3; Musicians 2; Farmers 7;—Total 18.

Not working, &c.

Carpenters 2; Ropemakers 3;—Total 5.

MASSACHUSETTS.

Working at their Trades, &c.

Blacksmiths 8; House Carpenters 9; Ship Carpenters 6; Boot and Shoemakers —; Dressmakers 26; Tailors 12; Horse Shoers 3; Sailmakers 3; Printers 5; Blockmaker 1; Painters 8; Caulkers 10; Jewelers 2; Gilders 4; Grain Inspector 1; Upholsterer 1; Masons 3; Stevedores 6; Milliners 4; Segar-makers 9; Store-keepers, (mostly clothing,) 22; Clergymen 11; Lawyers 3; Physician 1; Doctors 8; Clerks 6: Gymnastic Professors 2; Crayon Artist 1; Business Agent 1;—Total 187.

Not working, &c.

Blacksmiths 4; Marine and Landscape Artist 1; Boot and Shoemakers 4; Tailors 2; Masons 3; Printers 6; Musicians 22; Blockmaker 1;—Total 46.

RHODE ISLAND,—No Returns.

CONNECTICUT.

Working at their Trades, &c.

Blacksmiths 11; House Carpenters 6; Boot and Shoemakers 7; Dressmakers 20; Tailors 4; Vestm.. :er 1; Masons 6; Printer 1; Wheelwrights 2; Milliners 2; Painters 4: Coopers 6; Burnishers 2; Farmers 7; Gardener 1; Mates 6; Teachers 6; Clergymen 9; Doctors 2; Engineers 2; Merchant 1; Grocers 4;—Total 97.

Not working at their Trades.

Blacksmiths 6; House Carpenters 3; Boot and Shoemakers 6; Tailors 3; Tailoresses 3; Mason 1; Painters 2; Coopers 2; Printers 4; Milliner 1;—Total 31.

NEW YORK.

Working at their Trades and Professions.

Boot and Shoemakers 30; House Carpenters 15—Apprentices 5; Hat-Strawmakers 16; Cabinetmaker 1; Blacksmiths 6; Ship Carpenters 4; Machinists 10; Masons 7; Printers 4—Apprentices 2; Hatter 1; Milliners 2; Tailors 3—Apprentice 1; Second-hand Clothing Stores 27; Painters 4; Japanner 1; Chair-matters 6; Coopers 6; Merchants 4; Peddlers 6; Clergymen 21; Physicians 7; Drug Storekeepers 7—2 practical Chemists, the rest kept by Physicians—4 Drug Clerks and Chemists, and 3 apprentices; Tinsmiths 5—apprentices 3; Musicians 18; Engineers 2; Watchmakers and Jewelers 2—apprentices 2; Dressmakers 100; Tailoresses 10; Shirtmakers and Seamstresses 11; Preserve Manufacturers 4 —2 Clerks, 2 Stores; Gold Watch-casemaker 1; Caulker 1; Upholsterers 2—one apprentice; Artist and Engraver 1; Straw Hat Presser 1; Soap Boiler 1; Horse Shoer 1; Baker 1; Confectioners 10; Tobacconists 2; Speculators in general Merchandise 7: Teachers 35; Ship Brokers 4; Stock and Land Brokers 4; Lawyer 1; Profesor in College 1; Silver Plater 1;—Total 419.

Not working at their Trades and Professions.

Boot and Shoemakers 45; Carpenters 28; Blacksmiths 24; Ship Carpenters 3; Machinists 8; Masons and Bricklayers 13; Wheelwrights 4; Printers 10; Hatters 4; Milliners 10; Tailors 15; Painters 7; Coopers 5; Sailmakers 4; Joiners 2; Musicians 15; Engineers 3; Dressmakers 35; Tailoresses 20; Caulkers 5; Upholsterers 4; Type Founder 1; Soap Boilers 3; Stone Cutters 4; Brass Founders 4; Horse Shoers 5; Bakers 11; Confectioners 18; Tobacconists 4; Caulkers 6; Shipbuilders 2;—Total 325.

NEW JERSEY.

Working at their Trades.

Blacksmith 1; House Carpenters 2; Dressmakers 5; Masons 1; Milliners 2; Cooper 1; Shingle Shavers 4; Patent Leather Manufacturers 2; Tinsmith 1; Engineers 2; Corsetmakers 2; Clergymen 2; Doctor 1; Teachers 3; Musicians 4; —Total 33.

Not working at their Trades.

House Carpenters 1; Machinists 1; Horse Shoers 1; Cooper 1;—Total 4.

PENNSYLVANIA.

Working at their Trades.

Boot and Shoemakers 37; Bakers 10; Ship Carpenters 42; Blacksmiths 15; Joiners 4; Sailmakers 14; Clergymen 35; Painters and Glaziers 5; Dyers and Hatters 4; Confectioners 35; Musicians 37; Dressmakers 125; Tailoresses 14; Physician 1; Doctors 7; Plain Seamstresses 40; Speculators in Merchandise 12; Land and Stock-jobber 1; Merchants 10; Milliners 7; Engineers 4; Saddle Treemakers 1; Paper Hangers 2; Turners 6; Ornamental Chairworkers 2; Teachers 20; Masons 4; Practical Farmers 37; Lumber Merchants 4; Several gentlemen of Fortune reputed for their good breed of cattle;—Total 515.

Not working at their Trades.

Boot and Shoemakers 60; Ship Carpenters 2; Turners 7; Carpenters 30; Sailmakers 6; Painters and Glaziers 7; Musicians 15: Dressmakers 32; Tailoresses 4; Plain Seamstresses and Shirtmakers 10; Milliners 4; Horse Shoers 2; Machinists 2; Silver Plater 1; Mason and Bricklayers 4;— Total 186.

OHIO.

Working at their Trades.

House Carpenters 36; Blacksmiths 24; Ship Carpenter 1; Boot and Shoemakers 38; Dressmakers 49; Tailors 6; Carriagemakers 2; Horse Shoers 12; Machinists 4; Masons 12; Printers 2; Milliners 4; Painters 16; Composition Roofer 1;

Plasterers 8; Candymaker 1; Turners 3; Cabinetmakers 4; Tobaconists 30; Daguerreotypists 10; Coopers 6; Musicians 6; Teachers 10; Clergymen 16; Doctors 3; Engineer 1; Wagonmakers 3;—Total 308.

Not working at their Trades.

Blacksmiths 20; House Carpenters 25; Ship Carpenters 8; Dressmakers 20; Boot and Shoemakers 31; Masons and Plasterers 10; Milliners 6; Brickmakers 10; Coopers 9; Hatters 5; Tobacconists 15; Painters 6; Turners 6; Cabinetmakers 6; Engineers 2; Wagonmakers 4;—Total 167.

INDIANA,—No Returns.

ILLINOIS.

Working at their Trades.

Blacksmiths 8; House Carpenters 18; Ship Carpenters 2; Boot and Shoemakers 5; Dressmakers 25; Tailors 3; Horseshoers 3; Machinist 1; Masons 15; Printer 1; Milliners 6; Painters 4; Cabinetmaker 1; Coopers 2; Turner 1; Farmers 15; Clergymen 4; Doctor 1; Teacher 1; Musicians 3;—Total 111.

Not working at their Trades.

House Carpenters 3; Dressmakers 4; Boot and Shoemakers 4; Tailors 2; Cooper 1; Masons 4; Printer 1; Milliners 4; —Total 23.

MICHIGAN.

Working at their Trades and Professions.

Blacksmiths 3; Carpenters 12; Boot and Shoemakers 8; Dressmakers 10; Tailors 3; Machinist 1; Masons 15; Painters 2; Milliner 1; Printers 3; Clerks 6; Bakers 4; Captains and owners of sailing crafts 4; Saddlers 2; Lumber and Wood Donlors 2; Coopers 6; Musicians 12; Engineers 3; Teachers 2; Farmers 7;—Total 110.

Not working at their Trades.

Horse-shoer 1; Boot and Shoemakers 2; Ship Carpenter 1; —Total 4.

CALIFORNIA AND OREGON.

Working at their Trades.

Blacksmiths 10; House Carpenters 10; Boot and Shoemakers 4; Dressmakers 12; Tailors 6; Masons and Plasterers 8; Milliners 3; Painters 4; Turners 2; Tin Plate Workers 2; Caulkers 10; Sailmakers 2; Soap and Candlemaker 1; Clergymen 8; Doctors 2; Musicians 27; Teachers 4;—Total 105.

Not working at their Trades, &c.

Blacksmiths 7; House Carpenters 9; Engineers 4; Machinists 4; Whitesmiths 3; Cabinetmakers 7; Dressmakers 16; Tailors 7; Masons and Plasterers 9; Painters 6; Caulkers 10; Sailmakers 4; Ship Builders 3; Tin Plate Workers 6; Artists 3;—Total 98.

Your Committee believe that the result of the Conversational gatherings in the different localities, will result in effecting immediate needful action in the several communities where our people are found.

All of which is respectfully submitted.

EDWARD V. CLARK.

On motion, the report was adopted.

On motion, Rev. Sampson White, of Washington, D. C., was admitted a corresponding member.

Rev. Stephen Smith then presented a memorial from the citizens of San Francisco, Cal., which was referred to the Business Committee.

Rev. Charles Birch and Mr. Fuller, of Conn., and Mr. Martin, of Ohio, were elected corresponding members.

Mr. Robert Purvis, of Pa., then said, that he desired to present three resolutions concerning Passmore Williamson. A motion was then made to suspend the rules so as to admit the resolutions. This motion occasioned some debate, and was finally lost.

The Business Committee then offered the following resolutions:

Resolved, That this Convention gladly seizes the opportunity of expressing towards Passmore Williamson their sincere admiration for his fidelity to their principle, and his heroic devotion to the cause of freedom, and they beg him to accept for himself and his injured and bereaved family, assurance of their deepest and most heartfelt sympathy.

Resolved, That Mr. Williamson, by his promptness on this, as on all occasions when called upon to fly to the aid of the slave when striving for his freedom, has entitled him to the highest regard and the warmest admiration of every man who has a heart to appreciate the value of freedom, or despise the chains of oppression.

Resolved, That a committee of five be appointed to wait upon and present to Mr. Williamson this expression of the National Convention.

The resolutions were received with loud applause, and after some discussion were adopted.

The following persons were announced to form the Committee to visit Passmore Williamson:—Robert Purvis, Pa.; John S. Rock, M. D., Mass.; George T. Downing, R. I.; Stephen Myers, N. Y., and Charles L. Remond, Mass.

The following additional preamble and resolutions were subsequently read:

WHEREAS, every man and woman are by right the owners of themselves, and except under legal contract voluntarily entered into, or to appease justice violated by crime, this right cannot be alienated, all laws for the holding of slaves, and all Fugitive Slave Bills to reclaim them, to the contrary notwithstanding—therefore

Resolved, That this Convention approve of and honor the conduct of John Ballard, William Custis, John Braddock, William Still, James Martin and Josiah Moore, who bore off, in the face of difficulty, Jane Johnson and her children, from the steamer on the Delaware, and thus secured to her what she had been robbed of, her own and her children's freedom.

After some further debate, the foregoing preample and resolutions were adopted.

The committee appointed at the former Convention to take into consideration the feasibility of founding an Industrial School for colored persons, reported adversely, as the committee deemed the subject impracticable. The committee recommend that a Mechanical Bureau be established in its stead.

On motion, Mr. J. Watkins was appointed to prepare a record of the names and post office address of each of the members.

The following resolution was offered by Rev. E. Kelly, through the Business Committee:

Resolved, That this Convention adopt the platform of principles laid down by the late Rochester Convention, with a view of referring the same to the Business Committee, with instructions to amend that document by striking out every proscriptive feature, and inserting others more liberal, and to simplify it as much as possible, so as to make it as a whole acceptible to this Convention, and to the people generally.

Pending the adoption of this, the Convention adjourned.

SECOND DAY—AFTERNOON SESSION.

The Convention met pursuant to adjournment. Prayer was offered by Rev. Mr. Bolden.

Dr. Jas. McCune Smith then read the following resolutions as a substitute for the report from the Philadelphia delegation.

Resolved, That this Convention recommend that in all communities where there is a sufficient number of colored people, that they form associations to be called Industrial Associations, with such rules and regulations as they may deem best for the purpose of encouraging colored artizans of both sexes in the pursuit of Mechanical or Artistic employment.

Resolved, That these associations be requested to correspond with each other, and publish the facts effected by them.

Resolved, That these associations shall hold a convention on the — day of October, 1857, in the City of ———.

Mr. J. C. Bowers then moved that Dr. Smith's resolutions be indefinitely postponed.

After some discussion the President decided that a resolution offered by Rev. E. Kelly, before the close of the morning session, was in order. Mr. Kelly spoke in favor of his resolution. It was lost.

Dr. J. McCune Smith spoke in favor of his resolutions. They were opposed by Mr. J. C. Bowers.

Rev. Stephen Smith moved that each delegate pay one dollar to defray the expenses of the Convention.

Mr. Morrell moved to amend by saying that each delegate pay such an amount as he shall feel able. The amendment was carried. The roll was then called, and the collection taken up.

The Convention then agreed to hear a full report of the Finance Committee on the following morning.

The Convention then resumed the consideration of Dr. Smith's resolutions, which were discussed up to the hour of adjournment.

Second Day—Evening Session.

The Convention met pursuant to adjournment, J. J. Gould Bias in the Chair.

Dr. Smith's resolutions being in order, Dr. J. McCune Smith, Dr. J. J. G. Bias, Wm. J. Watkins and Frederick Douglass spoke in favor of said resolutions, and Josiah C. Wears, Charles H. Bustill and Robert Purvis against them.

Dr. J. McCune Smith moved that the report of the Philadelphia delegation be amended by striking out of it so much as deemed the establishment of an Industrial School as inadvisable, and incorporating the resolutions as a supplement. It was adopted.

The Convention adjourned till the following morning at 9½ o'clock.

Third Day—Morning Session.

The Convention met pursuant to adjournment, the President in the Chair.

By permission, Rev. Thomas P. Hunt addressed the Convention on the advantages of Agricultural pursuits. After which the Business Committee reported a number of letters from delegates elected, but unable to be present. Communications from Rev. J. W. C. Pennington and Rev. C. W. Gardiner were read, and ordered to be printed with the minutes.

A letter from Mr. Jacob Handy of Baltimore, eulogizing the Republic of Liberia, and advocating the colonization movement, was opposed by Messrs. C. L. Remond, Geo. T. Downing, P. A. Bell, Thos. Gray and J. J. Simons. After several propositions to return the letter, respectfully and otherwise, Mr. Geo. T. Downing, unwilling to incur the expense of three cents, moved that the communication be burned, and called for the previous question. Yeas 33—Nays 20.

The Business Committee then reported the following resolution, which was adopted:

Resolved, That the Constitution of the National Council be referred to a committee of one from each State, to suggest such revisions or alterations as in their judgment they may deem best.

The following, offered by the Business Committee, were also adopted:

Resolved, That education, the great elevator of mind, is what we need, and what we must have, to place us on an equal footing with other men, and we will improve such opportunities as are afforded us to secure it for ourselves and our children.

Resolved, That in the first place our people be made to feel the necessity of securing real estate, and that it requires union with us as a people to sustain each other, that we obtain the great object which we have in view, viz: our social, civil and political rights, and that we encourage our people in agricultural pursuits on lands of their own.

The Convention then adjourned.

Third Day—Afternoon Session.

The Convention met pursuant to adjournment, the President in the Chair.

Prayer was offered by Mr. S. Golden.

The Business Committee then reported the following resolutions:

Resolved, That we rejoice in the legislative act of Massachusetts, by which her common schools are open to every class of her citizens, believing that the school-room is, when really free, the greatest leveller of all species of prejudice.

Resolved, That as no one class can elevate another, so we believe that all the general plans that may be adopted by this and other National Conventions will fail of their purpose, unless the people realize the necessity of individual application and effort.

Resolved, That we recommend to our mothers and sisters to use every honorable means to secure for their sons and brothers places of profit and trust in stores and other places of business, such as will throw a halo around this proscribed people, that shall in coming time reflect honor on those who have laid the corner stone to our platform of improvement.

Resolved, That we use our influence to prevent our boys from taking employment in cities at places of amusement, where marked distinction on account of color is made the order of exercises.

Resolved, That considering our relative position as a part of the nation, in the capacity of the real producers of the wealth of the nation and this country, we therefore recommend to all our youth to learn some useful trade or some mechanical art, as a means of doing away with prejudice against color, and thus show to the world that we aspire to, and can arrive at, the highest eminence from which slavery and social and civil oppression have debarred us.

Mr. Robert Purvis, Chairman of the Committee to visit Passmore Williamson in Moyamensing Prison, reported verbally that the Committee had waited upon Mr. Williamson, and tendered him the resolutions of sympathy; that Mr. Williamson received the resolutions, and tendered his best wishes to the Convention, and assured them that no matter what the consequences may be, he will not sacrifice a single principle upon the altar of slavery. The Committee have only to fear that Mr. Williamson's health will suffer from his long confinement.

The following address was then offered by Dr. J. McCune Smith:

AN ADDRESS

TO THE PEOPLE OF THE UNITED STATES.

FELLOW CITIZENS:—In behalf of three millions of our brethren, held in Slavery, in the United States:

In behalf of two hundred and fifty thousand, so called, free persons of color, occupying various grades of social and political position, from equal citizenship in most of the New England States, to almost chattel slavery in Indiana and the Southern States:

In behalf of three hundred thousand slaveholders, embruted with the lawlessness, and drunken with the blood-guiltiness of slaveholding:

In behalf of the Constitution of these United States, during sixty years perverted and misconstrued, so as to read things for persons, and Slavery for Liberty:

In behalf of the religion of Jesus Christ, brought into shame and disrepute by the evil constructions and worse practices fastened upon it by the American Church:

In behalf of the sacred cause of HUMAN FREEDOM, beaten down and paralyzed by the force of American Example—

The undersigned, delegates to a Convention of the People of Color, held in the city of Philadelphia, October 18th, 1855, beg leave, most respectfully, to address you:—

We claim that we are persons not things, and we claim that our brethren held in slavery are also, *persons* not *things;* and that they are, therefore, so held in slavery in violation of the Constitution, which is the supreme law of the land.* For the Constitution expressly declares, that all human beings, described under it, are *persons,*† and afterwards declares, that "NO PERSON shall be deprived of liberty without due process of law;"‡ and that the right of the people to be secure in their *persons* shall not be violated.§ And as no law has ever been enacted,¶ which reduced our brethren to slavery, we demand

---

* Art. 6. § 2.
† Art. 1. sect. 2. § 3. and sect. 9. § 1. and Art. 4. sect. 2. § 3.
‡ Amendments Art. 1. § 5.
§ Ib. § 4.
¶ Speech of Judge Mason on Fugitive Slave Bill in Congress 1850. "If it be required that proof shall be brought that Slavery is established by existing laws, it is impossible to comply with the requisition, for no such proof can be produced, I apprehend, in any of the slave States. I am not aware there is a single State in which the Institution is established by peculiar law."—Aug. 19th, 1850.

their immediate emancipation, and restoration to the rights secured to every person under the Constitution, as the instant result of that personality with which the Constitution itself clothes them, and which it was ordained to protect and defend.

All human beings who may be born in this land, in whatever condition, and all who may come or may have been brought to this land, under whatever circumstances, are declared by the Constitution to be PERSONS : the idea that such may be property, or may become property, is no where recognized, but every where excluded by the Constitution.||

The Constitution, moreover, endows Congress with the power, and calls on Congress to exercise the power to abolish Slavery in the Slave States, when it declares that " Congress shall provide for the general welfare ;" and announces that " the United States shall guarantee to every State in this Union a republican form of government :" and that "this Constitution, and the laws of the United States, which shall be made in pursuance thereof, shall be the supreme law of the land ; and the judges in every State shall be bound thereby, any thing in the Constitution or laws of any State to the contrary notwithstanding." (Art. 6, sec. 2.)

It is not needful to prove that slavery inhibits, obstructs and threatens to destroy the " general welfare," and is therefore an institution which Congress is competent, and in duty bound, to abolish everywhere where it may cause such obstruction. Nor is it necessary to show that slavery is a contradiction of the Republican form of Government, which the United States, that is Congress is constitutionally bound " to guarantee" to each and " every State in the Union :" which guarantee can only be accomplished by immediately abolishing slavery in every State where it may exist. These things contain their own proof in the very statement of them.

We claim, therefore, that the right and duty of Congress to abolish slavery in the slave States, is just as clear and well defined in the Constitution as the right to levy duties, declare war, or make a treaty.

To uphold a contrary view of the Constitution, requires that that instrument should contradict itself, and requires also that the idea of personal liberty, as defined by it, and on which you

---

|| " I deny that the Constitution recognizes property in man. I submit, on the other hand, most respectfully, that the Constitution not merely does not affirm that principle, but, on the contrary, altogether excludes it."—Hon. Wm. H. Seward's Speech in admission of California, in Senate, March 11, 1850.

all, fellow-citizens, so confidently rely, shall be entirely erased therefrom. The personality of the negro and of the white man stand therein side by side; you cannot destroy the one without also destroying the other; you cannot uphold the one without also upholding both.

We solemnly believe, fellow-citizens, that a vast majority of you ardently wish that slavery may be abolished, and are willing to join in any lawful movement to accomplish this great purpose. We call upon you, therefore, at once to set about this glorious work in accordance with the provisions of the Constitution which is the "supreme law of the land." Elect such a Congress, such a President, and thereby secure the appointment of such a Judiciary as will guarantee to each man, woman and child, in the land, the right to their own persons, which the Constitution guarantees. There is no other way, there never has been, there can be no other way to abolish slavery and the slave power throughout the land.

It is idle to talk of preventing the extension or circumscribing the limits of slavery: there is no foot of American Territory over which slavery is not already triumphant, and will continue triumphant, so long as there remains any foot of American Territory on which it is admitted that man can hold property in man. It is imbecile for you, fellow-citizens, with the gyves on your wrists, and your chains clanking audibly to the rest of mankind, any longer to boast the possession, or speak of the maintenance of your personal rights and franchises. During sixty-eight years you have suffered us to be robbed of these rights and franchises, in the belief that your own continued unimpaired. But now, after the experience of two generations, you find your own rights invaded and your own privileges taken away in like manner with ours. It is now, therefore, demonstrated, by incontrovertible History, that you cannot, by whatever neglect or suffered misinterpretation of the Constitution, imperil or abandon our rights, without, in like manner, imperiling and abandoning your own. It stands forth, in letters of living light, that there can be not one white free-man while there remains one black slave in the Union. And there can be no higher praise of the Constitution, than that its workings are absolute—if rightly interpreted, for Freedom—if wrongly, for Slavery—to all.

As at present misisterpreted and carried out, your own rights under the Constitution, fellow-citizens, are not a shade higher than those of the veriest slave in the South: your local elective franchises are exercised, your very territory occupied, your relations at home and abroad regulated at the bidding of the slave power; and you must either remain the willing victims of their atrocious institution, and hug the chains daily accumulating upon you, or you must at once rise and rend them, and regain your own liberties while you establish those of your brethren in bonds.

We earnestly call upon you, therefore, fellow-citizens, in behalf of the down-trodden slave, in behalf of your own imperiled liberties, in behalf of the cause of civil and Religious Freedom throughout the world, in behalf and in vindication of our glorious Constitution, we solemnly call upon you, peacefully, lawfully and constitutionally, to abolish slavery in the slave States.

Mr. F. Douglass moved the adoption of the address.

Messrs. J. C. Morrell and C. L. Remond opposed the address, and Mr. Robert Purvis read Mr. Wm. J. Bowditch's opinion of the pro-slavery character of the Constitution, from No. 1 of the series of Anti-slavery tracts.

Mr. F. Douglass and Dr. J. McCune Smith advocated the address. The yeas and nays were called for, and decided in the affirmative.

The vote to burn Mr. Handy's Communication was reconsidered, and it was agreed to return it to Mr. Handy.

The Convention then adjourned.

THIRD DAY—EVENING SESSION.

The Convention met pursuant to adjournment, the President in the Chair. Prayer was offered by Rev. Wm. Douglass.

The Committee appointed to revise the Constitution of the National Council, then made the following report:—

To the President and Members of the National Convention:

Your Committee appointed to revise the Constitution of the National Council beg respectfully to submit the following

REPORT.

Owing to the late hour of the appointment of your Committee, they have been unable to attend to the revision of the Constitution of the National Council. And the Committee have unanimously agreed to recmmend the Convention to empower the National Council to revise said Constitution.

J. S. ROCK,	C. L. REASON,
J. C. BEEMAN,	W. J. WATKINS.

The Report of the Committee was adopted.

The Committee on Statistics then submitted the following

REPORT.

1. That the Statistics presented to them in this Convention are entirely too few to make up a Report upon.

2. The Committee have in possession, however, copious statistics in relation to the colored population, free and slave, which they think it important should be published as a reply to the many slanders recently heaped upon us.

3. The cost of Printing 5000 copies of these statistics will be not less than two hundred dollars; and as the Committee have not the means for such publication, they respectfully request the direction of the Convention as to the best mode of procuring their publication.

Respectfully submitted.

A. S. DRIVER,	WM. C. NELL,
J. McCUNE SMITH,	STEPHEN SMITH,
SAMUEL T. GRAY.	

The Report was adopted, and ordered to be incorporated in the Minutes.

The resolutions offered in the afternoon session were discussed by Messrs. F. Douglass, Wm. J. Watkins, Rev. J. C. Beman, and Messrs. J. C. Bowers, J. C. Wears, C. L. Remond and Dr. J. S. Rock, and were adopted.

The following resolutions were also discussed separately:

Resolved, That we recommend the colored people to turn their attention to inter-state traffic and trade, and to commerce with foreign countries. Adopted.

Resolved, That the devoted labors of the abolitionists of the land, to bring about immediate emancipation, endear them to us, and we give to all of them in these endeavors the right hand of fellowship. Laid on the table.

A vote of thanks was then tendered to Mr. E. V. Clark for his report, and it was ordered to be incorporated in the minutes.

After which the following resolutions were adopted :

Resolved, That we adopt "Frederick Douglass's Paper" as our Organ.

Resolved, That we print 1500 copies of the Minutes, and divide them equally among the delegates who have paid the expenses of the Convention.

Resolved, That the President appoint a Publishing Committee of five, to be located in the City of Philadelphia.

The President then appointed Messrs. Franklin Turner, Frances A. Duterte, Ulysses B. Vidal, Isaiah C. Wears and Robert Purvis.

A vote of thanks was tendered to the Philadelphia delegation for their kindness and attention to the delegates, and also a vote of thanks to the officers of the Convention, and to the Reporters of the press.

The Convention then adjourned *sine die*, and the members and audience all joined in singing the doxology—

"Praise God from whom all blessings flow."

APPENDIX.

——o——

COMMUNICATIONS RECEIVED BY THE CONVENTION.

29 Sixth Avenue, New York, October 15, 1855.

To the Chairman of the National Convention at Philadelphia:

As a member of the New York Delegation, I deeply regret that circumstances unforseen and beyond my control prevent me from taking my seat in your Assembly. Be assured, however, sir, that I am cordially with you in the object of this great meeting. I well remember, sir, to have been a member of the 1st, 2d, and 3d National Conventions of our people, held in the City of Brotherly Love, (held severally) in the years 1831, '32 and '33. Those were glorious gatherings, where our Bowerses, Sipkinses, Hamiltons, Jinnings, Shads, Pecks, Morrells, Whippers and Bells were chief men among our brethren; and in my humble opinion it was a great mistake on our part when, in 1834, we abandoned our National Convention for a mode of operation which disappointed us. But it is not too late to return to the good old path;—better late than never. I say, then, sir, let this be the beginning of a new series of National Conventions of our people. The time has fully come when a most vigorous and uncompromising stand must be made against the slave power on this vast Continent. We are competent to resist it; and, "we must do or die!"

The population of this Continent ranges between 50 and 60 millions. Nearly seven millions of that number are of African descent.

The Governments of this Continent, about 40 in number, are prevailingly Republican or liberal monarchies, or provinces under the government of liberal monarchies. Now, sir, the liberal parties of all the parties and races of this Continent must combine in order to withstand the slave power of *this* Republic. Nay, by such a combination alone can that huge power be overthrown. That power is making headway against all races; hence, of course, all races must combine against it.

Let there be a grand fusion Western Continent Anti-slavery

Extension Convention held. Let it be held at some place or point where gentlemen of talent from the British, French, Spanish and Danish Dominions, and also from Mexico and Central America—I say let such a Convention be held, and let it be held at some point where civilized law and order prevail—Jamaica, Hayti—and let it be a great Congress of Liberty, to be attended by all the friends of Liberty, who will unite to oppose the slave power of this Continent. Sir, this is a grand idea, worthy to be entertained by this Convention; and, sir, why not appoint a committee to mature this idea?

I tell you in this Convention, that if ever we compete successfully with the slave power of this Republic, we must now act with all the oppressed and insulted races.

Where are Walker and Kinney? Trampling upon the necks of portions of the inoffensive inhabitants of Central and South America.

I am sorry, sir, that the same causes which prevent my presence with you, also prevent me from elaborating these views.

In regard to the report of the religious state of the Colored people, which I believe was assigned me at the meeting of our State Council, I will state that my esteemed Baptist Brother, Rev. James Leonard of Rhode Island, is preparing a book on that subject, embracing all denominations. Mr. L. is a scholar of no mean order. The subject is safe in his hands. I have placed at his disposal such materials as I had. I commend his book.

Finally, Mr. Chairman, in your deliberations remember PASSMORE WILLIAMSON. "I SPEAK AS UNTO WISE MEN—JUDGE YE WHAT I SAY."

Yours, as ever,
J. W. C. PENNINGTON,
Pastor of Shiloh Pres. Church, N. Y.

Newport, R. I., October 15, 1855.

To the National Convention at Philadelphia:

RESPECTED BRETHREN—It was not my lot to receive an appointment to your Convention, as the people of Newport, R. I., in most other cases took no action thereon. Nevertheless, I deemed it proper to lay my views before you.

Some 25 or 26 years since, we formed the parent society in Philadelphia. Eighteen years since I was chosen one of the assessors of Philadelphia, to ascertain the number of the colored inhabitants, &c., &c., in the city. At both of these periods I stated my views of our best mode of action, which I shall now lay before your body, viz:—That your Convention recommend to our people to submit to a taxation of $1.00 per year, on all males of 21 years of age, (not excluding others that may see proper to pay it) or larger sums if preferred—that in every city or large village, where 200 colored persons are located, there be one assessor, or more if necessary, whose duty it shall be to assess the people and collect the money quarterly—that there be a committee of three in each city, &c., to whom he shall be amenable ; and render his accounts quarterly, and they so do to the general Committee, who shall superintend the whole, and be located where your wisdom may direct. There would be little or no objection to such collections even in Slave States for educational purposes, when the persons were to be educated out of the State. There is no doubt in my mind that the sum of $100,000 could be collected annually, which would afford a handsome sum after the necessary expenses were met, which fund should be appropriated after the order of the Presbyterian Board of Education, the candidates being subject to an examination by your Committee ; and when recommended to your board let them receive such aid as your laws shall direct.

Thus having the funds on hand assistance can be given when and where it is needed. As to schools or colleges, though I have passed my three score years and ten I am certain if the support and qualifications were present that I could find doors open in High Schools, Academies, Seminaries and Colleges, for five hundred young ladies and gentlemen of color, within the States of New England, New York and Pennsylvania.

Respected brethren, you will see that my plan is simple and comatable, and must recommend itself to your honorable notice. I have given no argument or direction, believing and knowing that your united wisdom will be sufficient for all such purposes.

At the same time you will see that I do not approve of separate colored schools, believing that education is the right of all, and that the only plan to lay the sure foundation of true Republicanism is, as far as practicable to educate male and female, white and colored, rich and poor, together, and so teach them that they are all human beings, united in a common brotherhood of universal love.

All of which I submit to your united wisdom. And may the Great Spirit of Light and Truth preside in all your councils, and rule to his glory and the good of all men—

While I subscribe myself yours for universal advancement and education.

CHARLES W. GARDNER.

The Convention
of 1864

THE NATIONAL CONVENTION OF 1864 STANDS IN LONELY splendor, nine years after the last preceding conclave had killed the revived effort for a black institution of higher education under the auspices of the National Convention, and had realigned the Negro community with the pro United States Constitution segment of American thinking. By 1864, the stand in favor of the Constitution had been vindicated, temporarily at least; black institutions of higher education were being formed, but not under the auspices of the National Convention; and emigrationism was laid to rest as Henry Highland Garnet and J. Sella Martin lectured in England in favor of the Union, and as Martin R. Delany joined the Union Army to fight for the nation from which he had tried for a decade to escape.

This was a time for evaluation of the work of a whole generation—thirty-five years—and most of the delegates who had passed through a substantial portion of those years could look back with justifiable pride on their achievements. They could point to better schools, increased recognition of the Negro American's position in America, increased participation in the body politic. But this backward look was not the reason for the convention. If any one reason for calling a convention in the fall of 1864 is to be named, it is that the fate of the Negro and the fate of the nation hung in delicate balance.

George B. McClellan, twice removed from command of the Army of the Potomac and for cause, was the Democratic party candidate running on an appeasement platform. Lincoln, with far too few recent victories to command confidence in an early and favorable settlement of the war, was hard pressed to hold his own in the coming election. He had sought to improve his position by accepting a southern Democrat as a running mate; he was toying with the idea of allowing the wartime measures (Emancipation Proclamation and all) to go before the courts as a means of winning the election.

Frederick Douglass, president of the convention, pointed to the all too obvious danger to the Negro and to the nation. With McClellan and the Democrats openly advocating a negotiated peace, and with Lincoln and the Republicans ready to compromise the gains already won, the National Convention warned that the only hope left was that the South would stubbornly fight on until it was completely crushed.

In one of the most challenging passages of the entire thirty-five years, the convention once more reminded the nation of the discrepancy between the claims of the democracy and the actions of that democracy; they reminded the nation that Negro troops, although at first refused the privilege of defending their country, had, when belatedly given the opportunity, acquitted themselves well. And once again they reminded America that the debasement of one was the debasement of all.

A Declaration of Wrongs and Rights (notice the word order), and the organization of a National Equal Rights League wound up the business of the last great meeting of the black men who had matured in adversity and had proven over and over again—if proof were still needed —that the Negro American was ready to carry his share of the load in building the great democracy which the American Revolution had promised, but had thus far failed to deliver.

PROCEEDINGS

OF THE

National Convention of Colored Men,

HELD IN

THE CITY OF SYRACUSE, N. Y.,

OCTOBER 4, 5, 6, AND 7, 1864;

WITH THE

BILL OF WRONGS AND RIGHTS,

AND THE

ADDRESS TO THE AMERICAN PEOPLE.

———————

BOSTON:
PUBLISHED BY J. S. ROCK AND GEO. L. RUFFIN,
6 TREMONT STREET AND 28 STANIFORD STREET,

1864.

To the Members of the National Convention.

PRESS OF GEO. C. RAND & AVERY, 3 CORNHILL, BOSTON.

NATIONAL CONVENTION OF COLORED MEN,

HELD IN THE CITY OF SYRACUSE, N. Y.,

OCTOBER 4TH, 5TH, 6TH AND 7TH, 1864.

The National Convention of Colored Men assembled in the Wesleyan Methodist Church, in Syracuse, N. Y., October 4, 64,. at 7 o'clock, P. M. Rev. Henry Highland Garnet, of Washington, D. C., called the Convention to order, and read the call. John M. Langston, Esq., of Oberlin, O., was chosen temporary Chairman; and Wm. Howard Day, of New Jersey, and St. George R. Taylor, of Pennsylvania, Secretaries.

The Convention then united in singing, —

"Blow ye the trumpet, blow;"

after which, Rev. Mr. Garnet offered up a fervent and eloquent prayer.

On motion, the Chairman appointed a Committee on Credentials, consisting of—

FREDERICK DOUGLASS, of *New York;*
PETER H. CLARK, of *Ohio;*
WILLIAM W. BROWN, of *Massachusetts.*

A motion was made to appoint a committee of one from each State, to nominate permanent officers for the Convention.

Mr. Stephen Myers, of Albany, moved, as a substitute, that the Convention proceed to elect its officers *vivâ voce.*

Rev. Elisha Weaver, of Philadelphia, moved that the original motion and the substitute lie upon the table until the Committee on Credentials made their report. **Carried.**

Rev. Mr. Garnet was now called upon, and addressed the Convention. He eloquently discussed the propriety and necessity for holding conventions, and the duty of this Convention to strengthen the hands of the soldier, and to use its influence towards promoting education and temperance. ɪe address was received with favor, and was frequently applauded.

The Committee on Credentials reported the names of delegates whose seats were not contested. The full list, as corrected, is as follows: —

MAINE.

SAMUEL J. MURRAY, Portland.
WILLIAM W. RUBY, "
JAMES F. MURRAY, Bangor.

MASSACHUSETTS.

JOHN S. ROCK, Boston.
GEORGE L. RUFFIN, "
JOHN B. SMITH, "
WM. W. BROWN, Cambridgeport.
EBENEZER HEMMENWAY, Worcester.
SAMUEL HARRISON, Pittsfield.

RHODE ISLAND.

GEO. T. DOWNING, Newport.
JAS. JEFFERSON, Providence.

CONNECTICUT.

F. L. CORDOZO, Hartford.
PETER H. NOTT, "
MINOR MARS, "
EDW. C. FREEMAN, "
WM. F. JOHNSON, Bridgeport.
ABRAM J. MORRISON, New M'ford.
R. J. COWES, New Haven.

NEW YORK.

ROBT. HAMILTON, N. Y. City.
SINGLETON T. JONES, "
J. W. C. PENNINGTON, "
P. B. RANDOLPH, "

HENRY H. GARNET, N. Y. City.
J. SELLA MARTIN, Brooklyn.
R. H. CAIN, "
LEWIS H. PUTNAM, "
PETER H. WILLIAMS (honorary), Brooklyn.
PETER W. RAY, Brooklyn.
WILLIAM H. JOHNSON, Albany.
GEORGE W. JOHNSON, "
STEPHEN MYERS, "
JAMES C. MATTHEWS, "
—— ELKINS (honorary), "
ROBERT JACKSON, "
JOHN CUTLER, "
H. W. JOHNSON, Canandaigua.
ANDREW B. SLATER, "
W. W. DeNIKE (honorary), Utica.
WILLIAM GREY, "
F. P. LAPIERRE, "
F. C. LIPPINS, "
PETER FREEMAN, "
SAMUEL DOVE, "
JAMES H. WASHINGTON, "
FRANCIS J. PECK, Buffalo.
GEORGE WEIR, "
GEORGE DOVER, "
SAMUEL MURRAY, "
PEYTON HARRIS (honorary), Buffalo.
FRED'K DOUGLASS, Rochester.
JAMES TAYLOR, "
THOMAS JAMES, "
WILLIAM H. BRUCE, "

J. W. LOGUEN, *Syracuse.*
W. H. BROWN, "
T. A. KEEN, "
ISAAC DEYO, *Poughkeepsie.*
A. BOLDEN, "
WILLIAM VIRGINIA, *Rome.*
THOMAS JOHNSON, "
JAMES SCHEMEOHORN, *Binghampton.*
W. H. DECKER, *Newburg.*
WALTER K. MOWER, *Amenia.*
SAMUEL J. HOLLINSWORTH, *Owego.*
THOMAS H. THOMAS, *Ithaca.*
WILLIAM RICH, *Troy.*
JACOB THOMAS, "
C. W. ROBINSON, *Waterville.*
A. J. BARRIER, *Brockport.*
NORRIS LEE, *Watertown.*
ENOCH MOORE, *Little Falls.*

NEW JERSEY.

WM. HOWARD DAY, *Newark.*
EDWIN H. FREEMAN, "
THOMAS G. GOULD, *Trenton.*
THOMAS H. COOPER, "
D. P. SEATON, *Morristown.*

PENNSYLVANIA.

E. D. BASSET, *Philadelphia.*
J. C. GIBBS, "
JOHN B. REEVE, "
ELISHA WEAVER, "
THOMAS J. BOWERS, "
ALFRED M. GREEN, "
H. J. BROWN, "
GEORGE W. GOINES, "
JOHN W. PAGE, "
P. N. JUDAH, "
A. BRYAN, "
D. D. TURNER, "
JOHN W. SIMPSON, "
THEO. D. MILLER, "
JOSEPH C. BUSTILL, "
CHARLES B. COLLY, "
OCTAVIUS V. CATTO, "

JAMES NEEDHAM, *Philadelphia.*
JACOB C. WHITE, "
ST. GEO. R. TAYLOR, "
JAMES H. WILSON, "
JAS. M'CRUMMELL, "
SAMUEL MORRIS, *Frankfort.*
WILLIAM NESBIT, *Altoona.*
DANIEL WILLIAMS, *Hollidaysburg.*
O. C. HUGHES, *Harrisburg.*
JOSEPH A. NELSON, "
GEO. B. VASHON, *Pittsburg.*
JOHN PECK, "
B. W. ARNETT, *Brownsville.*
P. HOUSTON MURRAY, *Reading.*
J. J. WRIGHT, *Montrose.*
WLLIAM DOUGLASS (honorary), *Corrie.*
JAMES DAVENGER, *Pittston.*
GEORGE BUTLER, "
SOLOMON COOPER, *Towanda.*

VIRGINIA.

R. D. BECKLEY, *Alexandria.*
SAMPSON WHITE, "
JAS. P. MORRISON, *Portsmouth.*
E. G. CORPREW, "
WILLIAM KEELING, *Norfolk.*

NORTH CAROLINA.

A. H. GALLOWAY, *Newbern.*
SAMUEL J. WILLIAMS, *Roanoke Island.*

FLORIDA.

JAS. M. SCOTTRON, *Jacksonville.*

LOUISIANA.

JAMES H. INGRAHAM, *New Orleans.*
SAMUEL SCOTT (honorary), *N. Orleans.*

OHIO.

PETER H. CLARK, *Cincinnati.*
JOHN P. SAMPSON, "

WM. P. NEWMAN, *Cincinnati.*
JOHN MALVIN, *Cleveland.*
J. A. DAVIS, "
JOHN M. LANGSTON, *Oberlin.*
HENRY LEE, "
J. M·C. SIMPSON, *Zanesville.*
G. W. BRYANT, *Xenia.*
B. K. SAMPSON, *Springfield.*

MICHIGAN.
H. P. HARRIS, *Adrian.*
HENRY F. BUTLER, "
JOHN D. RICHARDS, *Detroit.*
GEORGE H. PARKER, "

ILLINOIS.
J. HOUSTON, *Springfield.*

MISSISSIPPI.
CHARLES P. HEAD, *Vicksburg*

TENNESSEE.
PETER LOWREY, *Nashville.*
ABRAHAM SMITH, ·
RANSOM HARRIS, "
MORRIS HENDERSON, *Memphis.*
HORATIO N. RANKIN, "

MISSOURI.
PRESTON G. WELLS, *St. Louis.*

DISTRICT OF COLUMBIA.
WILLIAM WILSON, *Washington.*

Mr. Green, of Pennsylvania, moved that the delegates whose seats are contested be not allowed to participate in the proceedings of the Convention, until the Committee on Credentials report them as entitled to full membership.—Agreed to.

On motion, W. H. Decker, from Newburg, New York, was received as a member.

Rev. H. H. Garnet moved that Mr. William Douglass, of Pennsylvania, who had lately invented a battery, which would fire six thousand times in a minute, be made an Honorary Member.—Carried with applause.

On motion of Rev. H. H. Garnet, Mr. Peyton Harris, of Buffalo, New York, was, after discussion, made an Honorary Member.

Mr. Lewis H. Putnam moved that the report of the Committee on Credentials stand as the roll of the Convention.—Agreed to.

The Committee on Credentials were, on motion, continued.

Moved by Professor E. D. Bassett, of Pennsylvania, that the delegation from each State now proceed to select one from its number; the persons so selected to constitute a Committee to nominate permanent officers for the Convention.

Dr. Randolph, of New York, moved as an amendment, that the nomination and election of permanent officers be in open Convention.

The amendment was sustained by Stephen Myers, and Wm. H. Johnson, of New York, and opposed by E. Weaver, of Pennsylvania.

Robert Hamilton, of New York, moved to amend the amendment, so as to elect by ballot.

Mr. Downing, of Rhode Island, opposed Mr. Hamilton's amendment. He thought that the appointment of a Nominating Committee would relieve the matter of all difficulty.

The Convention then negatived both amendments, and adopted the original motion made by Professor Bassett.

Dr. P. W. Ray, of New York, moved that the Convention take a recess of five minutes, to enable the delegations to agree upon their representatives.—Carried.

The following persons were then named members of the Committee upon Permanent Organization: —

Maine	SAMUEL J. MURRAY,
Massachusetts	GEORGE L RUFFIN,
Rhode Island	GEORGE T. DOWNING.
Connecticut	PETER H. NOTT,
New York	ROBERT HAMILTON,
New Jersey	WILLIAM HOWARD DAY,
Pennsylvania	J. C. GIBBS,
Virginia	WILLIAM KEELING,
North Carolina	A. H. GALLOWAY,
Mississippi	CHARLES P. HEAD,
Louisiana	JAMES H. INGRAHAM,
Tennessee	PETER LOWREY,
Florida	JAMES M. SCOTTRON,
Missouri	P. G. WELLS,
Ohio	PETER H. CLARK,
Michigan	H. P. HARRIS.

The Committee on Permanent Organization retired, and Mr. Frederick Douglass was called upon to address the Convention. Mr. Douglass came forward and addressed the Convention at length, making one of his most able and eloquent speeches, which was frequently applauded.

The Nominating Committee, through their Chairman, Mr. Robert Hamilton, unanimously reported the following: —

For President:

FREDERICK DOUGLASS, *of New York.*

Vice-Presidents:

W. W. RUBY, *Maine.*
JOHN B. SMITH, *Massachusetts.*
JAMES JEFFERSON, *Rhode Island.*
ABRAHAM J. MORRISON, *Connecticut.*
WILLIAM RICH, *New York.*
S. G. GOULD, *New Jersey.*
JOHN B. REEVE, *Pennsylvania.*
WILLIAM KEELING, *Virginia.*
ABRAM H. GALLOWAY, *North Carolina.*
CHARLES P. HEAD, *Mississippi.*
JAMES H. INGRAHAM, *Louisiana.*
PETER LOWREY, *Tennessee.*
JAMES M. SCOTTRON, *Florida.*
PRESTON G. WELLS, *Missouri.*
JOHN MALVIN, *Ohio.*
H. P. HARRIS, *Michigan.*

Secretaries:

EBENEZER D. BASSETT, *Pennsylvania.*
ABRAM SMITH, *Tennessee.*
JOHN P. SAMPSON, *Ohio.*
ROBERT HAMILTON, *New York.*
EDWIN C. FREEMAN, *Conn.*

The report of the Committee was received, the name of Frederick Douglass being greeted with great applause.

The report of the Committee was then adopted as a whole.

The temporary Chairman then conducted the President elect to the chair, and introduced him to the Convention.

Mr. Douglass, upon taking the chair, said: —

" Gentlemen, — I thank you very sincerely for the honor you have conferred upon me, by selecting me from among your number to preside over the deliberations of this Convention. While I am grateful for the position you have been pleased to assign me, — I say it without the least affectation, — I accept it with the utmost diffidence, and distrust of my ability. There are, at least, a score of gentlemen present who could preside better than I can. If you have chosen me because of any belief in my ability to conduct the proceedings of this Convention with special decorum and dignity, I fear you have made a mistake, which will become more and more apparent during the progress of the Convention; but if, as I suppose is the case, you have called me to this position as a mark of your consideration for my labors in our common cause, I am vain enough to admit that the compliment is not wholly undeserved; and, as such, I am grateful for it. For the order and decorum which may prevail here, gentlemen, I look to you. With your assistance and support we shall have harmony, which is essential to our deliberations. The cause which we come here to promote is sacred. Nowhere, in the ' wide, wide world,' can men be found coupled with a cause of greater dignity and importance than that which brings us here. We are here to promote the freedom, progress, elevation, and perfect enfranchisement, of the entire colored people of the United States; to show that, though slaves, we are not contented slaves, but that, like all other progressive races of men, we are resolved to advance in the scale of knowledge, worth, and civilization, and claim our rights as men among men. In doing this, we shall give offence to none but the mean and sordid haters of our race; while we shall command the sympathy and encouragement of all men who love impartial freedom, and the welfare of the human race."

It was moved by Mr. Johnson, of Albany, N. Y., that the thanks of this Convention be hereby tendered to J. Mercer Langston, of Ohio, temporary Chairman; to Wm. Howard Day, of New Jersey; and St. George R. Taylor, of Pennsylvania, Secretaries, — for the acceptable services they have rendered the Convention.

The motion was unanimously adopted.

Mr. Hamilton, of New York, moved that the thanks of this Convention be hereby tendered the officers of the Wesleyan Methodist Church, for their kindness in permitting the use of the Church for the deliberations of the Convention. Adopted, with applause.

The Convention, on motion, adjourned to meet in Wieting Hall, Wednesday morning, Oct. 5, at 9 o'clock.

SECOND DAY.

Morning Session.

Wednesday Morning, 9 o'clock.

The Convention met in Wieting Hall, pursuant to adjournment; the President in the chair.

2

Prayer was offered by Rev. William P. Newman, of Cincinnati, O.

The minutes of the previous meeting were read and approved.

On motion of Mr. Stephen Myers, of Albany, Mr. James F. Murray, of Bangor, Maine, and Mr. Samuel Scott, of New Orleans, La., were elected honorary members.

On motion of Rev. Mr. James, Mr. Bruce, of Rochester, N. Y., was elected to fill the vacancy in the Committee upon Credentials, caused by the election of Mr. Douglass as President of the Convention.

Mr. Davenger, of Pennsylvania, moved that the President appoint one from each delegation, to constitute a Business Committee.

Mr. Basset, of Philadelphia, moved, as an amendment, that the President appoint one or more from each delegation; and that said Committee be allowed to choose from its members its own chairman.

Mr. Green, of Pennsylvania, moved that this motion be laid upon the table; which, after discussion, was rejected.

Mr. Lee, of Ohio, moved, as an amendment, that each delegation appoint its member of that Committee. Lost.

After considerable discussion, the original amendment prevailed; and the motion, as amended, was adopted.

Mr. Clark, of Ohio, moved that a Committee of five be appointed by the chair, to report a schedule of rules for the government of the Convention. Carried.

Mr. Clark, of Ohio, moved that the chair appoint a Committee upon Finance. Carried.

Mr. Brown, of Massachusetts, moved that all business must come before the Convention through the Business Committee. Carried.

The President appointed the following-named gentlemen as a Business Committee: —

H. H. GARNET, *District of Columbia.*

EBENEZER D. BASSETT, *Pennsylvania.*

J. C. GIBBS, *Pennsylvania.*

PETER H. CLARK, *Ohio.*

J. M. LANGSTON, "

JOHN S. ROCK, *Massachusetts.*

GEORGE L. RUFFIN, *Massachusetts.*

GEORGE T. DOWNING, *Rhode Island.*
WM. H. JOHNSON, *New York.*
P. B. RANDOLPH, "
J. SELLA MARTIN, "
W. H. DECKER, "
J. H. INGRAHAM, *Louisiana.*
D. P. SEATON, *New Jersey.*
RANSOM HARRIS, *Tennessee.*
MORRIS HENDERSON, *Tennessee.*

CHARLES P. HEAD, *Mississippi.*
SAMUEL M. SCOTTRON, *Florida.*
E. G. CORPREW, *Virginia.*
P. G. WELLS, *Missouri.*
A. H. GALLOWAY, *North Carolina.*
J. D. RICHARDS, *Michigan.*
F. L. CORDOZA, *Connecticut.*
J. HOUSTON, *Illinois.*
S. J. MURRAY, *Maine.*

COMMITTEE ON RULES:

PETER W. RAY, M. D.
W. H. JOHNSON.
ALFRED M. GREEN.

PROF. G. B. VASHON,
WILLIAM NESBITT.

COMMITTEE ON FINANCE:

ROBERT HAMILTON.
J. W. LOGUEN.
EBENEZER HEMMENWAY.

GEORGE B. VASHON.
H. H. BRUCE.

Mr. J. M. Langston, of Ohio, moved that we set aside the evenings of the Convention for public speaking. Carried.

The Chair appointed, as Committee upon Public Speaking, Messrs. J. M. Langston, James Jefferson, and John Malvin. Mr. Langston declined; and P. B. Randolph, of New York, was substituted.

Mr. Langston, of Ohio, moved that Rev. Mr. Bryant, of Ohio, act as Chaplain of the Convention. Carried.

Mr. Bassett asked to be excused from acting as Secretary. The Convention at first refused, but finally excused him; and O. C. Hughes was elected to fill the vacancy.

Mr. Frederick Douglass was requested to entertain the Convention during the absence of the Business Committee. He declined; and introduced Mr. William Wells Brown, of Massachusetts, who addressed the Convention at length.

After which, Messrs. B. K. Sampson, of Ohio, Mr. Wright, of New York, and others, addressed the Convention

The Committee on Public Speaking reported F. Douglass, J. M. Langston, and J. C. Gibbs, as speakers for Wednesday evening.

The Committee on Rules reported a set of rules for the government of the Convention; which were adopted.

Messrs. J. W. Loguen, W. W. Brown, and James Jefferson, were appointed a Committee to investigate the case of three destitute children brought before the Convention.

On motion of Mr. Stephen Myers, of New York, Mr. S. J. Murray was elected an honorary member of the Convention.

Mr. Murray asked the Convention to replace, by contribution, the cane taken from Rev. Mr. Garnet by some rowdies in Syracuse. The motion was agreed to; and over forty dollars were collected for this purpose.

The Convention then adjourned.

AFTERNOON SESSION.

At two o'clock, the Convention was called to order by the President; Rev. G. W. Bryant addressing the Throne of Grace.

A motion was made by Mr. Myers, of New York, to admit W. W. De Nike, of Utica, N. Y.; Dr. Elkins, of Albany, N. Y.; and Henry Moore, — to honorary membership in this Convention. Adopted.

On motion, H. H. Garnet and Enoch Moore were appointed a Committee to borrow the battle-flag of the First Louisiana Colored Troops, to suspend across the platform.

The Business Committee reported Resolution No. 1 (see Appendix, page 33), relating to the petition to the President of the United States in reference to colored soldiers.

This resolution was ably discussed by Mr. Richards, of Michigan; Mr. Garnet, of New York; Mr. Green, of Pennsylvania; and Mr. Newman, of Ohio.

At this juncture, the Committee which was appointed to borrow the flag came in, and desired to report.

Dr. J. B. Smith, of Massachusetts, made a motion to lay the pending resolution upon the table until the Committee made its report. Carried.

The beautiful flag was then presented by Rev. Mr. Garnet. He alluded to Capt. Ingraham, who led the attack at Port Hudson when the brave Cailloux fell. Capt. Ingraham then gave a feeling narrative of the events connected with the flag. His remarks were greeted with great applause. The whole audience rose, and united in giving three hearty cheers for Capt. Ingraham, the brave men who were with him, and the battle-flag which they bore.

The Finance Committee then proceeded to collect two dollars, being the amount which had been levied upon each delegate by the Convention, to enable it to defray its expenses.

The Convention adjourned.

WEDNESDAY EVENING, 7 O'CLOCK.

The Convention assembled, the President in the chair. The audience joined in singing "The John Brown Song."

The Business Committee, through their chairman, reported a Declaration of Wrongs and Rights, for which see Appendix, page 41.

SPEECHES.

As the evening, by the vote of the Convention, was to be devoted to speeches, a large assemblage was present. The President, Frederick Douglass, said that his name had been mentioned as one of the speakers of the evening; but he did not intend to detain the audience long. He said that there were younger men behind him upon the platform, who had come up in this time of whirlwind and storm, and who would very naturally give them thunder.

Mr. Douglass first answered the question, Why need we meet in a National Convention? He showed its necessity from the state of feeling in the country toward the colored man; to answer the question, as we pass to and from this hall, by the men on the streets of Syracuse, "Where are the d—d niggers going?"

He recapitulated the acts passed by the Congress of the nation favorable to the colored people of the country, and rendered a tribute of praise to the parties instrumental in securing them; but he wanted, at the same time, to have the colored people of the country look the facts of the case in the face, and to consider the dangers which threaten them even now. The tardiness of justice awarded was then forcibly dwelt upon, and the late speech of Mr. Secretary Seward submitted to a pointed review in brief, so far as it intimates that if peace by any means be secured the status of the colored people should remain as it is to-day. Mr. Douglass was not unmindful of the hopeful side of the question, but felt that we were safest when we knew our danger.

The President then introduced Rev. J. Sella Martin, of New York. Mr. Martin began by referring to the principles which could be seen underlying the present contest in this land, and especially to the hand of Providence in behalf of the colored man. God had interfered mercifully for the oppressed, and had offset the nation's acts against the black man by meeting them at every point. When the war began, the colored man was employed only to dig ditches. The colored man wrought there, and wrought worthily; but the nation was not prepared to advance him to any point beyond that, until, in the order of Providence, there was removed from command the great ditch-digger of the nineteenth century. So from one point to another had the colored people, in the order of Providence, passed on and up to their proud position to-day.

Mr. Martin was hopeful in God and in the nation, and looked forward to see liberty and enfranchisement blessing the whole people. The speech was compact, earnest, eloquent; and, like Mr. Douglass's, well received.

The President said, as the audience were now in such good humor, he proposed that they keep so until they should be visited by the Finance Committee, after which they would be addressed by a young colored lady. He said, "You have your Anna Dickinsons; and we have ours. We wish to meet you at every point."

While the financial visit was pending, a song was called for, and sung finely by Mr. Robert Hamilton. The President then introduced Miss Edmonia Highgate, an accomplished young lady of Syracuse. Miss Highgate urged the Convention to trust in God and press on, and not abate one jot or tittle until the glorious day of jubilee shall come.

Mr. J. Mercer Langston, Esq., of Ohio, was the next speaker. He began by saying that he was a believer in the Declaration of American Independence; and proceeded to show that all people in the land, white and colored, were slaves to the oligarchy which inaugurated the present rebellion; and that the effort we are making to secure rights for the colored men was also one to secure the recognition of the rights of the white men of the country. Mr. Langston referred at length to Attorney-General Bates's opinion as to the citizenship of colored men, and claimed that that was a complete answer to the arguments and cavils against us.

As a voter in Ohio, under the law as construed, which enables men to vote who are more white than black, he had supported the Republican party, and he expected to do it again.

He ascribed the good done, however forced, to that party; and he meant to vote with and for them.

Mr. Langston's speech had many good points, all worthy of consideration. The argument to our opponents was full and convincing, and the speech was frequently interrupted with hearty applause.

Rev. J. C. Gibbs, of Pennsylvania, was called for by the President as one of the appointees for the evening; but he declined to speak.

The President then called upon Rev. Henry Highland Garnet; but, at that late hour, he also declined.

A motion was then made that Rev. Mr. Garnet be appointed the first speaker for the following (Thursday) evening, which motion was unanimously adopted.

The President then referred briefly to the position taken by the preceding speakers, and closed by calling attention to the sessions of the Convention. After the singing of the " Battle-cry of Freedom," in which all joined, the Convention adjourned.

THIRD DAY.

Thursday morning, Oct. 6.

The Convention met pursuant to adjournment; the President in the chair.

The minutes of the morning, afternoon, and evening sessions of Wednesday were read, corrected, and approved.

Mr. A. M. Green, of Pennsylvania, offered the following: —

Resolved, That there be a committee appointed on the general state of the country, and on military affairs, consisting of one member from each State ; and that so much of the report of the Business Committee as relates to military affairs, together with the Declaration of Sentiments, read at a previous session, be referred to said committee.

Dr. J. B. Smith, of Massachusetts, moved to proceed with the consideration of the resolution reported by the Business Committee in the afternoon session of Wednesday. The President then ruled, that, as the Convention adjourned while the resolution of the Business Committee was under discussion, it would necessarily come up as unfinished business.

Mr. Green stated that it was his intention to include that resolution, and refer all such matters to a special committee.

The President then ruled Mr. Green's motion in order.

Mr. Harrison, of Massachusetts, and Mr. Garnet, of New York, opposed the resolution; and Mr. Cain, of New York, supported it. After considerable discussion, on motion of Dr. Randolph, of New York, it was laid on the table. The previous question was ordered, and the resolution presented by the Business Committee was adopted.

Mr. Garnet moved to reconsider this vote; which, after some discussion, was carried.

Mr. Garnet then moved to amend the resolution by directing it to Congress rather than to the President of the United States; which amendment was adopted.

The resolution, as amended, was then adopted.

The Bill of Wrongs and Rights was then unanimously adopted.

The Business Committee, through their chairman, reported

an Address to the People of the United States; which was read and received. [See Appendix, page 45.]

Mr. A. M. Green offered the following: —

Resolved, That the Address just read be received with the unanimous indorsement of the Convention, and published separately.

Rev. H. H. Garnet moved to amend, by ordering it to be published in the minutes.

Mr. D. D. Turner, of Pennsylvania, moved to adopt the Address; and to have printed, for general circulation, ten thousand copies. Carried.

The chairman of the Business Committee reported a plan of organization for an Equal-Rights League. [See Appendix, page 36.]

Mr. Putnam, of New York, moved to receive the report, and make it the special order for the afternoon session. Agreed to.

The Business Committee reported Resolutions 5, 6, and 7; which were read and adopted. The Convention then adjourned.

AFTERNOON SESSION.

The Convention met at half-past 2 o'clock, the President in the chair. Prayer was offered by Rev. Mr. Thomas.

The minutes of the previous session were read and approved.

Mr. Peter H. Clark, of Ohio, moved that the Finance Committee now make a report. The motion was adopted, and the committee proceeded to report by calling the roll of more than one hundred and sixty names; most of whom had responded to the call to pay their assessment towards defraying the expenses of the Convention.

On motion of Mr. Hamilton, of New York, Mr. P. H. Williams, of Brooklyn, N. Y., was received as an honorary member.

A motion was made that the Plan in regard to the Equal-Rights League be considered section by section; which motion was adopted.

3

The plan was then taken up, and fully discussed by Messrs. P. H. Clark, H. H. Garnet, L. H. Putnam, W. H. Johnson, William F. Murray, and D. D. Turner, — amended, and adopted as it stands.

It was moved by Mr. Johnson, of Albany, N. Y., that the first blank in the constitution of the National Equal-Rights League be filled by inserting " Philadelphia."

Rev. William P. Newman proposed the city of Cincinnati, Ohio, and argued that the meeting should be held more towards the South and South-west.

Cincinnati was also urged by Mr. J. P. Sampson, of Ohio.

Mr. Stephen Myers, of Albany, N. Y., suggested that Cleveland, O., had the best claim as a central place, and earnestly urged that it be the location for the bureau.

That proposition was seconded by Mr. J. M. Langston, of Ohio ; who advocated it on the ground that Cleveland would be central, and that the association would there have the full sympathy of the white as well as the colored portion of the population.

Mr. D. D. Turner, of Pennsylvania, proposed Philadelphia as the proper place for the bureau. Mr. Turner contended that Philadelphia has a larger number of people of color than any other city, and thought that the thrift and noted moral worth of its people ought to have earned for them some consideration.

Prof. Bassett, of Pennsylvania, supported the proposition to establish the bureau in Philadelphia.

The hour of adjournment, according to the rules, having arrived, the time was, on motion, extended twenty minutes ; and Rev. J. Sella Martin obtained the floor. Mr. Martin contended that we needed to establish the bureau near the freedmen, and urged Philadelphia as the best place for it.

After a separate vote on each place named for the permanent bureau of the League, Cleveland, O., was declared to be the location.

On motion of Mr. J. M. Langston, the time of the annual meeting proposed and adopted was the third Tuesday of September, at 10 o'clock. A. M.

The Convention then adjourned to meet at half-past 6 o'clock, P. M.

EVENING SESSION.

Convention met pursuant to adjournment; the President in the chair. Prayer was offered by the Rev. W. P. Newman, of Ohio.

A motion was made, that the case of the destitute children be referred to the Finance Committee, with instructions to make arrangements for relieving their present wants.

Rev. Elisha Weaver, of Pennsylvania, moved to reconsider the vote locating the Bureau of the League at Cleveland, and that Philadelphia be substituted.

After some discussion, Mr. Weaver's motion prevailed.

Resolution 8th, returning thanks to the President, Cabinet, and others, was then unanimously adopted.

Resolution 9th, appointing a Committee upon Publication, consisting of John S. Rock and George L. Ruffin, of Boston, and William Howard Day, of New Jersey, was adopted.

A motion was made by Mr. Green, of Pennsylvania, that Mr. J. M. Langston, of Ohio, be made President of the National Equal-Rights League.

Mr. Robert Hamilton, of New York, offered the name of Rev. Henry Highland Garnet.

A spirited discussion ensued. When the vote was about to be taken, Mr. P. H. Clark, of Ohio, offered an amendment, that the election of officers for the National League be referred to a committee, and that said committee be appointed by the Chair. Adopted.

A motion was then made, that, when the Convention adjourn, it adjourn to meet Friday morning, at 9 o'clock.

A call was then made for the speakers of the evening.

Mr. Douglass introduced Rev. H. H. Garnet as the first speaker.

Mr. Garnet said he had been asked that night to define his position; but he felt that such a request of him, at this late day in his career, was exceedingly humiliating. There had been a strong disposition to throw him on the shelf, on account of his connection with the African Civilization Society. He had acted in accordance with his convictions. He believed in a "Negro nationality," and referred to the brave deeds of the colored soldiers, and the effect their brave conduct had produced upon the public mind. The Convention had a right to do as it pleased; but, if taken to the stake, he would utter his honest convictions.

Mr. Garnet drew a picture of the shadows which fell upon New-York city in July, 1863, where demoniac hate culminated in that memorable mob. He told us how one man was hung upon a tree; and that then a demon in human form, taking a sharp knife, cut out pieces of the quivering flesh, and offered it to the greedy, blood-thirsty mob, saying, "Who wants some nigger meat?" and then the reply, "I!" "I!" "I!" as if they were scrambling for pieces of gold.

Mr. Garnet referred to the nationality of those composing that mob, and said he could not tell how it was that men crossing the ocean only should change as much as they. He had travelled from Belfast to Cork, and from Dublin to the Giant's Causeway, and the treatment he received was uniformly that of kindness. He had stood in public beside the great O'Connell; and we know what his hatred of oppression was. He attributed the change in the Irish people to the debasing influence of unprincipled American politicians. The name of O'Connell was received with great applause. Mr. Garnet was heartily cheered during his speech.

The Finance Committee then took up a collection for the purposes of the Convention.

During this visit of the Finance Committee, Mr. Robert Hamilton was detailed, at the call of the audience, to sing a stirring song.

The President then introduced Dr. P. B. Randolph, of New York, as the next speaker.

Dr. Randolph opened by saying that history constantly repeated itself; that an All-Wise Providence dictated the paths which men and nations must pursue; and, whenever they wilfully forsook those paths, they were certain to be brought back, sooner or later, by the resistless right hand of the Eternal God. The overruling Father brought out the sons of Abraham from Egyptian bondage three thousand years ago, and to-day he leads us — the negro race — with a strong arm from out of the swamps of slavery. He led the Israelites

through the Red Sea, over sandy wastes, into the land of
promise and plenty, — glorious Canaan ; and so now he is
leading us, and with us this nation, through the Red Sea of
human blood, towards the glorious highlands of Justice and
Freedom. [Applause.] In the olden time, God passed in wrath
over Egypt's hoary strand, and smote the first-born of the
oppressor with quick and sudden death, and lo ! where is
the house in this land, whether of the black man or the white,
whose lintels and door-posts bear not the red sign? which
have not been smitten with the splash of human gore?

And yet his paths are plain. Let the nations take warning !
God never sleeps ! Wherefore let us all take heart. He
fights our battles; and, where he fights, he wins. Wagner,
Hudson, Petersburg, and all the other battles of this war, have
not been fought in vain ; for the dead heroes of those and
other bloody fields are the seeds of mighty harvests of
human goodness and greatness, yet to be reaped by the
nations and the world, and by Afric's sable descendants on
the soil of this, our native land. Be of good cheer ! Behold
the starry flag above our heads ! What is it ? It is the pledge
of Heaven, that we are coming up from the long dark night of
sorrow towards the morning's dawn : it is the rainbow of
eternal hope, set in our heaven, telling us that we shall never
again be drowned in our own salt tears, forced up from our
very souls' great depths by the worshippers of Moloch, —
bloody-handed Mammon : it is a guaranty, by and from the
God of heaven, that we, the mourners, may and shall be
happy yet. My very soul leaps onward a full century ; and
its vision falls on fertile fields, with no slave-driver there, no
hearts crushed by fierce oppression, no more heads bowed
down. Ay ! my soul listens already to the glad prelude of
a song of triumph welling up from myriad hearts, and swelling
into a pæan that fills the vast concave of heaven itself with
the deep-toned melodies of an universal jubilee. [Great applause.]

The body I now address is to be not only an historical one ;
but if we do our duty, as we will, the most important in its
results and effects, not only upon us here banded together in
the firm concord of brotherhood, but to the nations of the

world and the ages yet to come. [Cheers.] Here we are met, not to hear each other talk, not to mourn over the terrible shadows of the past; but we are here to prove our right to manhood and justice, and to maintain these rights, not by force of mere appeal, not by loud threats, not by battle-axe and sabre, but by the divine right of brains, of will, of true patriotism, of manhood, of womanhood, of all that is great and noble and worth striving for in human character. We are here to ring the bells at the door of the world; proclaiming to the nations, to the white man in his palace, the slave in his hut, kings on their thrones, and to the whole broad universe, that WE ARE COMING UP! [Applause.] Yes: we are, at last; and going up to *stay*. He loveth and chasteneth: but he also saves; but saves those first who help themselves. Sheer folly to expect to be raised to a coveted position without self-endeavor. There are two great principles in operation in this world. One is that of progression; the other, that of development: one is the body of success; the other is its soul: the one makes us scholars merely; and the other makes us MEN,— and *that*, and that only, is the pearl for which we are seeking. Progress means acquisition of knowledge; and it is very good, if well applied: and yet a man may have a hundred libraries by heart; he may be master of a hundred sciences; a walking encyclopædia, — and yet be a worthless drone in the world. It is not the thought-gatherer who makes his mark in the world; but it is the thought-producer who is the man of mark and value. Development means persistent culture of our latent powers; and we need it. Slavery and ignorance, liberty and light! It is the mind, not the dollars, that makes the man. Here the orator turned toward the blood-stained flag of the Louisiana regiment, apostrophized it, spoke of Cailloux and Ingraham who fought and bled upon the field where it waved, and with all his power besought his hearers never to disgrace it by word, act, or thought. [Applause.]

Rev. Jonathan C. Gibbs, of Pennsylvania, was then introduced, and spoke in a highly interesting manner. We regret we have no report of Mr. Gibbs's speech.

John S. Rock, Esq., of Boston, was the next speaker. He

said, "I come from Massachusetts, where we are jealous of every right. I received information a few days ago that a sergeant in the Fifty-fourth Massachusetts Regiment, who is a splendid penman, had been detailed by his captain as a clerk in his department; and that, when the officer in command learned this, he immediately ordered the sergeant back to his regiment, saying in his order, that 'no Negro will be allowed to hold any position in this department except that of a cook or a laborer.' A copy of this order was forwarded to me; and I immediately presented the case to our most excellent Governor, who was going to Washington that evening. The result is, the sergeant is restored back to his position as clerk, and the officer who made the order has suddenly left for the North. [Applause.] This result was at once forwarded to me; and I immediately communicated it to his Excellency the Governor, when he sent me this noble reply: —

COMMONWEALTH OF MASSACHUSETTS,
EXECUTIVE DEPARTMENT,
BOSTON, Oct. 4, 1864.

JOHN S. ROCK, ESQ.

DEAR SIR, — I am glad to hear of the favorable result in the case referred to. I had no doubt what the result would be; but it is through you that I first learn it definitely. I thank you for your kind expressions of acknowledgment to me personally; and with a constant willingness to do my part, always, to insure equal opportunities for usefulness and success in all the occupations and duties of life, to men of equal intelligence, industry, and integrity, whether they be white or black,

I am, very truly, yours,

JOHN A. ANDREW.

[Great applause.]

"All we ask is equal opportunities and equal rights. This is what our brave men are fighting for. They have not gone to the battle-field for the sake of killing and being killed; but they are fighting for liberty and equality. [Applause.] We ask the same for the black man that is asked for the white man; nothing more, and nothing less. When our men fight bravely, as they always do, they don't like to be cheated out of the glory and the positions they so dearly earn. Many of our grandfathers fought in the Revolution, and they thought they were fighting for liberty; but they made a sad mistake, and we are now obliged to fight those battles over again, and I hope, this time, to a better purpose. We are all loyal. Why are we not treated as friends? This nation spurned our offers to rally around it, for two long years, and then, without any guaranties, called upon us at a time when the loyal white men of the North hesitated. We buried the terrible outrages of the past, and came magnanimously and gallantly forward. In the heroism displayed at Milliken's Bend, Port Hudson, Fort Wagner, Olustee, in the battles now going on before Richmond, and everywhere where our men have faced the foe, they have covered themselves all over with glory. [Applause.] They have nobly written with their blood the declaration of their right to have their names recorded on the pages of history among the true patriots of this American Revolution for Liberty. [Applause.] Witness, if you please, the moral heroism of the Massachusetts soldiers, spurning the offers of seven dollars a month, which the Government insultingly tempted them with for eighteen months, when it was known that they were without means, and that many of them had wives at home and children crying to them for bread when there was none to give them. But they bore it manfully, and have lived to see the right triumph. [Applause.] My friends, we owe much to the colored soldiers; not only to the Massachusetts men, but to every brave man who has taken up the musket in defence of liberty. [Applause.] They have done wonders for the race. Let us stand by them and their families, and be ready at any and at all times to assist them, and to give them a word of cheer.

"Though we are unfortunately situated, I am not discouraged. Our cause is flying onward with the swiftness of Mercury. Every day seems almost to be an era in the history of our country. We have at last reached the dividing-line. There are but two parties in the country to-day. The one headed by Lincoln is for Freedom and the Republic; and the other, by McClellan, is for Despotism and Slavery. There can be no middle ground in war. The friends and the enemies of the country are defined, and the one or the other must triumph. We are to have but one government throughout the broad territory of the United States. Two systems of government so innately hostile to each other as that of the North is to that of the South could not exist on the same soil. We should be like the Romans and Carthaginians; among whom, says Patercules, 'there always existed either a war, preparations for a war, or a deceitful peace.' The fate of this Republic will be settled in this contest; and its enemies must either be subdued or annihilated, and it is of but little consequence which." [Applause.]

Rev. J. Sella Martin was called for, and delivered an able and eloquent speech.

Mrs. Frances Ellen Watkins Harper was then introduced, and spoke feelingly and eloquently of our hopes and prospects in this country.

The Chairman then appointed the following-named committee to nominate officers for the National League: John M. Langston, of Ohio; William Wilson, of Washington, D. C.; and P. N. Judah, of Pennsylvania,

The Convention then adjourned to meet Friday morning at 9 o'clock.

FOURTH DAY.

FRIDAY MORNING, Oct. 7.

The Convention met in Wieting Hall, pursuant to adjournment; the President in the chair.

Prayer was offered by Rev. William Wilson, of Washington City.

On motion of Mr. Johnson, of Albany, the minutes of the Convention were adopted.

The chairman of the Business Committee presented the resolution in relation to the associations for freedmen, naming the "National Freedmen's Relief" and "American Missionary Association." [As passed, see Appendix, — "Resolutions."]

Rev. Mr. Cain, of New York, moved to amend by inserting

the name of the "African Civilization Society," and defended the motion in an earnest, pertinent speech; giving in that speech the history of the success attending the establishment of schools in Washington City. Mr. Cain at the same time labored to show that the object of the African Civilization Society is not to colonize the colored people.

He then read the instructions given by his constituents, especially that part relating to the freedmen, and suggested respectfully that the interest of the freedmen had not been sufficiently considered by this Convention; that the African Civilization Society was now doing a noble part in caring for them and their children, and ought, as a society of colored men, to have the support of this Convention and the people generally.

The Rev. W. P. Newman, of Ohio, rose to enforce the idea, that the work of elevating our brethren must be committed to the colored men of the country. Mr. Newman was very pointed in reference to the present action of the Baptist Home-Mission Society; which society was now holding sacredly, for the rebels who should be left, the church property in the South, just as far as they were able so to do. Mr. Newman referred to the Ex-Secretary of the Treasury, Mr. Chase; who, he said, was far ahead, on this subject, of the religious organizations of the land. Mr. Chase said, in a letter urging him to return from the West Indies to the United States, that the great work of lifting up the freedmen must be committed to the colored people of the country.

Mr. George T. Downing, of Rhode Island, said, "I regret the introduction of this subject at so late a period in the Convention, when so many delegates have already left for home; but when that Society, through its representatives, asks this Convention for what may be used as an indorsement of that Society, it seems to me there is deception involved in it! I think it well to thank all who have aided the freedmen; but we must be careful not to be made tools of. The exertions of this Society have been where friends have been numerous and where schools are springing up daily: where the Society was needed, it did not go. I do not charge all with the motives of its founders. It is the child of prejudice; and its originators assert that the colored man cannot be elevated in the United States; that black men must be 'massed to themselves,' and have a grand fight for a 'Negro nationality,' before they can be respected! Look at the history of this Society: a colonizationist was its founder, and it invites no abolitionist to its platform; and they have declared from their platform, that we are out of our place here, and that 'it would be well if every colored man was out of the country.' A gentleman here, who defended that Society, presided at the meeting when these remarks were made; and, though one of the speakers on that occasion, he had no word of censure, and did not even disapprove of these insulting remarks made in his presence. This Society is in perfect harmony with our old enemy, the Colonization Society. The agents of both societies act in concert, and both use the same rooms. It must publicly atone for its disgraceful past conduct, before it can have an indorsement at my hands."

Rev. J. Sella Martin rose to deny that he and others are being used by white men. He said, if the Society in the beginning, and under other auspices, looked mainly Africa-ward, and upon that account it had acquired a taint, he, for one, meant, with others, to redeem it from that odium.

Rev. H. H. Garnet rose to thank Mr. Cain for his remarks in reference to the work of the Society at Washington. He (Mr. Garnet) resided there, and he well knew the benefits resulting from those schools. As to the personal matters referred to by Mr. Downing, he would say he might appeal to all present whether they believed, that now, so late in his public life, he had begun to falsify himself by putting himself under the direction, and being made the tool, of white men. He had during all that life been unpopular, for the very reason that he was too independent to be used as a tool. For that independence he had sacrificed something, and to-day was poor because of it. Mr. Downing made the objection, that the African Civilization Society takes money from white men. "I think," said Mr. Garnet, "that when this hall was filled, — the major portion white people, — the Finance Committee of this Convention passed among them, and I was not aware that they refused any means because a white man gave it. If Jeff.

Davis would send an amount to educate the colored children, I would gladly receive it; and I would say to him, 'That is one good act you have done, if you have done no other.' Mr. Downing, even, takes money from white men. As regards the other personal remarks of Mr. Downing, I pass them by. Those who know me, know well that I could retort if I chose. But I will not retort. Mr. Downing and I have in days gone by had many hard intellectual battles. He has hurled against me all the force of his vigorous logic, and I struck him back again with all my power. If I smarted from his blows, I think I may say he went away a little lame; and he has never forgotten it. If Mr. Downing has intended to cripple my influence in this Convention, to keep me out of office and off of committees, he has successfully accomplished that purpose. But we will work in our humble way, as we are laboring now, to lift up the race with which we are identified, but especially to give to the children of the people the education of which for so long they have been deprived."

Prof. Vashon, of Pennsylvania, deprecated the turn which the discussion had taken. He did not consider the Convention the place for gentlemen to come to settle their old difficulties, but felt that we ought to unite for one great end, harmonizing as much as possible. He intended to make a proposition which he thought would harmonize all parties, and he would move it as a suplementary resolution, by way of amendment.

Resolved, That, while we have no sympathy with any feature of the African Civilization Society looking to colonizing Africa with colored Americans, we still readily accord that organization all praise for their important labors in behalf of freedom.

Rev. H. H. Garnet remarked that he would prefer no resolution rather than the one proposed by Prof. Vashon.

Mr. Johnson, of Albany, N. Y., sustained the amendment proposed by Mr. Cain. He was as much opposed to the *name* of the African Civilization Society as any one; but he believed that that Society was just what Mr. Cain said it was.

The previous question was called for, and ordered; when the amendment of Prof. Vashon was lost.

The amendment proposed was then voted upon, and carried; and the resolution was adopted as amended.

The Chairman of the Business Committee then reported Resolutions 12 and 13. [See Appendix, pp. 35, 36.]

Mr. Martin moved to amend by striking out all that part of the Report referring to private enterprises.

The amendment was opposed by Mr. Langston; who concluded his remarks by asking Mr. Martin to explain what he meant by private enterprises.

Mr. Martin replied that he regarded all newspapers as private enterprises.

Mr. Martin's motion was lost.

The chairman of the Nominating Committee for the League appeared, and asked leave to make a report. The Report was read, and a motion made to accept it, when—

Mr. Green, of Pennsylvania, offered the following resolution as an amendment:—

Resolved, That so much of the plan organizing a National Equal-Rights League as refers to Vice-Presidents and Secretaries be reconsidered; and that the Board of Vice-Presidents shall consist of one from each State represented in the Convention; and that there be one additional Secretary elected by the Convention.

This amendment was discussed at some length by several gentlemen, and was finally agreed to.

The vote was then taken upon the main question, and carried unanimously. The Report was, on motion, adopted as follows:—

For President.

J. MERCER LANGSTON.

Vice-Presidents.

J. S. ROCK.	WILLIAM WILSON.
P. G. WELLS.	J. SELLA MARTIN.
J. H. INGRAHAM.	JAMES JEFFERSON.
F. L. CORDOZA.	GEORGE H. PARKER.
W. P. NEWMAN.	JOHN PECK.
S. J. MURRAY.	JAMES COCHRAN.
J. HOUSTON.	ABRAM SMITH.
A. H. GALLOWAY.	D. P. SEATON.

RECORDING SECRETARIES.

ST. GEORGE R. TAYLOR.
DAVIS D. TURNER.

CORRESPONDING SECRETARY.

GEORGE B. VASHON.

TREASURER.

WILLIAM RICH.

MEMBERS OF EXECUTIVE BOARD.

J. D. RICHARDS.   A. H. GALLOWAY.
RANSOM HARRIS.   W. KEELING.

The following was submitted by the Rev. Singleton T. Jones, of New York, and adopted : —

Resolved, That we regard with deep interest and solicitude the recent movement on the part of the two great colored Methodist denominations in the United States, through a Convention held in Philadelphia in June last, looking to their union and consolidation into one organization, having for its object the religious, moral, social, and intellectual advancement and improvement of our people ; and that, regarding a more intimate union of interest as an essential element to our strength and success, we earnestly recommend the speedy consummation of that contemplated union ; and we as earnestly urge the recognition and cultivation of the great principle of union among our people everywhere.

The Finance Committee then made their final Report. [See Appendix, pp. 32, 33.]

Moved by J. M. Langston, that all money in the hands of the Finance Committee be placed in the hands of the Treasurer of the League, William Rich, to pay for the printing of the Minutes, and the other expenses connected therewith. Carried.

Pending a motion for adjournment, the President briefly addressed the Convention; and, on suggestion, all joined in singing, —

"From all that dwell below the skies."

The Convention, at twelve o'clock, adjourned *sine die.*

O. C. HUGHES, *Secretary.*

APPENDIX.

REPORT OF COMMITTEE ON RULES.

1st, There shall be two regular sessions of the Convention daily.

Morning Session. — The Convention shall meet at 9 o'clock, A. M., and adjourn at 12 o'clock.

Afternoon Session. — The Convention shall meet at 2 o'clock, and adjourn at 5 o'clock, P. M.

2d, The majority of the members of the Convention shall constitute a quorum for the transaction of business at either of its sessions.

3d, The rules of order as laid down in "Mathias's Manual" shall be the standing rules of order of this Convention, in all points not herein provided for.

4th, No member shall be allowed to speak more than twice upon the same subject, without special leave of the Convention; and not longer than ten minutes the first time, and five minutes the second.

REPORT OF THE COMMITTEE ON FINANCE.

Received from regular members of the
Convention $277 00
Received from collections and honorary
members 102 00
Whole amount collected . ——— $379 00
Amount carried forward, $379 00

Amount brought forward, $379 00

Paid to Mr. James Jefferson to assist the destitute children . . .	$24 50	
Stationery	2 25	
Hire of Hall	60 00	
Mr. Robert Hamilton's bill for printing the call of the Convention . .	70 00	
Amount paid out . .	—— 156 75	
Balance on hand	$222 25	

RESOLUTIONS.

1. *Resolved,* That a petition be sent to the Congress of the United States, in the name of this Convention, asking them respectfully, but most earnestly, to use every honorable endeavor that they may, to have the rights of the country's colored patriots now in the field respected, without regard to their complexion; and that our Goverment cease to set an example to rebels, in arms against it, by making invidious distinctions, based upon color, as to pay, labor, and promotion.

2. *Resolved,* That the unquestioned patriotism and loyalty of the colored men of the United States — as shown in the alacrity with which, shutting their eyes to the past, and looking steadfastly to the future, at the call of the country, without pay, without bounty, without prospect of promotion, without the protection of the Government, they have rallied to the defence of "Liberty and Union" — vindicate our manhood, command our respect, and claim the attention and admiration of the civilized world.

3. *Resolved,* That we hereby assert our full confidence in the fundamental principles of this Government, the force of acknowledged American ideas, the Christian spirit of the age, and the justice of our cause; and we believe that the generosity and sense of honor inherent in the great heart of this

5

nation will ultimately concede us our just claims, accord us our rights, and grant us our full measure of citizenship, under the broad shield of the Constitution.

4. *Resolved*, That, should an attempt be made to reconstruct the Union with slavery, we should regard such a course as a flagrant violation of good faith on the part of the Government, false to the brave colored men who have fallen in its defence, unjust to the living who are perilling their lives for its protection, and to be resisted by the whole moral power of the civilized world.

5. *Resolved*, That we extend the right hand of fellowship to the freedmen of the South, and express to them our warmest sympathy, and our deep concern for their welfare, prosperity, and happiness ; and desire to exhort them to shape their course toward frugality, the accumulation of property, and, above all, to leave untried no amount of effort and self-denial to acquire knowledge, and to secure a vigorous moral and religious growth. We desire, further, to assure them of our co-operation and assistance ; and that our efforts in their behalf shall be given without measure, and be limited only by our capacity to give, work, and act.

6. *Resolved*, That we recommend to colored men from all sections of the country to settle, as far as they can, on the public lands.

7. *Resolved*, That, as Congress has exclusive control over the elective franchise in the District of Columbia, we earnestly pray that body to extend the right of suffrage to the colored citizens of said District.

8. *Resolved*, That the President of the United States, his Cabinet, and the Thirty-seventh Congress, are hereby tendered our warmest and most grateful thanks, —

For revoking the prohibitory law in regard to colored people carrying the mails ;

For abolishing slavery in the District of Columbia ;

For recognizing the National Independence of Liberia and Hayti ;

For Military Order 252, retaliating for the unmilitary and barbarous treatment of the colored soldiers of the Union army by the rebels.

The Convention further tenders its thanks to Senator Sumner, for his noble efforts to cleanse the statute-books of the nation from every stain of inequality against colored men.

And also to Gen. Butler, for the course he has taken in suggesting a way for lifting the slaves first to the condition of contrabands, and then to the position of freedmen.

And to all other noble workers, both in our legislative halls and elsewhere, who have contributed to bring about the improved state in which, as colored men, we find ourselves to-day.

9. *Resolved,* That we witness, with the most grateful emotions, the generous and very successful efforts that have been made, and are still in operation, by the " National Freedmen's Relief Association," the "American Missionary Society," the "African Civilization Society," and their auxiliary and kindred bodies, for the mental and moral instruction, and the domestic improvement, of the colored people in our Southern States, who have hitherto been the victims of that impious slaveholding oligarchy, that is now in open rebellion against our American Republic.

10. *Resolved,* That we view with pride, and heartily indorse, the efforts of the gentlemen composing the faculties and executive boards of the "Institute for Colored Youth" at Philadelphia; the "Avery College" at Alleghany City, Penn.; the "Wilberforce University" at Zenia, O.; and the "Albany Enterprise Academy" at Albany, O., to develop the intellectual powers of our youth, and for opening a field for the honorable employment of those powers.

11. *Resolved,* That we are indebted to the publishers of the "Anglo-African," "Christian Recorder," and "Colored Citizen," for the manifestation of intellectual energy and business tact which they have shown to the American people by the publication of those journals; the contents of which are complimentary to the heads and hearts of their conductors, and the people whom they represent.

12. *Resolved,* that a committee of three — consisting of John S. Rock and George L. Ruffin of Boston, and William H. Day of New Jersey — be appointed to revise, correct, and

publish the proceedings of this National Convention for general distribution.

13. *Resolved,* That this Convention returns .its sincere thanks to its officers for the manner in which they have conducted its business; to the Rev. J. W. Loguen, and those citizens of Syracuse who have composed and co-operated with the Reception Committee; also to such of the newspapers as have made a just report of our proceedings.

PREAMBLE AND CONSTITUTION OF THE NATIONAL EQUAL-RIGHTS LEAGUE.

Whereas, The purposes entertained by the callers of this Convention, and those who have responded to that call, can be best promoted by a close union of all interested in the principles of justice and right sought to be established; therefore, be it—

Resolved, That we proceed to organize an association, to be called the National Equal-Rights League, with auxiliaries and subordinate associations in the different States.

Resolved, That, in the establishment of the Colored Men's National League, we do not seek to disorganize or in any way interfere with any existing society or institution of a benevolent or other character; but, believing that the interests of colored men generally will be best subserved and advanced by a union of all our energies and the use of all our means in a given direction, we therefore invite the co-operation of such societies in the advancement of the objects of the League.

SECTION 1. The objects of this League are to encourage sound morality, education, temperance, frugality, industry, and promote every thing that pertains to a well-ordered and dignified life; to obtain by appeals to the minds and conscience of the American people, or by legal process when possible, a recognition of the rights of the colored people of the nation as American citizens.

SEC. 2. The members of this Convention shall be constituted

the members of the National Equal-Rights League for the first year. Hereafter such persons as shall be duly accredited representatives of the auxiliary associations herein provided for shall constitute its members; provided that no auxiliary society shall be entitled to more than one representative for each fifty dollars contributed by such society, with an additional member for any amount over thirty dollars thus contributed.

SEC. 3. The officers shall be a President, one Vice-President from each State represented in this Convention, Recording and Corresponding Secretaries, a Treasurer, and an Executive Committee consisting of the President, First Vice-President, Recording Secretaries, and four other persons to be elected by the League at the same time with the other officers.

SEC. 4. The President shall preside at all regular meetings of the League and of the Executive Committee, see that all decrees of the League are duly executed, and perform such other duties as may be impose 1 by the League. .

The Vice-Presidents in the order of their election shall in the absence of the President perform his duties.

The Recording Secretary shall duly record the proceedings of the League and of the Executive Committee; draw all orders on the Treasurer when directed by the proper authority; receive all money paid to the League, pay the same to the Treasurer, and take his receipt therefor.

The Corresponding Secretaries shall, under the guidance of the League and the Executive Committee, conduct the correspondence of the League; receive from the agents of the League or other persons all documents of historical, statistical, or general interest; and shall carefully preserve, arrange, and tabulate such documents for the use of the League.

The Treasurer shall keep all money collected by the agents, or contributed by the auxiliary Leagues. He shall report to the League annually, and to the Executive Committee whenever required, the condition of the treasury. He shall pay out money only upon order of the Executive Committee, and when properly signed by the President and Recording Secretary.

SEC. 5. The Executive Committee shall establish an office

in the city of Philadelphia, Penn.; in which place they shall hold such sessions as may be necessary to promote the purposes of the League. They shall hire an agent or agents, who shall visit the different States of the nation accessible to them, and shall call the people of those States together in convention or otherwise, and urge them to take the steps necessary to secure the rights and improvements for the attainment of which this League is formed. They shall encourage the publication of such documents as may be of advantage to our cause; and may, at their discretion, publish brief appeals, arguments or statements of fact, which may have a tendency to promote the ends of the Association, provided that such documents shall be furnished to the public at such rates as shall admit of their general distribution. They shall apportion among the auxiliary leagues, according to the number of members reported, the amounts which the League shall determine to raise, and shall urge upon the officers of such auxiliary societies a prompt response to such demands. They shall cause orders to be drawn on the Treasurer for the payment of such expenses as may be incurred in the carrying-out the purposes of the Association.

They shall make an annual report to the Association of their labors, and shall recommend such improvements as may be suggested by their official experience.

SEC. 6. The officers shall hold their offices for one year, or until their successors are elected. The officers of the League may receive such compensation as may be determined by the Executive Committee.

SEC. 7. Persons in the different States friendly to the purposes of this League may form State Leagues auxiliary to this, with such subordinate organizations as they may deem proper, provided that no distinction on account of color or sex shall be permitted in such auxiliary or subordinate association. Such Leagues may, at their discretion, employ agents, and issue such documents as they may deem conducive to the ends for which this League is formed. They shall collect and pay into the treasury of the National Equal-Rights League such sums as may be assessed upon them by vote of the majority at the annual meeting, and shall co-operate with that Association in all movements which it shall inaugurate for the accomplishment of the purposes for which it was formed.

SEC. 8. The sessions of the National Equal-Rights League shall be held annually; on the third Tuesday of September, at at ten o'clock, A. M., for the election of officers, and the transaction of such other business as may be brought before it.

SEC. 9. At any annual meeting of the National Equal-Rights League, this Constitution may be altered or amended by a vote of the majority of the members present.

On motion of Mr. Downing, of Rhode Island, the Executive Board of the League were authorized to fill any vacancies occurring during the year in the official direction of the League.

LIST OF THE COMMITTEES IN THE CONVENTION.

COMMITTEE ON CREDENTIALS.

FREDERICK DOUGLASS.   PETER H. CLARK.
WILLIAM WELLS BROWN.

Mr. Bruce was afterwards added, to supply the place made vacant by electing Mr. Douglass as President of the Convention.

COMMITTEE ON PERMANENT ORGANIZATION.

SAMUEL F. MURRAY.............................Maine.
GEORGE L. RUFFIN.............................Massachusetts.
GEORGE T. DOWNING......,.................;...Rhode Island.
PETER H. NOTT...............................Connecticut.
ROBERT HAMILTON.............................New York.
WILLIAM HOWARD DAY.........................New Jersey.
JONATHAN C. GIBBS..........................Pennsylvania.
WILLIAM KEELING............................Virginia.
A. H. GALLOWAY..............................North Carolina.
CHARLES P. HEAD............................Mississippi.
J. H. INGRAHAM.............................Louisiana.
PETER LOWERY...............................Tennessee.
JAMES M. SCOTTRON..........................Florida.
P. G. WELLS................................Missouri.
PETER H. CLARK.............................Ohio.
H. P. HARRIS...............................Michigan.

ROBERT HAMILTON, Chairman; Peter H. Clark, Secretary.

BUSINESS COMMITTEE.

HENRY H. GARNET.
EBENEZER D. BASSETT.
JONATHAN C. GIBBS.
PETER H. CLARK.
JOHN M. LANGSTON.
JOHN S. ROCK.
GEORGE L. RUFFIN.
GEORGE T. DOWNING.
WILLIAM H. JOHNSON.
PASCHAL B. RANDOLPH.
J. SELLA MARTIN.

J. H. INGRAHAM.
D. P. SEATON.
RANSOM HARRIS.
MORRIS HENDERSON.
CHARLES P. HEAD.
JAMES M. SCOTTRON.
WILLIAM KEELING.
P. G. WELLS.
A. H. GALLOWAY.
J. D. RICHARDS.
W. H. DECKER.

The Committee elected JOHN M. LANGSTON, Chairman; and JOHN S. ROCK, Secretary. Mr. Garnet declined to serve.

FINANCE COMMITTEE.

EBENEZER HEMMENWAY.
ROBERT HAMILTON.

J. W. LOGUEN.
GEORGE B. VASHON.
W. H. BRUCE.

COMMITTEE ON RULES.

PETER W. RAY, M.D.
SERGT. ALFRED M. GREEN.

GEORGE B. VASHON.
WILLIAM H. JOHNSON.
WILLIAM NESBIT.

P. W. RAY, *Chairman.*

PUBLISHING COMMITTEE.

JOHN S. ROCK.
GEORGE L. RUFFIN.
WILLIAM HOWARD DAY.

DECLARATION OF WRONGS AND RIGHTS,

MADE BY THE COLORED MEN OF THE UNITED STATES OF AMERICA IN
CONVENTION ASSEMBLED, IN SYRACUSE, N. Y., OCT. 4, 1864.

1st. As a branch of the human family, we have for long ages been deeply and cruelly wronged by people whose might constituted their right; we have been subdued, not by the power of ideas, but by brute force, and have been unjustly deprived not only of many of our natural rights, but debarred the privileges and advantages freely accorded to other men.

2d. We have been made to suffer well-nigh every cruelty and indignity possible to be heaped upon human beings; and for no fault of our own.

3d. We have been taunted with our inferiority by people whose statute-books contained laws inflicting the severest penalties on whomsoever dared teach us the art of reading God's word; we have been denounced as incurably ignorant, and, at the same time, have been, by stern enactments, debarred from taking even the first step toward self-enlightenment and personal and national elevation; we have been declared incapable of self-government by those who refused us the right of experiment in that direction, and we have been denounced as cowards by men who refused at first to trust us with a musket on the battle-field.

4th. As a people, we have been denied the ownership of our bodies, our wives, homes, children, and the products of our own labor; we have been compelled, under pain of death, to submit to wrongs deeper and darker than the earth ever witnessed in the case of any other people; we have been forced to silence and inaction in full presence of the infernal spectacle of our sons groaning under the lash, our daughters ravished, our wives violated, and our firesides desolated, while we ourselves have been led to the shambles and sold like beasts of the field.

5th. When the nation in her trial hour called her sable sons to arms, we gladly went to fight her battles: but were denied the pay accorded to others, until public opinion demanded it; and then it was tardily granted. We have fought and conquered, but have been denied the laurels of victory. We have fought where victory gave us no glory, and where captivity meant cool murder on the field, by fire, sword, and halter; and yet no black man ever flinched.

6th. We are taxed, but denied the right of representation. We are practically debarred the right of trial by jury; and institutions of learning which we help to support are closed against us.

We submit to the American people and world the following Declaration of our Rights, asking a calm consideration thereof:

1st. We declare that all men are born free and equal; that no man or government has a right to annul, repeal, abrogate, contravene, or render inoperative, this fundamental principle, except it be for crime; therefore we demand the immediate and unconditional abolition of slavery.

2d. That, as natives of American soil, we claim the right to remain upon it: and that any attempt to deport, remove, expatriate, or colonize us to any other land, or to mass us here against our will, is unjust; for here were we born, for this country our fathers and our brothers have fought, and here we hope to remain in the full enjoyment of enfranchised manhood, and its dignities.

3d. That, as citizens of the Republic, we claim the rights of other citizens. We claim that we are, by right, entitled to respect; that due attention should be given to our needs; that proper rewards should be given for our services, and that the immunities and privileges of all other citizens and defenders of the nation's honor should be conceded to us. We claim the right to be heard in the halls of Congress; and we claim our fair share of the public domain, whether acquired by purchase, treaty, confiscation, or military conquest.

4th. That, emerging as we are from the long night of gloom and sorrow, we are entitled to, and claim, the sympathy and aid of the entire Christian world; and we invoke the considerate aid of mankind in this crisis of our history, and in this hour of sacrifice, suffering, and trial.

Those are our wrongs; these a portion of what we deem to

be our rights as men, as patriots, as citizens, and as children of the common Father. To realize and attain these rights, and their practical recognition, is our purpose. We confide our cause to the just God, whose benign aid we solemnly invoke. To him we appeal.

ADDRESS

OF THE

COLORED NATIONAL CONVENTION

TO THE

PEOPLE OF THE UNITED STATES.

FELLOW-CITIZENS, —

The members of the Colored National Convention, assembled in Syracuse, State of New York, October the 4th, 1864, to confer with each other as to the complete emancipation, enfranchisement, and elevation of our race, in essaying to address you on these subjects, warmly embrace the occasion to congratulate you upon the success of your arms, and upon the prospect of the speedy suppression of the slaveholders' rebellion. Baptized in the best blood of your noblest sons, torn and rent by a strife full of horrors, — a strife undertaken and prosecuted for aims and objects the guiltiest that can enter the wicked hearts of men long in the practice of crime, — we ardently hope with you that our country will come out of this tremendous conflict, purer, stronger, nobler, and happier than ever before. Having shared with you, in some measure, the hardships, perils, and sacrifices of this war for the maintenance of the Union and Government, we rejoice with you also in every sign which gives promise of its approaching termination, and of the return of our common country again to those peaceful, progressive, and humanizing activities of true national life, from which she has been so wantonly diverted by the insurrection of slaveholders.

In view of the general cheerfulness of the national situation, growing brighter every day ; the rapid dispersement of the heavy clouds of dismal terror, which only a few weeks ago mantled our land with the gloomiest forebodings of national disaster and ruin,—we venture to hope that the present is a favorable moment to commend to your consideration the subject of our wrongs, and to obtain your earnest and hearty co-operation in all wise and just measures for their full redress.

When great and terrible calamities are abroad in the land, men are said to learn righteousness. It would be a mark of unspeakable national depravity, if neither the horrors of this war, nor the dawning prospect of peace, should soften the heart, and dispose the American people to renounce and forsake their evil policy towards the colored race. Assuming the contrary, we deem this a happily chosen hour for calling your attention to our cause. We know that the human mind is so constituted, that all postponement of duty, all refusal to go forward when the right path is once made plain, is dangerous.

After such neglect of, and disobedience to, the voice of reason and conscience, a nation becomes harder and less alive than before to high moral considerations. If won to the path of rectitude at all, thereafter, it must be by means of a purer light than that which first brought right convictions and inclinations to the national mind and heart. We speak, then, fellow-citizens, at an auspicious moment. Conviction has already seized the public mind. Little argument is needed. We shall appeal rather than argue ; and we may well implore an attentive hearing for our appeal. The nation is still in tears. The warm blood of your brave and patriotic sons is still fresh upon the green fields of the Shenandoah. Mourning mingles everywhere with the national shout of victory ; and though the smoke and noise of battle are rolling away behind the southern horizon, our brave armies are still confronted in Georgia and Virginia by a stern foe, whose haughtiness and cruelty have sprung naturally from his long and undisputed mastery over men. The point attained in the progress of this war is one from which you can if you will view to advantage the calamities which inevitably follow upon long and persistent violation of manifest duty; and on the other hand, the signs of final triumph enable you to anticipate the happy results which must always flow from just and honorable conduct. The fear of continued war, and the hope of speedy peace, alike mark this as the time for America to choose her destiny. Another such opportunity as is now furnished in the state of the country, and in the state of the national heart, may not come again in a century. Come, then, and let us reason together.

We shall speak, it is true, for our race, — a race long oppressed, enslaved, ignored, despised, slandered, and degraded; but we speak not the less for our country, whose welfare and permanent peace can only result from the adoption of wise and just measures towards our whole race, North and South.

Considering the number and the grievous character of the wrongs and disabilities endured by our race in this country, you will bear witness that we have borne with patience our lot, and have seldom troubled the national ear with the burden of complaint. It is true that individuals among us have constantly testified their abhorrence of this injustice; but as a people, we have seldom uttered, as we do this day, our protest and remonstrance against the manifold and needless injustice with which we are upon all sides afflicted. We have suffered in silence, trusting that, though long delayed, and perhaps through terrible commotions, the hour would come when justice, honor, and magnanimity would assert their power over the mind and heart of the American people, and restore us to the full exercise and enjoyment of the rights inseparable from human nature. Never having despaired of this consummation so devoutly wished, even in the darkest hours of our history, we are farther than ever from despairing now. Nowhere in the annals of mankind is there recorded an instance of an oppressed people rising more rapidly than ourselves in the favorable estimation of their oppressors. The change is great, and increasing, and is viewed with astonishment and dread by all those who had hoped to stand forever with their heels upon our necks.

Nevertheless, while joyfully recognizing the vast advances made by our people in popular consideration, and the apparent tendency of events in our favor, we cannot conceal from ourselves, and would not conceal from you, the fact that there are many and powerful influences, constantly operating, intended and calculated to defeat our just hopes, prolong the existence of the source of all our ills, — the system of slavery, — strengthen the slave power, darken the conscience of the North, intensify popular prejudice against color, multiply unequal and discriminating laws, augment the burdens long borne by our race, consign to oblivion the deeds of heroism which have distinguished the colored soldier, deny and despise his claims to the gratitude of his country, scout his pretensions to American citizenship, establish the selfish idea that this is exclusively the white man's country, pass unheeded all the lessons taught by these four years of fire and sword, undo all that has been done towards our freedom and elevation, take the musket from the shoulders of our brave black soldiers, deny them the constitutional right to keep and bear arms, exclude them from the ballot-box where they now possess that right, prohibit the extension of it to those who do not possess it, overawe free speech in and out of Congress, obstruct the right of peaceably assembling, re-enact the Fugitive-slave Bill, revive the internal slave-trade, break up all diplomatic relations with Hayti and Liberia, re-open our broad territories to the introduction of slavery, reverse the entire order and tendency of the events of the last three years, and postpone indefinitely that glorious deliverance from bondage, which for our sake, and for the sake of the future unity, permanent peace, and highest welfare of all concerned, we had fondly hoped and believed was even now at the door.

In surveying our possible future, so full of interest at this moment, since it may bring to us all the blessings of equal liberty, or all the woes of slavery and continued social degradation, you will not blame us if we manifest anxiety in regard to the position of our recognized friends, as well as that of our open and declared enemies; for our cause may suffer even more from the injudicious concessions and weakness of our friends, than from the machinations and power of our enemies. The weakness of our friends is strength to our foes. When the "Anti-slavery Standard," representing the American Anti-slavery Society, denies that that society asks for the enfranchisement of colored men, and the "Liberator" apologizes for excluding the colored men of Louisiana from the ballot-box, they injure us more vitally than all the ribald jests of the whole proslavery press.

Again: had, for instance, the present Administration, at the beginning of the war, boldly planted itself upon the doctrine of human equality as taught in the Declaration of Independence; proclaimed liberty to all the slaves in all the Slave States; armed every colored man, previously a slave or a freeman, who would or could fight under the loyal flag; recognized black men as soldiers of the Republic; avenged the first act of violence upon colored prisoners, in contravention of the laws of war; sided with the radical emancipation party in Maryland and Missouri; stood by its antislavery generals, instead of casting them aside,—history would never have had to record the scandalous platform adopted at Chicago, nor the immeasurable horrors of Fort Pillow. The weakness and hesitation of our friends, where promptness and vigor were required, have invited the contempt and rigor of our enemies. Seeing that, while perilling every thing for the protection and security of our country, our country did not think itself bound to protect and secure us, the rebels felt a license to treat us as outlaws. Seeing that our Government did not treat us as men, they did not feel bound to treat us as soldiers. It is, therefore, not the malignity of enemies alone we have to fear, but the deflection from the straight line of principle by those who are known throughout the world as our special friends. We may survive the arrows of the known negro-haters of our country: but woe to the colored race when their champions fail to demand, from any reason, equal liberty in every respect!

We have spoken of the existence of powerful re-actionary forces arrayed against us, and of the objects to which they tend. What are these mighty forces? and through what agencies do they operate and reach us? They are many; but we shall detain by no tedious enumeration. The first and most powerful is slavery ; and the second, which may be said to be the shadow of slavery, is prejudice against men on account of their color. The one controls the South, and the other controls the North. Both are original sources of power, and generate peculiar sentiments, ideas, and laws concerning us. The agents of these two evil influences are various : but the chief are, first, the Democratic party ; and, second, the Republican party. The Democratic party belongs to slavery ; and the Republican party is largely under the power of prejudice against color. While gratefully recognizing a vast difference in our favor in the character and composition of the Republican party, and regarding the accession to power of the Democratic party as the heaviest calamity that could befall us in the present juncture of affairs, it cannot be disguised, that, while that party is our bitterest enemy, and is positively and actively re-actionary, the Republican party is negatively and passively so in its tendency. What we have to fear from these two parties, — looking to the future, and especially to the settlement of our present national troubles, — is, alas ! only too obvious. The intentions, principles, and policy of both organizations, through their platforms, and the antecedents and the recorded utterances of the men who stand upon their respective platforms, teach us what to expect at their hands, and what kind of a future they are carving out for us, and for the country which they propose to govern. Without using the word " slavery," or " slaves," or " slaveholders," the Democratic party has none the less declared, in its platform, its purpose to be the endless perpetuation of slavery. Under the apparently harmless verbiage, "private rights," "basis of the Federal Union," and under the language employed in denouncing the Federal Administration for " disregarding the Constitution in every part," "pretence of military necessity," we see the purpose of the Democratic party to restore slavery to all its ancient power, and to make this Government just what it was before the rebellion, — simply an instrument of the slave-power. " The basis of the Federal Union " only means the alleged compromises and stipulations, as interpreted by Judge Taney, by which black men are supposed to have no rights which white men are bound to respect ; and

7

by which the whole Northern people are bound to protect the
cruel masters against the justly deserved violence of the
slave, and to do the fiendish work of hell-hounds when slaves
make their escape from thraldom. The candidates of that
party take their stand upon its platform; and will, if elected,
— which Heaven forbid! — carry it out to the letter. From
this party we must look only for fierce, malignant, and unmitigated hostility. Our continued oppression and degradation is
the law of its life, and its sure passport to power. In the
ranks of the Democratic party, all the worst elements of
American society fraternize; and we need not expect a single
voice from that quarter for justice, mercy, or even decency.
To it we are nothing; the slave-holders every thing. We
have but to consult its press to know that it would willingly
enslave the free colored people in the South; and also that it
would gladly stir up against us mob-violence at the North, —
re-enacting the sanguinary scenes of one year ago in New
York and other large cities. We therefore pray, that whatever wrath, curse, or calamity, the future may have in store
for us, the accession of the Democratic party to the reins of
power may not be one of them; for this to us would comprise
the sum of all social woes.

How stands the case with the great Republican party in
question? We have already alluded to it as being largely
under the influence of the prevailing contempt for the character and rights of the colored race. This is seen by the
slowness of our Government to employ the strong arm of the
black man in the work of putting down the rebellion: and in
its unwillingness, after thus employing him, to invest him with
the same incitements to deeds of daring, as white soldiers;
neither giving him the same pay, rations, and protection, nor
any hope of rising in the service by meritorious conduct. It
is also seen in the fact, that in neither of the plans emanating
from this party for reconstructing the institutions of the
Southern States, are colored men, not even those who had
fought for the country, recognized as having any political existence or rights whatever.

Even in the matter of the abolition of slavery, — to which, by
its platform, the Republican party is strongly committed, as

well by President Lincoln's celebrated Proclamation of the first of January, 1863, and by his recent letter "To whom it may concern,"—there is still room for painful doubt and apprehension. It is very evident, that the Republican party, though a party composed of the best men of the country, is not prepared to make the abolition of slavery, in all the Rebel States, a consideration precedent to the re-establishment of the Union. However antislavery in sentiment the President may be, and however disposed he may be to continue the war till slavery is abolished, it is plain that in this he would not be sustained by his party. A single reverse to our arms, in such a war, would raise the hands of the party in opposition to their chief. The hope of the speedy and complete abolition of slavery, hangs, therefore, not upon the disposition of the Republican party, not upon the disposition of President Lincoln; but upon the slender thread of Rebel power, pride, and persistence. In returning to the Union, slavery has a fair chance to live; out of the Union, it has a still better chance to live: but, fighting against the Union, it has no chance for any thing but destruction. Thus the freedom of our race and the welfare of our country tremble together in the balance of events.

This somewhat gloomy view of the condition of affairs — which to the enthusiastic, who have already convinced themselves that slavery is dead, may not only seem gloomy, but untruthful—is nevertheless amply supported, not only by the well-known sentiment of the country, the controlling pressure of which is seriously felt by the Administration; but it is sustained by the many attempts lately made by the Republican press to explain away the natural import of the President's recent address "To whom it may concern," in which he makes the abolition of Slavery a primary condition to the restoration of the Union; and especially is this gloomy view supported by the remarkable speech delivered only a few weeks ago at Auburn, by Hon. William H. Seward, Secretary of State. Standing next to the President in the administration of the government, and fully in the confidence of the Chief Magistrate, no member of the National Cabinet is better qualified than Mr. Seward to utter the mind and policy of the Administration upon this momentous subject, when it shall come up at the close of the war. Just what it will do in the matter of slavery, Mr. Seward says, —

"When the insurgents shall have disbanded their armies, and laid down their arms, the war will instantly cease; and all the war measures then existing, including those which affect slavery, will cease also; and all the moral, economical, and political questions, as well affecting slavery as others, which shall then be existing between individuals and States and the Federal Government, whether they arose before the civil war began, or whether they grew out of it, will, by force of the Constitution, pass over to the arbitrament of courts of law, and the counsels of legislation."

These, fellow-citizens, are studied words, full of solemn and fearful import. They mean that our Republican Administration is not only ready to make peace with the Rebels, but to make peace with slavery also; that all executive and legislative action launched against the slave-system, whether of proclamation or confiscation, will cease the instant the Rebels shall disband their armies, and lay down their arms. The hope that the war will put an end to slavery, has, according to this exposition, only one foundation; and that is, that the courts and Congress will so decree. But what ground have we here? Congress has already spoken, and has refused to alter the Constitution so as to abolish Slavery. The Supreme Court has yet to speak; but what it will say, if this question shall come before it, is very easily divined. We will not assert positively what it will say; but indications of its judgment are clearly against us. What then have we? Only this, as our surest and best ground of hope; namely, that the Rebels, in their madness, will continue to make war upon the Government, until they shall not only become destitute of men, money, and the munitions of war, but utterly divested of their slaves also.

But, fellow-citizens, the object of this Address is not merely to state facts, and point out sources of danger. We would distinctly place our whole cause before you, and earnestly appeal to you to make that cause practically your cause; as we believe it is the cause of justice and of our whole country.

We come before you altogether in new relations. Hitherto we have addressed you in the generic character of a common humanity: only as men: but to-day, owing to the events of the last three years, we bring with us an additional claim to consideration. By the qualities displayed, by the hardships endured, and by the services rendered the country, during these years of war and peril we can now speak with the confidence of men who have deserved well of their country. While conscious of your power and of our comparative weakness, we may still claim for our race those rights which are not less ours by our services to the country than by the laws of human nature. All, therefore, that justice can demand, and honor grant, we can now ask, without presumption and without arrogance, of the American people.

Do you, then, ask us to state, in plain terms, just what we want of you, and just what we think we ought to receive at your hands? We answer: First of all, the complete abolition of the slavery of our race in the United States. We shall not stop to argue. We feel the terrible sting of this stupendous wrong, and that we cannot be free while our brothers are slaves. The enslavement of a vast majority of our people extends its baleful influence over every member of our race; and makes freedom, even to the free, a mockery and a delusion: we therefore, in our own name, and in the name of the whipped and branded millions, whose silent suffering has pleaded to the humane sentiment of mankind, but in vain, during more than two hundred years for deliverance, we implore you to abolish slavery. In the name of your country, torn, distracted, bleeding, and while you are weeping over the bloody graves of more than two hundred thousand of your noblest sons, many of whom have been cut down, in the midst of youthful vigor and beauty, we implore you to abolish slavery. In the name of peace, which experience has shown cannot be other than false and delusive while the rebellious spirit of Slavery has an existence in the land, we implore you to abolish slavery. In the name of universal justice, to whose laws great States not less than individuals are bound to conform, and the terrible consequences of whose violation are as fixed and certain as the universe itself, we implore you to abolish slavery; and thus place your peace and national welfare upon immutable and everlasting foundations.

Why would you let slavery continue? What good thing has it done, what evil thing has it left undone, that you should allow it to survive this dreadful war, the natural fruit of its existence? Can you want a second war from the same cause? Are you so rich in men, money, and material, that you must provide for future depletion? Or do you hope to escape the consequences of wrong-doing? Can you expect any better results from compromises in the future, than from compromises with slavery in the past? If the South fights desperately and savagely to-day for the possession of four millions of slaves, will she fight less savagely and desperately when the prize for which she fights shall become eight instead of four millions? and when her ability to war upon freedom and free institutions shall have increased twofold?

Do you answer, that you have no longer any thing to fear? that slavery has already received its death-blow? that it can only have a transient existence, even if permitted to live after the termination of the war? We answer, So thought your Revolutionary fathers when they framed the Federal Constitution; and to-day, the bloody fruits of their mistake are all around us. Shall we avoid or shall we repeat their stupendous error? Be not deceived. Slavery is still the vital and animating breath of Southern society. The men who have fought for it on the battle-field will not love it less for having shed their blood in its defence. Once let them get Slavery safely under the protection of the Federal Government, and ally themselves, as they will be sure to do, to the Democratic party of the North; let Jefferson Davis and his Confederate associates, either in person or by their representatives, return once more to their seats in the halls of Congress,—and you will then see your dead slavery the most living and powerful thing in the country. To make peace, therefore, on such a basis as shall admit slavery back again into the Union, would only be sowing the seeds of war; sure to bring at last a bitter harvest of blood! The sun in the heavens at noonday is not more manifest, than the fact that slavery is the prolific source of war and division among you; and that its abolition is essential to your national peace and unity. Once more, then, we entreat you — for you have the power — to put away this monstrous abomination. You have repeatedly during this wanton slaveholding and wicked Rebellion, in the darkest hours of the struggle, appealed to the Supreme Ruler of the universe to smile upon your armies, and give them victory: surely you will not now stain your souls with the crime of ingratitude by making a wicked compact and a deceitful peace with your enemies. You have called mankind to witness that the struggle on your part was not for empire merely; that the charge that it was such was a gross slander: will you now make a peace which will justify what you have repeatedly denounced as a calumny? Your antislavery professions have drawn to you the sympathy of liberal and generous minded men throughout the world, and have restrained all Europe from recognizing the Southern Confederacy, and breaking up your blockade of Southern ports. Will you now proclaim your own baseness and hypocrisy by making a peace which shall give the lie to all such professions? You have over and over again, and very justly, branded slavery as the inciting cause of this Rebellion; denounced it as the fruitful source of pride and selfishness and mad ambition; you have blushed before all Europe for its existence among you; and have shielded yourselves from the execrations of mankind, by denying your constitutional ability to interfere with it. Will you now, when the evil in question has placed itself within your constitutional grasp, and invited its own destruction by its persistent attempts to destroy the Government, relax your grasp, release your hold, and to the disappointment of the slaves deceived by your proclamations, to the sacrifice of the Union white men of the South who have sided with you in this contest with slavery, and to the dishonor of yourselves and the amazement of mankind, give new and stronger lease of life to slavery? We will not and cannot believe it.

There is still one other subject, fellow-citizens, — one other want, — looking to the peace and welfare of our common country, as well as to the interests of our race; and that is, political equality. We want the elective franchise in all the

States now in the Union, and the same in all such States as may come into the Union hereafter. We believe that the highest welfare of this great country will be found in erasing from its statute-books all enactments discriminating in favor or against any class of its people, and by establishing one law for the white and colored people alike. Whatever prejudice and taste may be innocently allowed to do or to dictate in social and domestic relations, it is plain, that in the matter of government, the object of which is the protection and security of human rights, prejudice should be allowed no voice whatever. In this department of human relations, no notice should be taken of the color of men; but justice, wisdom, and humanity should weigh alone, and be all-controlling.

Formerly our petitions for the elective franchise were met and denied upon the ground, that, while colored men were protected in person and property, they were not required to perform military duty. Of course this was only a plausible excuse: for we were subject to any call the Government was pleased to make upon us, and we could not properly be made to suffer because the Government did not see fit to impose military duty upon us. The fault was with the Government, not with us.

But now even this frivolous though somewhat decent apology for excluding us from the ballot-box is entirely swept away. Two hundred thousand colored men, according to a recent statement of President Lincoln, are now in the service, upon field and flood, in the army and the navy of the United States; and every day adds to their number. They are there as volunteers, coming forward with other patriotic men at the call of their imperilled country; they are there also as substitutes filling up the quotas which would otherwise have to be filled up by white men who now remain at home; they are also there as drafted men, by a certain law of Congress, which, for once, makes no difference on account of color: and whether they are there as volunteers, as substitutes, or as drafted men, neither ourselves, our cause, nor our country, need be ashamed of their appearance or their action upon the battle-field. Friends and enemies, rebels and loyal men, — each, after their kind,—have borne conscious and unconscious testimony to the gallantry and other noble qualities of the colored troops.

Your fathers laid down the principle, long ago, that universal suffrage is the best foundation of Government. We believe as your fathers believed, and as they practised; for, in eleven States out of the original thirteen, colored men exercised the right to vote at the time of the adoption of the Federal Constitution. The Divine-right Governments of Europe, with their aristocratic and privileged classes of *priests* and *nobles*, are little better than cunningly devised conspiracies against the natural rights of the people to govern themselves.

Whether the right to vote is a natural right or not, we are not here to determine. Natural or conventional, in either case we are amply supported in our appeal for its extension to us. If it is, as all the teachings of your Declaration of Independence imply, a *natural right*, to deny to us its exercise is a wrong done to our human nature. If, on the other hand, the right to vote is simply a conventional right, having no other foundation or significance than a mere conventional arrangement, which may be extended or contracted, given or taken away, upon reasonable grounds, we insist, that, even basing the right upon this uncertain foundation, we may reasonably claim a right to a voice in the election of the men who are to have at their command our time, our services, our property, our persons, and our lives. This command of our persons and lives is no longer theory, but now the positive practice of our Government. We say, therefore, that having required, demanded, and in some instances compelled, us to serve with our time, our property, and our lives, coupling us in all the obligations and duties imposed upon the more highly favored of our fellow-citizens in this war to protect and defend your country from threatened destruction, and having fully established the precedent by which, in all similar and dissimilar cases of need, we may be compelled to respond to a like requisition,—we claim to have fully earned the elective franchise; and that you, the American people, have virtually contracted an obligation to grant it, which has all the sanctions of justice, honor, and magnanimity, in favor of its prompt ful-

8

filment. Are we good enough to use bullets, and not good
enough to use ballots? May we defend rights in time of
war, and yet be denied the exercise of those rights in time
of peace? Are we citizens when the nation is in peril, and
aliens when the nation is in safety? May we shed our blood
under the star-spangled banner on the battle-field, and yet be
debarred from marching under it to the ballot-box? Will the
brave white soldiers, bronzed by the hardships and exposures
of repeated campaigns, men who have fought by the side of
black men, be ashamed to cast their ballots by the side of
their companions-in-arms? May we give our lives, but not
our votes, for the good of the republic? Shall we toil with
you to win the prize of free government, while you alone shall
monopolize all its valued privileges? Against such a conclusion, every sentiment of honor and manly fraternity utters an
indignant protest.

It is quite true, that some part of the American people may,
with a show of plausibility, evade the force of this appeal and
deny this claim. There are men in all countries who can
evade any duty or obligation which is not enforced by the
strong arm of the law. Our country is no exception to the
rule. They can say in this case, "Colored men, we have
done you no wrong. We have purchased nothing at your
hands, and owe you nothing. From first to last, we have objected to the measure of employing you to help put down
this rebellion; foreseeing the very claim you now set up.
Were we to-day invested with the power and authority of
this Government, we would instantly disband every colored
regiment now in front of Richmond, and everywhere else in
the Southern States. We do not believe in making soldiers
of black men." To all that, we reply, There need be no doubt
whatever. No doubt they would disband the black troops if
they had the power; and equally plain is it that they would
disband the white troops also if they had the power.

They do not believe in making black men soldiers; but
they equally do not believe in making white men soldiers
to fight slaveholding rebels. But we do not address ourselves here to particular parties and classes of our countrymen: we would appeal directly to the moral sense, honor,

and magnanimity of the whole nation : and, with a cause so good, cannot believe that we shall appeal in vain. Parties and classes rise and fall, combine and dissolve : but the national conscience remains forever; and it is that to which our cause is addressed. It may, however, be said that the colored people enlisted in the service of the country without any promise or stipulation that they would be rewarded with political equality at the end of the war; but all the more, on this very account, do we hold the American people bound in honor thus to reward them. By the measure of confidence reposed in the national honor and generosity, we have the right to measure the obligation of fulfilment. The fact, that, when called into the service of the country, we went forward without exacting terms or conditions, to the mind of the generous man enhances our claims.

But, again, why are we so urgent for the possession of this particular right? We are asked, even by some Abolitionists, why we cannot be satisfied, for the present at least, with personal freedom ; the right to testify in courts of law ; the right to own, buy, and sell real estate ; the right to sue and be sued. We answer, Because in a republican country, where general suffrage is the rule, personal liberty, the right to testify in courts of law, the right to hold, buy, and sell property, and all other rights, become mere privileges, held at the option of others, where we are excepted from the general political liberty. What gives to the newly arrived emigrants, fresh from lands governed by kingcraft and priestcraft, special consequence in the eyes of the American people? It is not their virtue, for they are often depraved; it is not their knowledge, for they are often ignorant; it is not their wealth, for they are often very poor: why, then, are they courted by the leaders of all parties? The answer is, that our institutions clothe them with the elective franchise, and they have a voice in making the laws of the country. Give the colored men of this country the elective franchise, and you will see no violent mobs driving the black laborer from the wharves of large cities, and from the toil elsewhere by which he honestly gains his bread. You will see no influential priest, like the late Bishop Hughes, addressing mobocrats and murderers as " gentlemen ; " and no influential politician, like Governor Seymour, addressing the "misguided" rowdies of New York as his "friends." The possession of that right is the keystone to the arch of human liberty : and, without that, the whole may at any moment fall to the ground ; while, with it, that liberty may stand forever, — a blessing to us, and no possible injury to you. If you still ask why we want to vote, we answer, Because we don't want to be mobbed from our work, or insulted with impunity at every corner. We are men, and want to be as free in our native country as other men.

Fellow-citizens, let us entreat you, have faith in your own principles. If freedom is good for any, it is good for all. If you need the elective franchise, we need it even more. You are strong, we are weak ; you are many, we are few ; you are protected, we are exposed. Clothe us with this safeguard of our liberty, and give us an interest in the country to which, in common with you, we have given our lives and poured out our best blood. You cannot need special protection. Our degradation is not essential to your elevation, nor our peril essential to your safety. You are not likely to be outstripped in the race of improvement by persons of African descent ; and hence you have no need of superior advantages, nor to burden them with disabilities of any kind. Let your Government be what all governments should be, — a copy of the eternal laws of the universe ; before which all men stand equal as to rewards and punishments, life and death, without regard to country, kindred, tongue, or people.

But what we have now said, in appeal for the elective franchise, applies to our people generally. A special reason may be urged in favor of granting colored men the right in all the rebellious States.

Whatever may be the case with monarchical governments ; however they may despise the crowd, and rely upon their *prestige*, armaments, and standing armies, to support them, — a republican government like ours depends largely upon the friendship of the people over whom it is established, for its harmonious and happy operation. This kind of government must have its foundation in the affections of the people : otherwise the people will hinder, circumvent, and destroy it. Up

to a few years of the rebellion, our government lived in the
friendship of the masses of the Southern people. Its enemies
were, however, numerous and active; and these at last prevailed, poisoned the minds of the masses, broke up the government, brought on the war. Now, whoever lives to see this rebellion suppressed at the South, as we believe we all shall, will
also see the South characterized by a sullen hatred towards the
National Government. It will be transmitted from father to
son, and will be held by them "as sacred animosity." The treason, mowed down by the armies of Grant and Sherman, will be
followed by a strong undergrowth of treason which will go far
to disturb the peaceful operation of the hated Government.

Every United-States mail-carrier, every custom-house officer,
every Northern man, and every representive of the United-
States Government, in the Southern States, will be held in abhorrence; and for a long time that country is to be governed
with difficulty. We may conquer Southern armies by the
sword; but it is another thing to conquer Southern hate. Now
what is the natural counterpoise against this Southern malign
hostility? This it is: give the elective franchise to every colored man of the South who is of sane mind, and has arrived at
the age of twenty-one years, and you have at once four millions
of friends who will guard with their vigilance, and, if need be,
defend with their arms, the ark of Federal Liberty from the
treason and pollution of her enemies. You are sure of the enmity of the masters, — make sure of the friendship of the
slaves; for, depend upon it, your Government cannot afford to
encounter the enmity of both.

If the arguments addressed to your sense of honor, in these
pages, in favor of extending the elective franchise to the colored people of the whole country, be strong, that which we are
prepared to present to you in behalf of the colored people of
rebellious States can be made tenfold stronger. By calling
them to take part with you in the war to subdue their rebellious masters, and the fact that thousands of them have done
so, and thousands more would gladly do so, you have exposed
them to special resentment and wrath; which, without the
elective franchise, will descend upon them in unmitigated
fury. To break with your friends, and make peace with your

enemies; to weaken your friends, and strengthen your enemies; to abase your friends, and exalt your enemies; to disarm your friends, and arm your enemies; to disfranchise your loyal friends, and enfranchise your disloyal enemies,—is not the policy of honor, but of infamy.

But we will not weary you. Our cause is in some measure before you. The power to redress our wrongs, and to grant us our just rights, is in your hands. You can determine our destiny,—blast us by continued degradation, or bless us with the means of gradual elevation. We are among you, and must remain among you; and it is for you to say, whether our presence shall conduce to the general peace and welfare of the country, or be a constant cause of discussion and of irritation,—troubles in the State, troubles in the Church, troubles everywhere.

To avert these troubles, and to place your great country in safety from them, only one word from you, the American people, is needed, and that is JUSTICE: let that magic word once be sounded, and become all-controlling in all your courts of law, subordinate and supreme; let the halls of legislation, state and national, spurn all statesmanship as mischievous and ruinous that has not justice for its foundation; let justice without compromise, without curtailment, and without partiality, be observed with respect to all men, no class of men claiming for themselves any right which they will not grant to another,—then strife and discord will cease; peace will be placed upon enduring foundations; and the American people, now divided and hostile, will dwell together in power and unity.